STRESS IN CHILDHOOD

AMS Studies in Modern Society: Political and Social Issues: No. 17

Other Titles in This Series:

No. 1. Jackwell Susman, ed. *Drug Use and Social Policy.* 1972. 616 pp.

No. 2. Helen Wortis and Clara Rabinowitz, ed. *The Women's Movement: Social and Psychological Perspectives.* 1972. 151 pp.

No. 3. Yonah Alexander and Nicholas N. Kittrie, eds. *Crescent and Star: Arab & Israeli Perspectives on the Middle East Conflict.* 1973. 486 pp.

No. 4. Virginia Paulus. *Housing: A Bibliography, 1960-1972.* 1974. 339 pp.

No. 5. Henry John Steffens and H. N. Muller, eds. *Science, Technology and Culture.* 1974. 204 pp.

No. 6. Parker G. Marden and Dennis Hodgson, eds. *Population, Environment, and the Quality of Life.* 1975. 328 pp.

No. 7. Milton F. Shore and Fortune V. Mannino, eds. *Mental Health and Social Change.* 1975. 330 pp.

No. 8. Nicholas N. Kittrie, Harold L. Hirsh, and Glen Wegner, eds. *Medicine, Law, and Public Policy.* 1975. 605 pp.

No. 9. William Barclay, Krishna Kumar, and Ruth P. Simms, eds. *Racial Conflict, Discrimination, and Power: Historical and Contemporary Studies.* 1976. 437 pp.

No. 10. Hugo Adam Bedau and Chester M. Pierce, eds. *Capital Punishment in the United States.* 1976. 576 pp.

No. 11. Ethel Tobach and Harold M. Proshansky, eds. *Genetic Destiny: Scientific Controversy and Social Conflict.* 1976. 163 pp.

No. 12. Virginia P. Robinson. *The Development of a Professional Self: Teaching and Learning in Professional Helping Processes. Selected Writings, 1930-1968.* 1978. 438 pp.

No. 13. David G. Gil, ed. *Child Abuse and Violence.* 1979. 614 pp.

No. 14. Ronald J. Kase. *The Human Services.* 1979. 353 pp.

No. 15. Anthony M. Scacco, Jr., ed. *Male Rape: A Casebook of Sexual Aggressions.* 1982. 326 pp.

No. 16. Roger E. Schwed. *Abolition and Capital Punishment: The United States' Judicial, Political, and Moral Barometer.* 1983. 227 pp.

ISSN 0275-8407

STRESS IN CHILDHOOD

Edited by

James H. Humphrey

AMS PRESS, INC.
New York

University of Charleston Library
Charleston, WV 25304

Library of Congress Cataloging in Publication Data
Main entry under title:
Stress in childhood.

(AMS studies in modern society: political and social issues; no. 17)
Includes index.
1. Stress in children. I. Humphrey, James Harry, 1911-   . II. Series: AMS studies in modern society; no. 17.
BF723.S75S78   1984   155.4   83-45028
ISBN 0-404-61624-0

Copyright © 1984 by AMS Press, Inc.
All rights reserved.

Manufactured in the United States of America.

CONTENTS

	Page
Preface	vii
Contributors	ix

PART I

FACTORS CONCERNED WITH STRESS IN CHILDHOOD

Chapter

1. Some General Causes of Stress in Children
   JAMES H. HUMPHREY ... 3
2. Growth and Development—A Source of Stress
   CAROL SEEFELDT ... 19
3. Behavioral Responses of Children to Stress
   LOUIS A. CHANDLER ... 47
4. Stressful Environments and Their Impact on Children
   CYNTHIA LONGFELLOW and DEBORAH BELLE ... 63
5. Environmental Change and Children of Divorce
   SHARLENE A. WOLCHIK, BRUCE S. FOGAS and IRWIN N. SANDLER ... 79
6. Measuring the Stressfulness of a Child's Environment
   R. DEAN CODDINGTON ... 97
7. Stress and Competence
   BERNARD BROWN and LILIAN ROSENBAUM ... 127

PART II

CONTROLLING AND REDUCING STRESS IN CHILDREN

8. Teaching Children About Stress
   JOY N. HUMPHREY ... 157
9. The Individuality Profile: A Tool for Personalizing Stress Management
   BARBARA S. KUCZEN ... 165
10. Dealing with Emotional Stress in Childhood
    JAMES H. HUMPHREY ... 195
11. Use of Systematic Desensitization in the Treatment of Children's Fears
    D'ANN WHITEHEAD, MARIELA SHIRLEY and C. EUGENE WALKER ... 213

12 The Quieting Reflex: A Psychophysiologic Approach for Helping Children Deal with Healthy and Unhealthy Stress
　　ELIZABETH L. STROEBEL
　　and CHARLES F. STROEBEL　　251
13 Use of Biofeedback Relaxation Procedures with Learning Disabled Children
　　JOHN L. CARTER and HAROLD L. RUSSELL　　277
14 Creative Relaxation: A Stress Reduction Technique for Children
　　JOY N. HUMPHREY　　301
Index　　325

PREFACE

In the summer of 1980, my good friend Hans Selye, one of the most distinguished scientists of modern times and world famous pioneer in the area of stress, wrote to me expressing his keen interest in stress as it pertains to children and inviting me to prepare a chapter on the subject for *Selye's Guide to Stress Research*. It was during preparation of this chapter that the idea for the present volume was conceived.

An appropriate approach appeared to be one that would bring together a number of specialists who were concerned with stress and children with each preparing a chapter involving his/her own particular expertise. A brief glance at the list of contributors will reveal that some of the foremost authorities in the area of childhood stress have participated in this noteworthy project.

It should be mentioned that multiple authorship can present certain problems, not the least of which is the possibility of overlapping of content. Such overlapping that occurs in this volume is unavoidable, and at the same time desirable, because it helps to preserve continuity in those chapters where certain aspects of overlapping occur.

The book is divided into two highly interdependent and interrelated parts. Part I is devoted to various factors involving stress in childhood and Part II is concerned with controlling and reducing this stress. This plan of organization provides for a relatively reasonable degree of continuity and at the same time allows each individual chapter to stand on its own merits as a more or less separate entity. This means that the book could satisfactorily be used as a text for various courses in child development and also serve as a reference for all persons who deal in some way with children.

CONTRIBUTORS

DEBORAH BELLE, Ed.D., is assistant professor of Social Psychology at Boston University and director of the Stress and Families Project at the Harvard University Graduate School of Education. She is co-editor of *The Mental Health of Women* and editor of *Lives in Stress: Women and Depression*, a report on the Stress and Families Project.

BERNARD BROWN, Ph.D., is a Social Science research analyst in the Administration for Children, Youth and Families, Department of Health and Human Services. His research has included longitudinal studies of early intervention and child development, the relationship of physical to mental growth, social program evaluation of child physical and mental health. Dr. Brown's early training and research were in nuclear physics and biophysics. He is the author of *Found: Long-Term Gains from Early Intervention* (Westview Press, 1978).

JOHN L. CARTER, Ph.D., is director of the Diagnostic Education Center at the University of Houston at Clear Lake City, Texas. For over twenty-five years he has been working in the area of diagnostic evaluation of children with learning difficulties. He has published more than forty research studies most of which have dealt with enhancing the abilities of children.

LOUIS A. CHANDLER, Ph.D., is currently a clinical associate professor in the Department of Educational Psychology at the University of Pittsburgh and director of the University's Psychoeducational Clinic. He also serves as a consulting psychologist to various community agencies and school districts. He is the author of several articles on childhood stress. His most recent work is *Children Under Stress: Understanding Emotional Adjustment Reactions* (Charles C. Thomas Publisher, 1982).

R. DEAN CODDINGTON, M.D., is professor, Department of Psychiatry, and chief, Section of Child Psychiatry, at the Louisiana State University School of Medicine, New Orleans. Interested in the prevention of emotional disorders in children, he first sought training in pediatrics and subsequently in psychiatry and child psychiatry. He has taught medical students for twenty years and in recent years he has focused his research on the development of a method of measuring environmental stressors that affect the lives of children and adolescents.

BRUCE S. FOGAS, B.A., is a graduate student in the Ph.D. program in clinical psychology at Arizona State University. He received his Bachelor of Arts degree with honors in psychology from Rutgers University in 1981. His research interests include the impact of stress on children, behavior therapy with children, and methodological issues in behavioral observations.

JAMES H. HUMPHREY, Ed.D., editor of the volume, is professor emeritus at the University of Maryland. He has published forty books, the last three of which are in the area of stress education. His 200 articles and research reports have been published in more than twenty different national and international professional journals. Dr. Humphrey has received numerous educational honors and awards and he has been a Distinguished Visiting Scholar at four universities. Recently, the Walter Clinton Jackson Library at the University of North Carolina at Greensboro made a collection of his works for the purpose of providing a center for those who wish to study his contribution to child learning.

JOY N. HUMPHREY, M.S., a former elementary school teacher, is the co-author of two books on stress: *Ted Learns About Stress* (Kimbo Educational 1980) and *Reducing Stress in Children Through Creative Relaxation* (Charles C. Thomas Publisher, 1981). In addition, she has published stress research studies in *STRESS: The Official Journal of the International Institute of Stress* and *Health Education*. She developed the technique of using creative movement as a stress reduction procedure for children.

BARBARA S. KUCZEN, Ph.D., is professor of Early Childhood Education at Chicago State University. She is the author of the recently published popular book for parents, *Childhood Stress: Don't Let Your Child Be a Victim* (Delacorte Press, 1982). Dr. Kuczen has established a community education program and prepared materials for parents to use in working with their children at home.

CYNTHIA LONGFELLOW, Ed.D., is a research fellow with the Stress and Families Project at the Harvard University Graduate School of Education. A notable stress researcher, she is currently investigating how chldren cope with and are affected by stress.

LILIAN ROSENBAUM, Ph.D., is director of Biofeedback Programs and clinical associate professor at the Georgetown University Medical Center. She pioneered the application of biofeedback training combined with family systems therapy for the treatment of psychophysiological disorders. She has supervised the training of over 1200 patients and health professionals. Dr. Rosenbaum is treasurer of the Biofeedback Certificate Institute of America and she has held various positions in the Biofeedback Society of America.

HAROLD L. RUSSELL, Ph.D., is a practicing clinical psychologist in Galveston, Texas. For seventeen years he was involved in clinical training of psychologists and psychiatrists at the University of Texas Medical Branch. During this time period he spent the bulk of his time in investigating, developing, and perfecting comprehensive relaxation procedures for individuals and groups.

IRWIN N. SANDLER, Ph.D., is currently an associate professor of psychology at Arizona State University. He has worked as a staff psychologist at Phoenix South Community Mental Health Center from 1971 to 1975 and joined the faculty at Arizona State University in 1975. He has conducted research in the area of stress and coping over the past five years.

CAROL SEEFELDT, Ph.D., professor in the Institute for Child Study at the University of Maryland, has published five books and over sixty articles, manuals, and research reports. Her recent books have been on teaching young children and curriculum development for preschool children. Dr. Seefeldt is the recipient of various educational honors and awards. Her most recent citation is that of Distinguished Scholar-Teacher at the University of Maryland.

MARIELA SHIRLEY, Ph.D., received her doctorate in Clinical Psychology from Vanderbilt University in 1982. She did her internship training in Pediatric Psychology at the University of Oklahoma Health Sciences Center. Recently she has returned to her home in Panama City, Panama where she plans to teach.

CHARLES F. STROEBEL, Ph.D., M.D., is director of research, Institute of Living in Hartford, Connecticut, professor of Psychiatry at the University of Connecticut Medical School, and lecturer in Psychiatry at Yale University School of Medicine. His classic research in biofeedback has provided new insights into stress reduction. He has published numerous scientific articles and is author of *The Quieting Reflex: A Six-Second Technique for Coping with Stress Anytime, Anywhere* (Putnam, 1982).

ELIZABETH L. STROEBEL, M.Ed., M.S., is a member of the faculty of the College of Arts and Sciences at the University of Hartford. Her training is in humanities and psychophysiology and she has been a classroom teacher for 22 years. She is the author of *Kiddie QR: A Choice for Children* (QR Institute, Wethersfield, Connecticut 1980).

C. EUGENE WALKER, Ph.D., is professor of Psychology and director of Training in Pediatric Psychology at the University of Oklahoma Medical School. He is also associate chief of Mental Health Services and director of the Out-Patient Pediatric Psychology Clinic at the Oklahoma Children's Memorial Hospital. His first two books, *Learn to Relax* and *Clinical Procedures for Behavior Therapy,* were published by Prentice-Hall. His latest books include *The Practice of Clinical Psy-*

chology (Pergamon Press), *The Handbook of Clinical Child Psychology* (John Wiley Publishers), and *The Handbook of Clinical Psychology* (Dorsey-Dow Jones-Irwin Press).

D'ANN WHITEHEAD, Psy.D. is coordinator of Behavioral Services at Presbyterian Hospital in Oklahoma City. She received her doctorate in Clinical Psychology from Baylor University in 1982. She did her internship training at the University of Oklahoma Health Sciences Center. A large portion of her training was done in the Pediatric Psychology Training Program.

PART I

FACTORS CONCERNED WITH STRESS IN CHILDHOOD

PART 2

CHAPTER 1

SOME GENERAL CAUSES OF STRESS IN CHILDREN

James H. Humphrey, Ed. D.

This chapter explains how modern society is stressful for children. Consideration is given to such general causes of stress in childhood as self conerns of children themselves, home condition, and a variety of school anxieties.

There are so many general causes of stress that almost anything that occurs in life can cause stress to a certain degree. These general causes of stress include, among a host of others, all of the various factors concerned with our modern highly technological society such as air travel, which makes the world a "smaller place," the mass media, especially the daily news which bombards us with information, which, if taken too seriously, can provide stressful conditions. In addition, such factors as overcrowding, air and noise pollution, along with the every day "hustle and bustle to survive," combine to make life in general a somewhat frustrating experience. All of us, children and adults alike, are possible stress victims of these kinds of conditions. Moreover, some of us by the very nature of our specific environments are susceptible to many stress-inducing factors.

Most children encounter a considerable amount of stress in our complex modern society. The objectives of those adults who deal with children should be to help them reduce distress by making a change in the environment and/or making a change in the children themselves. It is well known that each person has a *tolerance level* as far as stress is concerned, and if the stress becomes considerably greater than the tolerance, a person will suffer from emotional stress and its consequent unhappy circumstances.

One of the problems of stress in children is that they are not likely to be able to cope with it as well as adults. The reason for this is that they do not have the readily available options that adults might have. Margaret Holland, a prominent child psychologist, makes the following comparisons between choices in coping with stress open to children and adults.[11]

1. An open display of anger is often considered unacceptable for children. For example, a teacher can be angry with a student, but children may not have the same right to be angry with a teacher.
2. Adults have the latitude of withdrawing or walking out, but this same option of freedom may not be available to children.
3. It is the belief of some child psychologists that *daydreaming* is therapeutic and productive. At the same time, children may be reprimanded for "daydreaming" in school.
4. An adult can get a prescription for "nerves" from a physician—another option not available to children.

It is very likely that more often than not children may be punished for using some of the same kinds of stress-coping techniques that are satisfactory for adults. Yet, some of these behaviors are considered socially unacceptable as far as children are concerned.

Indeed, the average child's environment abounds with many stress inducing factors—society in general, the home, and the school. Things such as various kinds of teacher and parent behaviors can have frustrating influences on children. The following discussions will identify and elaborate on some of the various causes of stress in children. When teachers and parents are more aware of some of these causes of stress, perhaps they can try to alleviate some of them and also try to help children deal with those situations that are difficult to eliminate.

SELF CONCERNS OF CHILDREN THAT CAN CAUSE STRESS

One of the important classifications of causes of stress in children is that which involves *personal* or *self concerns*. The following generalized descriptive list takes some of these factors into account.

1.–*Self concerns associated with the meeting of personal goals.* Stress is likely to result if adults set goals for children that are too difficult for them to accomplish. For example, goals may be much higher than a particular school or home environment will permit children to achieve. On the contrary, when goals are set too low, children may develop the feeling that they are not doing as much for themselves as they should. This aspect of stress is also concerned with the fear some children have that they will not reach their goals in life. It is interesting to note that this can sometimes happen early in a child's life.

2.–*Self concerns that involve self-esteem.* This involves the way one feels about himself, and one's self-esteem can often be highly related to the fulfillment of certain *ego needs*. Some children may feel that there are not enough opportunities offered in modern society for them to succeed. This is perhaps more true of those children who are in a low socioeconomic environment. It bothers some children, too, that adults do not praise them for what they consider to be a job well done.

3.—*Self concerns related to changing values.* It is frustrating to some children if they do not understand the system of values imposed on them in a given school or home environment. They may develop the feeling that adults are not inclined to place a value on those factors that children feel are important to them personally at their various stages of growth and development.

4.—*Self concerns that center around social standards.* In some cases children get confused with the difference in social standards required at the different levels of their development. It is sometimes difficult for them to understand that what was socially acceptable at one age level is not necessarily so at another.

5.—*Self concerns involving personal competence and ability.* This is probably the self concern that frustrates children the most. Certainly, lack of confidence in one's ability can be devastating to the morale of a child. Many children are becoming increasingly concerned with their ability, or lack thereof, to cope with problems such as expectations of parents and keeping up with school work.

6.—*Self concerns about their own traits and characteristics.* Certainly not the least of the concerns among children are those factors that are likely to make them different from the so-called average or normal child. This is concerned with the social need for *mutuality,* which means wanting to be like their peers. When children deviate radically from others in certain traits and characteristics, it can be a serious stress-inducing factor. A specific example is the child who is extremely overweight. Some child psychiatrists feel that they are likely to mature into overweight adults and studies show that overweight children may get lower grades in school, that in some cases they may be discriminated against by teachers, and that they often have poor social skills.

It should be mentioned that not all of these self concerns are characteristic of all children, particularly because of the individual differences among them. That is, what may be a serious self concern for one child may be a minimal concern for another.

HOME CONDITIONS THAT CAN CAUSE STRESS

Changes in society with consequent changes in conditions in some homes are likely to make child adjustment a difficult problem. Factors such as changes in standards of female behavior, larger percentages of both parents working, economic conditions, mass media such as television, as well as numerous others, can complicate the life of the modern-day child.

Some child psychiatrists are convinced that some home conditions can have an extremely negative influence on the personality and mental health of some children. Studies show that the interaction of stress factors is especially important. Most of these studies tend to identify the following factors to be strongly associated with childhood psychiatric disorders: (1) severe marital discord, (2) low social status, (3) over-crowding or large family size, (4) paternal criminality, (5) maternal psychiatric disorder, and (6) admission into the care of local authorities.[12]

It is estimated that with only one of the above conditions present, a child is no more likely to develop psychiatric problems than any other child; however, when two of the conditions occur the child's psychiatric risk increases fourfold.

In our own studies it was found that there were certain actions of parents that induced stress in teachers, and, according to the teachers, these parental attitudes might well be considered as stress inducing factors for their students.[4]

Actions of parents that induce stress in teachers can be classified into three areas: (1) lack of concern of parents for their children, (2) parental interference, and (3) lack of parental support for teachers.

In forty-five percent of the cases, *lack of parental concern for children* was stressful for teachers. They cited things such as parents not caring when a student did poorly, parents not willing to help their children with school work, a lack of home discipline, and stress placed on teachers by the difficult time they had in getting parents to conferences.

Thirty-two percent of the teachers said *parental interference* was a stressor for them. Such interference was often a result of parents having expectations too high for their children. This in turn resulted in parental pressure on children, particularly for grades, which may be one of the most serious conditions in our schools today. Incidentally, in this general connection, it is interesting to note that one authoritative source suggests that attitudes acquired during youth can affect the way an individual reacts to stress as an adult. This may be significant in the case of persons whose family has emphasized performance and achievement to the exclusion of all other characteristics.[10]

It has been suggested that pressure exerted by parents for grades could be a contributing cause of the increase in the suicide rate among students. Moreover, there are some who believe that parents are literally "driving their children to drink" because of an increase in alcohol consumption by children, possibly due to the "grade pressure syndrome."

The third classification of parental actions causing stress for teachers was that of *lack of parental support,* and twenty-three percent identified stress inducing factors here. They were stressed by factors such as not being backed by parents and a general poor attitude of parents toward teachers.

Another, and very important home condition that can induce stress in children is when a family itself is under stress. Parenting itself is an extremely difficult task, and the demands of this task are becoming more and more complicated. Consequently, many of the pressures that modern parents are called upon to endure cannot only cause stress for them but can also cause them to induce stress upon their children as well.

A recent publication by the United States Department of Health and Human Services entitled *Families in Stress*[7] suggests that parents who begin to feel stress because of their children ask themselves the following questions:

1. Is it so important that the child *always* do things my way?
2. Can I let the children have it their own way sometimes?
3. Do I really take enough time to try to understand what the children are saying to me?
4. Do I really know what the children want and need from me?
5. Is what I say or tell them to do really clear to them?

In addition to these criteria for evaluation for dealing with their children, the following "stress and tension relievers" are recommended:

1. Count to ten, put the child in a safe area (crib, playpen, child-proof room), and go to another room or outside for a few minutes.
2. Go into another room, close the door, and cry or scream. Then take ten minutes to read, knit, or do whatever relaxes you best.
3. Lie on the floor with your feet up on a chair; place a cool washcloth on your face, and think of the most peaceful scene you can imagine. Stay there for five minutes.
4. Tell your child exactly what is making you feel angry. Be really specific about what behavior needs to be changed in order to reduce your anger level.
5. After you have put the child down for a nap, forget what you "should" be doing. Take some time for yourself to relax, sleep, read, listen to music, take a bath—whatever makes you feel fresh again.
6. Designate a corner, chair, or some quiet spot as a "time-out" place

where you can go when you feel like losing your temper. Designate a separate one for your child. It gives both of you a few minutes to calm down, *and* it tells the other person that you are getting angry.

7. Save a special, quiet plaything to be used only at certain times. It will be a treat for your child and will provide some quiet time for you.

It is estimated that one million or more children are abused or neglected by their parents or other "overseers" in our country annually, and that as many as 2,000 die as a result of maltreatment. Authorities suggest that most of this is not caused by inhuman, hateful intent on the part of parents, but rather, it is the result of a combination of factors including the accumulation of stresses on families and the unmet needs of parents for support in coping with their child rearing responsibilities.

SCHOOL ANXIETIES THAT CAN CAUSE STRESS

There are a number of conditions existing in most schools that can raise stress levels of students. Several of these will be considered in the subsequent discussions.

Stress and the Child in the Educative Process

School anxiety as a child stressor is a phenomenon with which educators, particularly teachers and counselors, frequently find themselves confronted in dealing with children. Various theories have been advanced to explain this phenomenon and relate it to other character traits and emotional dispositions. Literature on the subject reveals the following characteristics of anxiety as a stress inducing factor in the educative process.

1. Anxiety is considered a learnable reaction that has the properties of a response, a cue of danger, and a drive.

2. Anxiety is internalized fear aroused by the memory of painful past experiences associated with punishment for the gratification of an impulse.

3. Anxiety in the classroom interferes with learning, and whatever can be done to reduce it should serve as a spur to learning.

4. Test anxiety is a near universal experience, especially in this country, which is a test-giving and test-conscious culture.

5. Evidence from clinical studies points clearly and consistently to the disruptive and distracting power of anxiety effects over most kinds of thinking.

It would seem that causes of anxiety change with age as do perceptions of stressful situations. Care should be taken in assessing the total life space of the child—background, home life, school life, age, and sex—in order to minimize the anxiety experienced in the school. It seems obvious that school anxiety, although manifested in the school environment, may often be caused by unrelated factors outside the school.

Teacher Behaviors That Induce Stress in Children

In the literature much emphasis has been placed on those factors that induce stress in teachers. It certainly seems appropriate to examine behavior of teachers that tends to induce stress in their students. The major reason for this, of course, is that teachers' behavior could possibly have a serious negative effect on those they teach. This is not a recent concern because over two decades ago, on the basis of minimum incidence statistics and pupil-teacher ratios, it was estimated that anxiety may affect as many as two hundred thousand teachers and that through them five million students may be affected.[8]

Equally important, if teachers induce stress in students, the students, in turn, are likely to manifest behavior that develops into stress inducing factors for teachers, and thus the *vicious circle* is allowed to perpetuate.

Perhaps one of the most satisfactory ways of identifying teacher behavior that is likely to cause stress among students is simply to ask students themselves. In this regard, a study was recently conducted with fifth and sixth grade children.[5] A question raised with some 200 fifth and sixth grade boys and girls was, "What is the one thing that worries you most in school?" As might be expected, there was a wide variety of responses. Nevertheless, the one general characteristic that tended to emerge was the emphasis that teachers placed on competition in so many school situations. Although students did not state this specifically, the nature of their responses clearly seemed to be along these general lines.

Certainly there are many conditions in the school situation that, if not carefully controlled, can cause *competitive stress*. This condition has been described as occurring when a child feels (perceives) that he will not be able to respond adequately to the performance demands of competition. When the child feels this way, he experiences a considerable threat to self-esteem that results in stress. Moreover, competitive stress is a negative emotion that a child experiences when he perceives the competition to be personally threatening.[13]

Whenever possible, teachers might try to guard against those conditions which may result in competitive stress and at the same time emphasize those kinds of conditions that will more likely promote *cooperation*. In this regard, it is interesting to note that the terms *cooperation* and *competition* are antonymous; therefore, the reconciliation of children's competitive needs and cooperative needs is not an easy matter. In a sense, we are confronted with an ambivalent condition that, if not handled carefully, could place children in a state of conflict. This was recognized by Karen Horney many years ago when she indicated that, although everything is done to spur us toward success—meaning that we must not only be assertive but also aggressive, able to push others out of the way—we are deeply imbued with ideals that declare that it is selfish to want anything for ourselves and that we should be humble, turn the other cheek, and be yielding.[3] Thus, modern society rewards not only one kind of behavior (cooperation) but also its direct opposite (competition). Perhaps more often than not our cultural demands sanction these rewards without provision of clear-cut standards of value in regard to specific conditions under which these forms of behavior might well be practiced. Thus, the child is placed in somewhat of a quandary about when to compete and when to cooperate.

In generalizing on the basis of the available evidence with regard to the subject of competition, it seems justifiable to formulate the following concepts:

    1. Very young children are not very competitive but become more competitive as they grow older.

    2. There is a wide variety in competition among children; that is, some are violently competitive, while others are mildly competitive, and still others are not competitive at all.

    3. Boys tend to be more competitive than girls.

    4. Competition should be adjusted so that there is not a preponderant number of winners over losers.

    5. Competition and rivalry effect effort and speed of accomplishment.[6]

Subject Anxiety as a Stress Inducing Factor

There are various subject areas that could be considered as perennial nemeses for many students. In fact, if you ask an elementary school pupil what he likes best in school, the invariable traditional response has been, "recess and lunch." Of course, neither of these are bona fide subjects and many pupils when pressed will respond with what they "hate the least."

Probably any subject could be a stress inducing factor for certain students. Prominent among those subjects that have a reputation for being more stress inducing than others are those concerned with the basic 3Rs. For example, it has been reported that for many children, attending school daily and performing poorly is a source of considerable and prolonged stress. If the children overreact to environmental stresses in terms of increased muscle tension, this may interfere easily with the fluid muscular movement required in handwriting tasks, decreasing their performance and further increasing environmental stresses. Most educators have seen children squeeze their pencils tightly, press hard on their paper, purse their lips, and tighten their bodies, using an inordinate amount of energy and concentration to write while performing at a very low level.[1]

Reading is another area of school activity that is loaded with anxiety, stress, and frustration for many children. In fact, one of the levels of reading recognized by reading specialists is called the "frustration level." In terms of behavioral observation this can be described as the level in which children evidence distracting tension, excessive or erratic body movements, nervousness, and distractability. This frustration level is said to be a sign of emotional tension or stress with breakdowns in fluency and a significant increase in reading errors.[1]

The subject that appears to stress the greatest majority of students is mathematics. This condition prevails from the study of arithmetic upon entering school through the required courses in mathematics in college. This has become such a problem in recent years that there is now an area of study called "Math Anxiety" that is receiving increasing attention. Prominent among those studying this phenomenon is Sheila Tobias,[14] some of whose thoughts on the matter are summarized in the following discussion.

There appears to be what could be called "math-anxious" and "math-avoiding" people who tend not to trust their problem-solving abilities and who experience a high level of stress when asked to use them. Even though these people are not necessarily "mathematically ignorant," they tend to feel that they are, simply because they cannot focus on the problem at hand or because they are unable to remember the appropriate formula. Thus, a feeling of frustration and incompetence are likely to make them reluctant to deal with mathematics in their daily lives. (And, certainly there are innumerable cases where they are almost required to do so). It is suggested that at the root of this self-doubt is a fear of making mistakes and appearing stupid in front of others.

People carry with them very distinct memories of their first encounters with mathematics, and most of these memories are very likely to be school-related. Indeed, long after they have left the classroom some people still experience stress and discomfort when confronting mathematics.

It is believed that there are at least three sources of anxiety commonly found in traditional mathematics classes: (1) time pressure, (2) humiliation, and (3) emphasis on one right answer.

As far as *time pressure* is concerned such things as flash cards, timed tests, and competitions in which the object is to finish first are among the first experiences that can make lasting negative impressions on many young mathematics learners. (The reader should recall that negative aspects of competitive stress were discussed previously). Speed becomes all important and slower learners are soon likely to become apprehensive when asked to perform a mathematics problem.

One of the strongest memories of math-anxious adults is the feeling of *humiliation* when being called upon to perform in front of the class. The child may be asked to go to the chalkboard to struggle over a problem until the solution is found. If an error is made the child may be prodded to locate and correct it. In this kind of stressful situation it is not surprising that the child is likely to experience "math block," which adds to his sense of humiliation and failure. This should not be interpreted to mean that the chalkboard should not be used creatively to demonstrate problem-solving abilities. A child who successfully performs a mathematical task in front of classmates can have the enjoyable experience of instructing others. Also the rest of the class can gain useful information from watching how another solves a problem. When using chalkboard practice, however, it is important to remember that children profit from demonstrating their competence and not their weaknesses.

Although mathematics problems do, in most cases have *right* answers, it can be a mistake to focus our attention only on accuracy. In putting too much emphasis on the end product, oftentimes overlooked is the valuable information about the process involved in arriving at that product. It would be well for teachers to reward creative thinking as well as correct answers. Again the reader should not interpret this as meaning that the right answer is not important. However, when it is emphasized to the exclusion of all other information, students can become fearful of making mistakes and possibly angry with themselves when they do.

Teachers who make an effort to reduce the number of stressful situations in mathematics programs will not only be helping their students to become better mathematics learners but at the same time they will also be helping them as future adults to be more confident and capable performers in mathematics tasks.

Test Anxiety as a Stress Inducing Factor

A few years ago The Society for Research in Child Development released two monographs that contained extensive longitudinal studies on test anxiety as it relates to school children.[2]

The first study represented a limited attempt to determine the relation over time between anxiety and indices of intellectual and academic performance. The following three major results were revealed:

1. The expected negative correlation between test anxiety and IQ tends to be small and insignificant in the first year, but increases significantly in the negative direction over time.
2. These tendencies are more marked and significant when measures designed to correct for sources of distortion of self-report are used.
3. The strength of the negative correlations between test anxiety and IQ scores are consistently stronger when third-grade rather than first-grade test anxiety scores are used as the predictor variable.

The second study is the summation of a longitudinal study of defensiveness to intelligence and achievement test performance and of school progress over the elementary school years. Some of the major findings indicated the following:

1. There was an increasingly negative relationship between anxiety and test performance over the entire elementary school experience.
2. Anxiety was greater on verbal than on nonverbal tests.
3. Unfamiliar tests aroused much anxiety.

In addition to the above reports, a great deal of research has appeared on test anxiety in various sources over the years. One literature review on the subject suggests the following generalizations:[9]

1. A critical factor is what the test situation means to a particular individual in terms of his learned patterns of response to anxiety. If the test is considered important to the individual and if he is anxious when taking tests, he is more likely to perform poorly on tests than one who is less anxious.

2. There is a negative relationship between level of ability and level of anxiety. Poorer students tend to be most anxious when facing a test.

3. There is a positive correlation between level of anxiety and level of aspiration. Those who are least anxious when facing a test tend to be those who have the least need or desire to do well in it.

4. Extreme degrees of anxiety are likely to interfere with test performance; however, mild degrees of anxiety facilitate test peformance.

5. The more familiar a student is with tests of a particular type, the less likely he is to suffer extreme anxiety.

6. Test anxiety can enhance learning if it is distributed at a relatively low level throughout a course of instruction rather than being concentrated at a relatively high level just prior to and during a test.

7. There are low-to-moderate negative relationships between measures of anxiety and performance on very complex tasks. This negative relationship tends to increase as the task becomes more test-like.

8. Test anxiety increases with grade level and appears to be long range rather than transitory.

What, then, does the nature of test anxiety imply for educational goals and practice? Perhaps there should be a continuing opportunity for all school personnel and parents to report on their experiences with the tests that have been used. This feedback should also place a great deal of emphasis on the students' reactions to their testing experience. It is essential that the reactions of children that give evidence to emotional disturbance in relation to tests be carefully considered, especially when test results are interpreted and used for instructional, guidance and administrative purposes.

The School Learning Environment Can Induce Stress in Boys

In general, emotional stress seems to have a greater effect on boys than on girls in both the school and home environment. One possible exception to this in the school situation is that girls are prone to suffer more anxiety over report cards than are boys. Most studies show that boys are much more likely to be stressed by family discord and disruption than are girls, although there does not seem to be a completely satisfactory explanation for this.

In any event, it is interesting to note that many people have been critical of the early school learning environment, particularly as far as boys are concerned. Some of these critics have gone so far as to say that young boys are being discriminated against in their early school years. Let us examine the premise.

A generally accepted description of the term *learning* is that it involves some sort of change in behavior. Many learning theorists maintain that behavior is a product of heredity and environment. Unquestionably, it is very apparent that environment plays a major role in determining one's behavior, and some tend to feel that man is, indeed, controlled by his environment. Nevertheless, we must remember that it is an environment largely of his own making. The issue here is whether or not an environment is provided that is best suited for learning for boys at the early age levels, and further whether such an environment is likely to cause more stress among young boys than young girls.

While the school has no control over ancestry, it can, within certain limitations, exercise some degree of control over the kind of environment in which the learner must function. Generally speaking, it is doubtful that all schools have provided an environment that is most conducive to learning as far as young boys are concerned. Many child development specialists have characterized the environment at the primary level of education as *feminized*.

A major factor to consider is that which concerns the biological differences between boys and girls in this particular age range, and it is questionable whether educational planning has always taken these important differences into account. Over the years there has been an accumulation of evidence on this general subject appearing in the literature on child development, some of which will be summarized here.

Due to certain male hormonal conditions, boys tend to be more aggressive, restless, and impatient. In addition, the male has more rugged bone structure, and as a consequence greater strength than the female at all ages. Because of this, males tend to display greater muscular reactivity that in turn expresses itself in a stronger tendency toward restlessness and vigorous overt activity. This condition is concerned with the greater oxygen consumption required to fulfill the male's need for increased energy production. The male organism might be compared to an engine that operates at higher levels of speed and intensity than the less energetic female organism.

Another factor to take into account is the difference in Basal Metabolic Rate (BMR) in young boys and girls. The BMR is indicative of the speed at which body fuel is changed into energy, as well as how fast this energy is used. The BMR can be measured in terms of calories per meter of body surface with a calorie representing a unit measure of heat energy in food. It has been found that on average BMR rises from birth to about three years of age and then starts to decline until the ages of approximately twenty to twenty-four. The BMR is higher for boys than for girls, particularly at the early age levels. Because of the higher BMR, boys in turn will have a higher amount of energy to expend. Because of differences in sex hormonal conditions and Basal Metabolic Rate, it appears logical to assume that these factors will influence the male in his behavior patterns.

From a growth and development point of view, while at birth the female is from one-half to one centimeter less in length than the male and around three hundred grams less in weight, she is actually a much better developed organism. It is estimated on the average that at the time of entrance into school, the female is usually six to twelve months more physically mature than the male. As a result, girls may be likely to learn earlier how to perform tasks of manual dexterity such as buttoning their clothing. In one of the present author's observational studies of preschool children, it was found that little girls were able to perform the task of tying their shoe laces at a rate of almost four times that of little boys.

Although all schools should not be categorized in the same manner, many of them have been captured by the dead hand of tradition and ordinarily provide an environment that places emphasis upon factors such as neatness, orderliness, and passiveness which is easier for girls to conform to than boys. Of course, this may be partly because our culture has forced females to be identified with many of these characteristics.

The authoritarian and sedentary classroom atmosphere that prevails in some schools that involves the "sit still and listen" syndrome, fails to take into account the greater activity drive and physical aggressiveness of boys. What have been characterized as feminization traits prevailing in many elementary schools tend to have an adverse influence on the young male child as far as learning is concerned.

Some studies have shown that as far as hyperactivity is concerned, boys may outnumber girls by a ratio of as much as nine to one. This may be one of the reasons why teachers generally tend to rate young males as being so much more aggressive than females, with the result that young boys are considered to be more negative and extroverted. Because of these characteristics, boys generally have poorer relationships with their teachers than girls, and in the area of behavior problems and discipline in the age range from five to eight years, boys account for twice as many disturbances as girls. The importance of this factor is borne out when it is considered that good teacher-pupil relationships tend to raise the achievement levels of both sexes.

Various studies have shown that girls generally receive higher grades than boys although boys may achieve as well as and in some instances better than girls. It is also clearly evident that boys in the early years fail twice as often as girls even when there is no significant difference between intelligence and achievement test scores of both sexes. This suggests that even though both sexes have the same intellectual tools, there are other factors that are against learning as far as boys are concerned.

If one is willing to accept the research findings and observational evidence appearing in the child development literature regarding the premise outlined here, then the question is: "What attempts, if any, are being made to improve the condition?" At one time it was thought that the solution might lie in defeminization of the schools at the early age levels by putting more men into classrooms. This apparently has met with little success because the learning environment remains essentially the same regardless of the sex of the teacher. Some educators have suggested that little boys start school later or that little girls start earlier. The problem with this, of course, is that state laws concerned with school entrance are likely to distinguish only in terms of age and not sex. In a few remote instances some schools have experimented with separating boys and girls at the early grade levels. In some cases this form of grouping has resulted in both groups achieving at a higher level than when the sexes were in classes together.

The major question that must be posed is: "What can be done at least partially to restructure an environment that will be more favorable to the learning of young boys?" One step in this direction recommended by various child development specialists is to develop curriculum content that is more *action* oriented, thus taking into account the basic need for motor activity involved in human movement. This is to say that deep consideration might well be given to learning activities through which excess energy, especially for boys, can be utilized. The extent to which this kind of curriculum content would make learning less stressful for boys is not entirely known; however, experimentation by the present author shows definite possibilities along these lines. (NOTE: For a detailed account of this approach the reader is referred to: Humphrey, James H., and Humphrey, Joy N., *Help Your Child Learn the 3R's Through Active Play,* Springfield, Illinois, Charles C Thomas Publisher, 1980).

Several causes and contributing causes of stress in children have been dealt with in the preceding discussions. It is possible to eliminate many of these stress inducing factors. For those that cannot be eliminated entirely, serious attempts should be made at least to keep them under control.

REFERENCES

1. Carter, John L. & Harold L. Russell, Relationship between reading frustration and muscle tension levels in children with reading disabilities. *American Journal of Clinical Feedback*, 1979, 2:2.
2. Hill, K. T. & S. B. Sarasen, *The relation of test anxiety and defensiveness to test and school performance over the elementary school years.* Monograph of the Society for Research in Child Development, 1966, 2 (Serial No. 104).
3. Horney, K. *The neurotic personality of our times.* New York: W. W. Norton & Company, Inc., 1937.
4. Humphrey, J. H., & J. N. Humphrey, Factors which induce stress in teachers. *Stress, The Official Journal of the International Institute of Stress,* 1981, 2:4.
5. ———, *Incidents in the school environment which induce stress in upper elementary school children.* College Park, Maryland, 1977.
6. Humphrey, J. H., *Child learning.* Dubuque: William C. Brown Company Publishers, 1974, p. 107.
7. Johnston, C. A., *Families in stress.* Washington, D. C.: U. S. Department of Health and Human Services, Publication No. (OHDS) 1979, 80–30162.
8. Kaplan, C., *Mental health and human relations.* New York: Harper & Row, 1959.
9. Kirkland, M. C. The Effect of Tension on Students and Schools. *Review of Educational Research,* 1971, 41.
10. Pellitier, K. R., *Mind as healer/mind as slayer.* New York: Dell Publishing Co., Inc., 1977, p. 104.
11. Report on a Proseminar Institute in Washington D. C., *The Washington Post,* June 13, 1980.
12. Rutter, M., Some grow up undisturbed: why? *The Spectrum,* Iowa City, Iowa, University of Iowa, Winter, 1977.
13. Scanlan, T. K. & M. W. Passer, *The psychological and social affects of competition.* Los Angeles, 1977.
14. Tobias, S., Stress in the math classroom. *Learning,* January, 1981.

CHAPTER 2

CHILD GROWTH AND DEVELOPMENT—A SOURCE OF STRESS?

Carol Seefeldt, Ph. D.

The demands of child growth and development require certain aspects of adjustment, a fact that is recognized by the proponents of the various theories of growth and development. In this chapter the author explores the three theoretical approaches—cognitive, psychoanalytic, and behavioral. Each theory is examined in detail and comparison of the theories provides insights into potential sources of anxiety and stress for young children, as well as implications for reducing stress in the lives of children.

"Stress is not something to be avoided. Indeed, by definition it cannot be avoided, since during every moment of our lives some demand for life-maintaining energy exists. Complete freedom from stress is death."[41] Given the definition of stress as a nonspecific response of the body to any demand, including the demand for readjustment, for performance of adaptive functions, then the normal process of growing, changing, adapting, adjusting, and learning involves a measure of stress.[41]

Major theories of child growth and development do recognize the demand for readjustment as a part of growth. The need for the human organism to reach homeostasis is a concept in the cognitive, psychoanalytic and behaviorial theories of child growth and development.

Cognitive theorists are quite clear about the role of stress as a necessary factor in learning.[34] The word disequilibrium is used to describe the unbalance children must experience in order to adjust their thinking to include new information. The cognitive development theories make the assumption that all human behavior is the product of thinking. Thinking itself, is a process of adaption and restructuring of cognitive structures. When children discover, through their own actions, the limitations of their cognitive schemas, or thought processes, they must readjust their thinking to obtain balance or equilibrium.

Stress may also result from the nature of children's thinking. As Piaget has documented, children's thinking is not only less complete and accurate than that of adults, it is structurally different from adults.[35] Children, below the age of seven or eight, who perceive the world in egocentric, magical ways, and who are unable to think logically, may become anxious and stressed simply because they are unable to comprehend everyday, benign, natural phenomena.

Psychoanalytic theory assumes that humans are born with internal, instinctive drives that push for release and discharge. Human behavior is explained on the basis of the fulfillment or nonfulfillment of these drives. The interplay between the tension of an unmet drive and the energy spent in the release of a drive, has been defined as a producer of anxiety or stress.[38] As children mature, they develop conscious thought, and control overdrives. This development of consciousness is related to their social, emotional, and intellectual development.

Behaviorists see anxiety or stress as coming from the external environment, not from internal states. Behavioral theories make the assumption that growth is directed by the external, not internal cognitive controls or instinctual drives, but by specific stimuli from the environment. In the past, little emphasis was placed on the ability of the human to mediate between the stimuli from the environment and their response. Today, however, behaviorists believe that behavior arises from a reaction to stimuli from the environment, as well as the accumulation of experiences based on past environmental conditions. Nevertheless, to the behaviorist, "anxiety and avoidance behaviors are responses elicited and maintained by specific proximal stimuli."[7]

Each of the three theoretical approaches, the cognitive, psychoanalytic, and the behaviorial, offers insights into children's growth and development. Each is useful in understanding the normal stress children must cope with as they grow and develop. Yet no one theory alone seems sufficient in and of itself to explain anxiety and stress. An examination and comparison of the theories permits insights into potential sources of anxiety and stress for young children, as well as offering implications for reducing stress in the lives of children.

COGNITIVE THEORIES

Human behavior is the result of thinking. According to the cognitive theories based on the works of Jean Piaget children's behavior is the result of their understanding of the situation.[34] Children do not behave

Growth and Development—A Source of Stress?

in response to any specific stimulus that comes from the environment. A child responds to a situation in a given way because of thinking about it. Thus, responses of fear, anxiety, and stress are the result of a child's understanding of the situation. This ability to think, to develop, and use cognitive structures, is not the result of associations between past and present experience, nor is it the result of teaching, but is created by the child.

The creation of cognitive structures arises from the need of the child to reach a state of equilibration with regard to the understanding of reality. Through repeated interactions with the environment, children take in information that does not fit with their understanding of the world. Their past understanding is no longer adequate to explain new experiences. The child, uncomfortable with this state of disequilibrium, and sensing the inadequacy of present cognitive structures, attempts to achieve equilibrium by constructing new schema or new ways of thinking.

For instance, young children are confident that it gets dark because they go to bed. After experiencing nightfall several times when they are not in bed, children are confronted by the inadequacy of their present ideas. Finding that their view of the world is not congruent with reality, they must accommodate new information into their cognitive structures and construct new ways of thinking for themselves.

It is true, this process of assimilation and accommodation involves physical interaction with the environment, as well as social interactions, yet it is the mental action that creates new and more adequate cognitive structures. This mental activity is not without a measure of stress.

> Equilibration—and therefore the development of new cognitive structures—results from a child's own activity in regulating exchanges with the environment, that is self regulation. Not only is the child's own activity essential in eliminating disequilbrium, it is also instrumental in creating a state of disequilbrium in the first place. A child gets himself into trouble and then gets himself out of it again.[38]

Getting oneself into trouble implies that thinking itself can produce anxiety or discomfort, yet it also suggests that children have a certain freedom or autonomy. Because children create their own cognitive structures, they are not tied to past or present experiences; they can adapt to the new and unique. Children's behavior is not a blind response to stimuli from the environment, because children themselves are in control of their own behavior. They are autonomous within the environment because they can think. The environment does provide opportunities for children to construct their own internal cognitive structures, but it is the cognitive structures, the child and not the environment, that controls thinking and thus behavior.

Theoretically this assumption has great implications. Because children are able to think, they are free to make choices and have the potential to control anxiety and to be in control of whatever situation the environment may present to them.

Cognitive theory is also a stage theory. Stages in children's thinking are believed to be hierarchical and invariant, with each stage representing an increasingly complex way of thinking or processing experiences. The stages are not prewired, nor do they unfold according to some predetermined genetic time table, but rather are shaped by children's thinking and interaction with their social and physical environment.[34]

A second source of stress is the nature of children's thinking. "The limited conceptual ability of children gives rise to a rather private and often false conception of how the world works."[36] Piaget, through structured interviews and observations, demonstrated that children under the age of seven or eight think in prelogical ways.[35] Young children view the world differently than adults. Their thinking is characterized by adualism, animism, and egocentrism. Each of these ways of viewing the world can become a source of stress.

Stages as Sources of Stress

Adualism

In the beginning, infants are believed not to be able to differentiate between self and the physical and human environment. The two major tasks of the infant and child up to around the age of two, are to build inner images of the outer world of people and things. The building of images of the outer world, and differentiation between self and environment, or progression from adualism to dualism, is not always pleasant for children, and may become stressful.

Differentiation of self from environment and others begins when the infant makes eye contact with others between six and twelve weeks of age. Next, children smile in response to any human face, or even in response to anything that resembles a human face.[1] The smiling response is considered the child's first act of social behavior. Between the ages of three and six months, smiling changes from indiscriminate to selective smiling. Now the baby smiles only at familiar people. This is an indication that the child is beginning to build mental images of familiar people against which to match other faces that enter her life. Once babies develop the ability to discriminate between familiar and unfamiliar faces, and smile selectively at the familiar, they begin to cry and exhibit anxiety and stress in the presence of strangers.

Stranger anxiety, and the discomfort that results from being in the presence of strangers, or being separated from the primary caregiver, is believed the result of cognition. The child has not developed the ability to internally represent the physical and social environment.[42] Although emotions and affections are involved, it is cognition that is responsible for the child's stress, not fear of being abandoned.

Even though stranger anxiety and separation from the primary caregiver are sources of stress, they are also positive experiences. First, these experiences provide children with the opportunity to cease to relate everything to their own state or action. The child:

> begins to substitute for a world of fluctuating tableau without spatio-temporal consistency or external physical causality, a universe of permanent objects structured according to its own groups of spatio-temporal displacement, and according to an objectified and spatialized causality, then his affectivity will also be attached to these localizable permanent objects and sources of external causality which persons come to be.[35]

Second, separation from the parent is a developmental task that must be accomplished and it gives children the chance to develop coping and adapting patterns. Bronson sees stranger anxiety and the stress resulting from it, as the beginnings of development of tolerance to stress.[8] Adults aid children in developing the ability to tolerate stress and cope with being separated from the primary caregiver by gradual introduction of surrogates, without deception, and in situations where the contact is otherwise pleasant.[43]

Animism

If not understood by adults, children's misinterpretation of the environment can be a source of profound stress. Before age seven or eight, children believe that the physical world is animistic, that everything is alive, has will and feelings. Therefore, the vacuum sweeper could "eat you up" just as grandma said "it eats the dirt right up." The sidewalk deliberately hurts the child stumbling and scraping a knee, and mother confirms this by saying "naughty sidewalk, you hurt my Ronnie." Cartoons, and the images in children's books and comics offer other confirming evidence for children's belief in animism.

Here children see trees that walk, cars that talk and lamps that chase cats dressed as people around the house. Surely the world is a place full of potential dangers!

Animistic thinking is also the source of children's fears of masks, clowns, and costumes. The young child simply does not understand that people stay the same even though they are dressed differently, or that the clown face, ghost costume or cat mask do not have the power, and will, to hurt them.

Children also believe their dreams are real, and this is another source of anxiety. A four year old reporting her dream tells of a giant. "It was really there, but it left when I woke up. I saw its footprints on the floor."[24] And even when adults reassure children, "don't worry, it wasn't realy, it was only a dream," children still hold onto their idea of the reality of dreams until they themselves master the idea that dreams are not real.

The primary function of the adult is to help children make sense of their world. "As the child's social contacts expand, the sense making function is shared by family, friends, teachers and peers."[36] Adults can establish and maintain routines for daily living that will give children a certain feeling of stability and familiarity with their world. Routines, that give children the idea the world is a stable place, a place they can depend on, as well as the presence of supportive, understanding adults, can help reduce the stress of this period of growth.

Egocentrism

"I'm hiding, I'm hiding, and no one knows where, for all they can see are my toes and my hair," from the poem "Hiding" by Dorothy Aldis,[1] is a perfect example of children's egocentric thought. With eyes covered, unable to see others, the child fully believes no one can see her either. Because of this egocentric thought, children fail to consider any perspective other than their own. They fail to understand that their own viewpoint may not be the same as another's and this thinking leaves them no choice but to see themselves at the center of things. This thinking makes for rocky social interactions as well as an exaggerated sense of power.

Egocentric thought places children, not only in the center of things, but at the cause of things as well. Anything bad that happens is because of something they have done, or did not do. A child who say, "I hate you, I wish you were dead" believes that it is she who caused her mother's illness because she wished it. A child experiencing painful separation, as well as painful, unexplained medical procedures upon hospitalization, believes this experience is the result of something she did.

The loss of egocentric thought, that reaches its height around the beginning of puberty, is believed to be the cause of the turbulence children experience during adolescence.

> During adolescence the young person develops a true "sense of self." Although children are aware of themselves, they are not able to put themselves in other people's shoes and to look at themselves from that perspective. Adolescents can do this and engage in such self-watching to a considerable extent. Indeed, the characteristic "self-consciousness" of the adolescent period results from the very fact that the young person is now very much concerned with how others react to her.[13]

Parents also command the critical eye of the now logically minded teenager. "Just as she is now able to see herself from the perspective of other people, she can now look at her home as others view it and frequently she finds it wanting."[13] The hositlity toward, and rejection of parents is the result of the teenager's understanding that others have opinions and that they, as well as their family, are being watched, observed, judged, and held up to others' opinions of them.

Implications of Cognitive Theories

"Stress occurs for anyone when needs are not being met."[45] Cognitive theory suggests that children need to have the freedom and opportunity to learn for themselves, whether at home, in school, or in the community. Children also need adults who understand their thinking, and provide them with necessary support as they try to make sense of their world. The concept of autonomy implies that children can develop, and then utilize, their internal resources to think, cope, and adapt to whatever stressful experiences they will meet.

Freedom to Learn

For children, driven by the need to learn and know through their own action, many school situations may be viewed as stressors. When faced with school environments that are characterized by teacher telling, rote learning, and paper and pencil tasks, young children's needs to learn are frustrated. Their need to reach a state of equilibrium in their thinking is thwarted, and they remain in a state of disequilibrium, anxious and frustrated.

Schools for young children, if accepting of the idea of learning through action, would be places of high activity. Children would have the freedom to learn from their interactions with the physical and social environment, and through their own mental activity. Children would be able to create their own knowledge through the processes of assimilation and accommodation as they worked with others, with raw materials, and were presented with open-ended activities.

Understanding Thinking

Adults could also minimize stress for children by developing the ability to understand children's thought processes. Adults who really listen to children, who can question children skillfully, who can open their minds to children's thinking, can do much to support children in their attempts to make sense of the world.

Certainly, cognitive theory is based on the assumption that children must do their own learning, yet adults who do understand children's thinking can plan experiences for them that will enable children to see incongruities between their own thinking and the reality of the world. Instead of telling children "the vacuum eats up dirt" adults could assist children in learning to plug the sweeper in, and in turning it on and off, continually reassuring children that it is only a machine, inanimate and without life.

Programs designed to prepare children for hospitalization provide an example of how adults can plan experiences to minimize stress, as well as how adults fail to consider children's thinking and inadvertently add stress. Hospital preparation programs make the assumption that children are rational, cognitive beings. By giving children simple explanations, based on specific stages of children's thinking, children will be better able to prepare themselves to cope with separation, as well as with whatever medical procedures required. Assuring children that they did not cause their illness, is a part of this preparation. Yet, these same programs fail to consider children's animistic thinking, and they present children with people dressed as clowns or big birds to prepare children for surgery, and puppet shows of talking stethoscopes and tongue depressors.

Developing Autonomy

"Stress is only stressful after cognitive processing."[10] As children think, they are in control. Through thinking, stressful events can be made more benign. Flavell[15] suggests that children can be taught to monitor their own cognitive processes; memory, comprehension, and understanding of the situation.[15] Through metacognition children could learn to gain control over their reaction to stressors. Children do appear to grow in self-reflective thought, and increase in volition as they mature.[11]

Instead of eliminating all sources of stress in children's lives, which would be impossible, adults could strengthen children's perceptions of themselves and their ability to cope with stress. As children experience minor stressors, and develop the ability to adapt and cope with stress, "gradually a perception of self and experience evolves."[27]

Children who perceive themselves as:
—competent and strong;
—possessing the ability, power, and control necessary to avoid, minimize or terminate an anticipated or actual stresful life experience;
—viewing the stressful experience as one which is surmountable, one that can be avoided, minimized or terminated; these are children who grow in perceiving themselves as generally able to manage, and in perceiving stressful life experiences as opportunities to manage and cope with stress.[28]

Although children must develop their own internal resources to manage and cope with stress, they still need the continuing support of understanding adults.

The tasks of adults wishing to help children cope with stress is not to attempt to eliminate stressful experiences from children's lives or protect them totally, but rather to try whenever possible to limit number and variety, intensity and duration of such experiences. Further, the adult's task is to provide immediate support and a bank of alternatives that the child may draw on in the future.[27]

PSYCHOANALYTIC THEORIES

Complex, yet rich, the psychoanalytic theories of Freud, followed by those of Adler, Jung, and Erikson, offer a systematic and organized framework for the study of children's growth and development. Based on the concepts that: 1) children's growth and develoment is connected with the need to control instinctual drives; 2) early forms of behavior are never lost, but can be activated and remain in a person's repertoire; and 3) current behavior can only be understood by knowing the developmental history of an individual, the theories present insights into causes of stress during childhood as well as implications for reducing potential sources of stress.

According to psychoanalytic theory, children are believed to be dynamic. Their growth is directed by an internal maturational plan that proceeds through invariant stages. Children develop mental structures that permit them to adapt to the environment and gain control over instinctual drives. According to the theory, there is a limited amount of energy to be spent in the fulfillment or delay of drives.

When growth proceeds normally, and each stage is without conflict, stress is not a problem. It may even serve as an organizer of experiences. Should something go wrong, however, should the environment hamper the unfolding of the genetic maturational plan, should some unbalance be present during a specific growth stage, or a lack of coordination between maturation, the environment and development occur, then stress would result.[43]

Nature of Growth

Based on the idea that behavior is determined from within an individual and directed by internal states or drives, the psychoanalytic theory is one of dynamism. This implies that there is a need, or a force, that directs children's behavior. This drive is not blind, but purposeful, and coordinated with an object, or set of objects, that will provide gratification by reducing the tension of the drive. Either fulfillment, or non-fulfillment of the drive, can be a source of stress.

If a child is driven by hunger, and cries, yet never receives the object, breast or bottle, that will fulfill the drive, she is likely to withdraw from the world, and give up. Yet if the same child is never permitted to cry, and has her needs met before she can develop mental images of objects that will fulfill the needs, she is just as hampered. Overgratification negates the development of autonomy and conscious thinking and the child is continually at the mercy of impulses and will fail to grow and develop.

Freud also suggested that there was a limited amount of energy to be spent in fulfillment of drives.[17] "It is assumed that if the drive energy is not discharged through one channel, it will be discharged through another."[38] If the child's drive of hunger is not fulfilled by breast or bottle, then the drive may be discharged internally, experienced within the child as affect.

If the breast or bottle is obtained, then there is a reduction of tension. The theory calls this reduction of an instinctual drive "pleasure" and if the drive is not fulfilled, an an increase in tension results, it is defined as "pain." The energy of an unreleased drive will become a source of anxiety for the child, especially if the child is unable to control her own behavior and drives. "When the individual is unable to control his own behavior, when he feels threatened that painful internal or external stimuli will overwhelm him, he experiences anxiety."[38] It is because of the anxiety a child feels that defense mechanisms develop. These defense mechanisms consist of cognitive processes, and serve to protect the child from excessive anxiety.

Thought, memory, language, perception and problem solving are among the cognitive structures that children develop as they grow and mature. These cognitive structures are considered ego functions, and they give children control over self, drives, and environment. Once children can think, they are no longer ruled by the need to release or fulfill instinctual drives, but can gain control over these drives. They are now autonomous, in charge of their own destiny, able to control drives, and anxiety and stress as well.

Primary thought processes, those developed as children create mental representations of objects that will fulfill drives, are closely related to drives. As children grow they achieve the ability to think in rational, logical, and orderly ways, ways that are orientated to problem solving. This thinking is termed *secondary* thinking, and permits children to govern their behavior by a reality principle. Now children are able to postpone immediate discharge or a drive, conserve energy, delay gratification, and achieve release from tension or stress through mental processes.

The Genetic Plan

Presenting a genetic point of view, psychoanalytic theory assumes that growth and development has a genetic determinant. Children develop according to an innate, genetic maturational plan, and each child follows the same stages of development. Each stage is characterized by a specific mode and zone, with the mode referring to a style of behavior, such as taking in or letting go, and the zone to a body part.

Along with the idea of invariant stages of development is the concept of critical periods. There is believed to be a time in development when psychological and physiological functions should combine to enable a person to function at a new and more complex level of psychological organization. If this coordination does not occur, the result is developomental imbalance or stress.[42]

Birth to Fifteen Months

The first stage of development—"Taking In"—occurs from birth to about fifteen months of age. During this time the child learns to differentiate self from others, and behavior and growth is characterized by taking in. Not only is food taken in, but everything else—sensory impressions, sounds, lights, warmth, comfort, and total physical care.

It is during this stage that separation anxiety occurs. To psychoanalytists, separation anxiety is viewed as more of an emotional phenomenon. Although Escalona[14] agrees with Piaget that children develop cognitive structures prior to separation anxiety, the anxiety is still believed to be the result of separation. Because the child is helpless and entirely dependent upon the mother for gratification of needs, separation is viewed as deprivation. If separation is abrupt, and long term, it will disrupt the normal establishment of attachments, first to the mother, and then to the world in general.[42]

Deprivation, stemming from lack of emotional gratification resulting from separation from the mother, can cause total withdrawal from the world.

> Without the expectation and experience of gratification from the external world, the young child has little reason to look, investigate, to learn. In extreme cases, such children become withdrawn, unresponsive to any external stimulus, appear with blank eyes, vacant stares, and with total indifference to the world about them.[17]

On the other hand, if the child is never separated from the mother, and if every need is met, even before the child fully realizes the need, overgratification occurs. When the child is overgratified, she fails to develop higher level modes of psychological functioning and reverts to the overgratified level under conditions of stress. "In either case, overgratification or deprivation, psychological development has failed to keep pace with maturation."[27]

An optimal balance between need gratification and delay is called for. Children who experience some stress from separation, or from having to wait for a need to be fulfilled, are gaining the opportunity to organize their psychological resources, and adapt to stress. Children who do not have this balance may be those who tend to become disorganized under stress. "From very early in life—even from infancy—their response to stress is for the mind to go blank. They disorganize."[38]

Fifteen Months to Two Years

From around fifteen months to two years of age children develop autonomy. "I Am What I Will" describes this period. Some sense of autonomy develops because the child can now move at will, darting and dashing wherever and whenever she wants. No longer does the child depend totally on others to meet her every need. Autonomy also results from the development of mental processes. Mental representations mature into cognitive processes. As perception, memory, and cognition develop, children gain freedom from instinctual drives. Now children can think about things, use language and satisfy drives by thinking.

A major source of stress arises from the process of toilet training. Psychoanalyists see this experience as one in which the child needs to express autonomy, but also needs to control impulses and drives and learn to cooperate with, and gain the approval, of others. If the child cooperates, and uses the toilet, she gains approval, but loses some autonomy. If she does not cooperate, and gives into her drives to hold on, she gains disapproval. If this conflict is not resolved satisfactorily, it is believed to resurface during adulthood, with either highly anxious, compulsive behavior or other undesirable behavior.

Three to Five Years

The third stage, from three to five years of age, is described by the phrase, "I Am What I Imagine Myself to Be." Now motor skills are firmly established and physical activity is more purposeful. Fantasies develop and children use the ability to daydream and make believe as outlets for their aggressive or impulsive drives. Make believe also permits them to be what they imagine—firefighters, mommies, or daddies. The ability to fantasize may be another source of stress for the child. Believing fully in the fantasies of their mind, they may become frightened by their daydreams. "Such fears can take rather elaborate forms, since the child may imagine committing some aggressive act against the parent, and then may fantasize that the parent will retaliate for this imagined aggression."[44]

Driven by curiosity, the child tests reality and tries to find out what makes the world work. "Why" is a frequent question, including the whys and hows of sex. Along with the curiosity about the development of sexual drives go the erotic feelings for the parents of the opposite sex. "The boy in love with his mother has a death wish toward his father, the girl in love with her father, wants her mother out of the way and sees herself already wounded because she has no penis."[44]

Typically, the child resolves the stress resultant from these oedipal feelings during the next stage of development. Nevertheless, oedipal feelings are believed to continue to exist in the unconscious and threaten to break into consciousness and exert strong influences during puberty as well as adulthood.[38]

Six to Ten Years

The fourth stage, "I Am What I Learn," is characterized by industry and occurs between six and ten years of age. Children, and their parents and teachers, have an easier time of life during these years. Children now gain great pleasure from making and doing. Going to school is natural, for children are driven by the need to learn, to find out how things work, to take things apart and put them together again. Instinctual energies are now directed into areas of endeavor, usually those that are socially valued, and will produce satisfaction from others.

During this stage, however, stress may arise from peers. Children are now becoming increasingly sensitive to other's views of them. Bruner describes this time as one of being "tutor prone" for children need to be accepted among a group of equals.[9] If a child is ostracized or held in low esteem by others, anxiety due to loss of self respect may arise and even become profound.

Adolescence

Who would argue with the concept that adolescence, the fifth stage of development, is a time of high stress? Now the child, experiencing rapid growth, uneven energy, increased activity levels, and the quest for identity is full of anxiety and stress. Anna Freud wrote extensively of the stress and behavior patterns of this stage.[16] She blamed the oedipal complex, not cognitive development or the culture, as the cause of this stress. She believed that teenagers experience a dangerous resurgence of the oedipal feeling. Because of these feelings, a child feels the need to escape, and therefore rebels against parents, rejecting them and their behavior. Anna Freud believed that adolescent turmoil was normal, as are the desperate defenses the teenager develops to work out her problems. It is the parents who need the help now, for "there are few situations in life which are more difficult to cope with than an adolescent son or daughter during the attempt to liberate themselves."[16]

Implications of the Theories

According to these theories, the role of the adult is to permit children to develop fully and freely. An understanding of each stage and age of development, and the behavioral characteristics of that stage, is required to reduce stress and permit freedom for growth. Parents, teachers, and others who work with children must understand how inner drives direct behavior at each age, and how they can provide for the release of these drives. It is not necessarily permissiveness that is required. Adults do not have to accept everything a child gives or wants to do, but rather to accept the childishness of the child that is required. Adults should give up restrictive or repressive ways of childrearing and educational practices that may hinder children from expressing their natural instincts and growing to full physical and pyschological maturity.

Balance is necessary in working with children. Freud did believe that discipline of children during the early 1900s was unnecessarily restrictive and could act to increase children's shame, guilt, and stress.[17] Yet, he maintained that all societies exact some instinctual renunciation, and that it would be unfair to the children to send them into the world believing they could behave as they pleased, acting on every drive and fulfilling every instinctual urge.

Recognizing Stages

Nevertheless, at each stage of development, adults must be willing to coordinate their guidance and educational practices with children's feelings, internal drives and maturity. For instance, during the first stage of development, infancy, the parent would try to meet each child's needs for food, clothing, comfort, sensory stimulation, and emotional support. It is during this stage that trust develops. When children's needs are met, they can tolerate their mother leaving for a short time, for they trust their environment, and trust her to return. If the child's needs are not met, then the child can never detach from the mother and will remain anxious, untrusting of self, others, and the environment.

Parents, teachers, and other adults working with children also protect children's need to express autonomy during the second stage of development. They give children choices they can make—"do you want to take a shower or a bath?" "wear your red or blue shirt?" "read a book or watch TV before going to bed?"—and otherwise protect children's rights to assert their will.

As toilet training is the highlight of this stage of development, and could result in stressful conflicts that may remain throughout an individual's life time, adults should also arrange for this process to be one where the child can express autonomy. Giving children clothing they can handle, without buttons, zippers, or complicated hooks, as well as equipment, benches, or toilet seats they can manage, permits them to "take charge." Now they can make their own decisions about using the toilet, and the adult has reduced sources of conflict between what she, the powerful parent, wants, and what the child desires.

When children enter school they need to find places where their need for industry and initiative can flourish. School structures—competition, grading, grouping, paper and pencil tasks, teacher talk—reduce children's opportunity to be industrious and take initiative. School should be a source of pleasure for children at this time, a place where they can develop basic, as well as social skills, and fulfill their need for industry.

Understanding adults are also required to help children through the turmoil of adolescence. Adults who recognize children's needs to be like others, who support them as they search for their identity and help them work through role confusion can do much to reduce the stress of the teen years.

Autonomy

The concept of autonomy is of equal importance in both the cognitive and psychoanalytic theories. Even though children are driven to fulfill instinctual drives, the psychoanalytic theory holds that they are capable of developing control over these drives. Autonomy arises as the secondary thought processes develop. The processes of thinking, memory, and language, can be used to control internal drives, and to deal with the environment in realistic ways. Children who are conscious of their internal drives, feelings or emotions, who can understand these drives, and perhaps verbalize them, are better able to develop controls over them.

As children's thought processes develop, they are also better able to engage in reality testing. Instead of giving into drives, or having temper tantrums when faced with stressful events, children use their mental images, memory and problem solving ability to test reality.

Children can learn to postpone the immediate discharge of energy and satisfy their urges through thinking.

The role of the adult is to help children develop secondary thought processes, the ability to test reality, and hence, autonomy over internal drives. Adults do not 'take over' for the child, nor do they limit the child's opportunities to experience anxiety or stress in normal living. Rather, they give children the chance to face unpleasantness, to become anxious, and solve problems, within safe, secure, and favorable conditions.

BEHAVIORAL THEORIES

To the behaviorists, reactions of fear, anxiety, and stress are responses to some immediately antecedent stimulus in the environment. Stress and fear are learned, reinforced, and maintained by environmental consequences. Rather than the child being driven by internal cognitive processes, or instinctual drives, behavior is attributed to environmental conditions and past learning.

Experiences, and the connections between experiences, produce behavior. "The organism's prewired repertory of behaviors is supplemented by continual rewirings that are produced by experience."[21] A young child, who has experienced an overly friendly, large dog, push her to the ground and lick her face, may become anxious as any dog approaches. She has learned to become apprehensive. This stress is not, according to the behaviorists, genetic, nor a result of a child's internal cognitive structures, nor is it stage or age related. There are no maturational processes, nor internal conflicts between fulfilled or unfilfilled drives, but only the connection between an act and its consequences. Thus any combination and any sequence of behavior including anxiety, stress, coping with stress, can be learned through experiences that are either reinforced or ignored.

Classical and Operant Theories

Anxiety, fear, or stress can be the result of classical conditioning. Just as Pavlov conditioned dogs to salivate upon hearing a bell, children can be conditioned to exhibit fear, anxiety, or stress. In Pavlov's study of dogs, the salivary response to food powder, occuring as essentially an inborn reflex, was the unconditioned stimulus. The conditioning process consisted of pairing some other stimulus with the unconditioned stimulus. A bell was rung slightly before the food powder was presented. The combination of the bell and the food was repeated, and the dogs began to salivate (the conditioned response) whenever they heard the bell (conditioned stimulus).

Instrumental, or operant conditioning, is also believed responsible in learning responses of fear, avoidance behavior, anxiety, or stress. Operant conditioning involves the process of changing the frequency of a response by controlling the consequences of the response. In classical conditioning, the conditioned stimulus and unconditioned stimulus are presented independently of the response of the animal or subject. In operant, or instrumental conditioning, the presentation of a reinforcer or punisher is contingent upon an appropriate response by the organism. The chicken, moving about the cage at random, does something, such as pressing a lever, which in turn produces a piece of food. After trials, the instrumental behavior, lever pressing, is influenced by its consequences.

Classical and operant conditioning go far beyond producing salivary responses in dogs or lever pressing in chickens. "We can only guess at the actual scope of classical and operant conditioning in human everyday life."[7] In human stress theories, the reinforcers may be pay, money, reduced work loads, or any other consequences that reinforce human behavior. Fear, avoidance behavior, compulsive rituals found in human anxiety, learned helplessness and other human emotions of adults and children have been attributed to the effects of classical and operant conditioning.

Perhaps the best known example of how classical conditioning can produce fear is Little Albert.[23] Albert was conditioned by Watson to fear white rats. Although the Little Albert study achieved the status of a myth, research continues to illustrate how emotions, such as fear, can function as learned drives.[22][30]

Operant conditioning has been studied in connection with avoidance behavior and its consequences. Although current theorists believe that avoidance learning involves at least some information processing,[3] operant techniques have been used to explain, as well as treat, avoidance behavior. In avoidance learning, animals are conditioned by being placed in a shuttle box, with two compartments. In one of the compartments, a tone or light is presented, followed by a shock. The animal upon receiving the shock in one compartment, moves to the other. Eventually the animal shuttles into the other compartment upon hearing the tone or light, thus avoiding the shock. Mowrer believed that fear is an aversive state that motivates the animal to engage in escape behavior.[31] The animal is escaping from the conditioned stimulus and the fear it elicits, thus avoiding the shock. The avoidance behavior is reinforced by fear induction, and as it is motivated by fear arousal elicited by the conditioned stimulus, and is reinforced by fear reduction, the presence of the unconditioned stimulus becomes irrelevant to maintain the response. Most research on avoidance learning has been conducted on animals; nevertheless, the theory is useful in explaining human avoidance behaviors.[7]

Current Theories

Today's behaviorists recognize some type of internal mediation between the environment and the behavioral response of the child to the environment. The current theorists, while still recognizing and accepting the role of environmental conditions and the association between a particular stimulus and response in learning, place much more emphasis on the power of the human to think. (see 4, 19, 21).

Gagné, for example, views learning as resulting from a combination of internal and external conditions.[19] The external conditions are the environment, which can be arranged to promote learning, eliminate stressors, or develop techniques for coping with stress. The environment is considered of great importance, but humans have control over environmental conditions and can exploit these external conditions to develop human thought and intellect.

> This enormous dependence of learning on environmental circumstances implies a great responsibility for all members of human society. The situations in which developing children are placed, whether deliberately or otherwise, are going to have great effects on them. . . . Learning is not simply an event that happens naturally; it is also an event that happens under certain observable conditions. Furthermore, these conditions can be altered and controlled; and this leads to the possibility of examining the occurrence of learning by means of the conditions under which learning takes place can be observed and described.[19]

Even with the importance of the environment in influencing human learning, Gagné believes in the concept of internal conditions that interact with the external to promote learning. These internal conditions, however, are not imposed on the child by some inherent cognitive struture or drive, but consist mainly of past learning and experiences. Gagné defines them as persisting effects of past learning. Previous learning can determine behavior that will occur in the presence of a particular external condition or stimuli. Thus behavior patterns such as fear, anxiety, or coping with stressors, are patterns produced by a combination of both external and internal conditions. Learning still consists of making connections or associations between a particular stimulus and response, yet this event is strongly influenced by internal conditions, past learning, and experience.[19]

Past learning is believed to mediate experiences as well as present conditions. This means that by understanding past learning, observing, and measuring the internal conditions of individual children, and by arranging external conditions, human growth, development, and learning could be controlled and enhanced.

Bandura also recognizes the principles of reinforcement and stimulus-response bonds, but believes that human learning involves much more than simple classical or operant conditioning.[5] The learning of fear, anxiety, or stress, as well as sex role, aggression, problem solving, and other human behaviors is much more complex than making chains between stimuli and responses, and involves the processes of attending, memory, observation and imitation.

By watching a model's behavior, a child can learn new behavior. This involves the child being able to attend to a model (attentional processes); to symbolically code, cognitively organize the observations (retention processes); to physically reproduce observed behaviors (motor reproduction processes), and involves external, vicarious as well as self, reinforcements (motivational processes).[6]

Bandura distinguishes between the acquisition and the performance of new responses.[3] One can observe a model, but not perform the response. Performances are governed by reinforcement and motivational variables. As well as vicarious and self reinforcements, direct ones can influence a child's performance. The evaluation children make of their own behavior (self reinforcement) also plays a role in the acquisition and performance of learning new behaviors.

Research evidence suggests that the theory of social learning can explain the socialization process. The process of observing and imitating models is the way in which children learn the "do's" and "don'ts" of a culture, and develop socially acceptable behavior. Given the evidence of research, the theory could also be used to explain how children develop anxiety, fear, or learn stress reactions and coping behavior.

In fact, Bandura[4] argues that other theories impede our understanding of how children learn to behave in stressful ways or react to stressful situations. According to Anna Freud the period of adolescence is extremely stressful.[16] She believed that the maturation of powerful sexual and aggressive drives throws the teenage child into a state of turmoil and the child thinks the only solution is to gain independence by rebelling from and rejecting the immediate family. Bandura believes this idea is a myth. He states:

> For most North American youth, adolescence is no more stressful than childhood. Nor is it a period of sudden independence-seeking; for parents already had taught their sons and daughters to become increasingly independent during childhood. Nor, finally, is it a period of rebellion against parents; for most teenagers continue to accept the advice and values of their parents, and they join peer groups that uphold and reinforce these values.[2]

For Bandura, the turmoil of adolescence is the result of our culture and social learning. It is the culture that dictates that teenagers become increasingly independent, and the peer group that serves to uphold and reinforce the values and behaviors of the teenager. Increased interest in the opposite sex during the teen years, according to Bandura, is also determined by the culture. For the American teenager, the culture expects and reinforces an intense interest in the opposite sex and this interest differs from culture to culture. Thus, we do not need to look for instinctual drives that have been hidden in the subconscious, nor maturational cognitive states, to explain the stress of adolescence, but rather to an examination of the specifics within a culture and the social learning variables that influence adolescent behaviors.[7]

Bandura's theory of social learning is moving away from the strict S-R theories of learning to the position of cognitive psychology.

> Bandura's learning theory differs from the traditional behavioristic theories in that it emphasizes, in addition to observational learning, symbolic representational and self-regulatory processes.[20]

Children are believed to be in control over their behavior because they think and regulate their behavior. To Bandura, the ability to feel in control of the situation, is the primary determinant of coping, defensive and anxious behaviors.[6]

Implications of the Theory

"In many ways, the behavioral perspective is primarily a treatment perspective."[7] If anxiety, fear, and stress are learned behaviors, learned through the processes of classical or operant conditioning, or through the process of modeling, then they can be unlearned through the same processes.

Behavior Modification

The techniques of behavior modification, based on the principles of classical and operant conditioning, can be systematically employed to reduce stress, change behaviors produced by stress or to desensitize children who are fearful, anxious, or stressed. There is an elegant simplicity and clarity to behavior modification techniques. First, the adult must identify the behavior of the child that is to be reduced or eliminated. It is not enough to say that the child's anxiety over separation is to be eliminated. The adult must identify in concrete behavioral terms, exactly which kind of behavior is to be eliminated—the crying, whining, clinging, or thumb sucking. When the adult identifies which behavior is appropriate and desired, the child upon separation will then not cry, will drop her mother's hand, and will join the other children.

The next step is to identify the events in the external environment that serve to reinforce the behavior to be eliminated. For instance, the child who clings and cries may be receiving rewards such as verbal promises from the mother or the attention of the teacher; or, her mother may pick her up, give her candy, or reinforce the inappropriate separation behavior in some other way.

The adult must also identify other approaches that do not reinforce the crying or separation behavior. Things the child would enjoy—feeding the rabbit, reading a story in the rocker with the teacher, serving snacks or other things that are liked, and may serve as reinforcers—are discovered. Then a schedule, based on principles of learning connections, would be designed. This schedule would be a plan for the withdrawal of the patterns of behavior that are reinforcing the child's anxiety at separation, and the rewarding of desired behavior with other reinforcers.

Conditions of Learning

Gagné identified how adults and teachers can analyze the internal and external conditions of learning to promote optimal environments for children. These have not been designed specifically for the reduction of stress or anxious behaviors; nevertheless, they could be a useful tool for those wishing to create supportive environments for children. The steps in planning conditions of learning include:
1. Stating objectives, and the terminal performance desired.
2. Analyzing performance and constructing learning hierarchies.
3. Specifying performances for prerequisites.

Growth and Development—A Source of Stress?

4. Identifying external conditions to promote prerequisite learning.
5. Gaining and maintaining the learner's attention.
6. Informing the learner of expected results.
7. Stimulating recall.
8. Presenting stimuli.
9. Providing guidance or prompting.
10. Providing feedback.
11. Encouraging self appraisal.
12. Providing for transfer.
13. Evaluating what is learned.[19]

These steps could be applied in any situation. They could be used to design a program to toilet train children without stress, to prepare children for separation, or to help a child learn new skills, concepts, or attitudes within the school setting.

Teachers wishing to reduce the potential stress of school could arrange the conditions of learning in the school environment. These conditions would provide a supportive environment, one in which children would achieve mastery and success. These steps include:

1. Individualizing of instruction so that the materials presented are on the child's level.
2. Utilizing mastery of teaching principles and errorless learning techniques (introduce material in small steps; distribute practice.)
3. Breaking the goal into components and rewarding efforts at each step toward the goal.
4. Setting up realistic goals; discouraging involvement in a situation for which the child lacks skills; providing realistic vocational guidance at the high school level.
5. Teaching at the level of the child's strengths; utilizing strengths to help the child compensate for deficits.[40]

Providing Models

The theory of social learning has applicability in stress reduction with children and in understanding children's reaction to stressors. Although the phrases "learning by doing" and "do as I say not as I do" imply that our folk culture has always recognized the role of observing and modeling in learning, it took the work of Bandura to formalize our understanding and increase our awareness of learning through models.

Just as Bandura showed children afraid of dogs models of other children calmly playing with peaceful dogs,[6] children experiencing stress, anxiety, or other fears could be presented with models calmly adapting and coping with those same stressors. The models could be live, of the same age, sex, and background of the children, or they could appear in movies, on television, video tape, or even be present as characters in children's books.

In a typical modeling paradigm, the child, who exhibits stress upon facing separation, would be exposed to another child, who can be apart from its mother without stress. The model would receive positive reinforcement, and perhaps the separation process would be broken into small, graduated steps and presented in a sequence. The child undergoing the stress may be asked to participate and be guided into experiencing separation without stress.

Teachers, parents, and others who work with children would constantly be aware of their role in modeling appropriate behavior for children. With the example of numerous models to learn from, children would be able to handle whatever stressful situation the environment should present to them.

CONCLUSION

All children experience stress of some sort. Whether one accepts the psychoanalytic, cognitive, or behavioral theories of child growth and development, it is clear that growth is characterized by situations of push and pull. These stem from either the external environment, or from within the child. Some are the result of a combination of both external and internal forces.

Many children may never have to cope with more than the normal stress that accompanies growth and development. Others, those who are separated from parents, hospitalized, facing the divorce of parents, death of siblings, wars, or other tragedies, are forced to cope with catastrophic stress.

McNamee believes that children can be categorized on three levels based on their ability to cope with stress.[28] The first group is made up of exceptionally good copers. These children recover spontaneously and integrate the stressful life experience into their life style in positive ways. They develop alternative ways of coping with stressful events. They believe in themselves. They see themselves as competent, and each time they face stress and handle it, they increase their feelings of competence.

The second group of children is comprised of those who have to work at coping with stress. They manage to cope adequately, and their self confidence grows. Yet, their successes are less frequent and their resource bank of successful alternatives grows more slowly than that of the exceptional copers.

Third level children are those who become disorganized by stress. These children must struggle hard to surmount even the stress of growing and developing, as well as the normal stresses that are a part of everyday life.

Knowledge of the theories of child growth and development may help adults understand how they can help all children to become good or exceptional copers. Taking bits and pieces from each of the theories enables adults to understand better children's growth, as well as to grasp their role in reducing stress and helping children develop the ability to cope with stress. With knowledge of the theories in mind, adults can work to provide children with optimal environments that are challenging as well as supportive. Adults can work to arrange conditions of learning that will enable children to develop the psychological resources required to cope, adapt, and master the stresses of daily life.

REFERENCES

1. Aldis, D., *All together*. New York: G. P. Putnam's Sons, 1925, p. 71.
2. Bandura, A., The stormy decade:fact or fiction. *Psychology in the Schools,* 1964, 1: 224–31.
3. ———The role of modeling processes in personality development. In W. W. Hartup & S. L. Smothergill (Eds.), *The Young Child: Review of Research*. Washington, D.C.: National Association for the Education of Young Children, 1967.
4. ———Social learning theory of identification processes. In D. A. Bostin (Ed.), *Handbook of socialization theory and research*. Chicago: Rand McNally & Company, 1969.
5. ———*Social learning theory*. Englewood Cliffs, N.J.: Prentice-Hall, 1977.
6. Bandura A. & R. H. Walters, *Social learning and personality development*. New York: Holt, Rinehart & Winston, 1963.
7. Bootzin, R. R. & D. Max, Learning and behavioral theories, In I. L. Kutash & L. B. Schlesinger (Eds.), *Handbook on stress and anxiety*. San Francisco: Jossey-Bass Publications, 1980, 36–48.
8. Bronson, G. W., *Infant's reactions to unfamiliar persons and novel objects*. Monograph of the Society for Research in Child Development, 1972, 37 (3 Serial No. 148).
9. Bruner, J. S., Nature and uses of immaturity. *American Psychologist,* 1972, 27: 687-700.
10. Coyne, J. C., & R. S. Lazarus, Cognitive styles, stress perception and

coping. In I. L. Kutash & L. B. Schlesinger (Eds.) *Handbook on stress and anxiety*. San Francisco: Jossey-Bass Publications, 1980, 145–158.
11. Damon, W. & D. Hart, The development of self understanding from infancy through adolescence. *Child Development*, 1982, 53, 4: 1–864.
12. Dennis, W., Causes of retardation among institutional children: Iran. *Journal of Genetic Psychology*, 1960, 96: 47–59.
13. Elkind, D., *A Sympathetic understanding of the child* (2nd Ed.) Boston: Allyn and Bacon, Inc., 1978.
14. Escalona, S., Patterns of infantile experience and the developmental process. *The Psychoanalytic Study of the Child*, 1963, 18: 197–244.
15. Flavell, J. H. & L. Ross (Eds.), *Social cognitive development: frontiers and possible futures*. Cambridge: Cambridge University Press, 1981.
16. Freud, A., Adolescence. *Psychological study of the child*, 1958, 13: 278–355.
17. Freud, S. (1907), *The sexual enlightment of children*. J. Riviere, Trans. *Collected papers*, II. New York: Basic Books, 1959.
18. ———(1914), *On narcissism: an introduction*. J. Riviere, Trans. *Collected papers*, II. New York: Basic Books, 1959.
19. Gagné, R. M., *The conditions of learning*. New York: Holt, Rinehart & Winston, 1977.
20. Gazda, G. M. & R. J. Corsini, *Theories of learning*. Itasca: Peacock Publishers, 1980.
21. Gleitman, H., *Psychology*. New York: W.W. Norton & Company, 1981.
22. Grings, W. W. & M. E. Dawson, *Emotions and bodily responses*. New York: Academic Press, 1978.
23. Harris, B., Whatever happened to Little Albert? *American Psychologist*, 1979, 34, 2: 151–161.
24. Kohlberg, L., Cognitive stages and preschool education. *Human Development*, 1966, 9: 5–17.
25. Lourie, R. S. & C. Schwarzbeck, When children feel helpless in the face of stress. *Childhood Education*, 1977, 55, 3: 141–184.
26. Mahoney, M. J., Reflections on the cognitive learning trend in psychology therapy. *American Psychologist*, 1977, 32, 1: 5–14.
27. McNamee, A. S., Introduction. *Children and stress*. Washington, D.C.: Association for the Education of Young Children. 1982, p. 5.
28. McNamee, A. & J. McNamee, *Self destructive behavior in children and adolescents*. New York: Van Nostrand Reinhold Co., 1981.
29. Meichenbaum, D., *Cognitive behavior modification*. New York: Plenum, 1977.
30. Miller, N. E., Learnable drives and rewards. In S. S. Stevens (Ed.), *Handbook of experimental psychology*. New York: John Wiley & Sons, 1951.
31. Mowrer, A., On the dual nature of learning: a reinterpretation of conditioning and problem solving. *Harvard Educational Review*, 1947, 17: 102–148.
32. Pavlov, I. P., *Conditioned reflexes*. London: Oxford University Press, 1927.

33. Perkins, D. G., Classical conditioning: Pavlov. In G. M. Gazda & R. J. Corsini (Eds.), *Theories of learning*. Itasca: Peacock Publishers, 1980.
34. Piaget, J., *The origins of intelligence in children*. New York: W. W. Norton, 1963.
35. Piaget, J. & B. Inhelder, *The psychology of the child*. New York: Basic Books, 1964.
36. Pozzuto, R., The child's community and the world at large. In A. S. McNamee (Ed.), *Children and stress*. Washington, D.C.: Association for the Education of Young Children, 1982, 68–74.
37. Rapaport, D., The structure of psychoanalytic theory: a systematic attempt. *Psychological Issues*, 1960, 2, 2: 7–158.
38. Rohwer, W. D., P. R. Ammon & P. Cramer, *Understanding intellectual development*. New York: Holt, Rinehart & Winston, 1974.
39. Rouck, L. A., Children's responses to hospitalization. In A. S. McNamee (Ed.). *Children and stress*. Washington, D.C.: Association for the Education of Young Children, 1982, 25–32.
40. Schaffer, M. P. & S. J. Schaffer, Stress related to organically based learning disorders. In A. S. McNamee (Ed.), *Children and stress*. Washington, D.C.: Association for the Education of Young Children, 1982, 14–15.
41. Selye, H., The stress concept today. In I. L. Kutash & L. B. Schlesinger, (Eds.), *Handbook on stress and anxiety*. San Francisco: Jossey-Bass Publishers, 1980, 127–144.
42. Spitz, R. A., Hospitalism: an inquiry into the genesis of psychiatric conditions in early childhood. *The psychoanalytic study of the child*, 1945, 153–174.
43. ———, *The first year of life*. New York: International Universities Press, 1965.
44. Wolff, S., *Children under stress*. New York: Penquin, 1969.

CHAPTER 3

BEHAVIORAL RESPONSES OF CHILDREN TO STRESS

Louis A. Chandler, Ph.D.

> *The possible options open to the individual in responding to stress are limited by genetic, psychological, social, and cultural variables. In the case of children, the options are further restricted because of developmental factors. Clinical experience suggests that the responses adopted by children in their efforts to cope with stress are limited to a few basic patterns. These patterns can be described by the model of personality functioning. This chapter discusses the stress response model and describes the resulting behavior patterns. It also presents an assessment instrument developed from the model, along with some preliminary data on its validity, reliability, and clinical use.*

Psychological stress has been criticized as a concept that is too vague and overly-inclusive.[1] Yet it is the very elasticity of the concept that lends it a particular value in psychosocial applications. Lerner addresses this point when he says: "A lot of the fuzziness about the concept of stress is what makes it so valuable."[23] He goes on to quote Aristotle to the effect that it is always an error to try to make a science more exacting than its subject allows.

One source of variance in attempts to define stress lies in the different contexts in which it is found. The contexts have been provided by the two main branches of research that have evolved: the psychophysiological and the psychosocial. Since Selye's pioneering work there has been a more or less ongoing interest in the relation of stress to physiological functioning.[32] In this context, stress is seen as a state consisting of nonspecific changes manifested in various physiological reactions. Selye's stress syndrome is a cluster of such reactions. Any agent which precipitates the nonspecific changes is, by definition, a stressor. The changes themselves are a *stress response*.

On the other hand, psychosocial researchers have tended to focus on stress as a problem arising out of a demand that taxes the system composed of the individual and his environment.[22] A key role is played by the appraisal that the individual makes of the demand, that is, seeing it as a threat with the probability of loss or harm as a consequence.[11] (In this context stress is viewed as a negative experience, although technically even positive actions or situations can be stressful in that they may serve to unbalance an individual's homeostasis.[18])

For our purposes stress may be defined as a state of tension arising from events or situations which the individual perceives as threatening. This state of emotional tension acts as a motivator as the individual, seeking drive reduction, attempts to cope with stress. That very attempt to cope may result in a number of stress responses ranging from healthy, effective ones to pathological ones that are not only ineffective but are often counterproductive. In the case of children extreme responses result in behavior that calls attention to itself and interferes with effective functioning at home, in school, and in social relations.

In any discussion of the stress response of children, the first consideration must be developmental. Significant differences are most obvious when comparing children to adults. Adults respond to stress in a number of ways based, in part, on their personality and, to a considerable extent, on previous experience. That is, they often tend to respond in ways that have been reinforced in the past. Children, with more limited experience in living, have a more limited repertoire of responses available to them.

In addition, many of the options open to adults simply do not exist for children since they are more dependent, less mobile, and have less freedom to choose. An adult who finds himself in a stressful job situation may be able to modify his duties, change jobs, arrange for a transfer, resign or relocate. The child who experiences school as a stressful situation may have few alternatives. Reducing stress by leaving the situation or consciously avoiding a potentially stressful situation are common responses that require a certain degree of independence, planning, and mobility.

Finally, children lack the adult reasoning powers that come with maturity. Adult reasoning provides the justification for the tradeoffs, compromises, and balances that are a necessary part of life. Adults are capable of foregoing immediate gratification in order to pursue long term goals. They are capable of tolerating stress, even extreme stress, for a period of time if they can see some ultimate benefit. Children have a more limited tolerance for frustration and for delaying gratification; and they seldom find convincing adult reasons that rationalize unpleasant experiences. Thus, developmental considerations serve to restrict the responses available to children. With these general remarks we can now turn to a closer examination of the specific response patterns likely to be found with children.

A STRESS RESPONSE MODEL

While there is considerable variation in the ways individuals respond to stress depending on personality, social, and cultural variables, the range of human response is not infinite. Ultimately human nature restricts the options that are available to the individual and genetic factors and previous learning further limits them to a rather fixed repertoire for any one individual. As a result, response patterns follow a few basic themes, although they may be manifested in a number of variations.

Some of the earliest psychological speculation involved the attempt to discover the basic themes or types of personality that could account for the variation seen among individuals. The Greek physician Hippocrates is credited with one of the first recorded attempts. His scheme was based on the then contemporary notion that the humours, or bodily fluids, determined the individual's temperament, that is, the way he was likely to respond. He postulated that four basic types of temperament could be identified: the phlegmatic, the sanguine, the melancholic, and the choleric, each associated with a specific humour.

Implicit in this idea were two elements which the modern researcher would recognize as contemporary issues. First, there is the notion that the physical is linked to, and to some extent determines, the psychological. The brain/mind problem has been a recurring research issue.

Second, a personality typology can be based on observable characteristics which are shared by all, although some individuals seem to have a predominance of one quality which assigns them to a certain type. The implication here is that the healthy personality is a well-balanced one showing, to some degree, many of the traits and attributes in less-than-extreme proportions. The view of personality traits as seen on a continuum from slight to extreme continues to influence psychological research.[25]

Various typologies have been proposed since Hippocrates for ordering and classifying personality. Shakespeare described his Danish prince as melancholic, giving us an Elizabethan example of the long-lasting influence of Hippocrates. A more contemporary effort has been made by Sheldon.[33,34]

Sheldon, like Hippocrates, believed that there were constitutional determinants of personality patterns. He proposed that such determinants were reflected in certain bodily types which could be described along morphological dimensions. Three dimensions, the endomorphic, the mesomorphic, and the ectomorphic, could be used to rate individuals with a three-digit number which would represent that person's body type. He then correlated these somatypes with three clusters of personality traits and found some agreement between bodily types and temperamental characteristics.

A more recent investigation into the temperament characteristics of children can be found in the work of Thomas and Chess.[36,37] They maintained that the behavioral characteristics of children could be used to define personality types. They identified nine such behavior patterns or temperament categories based in their observations of babies and young children in their clinic: activity level, rhythmicity, approach/withdrawal, distractability, adaptability, attention span and persistence, intensity of reaction, threshold of responsiveness, and quality of mood. These characteristics were first seen in infancy, and, although they did not make a strong case for a genetic or constitutional base for temperament patterns, their work does lend some support to that notion.[21]

While the various proposed typologies have some theoretical base, for some, the theoretical underpinnings are more comprehensive than for others. Freud, for example, in introducing the oral, anal, phallic, and genital character types, based his classification on a rather extensive theory of personality development and psychopathology.[17] Theoretical formulations supply the general principles which can be applied to all cases. One such fundamental principle is that man is a dynamic entity. He must reach out to interact with his environment if he is to survive. Some degree of activity, therefore, is always present. The infant, though restricted in his mobility, cries and struggles in an effort to reach out to his world. Later the child slowly builds a sense of mastery as he is able to affect objects and others in his home and school. Activity is a constant but the degree of activity varies across individuals. Some individuals seem by nature to be more passive and lethargic, while others are more active and energetic. Physiological studies have shown that the degree of activity is related to, among other things, the state of physiological arousal of the central nervous system.[12] Activity can be seen on a continuum as one of the underlying dimensions of personality.

A second dimension of personality has to do with the direction towards which activity is expended. Some individuals tend to turn their activity toward the world. They are allocentric, outward-looking, and overtly active. They are extroverts. At the other extreme are the more introverted who characteristically turn their activity inward, preferring to withdraw their energy from contact with the world. Jung is often credited with first introducing the introversion-extroversion dimension of personality.[19] This dimension has been called by far the most popular dimension utilized by personality theorists.[24] A review of the literature finds considerable support for an active-passive (see References 1, 26, 27, 28, 31, 35) and an extroversion-introversion dimension (see 3, 14, 15, 16). These two fundamental dimensions can be related by an orthogonal configuration in a circumplex model (Figure 1).

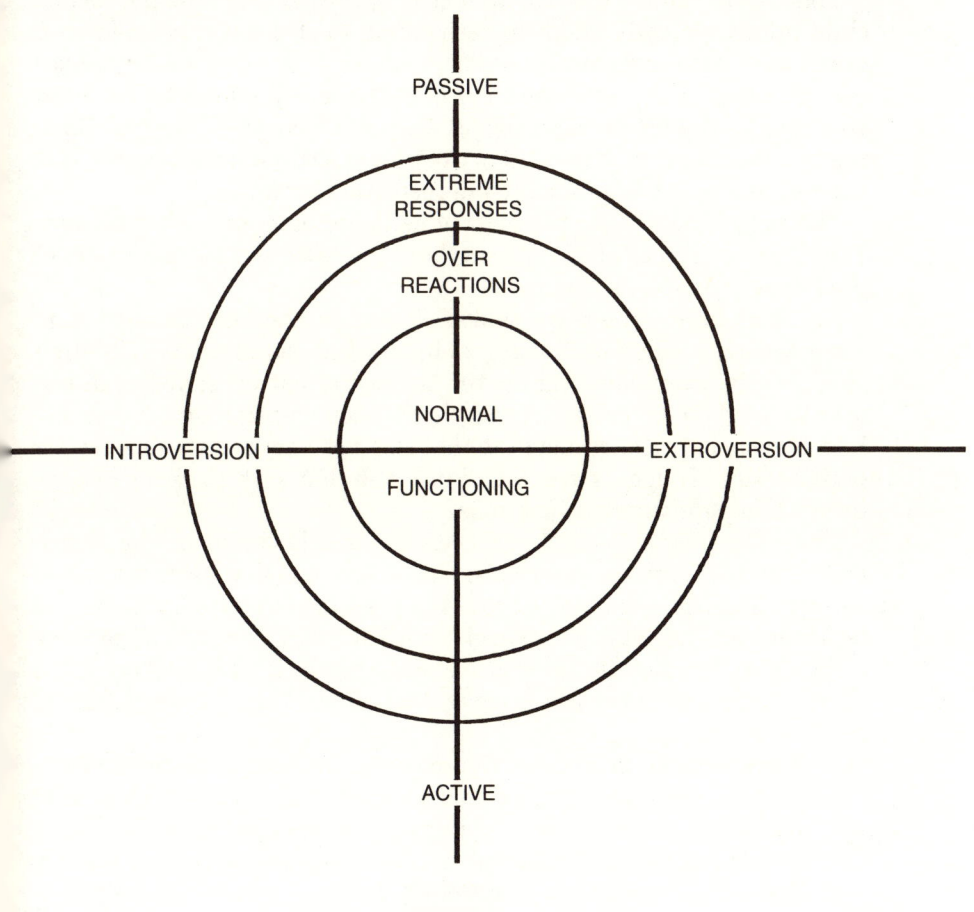

FIGURE 1
Two Dimensions of Personality

With this model the vertical axis describes the quantity of activity the child expends; while the horizontal axis represents the direction of that activity, that is, turned outward towards the environment or inward toward the self.

It is apparent from observations of children in schools and clinics that when children are under stress their activity levels vary. Some children become overactive; some become more withdrawn, almost lethargic and passive. Similiarly, they may turn their activity inward or outward toward the world. They may withdraw into quiet isolation or act out. These two basic dimensions then, the active-passive, and the introversion-extroversion, should be useful in describing the behavioral responses of children.

This model relates the two dimensions, illustrating how the style a child might typically adopt in responding to stress can be seen on a continuum with extreme behavior at either end. What distinguishes normal functioning from the kind of extreme behavior as seen in an emotional adjustment reaction, is simply a matter of degree. Emotional adjustment reactions then, can be defined as extreme patterns of normal coping behavior adopted in response to stress.

The model yields four patterns of behavior, one for each quadrant. These can be seen as ideal types in that they represent extreme cases of the behavior patterns (Figure 2).

As ideal types, they are seldom found as discrete, isolated, and consistently predictable patterns in clinical populations. Children vary widely, even adopting (at times) several patterns; although one usually tends to be preferred and can be seen as dominant. Nevertheless, clinical experience suggests that children showing these behavior patterns are commonly seen at clinics, and that such patterns may be useful as diagnostic classifications.

These diagnostic types have been frequently found in the literature [10,30] and similar syndromes have occasionally been identified through empirical studies.[13] From the literature and from a review of psychological reports of children, characteristics for each type were collated, and composite descriptive statements developed. The model then, yields four diagnostic categories which may be described as follows:

The Dependent Child is often passive, immature, and characterized by regressive habits and childish mannerisms. This child lacks independence in many areas of functioning, and usually avoids taking the initiative in learning and social situations. Some children, while dependent, are less passive and adopt a more assertive, demanding manner to have their needs met.

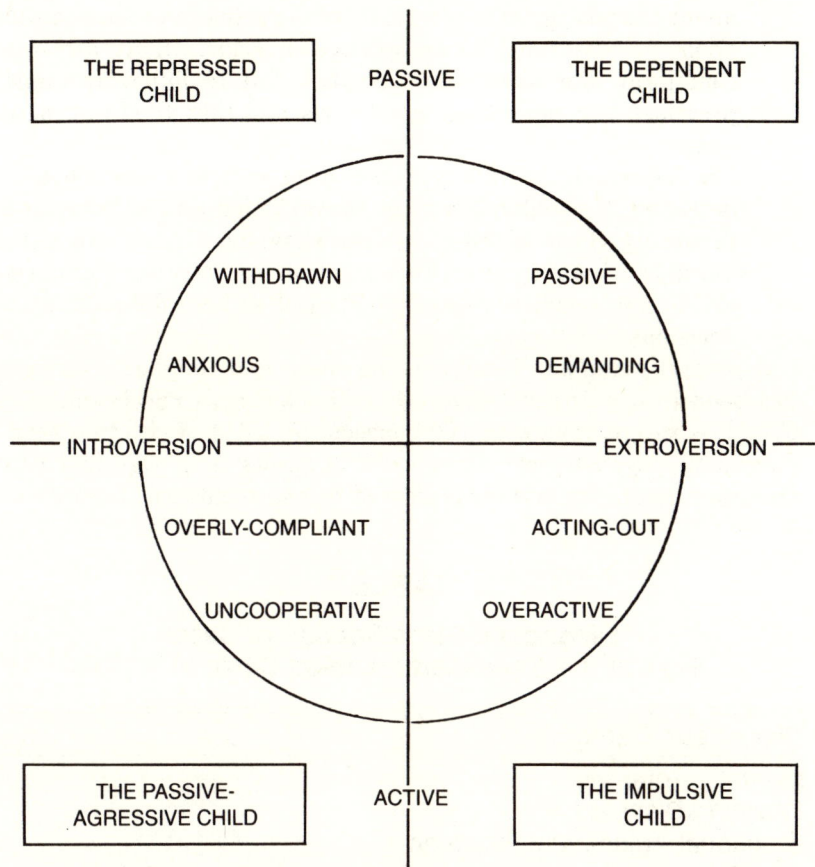

FIGURE 2
Four Common Response
Patterns to Stress

These children are often described as headstrong, defiant, selfish, and willful. They seek immediate need gratification.

The Impulsive Child is easily excited, impulsive, and generally overactive. If this child's activity is focused, it may be turned toward authority figures or peers. Such children are described as aggressive and hostile, subject to temper tantrums, violence, and acting out behavior. For both subtypes, the essential problem is a lack of appropriate controls.

The Passive-Aggressive Child is most often characterized by school underachievement, and is usually described as indifferent about his poor grades in school. While sometimes these children adopt an obstinate, uncooperative attitude, others are overly-compliant and agreeable, yet they fail to follow through on promises to complete assigned work and they tend to procrastinate.

The Repressed Child is typically quiet, reserved, shy, moody, and detached. He seldom initiates conversation and is prone to daydreaming. Some of these children show more symptoms of being anxious. This may involve fears, worries, nervous mannerisms, and overly-sensitive reactions. They often have difficulty making decisions.

A partial taxonomy incorporating these four diagnostic categories has been in use at the University of Pittsburgh's Psychoeducational Clinic. A recent review of 100 consecutive cases of children seen for diagnostic psychological assessment suggests that over half can be classified according to their preferred response pattern (Table 1).

TABLE 1

Diagnostic Classification of Cases Seen at the Psychoeducational Clinic (n = 100)

Diagnostic Category	n
Mentally Retarded	6
Learning Disabled	4
Emotional Adjustment Reaction	56
Dependent	(11)
Impulsive	(12)
Passive-Aggressive	(11)
Repressed	(17)
Mixed	(5)
Other Diagnosis	15
No Significant Problem	19

THE STRESS RESPONSE SCALE

In order to assess the child's response to stress, some behavioral descriptive measure is necessary. Such a measure should describe the *nature* and *severity* of the child's response. It should reflect the more common behavior patterns adopted by children in responding to stress and it should estimate the magnitude of that response along a continuum of severity.

Behavior rating scales have considerable potential value for assessment with children since they provide relatively objective, quantifiable data. However, one of the frequent criticisms of behavior rating scales has to do with their clinical relevance and usefulness in assessment. This problem reflects a fundamental validity weakness. While some of the better rating scales have proven empirical validity, they often lack conceptual validity or a theoretical foundation which could lend meaning to the results and which could provide a clinically-useful interpretation.[13] A scale constructed from the stress response model would have conceptual validity; and empirical validity could be tested by analyzing the data on its use with children. It could also provide the examiner with information on the child's preferred response pattern that could prove useful in designing intervention.

The Stress Response Scale was designed with concern for these validity issues. Psychological reports of children seen at the University of Pittsburgh's Psychoeducational Clinic were reviewed and descriptors extracted for each of the four types of behavior response patterns predicted by the model. These descriptors were arranged in a rating scale format. The current edition of the scale has 40 descriptors randomly assigned to item positions so that they can be rated on a six-point scale (0, never; 1, almost never; 2, sometimes; 3, often; 4, almost always; 5, always). The scale is designed to be completed by the adult making the referral, parent or teacher, and so the items are not situation-specific to home or school.

Validity

A series of developmental studies were conducted beginning in January 1979 with previous versions of the scale.[7] An initial factor analytic study with a sample of clinic-referred children (n = 120) found a five-factor solution consonant with the types predicted by the model, which accounted for 62% of the variance.[4] Replication with a modified version of the scale and a larger group of clinic-referred children (n = 200) also found a five-factor solution accounting for 70% of the variance.[29] One important finding was that a similar factor structure existed with a group of non-referred children (n = 376). This lent support to the notion that emotional adjustment reactions can be seen as extreme patterns of normal coping behavior.[5]

A factor analytic study of the current version of the scale with non-referred children (n = 167) yielded a five-factor solution which accounted for 64% of the variance. Thirty-four of the 40 items were included in the analysis, and the cluster sizes ranged from 6 to 12 items each. Three of the clusters seemed consistent with the predicted categories of the model and were labeled as Passive-Aggressive, Dependent, and Repressed. The two remaining clusters seemed to reflect a division of the fourth predicted type, the Impulsive, into two subtypes: Impulsive, overactive; and Impulsive, acting out. This analysis was then used to establish subscale scoring categories based on the clusters (Table 2).

TABLE 2
Items Used in Computing Category Subscale Scores

Category	Items*	n of Items
Impulsive (Acting Out)	5, 9, 11, 17, 23, 25, 26, 28, 29, 34, 37, 38, 39, 40	14
Passive-Aggressive	2, 7, 13, 15, 21, 23, 24, 27, 31, 34, 36, 39, 40	13
Impulsive (Overactive)	3, 8, 10, 19, 21, 22, 30, 35, 37	9
Repressed	1, 18, 27, 32, 33, 35	6
Dependent	10, 21, 27, 28, 36, 38	6

*Because of positive connotations or negative factor loadings certain items are reversed in scoring.

From the analysis five syndromes could be identified as typical behavior patterns adopted by children. They are:

I. Impulsive (Acting Out)

Acting out children are often described as demanding, selfish, and defiant with frequent temper outbursts. They are prone to fighting, and picking on other children. They are impulsive, uncooperative, and stubborn, and they have difficulty accepting criticism. They show a rather poor attitude toward school, usually not caring about schoolwork. They are sometimes mischievous, willful, and detached.

II. Passive-Aggressive

Passive-aggressive children are often described as underachievers who procrastinate, put things off, have a poor attitude toward school, seem detached, daydream, do not care about schoolwork, tend not to complete assignments and show declining grades. They also tend to be uncooperative and stubborn.

III. Impulsive (Overactive)

Overactive children are often described as easily excited, mischievous, playful, and talkative. They tend to participate in activities and are not at all withdrawn, passive, or shy.

IV. Repressed

Repressed children are often described as sensitive, easily hurt, worrying, jumpy, easily upset, and afraid of new situations. They tend to lack self-confidence.

V. Dependent

Dependent children are often characterized as dependent, seldom asserting their will. They lack self-confidence, and are unable to take criticism. They seldom participate in activities.

Reliability

Initial reliability was found to be good with children in regular education (n = 45) using teachers as raters and a test-retest interval of two weeks (80.7% of agreement across all items). A reliability study with the current version of the scale also showed good results (r_s = .86) with a similar population (n = 25) in a test-retest procedure over a one-month interval.

Clinical Use

Several studies have suggested that the Stress Response Scale can be used to discriminate between clinic-referred and non-referred children and to distinguish among five subgroups within the clinic-referred group (see 4, 9, 29). It has also been shown to discriminate between adolescents in regular classes and in special classes for the emotionally disturbed.[20]

For screening purposes, such as when identifying high-risk children, the total raw score may be useful. Table 3 shows the results of a recent study which compared 32 clinic-referred children against 208 non-referred children in regular education classes on the total raw scores.[8]

In this study a significant difference was found between the mean total raw scores for the boys in both groups (t = 4.36, $p < .001$), indicating that clinic-referred boys score higher as a group on their overall raw scores than do non-referred boys. No attempt was made to

TABLE 3

Means and Standard Deviations of Total Raw Scores for Two Groups by Sex

	Boys			Girls		
	n	M	SD	n	M	SD
Non-Referred	104	65.02	27.20	104	51.87	19.37
Clinic-Referred	24	90.95	21.19	8	94.37	12.11

compare the girls in both groups because of the small number of clinic-referred girls in the sample (n = 8).

When the scale is being used as part of a screening procedure, cut-off scores can be established to delineate the ranges of risk. As an example, some suggested cut-off scores were derived from the experimental norms and the clinic-referred boys in the study cited above were then compared against these cut-off scores. Table 4 shows the number of boys in each range.

For diagnostic assessment purposes subscale scores are the most useful. The subscale scores for 208 non-referred children in regular education classes are presented in Table 5. This group provided the data for the experimental norms for the Stress Response Scale.

TABLE 4

Suggested Cut-Off Scores for Boys

Total Raw Score	Range	n of C-R Boys
0-69	Little evidence to suggest further study	2
70-89	Possible evidence suggestive of further study	10
90+	Probable evidence suggestive of further study	12
	n =	24

TABLE 5
Total Raw and Subscale Scores for Non-Referred Subjects (n = 208)

	Boys (n = 104)		Girls (n = 104)	
	M	SD	M	SD
Total Raw Score	65.02	27.20	51.87	19.37
IMP (A)	21.10	12.39	14.19	8.75
P-A	19.85	12.15	14.74	8.83
IMP (O)	25.75	6.05	23.71	4.63
REP	10.10	4.43	9.59	4.11
DEP	13.70	4.10	13.52	4.59

Subscale scores can be converted to T scores and a profile can be constructed reflecting the child's preferred response pattern. Intervention methods can then be suggested based on what has been found to be effective with similar children as reported in the literature and/or through clinical experience. General guidelines for the behavior management of children with various types of response patterns can be developed for the significant adults in the child's life.[6]

The Stress Response Scale has shown considerable promise as a means of assessing the preferred response pattern children adopt in attempting to cope with stress in their lives. At the time of this writing it is still a prototypical instrument and further developmental work must be done before it can be routinely used in clinical, community, and school settings. While the scale's ultimate value in assessment is yet to be demonstrated, experience in working with the scale suggests that it serves another useful purpose. Because it characterizes the child's behavior as a stress response, it helps adults to understand the problem in terms of actual stress events and perceived stress situations in the child's life, as well as his attempts to cope with that stress.

REFERENCES

1. Achenbach, T.M., The classification of children's psychiatric symptoms: a factor-analytic study. *Psychological Monographs*, 1966, 80, 6.
2. Apply, M.H. & R. Trumbull, *Psychological stress*. New York: Appleton-Century-Crofts, 1967.
3. Cattel, R.B. & I.N. Schierer, *The meaning and measurement of neuroticism and anxiety*. New York: Ronald Press, 1961.

4. Chandler, L.A., *A classification scheme for behavior disorders.* Unpublished manuscript, University of Pittsburgh, 1979.
5. ———, *The Stress Assessment System: assessing emotional adjustment reactions.* Paper presented at the convention of the National Association of School Psychologists, Toronto, March, 1982.
6. ———, *Children under stress: understanding emotional adjustment reactions.* Springfield: Charles Thomas, Pub., 1982.
7. ———, *The Stress Response Scale: a preliminary report.* Paper presented at the convention of the American Psychological Association, Washington, D.C., August, 1982.
8. ———, *The Stress Response Scale: experimental norms.* Unpublished manuscript, University of Pittsburgh, 1982.
9. Chandler, L.A. & W.T. Lundahl, Empirical classification of emotional adjustment reactions. *American Journal of Orthopsychiatry.* In press.
10. Clarizio, H.F. & G.F. McCoy, *Behavior disorders of children.* New York: Thomas Crowell Co., 1970.
11. Coyne, J.C. & R.S. Lazarus, Cognitive style, stress perception and coping. In I.L. Kutash et al. (Eds.), *Handbook on stress and anxiety.* San Francisco: Jossey-Bass, 1980.
12. Duffy, E., *Activation and behavior.* New York: John Wiley & Sons, 1962.
13. Edelbrock, C.S., Empirical classification of children's behavior disorders: progress based on parent and teacher ratings. *School Psychology Digest,* 1979, 8, 4: 355–369.
14. Eysenck, H.J., Classification and the problem of diagnosis. In H.J. Eysenck (Ed.), *Handbook of abnormal psychology.* London: Pittman, 1960.
15. ———, A dimensional system in psychodiagnostics. In A.R. Mahrer (Ed.), *New approaches to personality classification.* New York: Columbia University Press, 1970.
16. Eysenck, H.J. & S.G. Eysenck, *Personality structure and measurement.* London: Routledge & Kegan Paul, 1967.
17. Freud, S., Character and anal eroticism (1908). In J. Riviere, (trans.) *Collected papers,* II. New York: Basic Books, 1959.
18. Garmezy, N., Children under stress: perspectives and antecedents and correlates of vulnerability and resistence to psychopathology. In A.I. Rabin et al. (Eds.), *Further explorations in personality.* New York: John Wiley & Sons, 1981.
19. Jung, C.G., *Psychological types.* New York: Harcourt, Brace and World, 1923.
20. Krotec, S.C., A comparison of behavior, personality and academic variables of learning disabled, emotionally disturbed and normal adolescents. Unpublished doctoral dissertation, University of Pittsburgh, 1981.
21. Lambert, N., Temperament profiles of hyperactive children. *American Journal of Orthopsychiatry,* 1982, 52, 3: 458–467.
22. Lazarus, R.S., The concepts of stress and disease. In L. Levi (Ed.), *Society, stress, and disease: the psychosomatic environment and psychosomatic diseases,* I. London: Oxford University Press, 1971.

23. Lerner, M., In S. Cunningham. Stress research moves from lab to workplace. *APA Monitor,* June 1982, 13, 6: p. 19.
24. Levy, L.H., *Conceptions of personality.* New York: Random House, 1970.
25. Lorr, E., Classification of the behavior disorders. In E.W. Farnsworth et al. (Eds.), *Annual Review of Psychology.* Annual Review, 1961.
26. Miller, J., *Pittsburgh Adjustment Survey Scales: A cross validation and normative study.* Unpublished manuscript, University of Louisville, 1968.
27. Patterson, G.R., An empirical approach to classification of disturbed children. *Journal of Clinical Psychology,* 1964, 20: 326–337.
28. Peterson, D.R., Behavior problems of middle childhood. *Journal of Consulting Psychology,* 1961, 25: 205–209.
29. Piso, C.N., A revision, factor analysis and concurrent validation study of a children's behavior scale. Unpublished doctoral dissertation, University of Pittsburgh, 1981.
30. Quay, H.C., Classification. In H.C. Quay & J.S. Werry, *Psychopathological disorders of childhood,* 2nd ed. New York: John Wiley & Sons, 1979.
31. Ross, A.O., *Psychological disorders of children.* New York: McGraw-Hill, 1974.
32. Selye, H., *The stress of life.* New York: McGraw-Hill, 1956.
33. Sheldon, W.H. & S. Stevens, *Varieties of temperament.* New York: Harper, 1942
34. Sheldon, W.H., W. Stevens, & W. Tucker, *The varieties of human physique.* New York: Harper, 1940.
35. Stover, D.O. & J.W. Glebnik, Inter-judge reliability of the Pittsburgh Adjustment Survey Scales. *Psychological Reports,* 1967, 21: 845–848.
36. Thomas, A. & S. Chess, *Temperament and development.* New York: Brunner/Mazel, 1977.
37. Thomas, A., S. Chess & J. Birch, *Temperament and behavior disorders.* New York: New York University Press, 1968.

CHAPTER 4

STRESSFUL ENVIRONMENTS AND THEIR IMPACT ON CHILDREN

Cynthia Longfellow, Ed. D.
and
Deborah Belle, Ed. D.

> *A better understanding of the impact of stress on children should be obtained when we are able to find out more about the social and psychological context in which life stressors occur. It was the purpose of the research presented in this chapter to acquire such information. The authors have provided important data concerned with the impact that certain stressful environments have on children.*

INTRODUCTION

Substantial research exists on the effects of stress on children, much of which has examined children's reactions to particular stressful events such as divorce, death, separation from a parent, or hospitalization (see 3, 5, 24). Other research focuses on the effects of particular life conditions on children's development, such as living with a single parent, living in a conflict-ridden home, living with a mentally ill parent, living in a large family, or living in poverty (see 4, 17, 23). By and large these studies show that both life events and life conditions can pose difficulties for children which result in impairment in their academic, social, and emotional adjustment.

One of the drawbacks in much of this research is the narrow focus on a single source of stress. In reality, one type of stress is often linked to other sources of stress. A familiar example is the likelihood that a

---

Note: Support for this project was provided by the W. T. Grant Foundation and by the National Institute of Mental Health, Mental Health Service Branch.

single-parent family is also an impoverished family.[14] A number of recent studies have addressed the question of multiple stressors in children's lives by gathering information on a variety of potential stressors and then determining which of these are most closely linked to children's adjustment problems (see 2, 6, 20, 29). These studies not only give a better picture of the context in which different types of stressors occur, they also place in perspective the relative impact of different environmental conditions and life events.

The purpose of our study was to examine a number of different stressors for their impact on children's behavioral adjustment and on their sense of well-being. We were particularly interested in whether stressors affecting mothers had a comparable impact on children. Differences in children's responses to stress based on income, age, and sex were also examined.

METHODS

The sample consisted of 160 mother-child pairs from low- and moderately low-income families in the Boston area. Families were recruited for the study by sending letters home with children from the public schools. There were 82 boys and 78 girls who ranged in age from 6 to 11 years. The sample included approximately equal numbers of working and non-working mothers; 40% of the mothers were single and 60% were "coupled"—the term we used for women who lived with a husband or boyfriend. Approximately 25% of the sample were Black and 75% were white. A three-to-four hour structured interview was administered to each mother. The interview included questions on demographics, sources of stress across different areas of life, availability of support, feelings of stress and strain, and current mental health status. Mothers were also asked about any physical, emotional, and learning problems their children might have. Children were administered a half-hour interview that asked among other things about their relationship with their parents.

Measuring stressors

Our measures of life stressors included the occurrence of discrete life events such as divorce or hospitalization and the existence of chronic life conditons—ongoing characteristics of the family's life which are known or believed to be stressful to children. In our work we have made a distinction between the term "stressors" which we define as those events or conditions which produce stress, and "stress" which is the feeling of upset, worry, and concern caused by stressors. From the child's point of view stressors include both the objective life difficulties reported by their mothers *and* their mothers' stress. Thus we are defining the mother's psychological distress as a potential stressor for the child.

(1) *Mother's physical and emotional health* was measured by four stressor scales: *health stressors,* a scale tapping the mother's current and recent illnesses, hospitalizations, health needs, and use of prescription drugs; *mental health stressors,* a scale reflecting a mother's history of contacts with mental health services and use of mood altering drugs; *role strain,* a scale tapping the mother's level of satisfaction in her various roles of homemaker, worker, and parent; and *depression,* the mother's score on the *CES-D Scale*,[10] a measure of depressive symptomatology. The scale asks respondents how frequently in the past week they have experienced twenty common symptoms of depression.

(2) *Family relationship stressors* tapped certain structural aspects of the family, e.g. whether or not the mother was *single,* and whether the man in the house was the child's biological father or *de facto stepfather.* A third stressor indicated whether a *separation or divorce* had occurred in the past two years. Two stressors tapped the quality of the relationship between a mother and her partner (referred to as *marital problems* although not all partners were legally married), and how much stress a mother felt over her relationship *(marital stress).* A final scale tapped the difficulties single women experienced by being without a partner *(single mother's stressors).*

(3) *Money troubles* were measured by two items: one was simple *annual per capita income.* The other was a *financial deprivation* scale which tapped the degree to which the mother was unable to afford adequate child care and health care, the frequency with which the household was without money, and the difficulty the mother had in getting money in an emergency.

(4) Two stressor events related directly to the *child's physical well-being:* whether the child had been *hospitalized* in the past two years and whether the child had had a *serious accident.*

(5) *Work-related stressors* included a mother's current *work status,* and for those mothers currently working, stressors relating to the conditions on her job. The *job stressors* scale included both characteristics of the job (e.g. long hours, physically demanding work, etc.) and the flexibility of the job in allowing a mother to attend to her children's needs.

(6) *Social network stressors* tapped the degree to which a mother's network of friends and relatives had problems that caused the respondent to worry.

(7) Finally, three background variables were included as stressors—mother's *level of education,* the ratio of children to adults living at home *(family size),* and mother's socioeconomic background—the degree of deprivation and stress experienced in her own youth *(family history stressors).*

Measuring well-being

The *CES-D Scale* was used to assess the mother's level of depressive symptomatology. Two measures of well-being were included for the 6 to 11-year-old children. One was the number of *adjustment problems* reported by the mother. Mothers were asked whether the child had any learning problems, behavioral or emotional problems, took any prescription drugs to control his/her behavior, had ever been expelled or suspended from school, had ever run away from home, or had ever been in trouble with the law. Over half of the children in the sample had no problems, 28% had one problem, and 14% had 2 or more problems. Children were administered the *Swanson Parent-Child Relationship Scale*[21] which asked them how happy they felt in their relationship with their parents.

FINDINGS

Pearson correlation coefficients were computed to examine the impact of each of the twenty stressors on mothers and children (see Table 1). Children's self-reported happiness in the parent-child relationship was significantly correlated ($p<.05$) with only one stressor—the amount of stress single mothers experienced over being single. This one correlation could well be significant by chance, particularly since there was no pattern of moderate but nonsignificant correlations between stressors and children's happiness.

The frequency of adjustment problems among children was significantly associated ($p<.05$) with a number of stressors in the predicted direction. Health problems, emotional problems, money problems, and social network problems all predicted adjustment problems. Mothers who reported more problems for their children were less likely to be working and had less education. Adjustment problems were also associated with the presence of a stepfather in the home and with a recent hospitalization of the child.

TABLE 1

Correlations of Stressors with Measures of Well-Being for Children and Mothers

Stressors	Children's Happiness	Children's Adjustment	Maternal Depression
Health stressors	.05	.17*	.25*
Mental health stressors	.10	.22*	.43*
Role strain	.07	.13*	.19*
Maternal depression	.10	.19*	—
Single parent	.03	.08	.10
Stepfather	−.05	.15*	.10
Separation/Divorce	−.07	.10	.17*
Marital problems (n = 94)	.03	.04	.17
Marital stress (n = 85)	.03	.18	.27*
Single mother's stressors (n = 66)	.21*	.14	.48*
Per capita income (n = 159)	−.07	−.11	−.30*
Financial deprivation	.01	.20*	.38*
Child hospitalized	.08	.15*	.01
Child had serious accident	−.05	.12	.16*
Work status	−.11	.14*	.19*
Job stressors (n = 82)	−.06	.19*	.03
Social network stressors	.05	.14*	.24*
Mother's education (n = 157)	.07	−.16*	−.27*
Family size	−.04	.00	.21*
Family history stressors	.01	.10	.23*

1. Higher scores on stressors indicate more stress except for per capita household income and number of years of education. High scores on outcome measures indicate poorer adjustment or emotional health.
2. N = 160 unless otherwise indicated.

Comparison of the magnitude of the correlation coefficients reveals little variation from one stressor to the next. For example, mental health stressors, which had the largest r explained five percent of the variance in children's adjustment problems while maternal role strain explained less than two percent of the variance. Neither the range nor the magnitude of explained variance is very large. Thus, no single stressor emerged as having a particularly strong effect on children. What is clear is that a wide range of stressors, tapping different areas of the child's social and psychological environment, was mildly associated with children's adjustment.

With few exceptions, stressors that were associated with children's behavioral adjustment were also associated with maternal depression in the predicted direction: maternal depression was significantly correlated ($p<.05$) with health stressors, mental health stressors, role strain, money stressors, marital stress, recent divorce or separation, the stress of being single, and social network stressors. Mothers with elevated depression scores had more children per adults living at home and had also weathered a recent serious accident of their child. Depressed mothers also came from more disadvantaged backgrounds, had lower educational attainment, and were less likely to be employed.

While comparisons between mothers' and children's reactions to the same stressors are somewhat crude because noncomparable outcome measures were used, two points are worth mentioning. First, an even broader range of life stressors affected mothers than children. Secondly, the impact of stressors on maternal depression was much greater than it was on either of the indicators of children's well-being. Whereas individual life stressors explained a maximum of five percent of the variance in children's adjustment, they explained up to twenty-three percent of the variance in maternal depression.

Maternal mental health as a mediator of life stressors.

Because children's adjustment problems were consistently linked to the stressor scales that reflected their mother's physical and emotional well-being, we investigated the possibility that maternal mental health mediated the impact of the other life stressors on children. In other words, were children's adjustment problems a direct response to the environmental stressors that their mothers also experienced, or were they, rather, a response to their mothers' depression?

In order to simplify the analysis, and because of the high intercorrelations among the various life stressors, we created two summary scores: one score represented the number of high scores on the stressor scales relating to maternal physical and emotional health (i.e. health stressors, mental health stressors, depression, and role strain); the other score represented the number of high scores on the remaining situational life stressors. High scores on the individual stressor scales were defined as the top third of all scores. A path analysis was used to determine to what degree situational stressors affected children's adjustment and their happiness directly, and to what degree their impact on children was indirect, mediated by the mother's well-being.

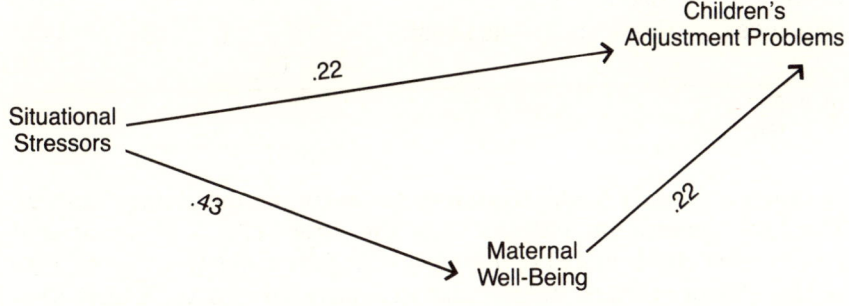

FIGURE 1

Figure 1 shows the path coefficients for the relationship between situational stressors, mother's well-being and the child's behavioral adjustment. Fourteen percent of the variance in children's adjustment was explained by these two sources of stress. Both sources of stress made significant unique, i.e. direct contributions to children's adjustment, each accounting for 5% of the variance. (See Table 2 for a summary of the multiple regression analysis.) Situational stressors explained four percent of the variance in problems indirectly through maternal mental and physical health. Thus the data support a model in which both situational stressors and maternal well-being have a direct effect on children's adjustment. In addition, the two sources of stress were highly correlated with each other; the path analysis further suggests that some of the impact of situational stressors on children is mediated by the mother's well-being.

The picture is somewhat different for children's happiness in the parent-child relationship as Figure 2 illustrates. Situational stressors and maternal mental health combined explained only three percent of

TABLE 2
Predictors of Children's Problems and Children's Happiness

Outcome	Predictor	Total R^2	beta	F^1
Children's Adjustment	Situational stressors		.22	6.96*
	Maternal mental health		.22	7.20*
		.14		12.37*
Children's Happiness	Situational stressors		−.09	1.15
	Maternal mental health		.18	4.06*
		.03		2.06

*p < .05
^{1}n = 160

the variance—a level which is not statistically significant (see Table 2). The path coefficients indicate that the direct effects of situational stressors on children's happiness were slightly negative, the opposite of the effects of maternal mental and physical health, which were positive. The indirect effect of situational stressors was in the predicted direction, i.e., more situational stressors were related to more maternal well-being stressors which in turn were associated with greater unhappiness among children. The indirect and direct effects of situational stressors appear to cancel each other, resulting in a near-zero simple correlation between situational stressors and children's happiness. It is worth noting that in the multiple regression analysis only the number of maternal mental health problems made a signifi-

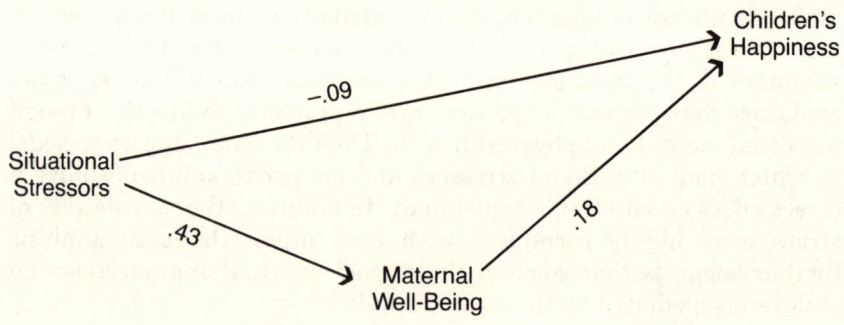

FIGURE 2

cant unique contribution to the variance in children's happiness scores (explaining three percent of the variance). Thus it appears that children's happiness in the parent-child relationship is mildly associated with their mother's mental health in the predicted direction, but *not* with other situational stressors.

Income as a moderator of the impact of life stress

Given the well-documented associations between poverty and life stressors and between poverty and emotional well-being for both mothers and children, we examined the data for evidence of this pattern. Simple correlations, computed between annual per capita income and each of the stressors, indicated that for over half of these stressors, lower income families were more likely than moderate-income families to have experienced them (see Table 3). Low-income

TABLE 3

Correlations of Per Capita Income with Stressors

	Pearson r
Health stressors	−.20*
Mental health stressors	−.20*
Role strain	.01
Maternal depression	−.30*
Single parent	.22*
Stepfather	−.01
Separation/Divorce	.06
Marital problems (n = 93)	−.27*
Marital stress (n = 84)	−.23*
Single mother's stressors (n = 66)	−.07
Financial deprivation	−.60
Child hospitalized	−.08
Child had serious accident	.06
Work status	.34
Job stressors (n = 82)	−.11
Social network stressors	−.15*
Mother's education (n = 156)	.29*
Family size	−.41*
Family history stressors	−.18

*p < .05
¹n = 159 unless otherwise indicated.

children tended to have more behavioral problems than their moderate income counterparts but there was no difference in children's self-reported happiness depending on income.

To understand better how money combined with other life stressors to affect children, we performed a multiple regression analysis using annual per capita income and a total life stressor score as predictor variables. The total stressor score was the sum of the situational stressor score and the maternal mental health score described above. Per capita income, but not money stressors, was excluded from the total score. Only children's adjustment was used as an outcome since analyses have already indicated that happiness in the parent-child relationship was not affected by most of the life stressors included in our study.

Multiple regression analysis showed that income did not make any unique contribution to predicting children's behavior problems. In contrast, the total life stressors score accounted for a highly significant proportion of the variance—fourteen percent—in their adjustment scores (see Table 4). We also examined the possibility that income

TABLE 4

Income, Age, and Sex as Predictors of Children's Adjustment to Life Stressors

Outcome	Predictor[1]	Cumulative R^2	beta	F of beta[2]
Children's Adjustment	Total Stressors	.14	.40	23.33*
	Income	.14	.07	0.66
	Income × Stressors	.14	−.15	0.72
Children's Adjustment	Total Stressors	.13	.34	20.65*
	Age	.15	.15	3.83*
	Age × Stressors	.16	.32	.48
Children's Adjustment	Total Stressors	.13	.34	21.37*
	Sex	.17	−.20	7.51*
	Sex × Stressors	.20	−.60	5.25*

*$p < .05$
1. The interaction term was added on the second step of the multiple regression analysis.
2. d.f. = 1,155

interacted with the level of stressors to affect children's adjustment by including an interaction term in the multiple regression equation entered on the second step (see Table 4). The data did not support this hypothesis, suggesting that the overall effect of life stressors on children is similar regardless of family income level.

Age and Sex Differences in Children's Response to Stress

Both age and sex were significantly associated with adjustment problems ($r = .20$ and $r = -.24$ respectively): boys and older children scored higher on the measure of problems. Older children may have had higher scores simply because some of the problems on the adjustment measure, namely school suspensions and expulsions, running away from home, and encounters with the law, are more likely to occur among older children. Multiple regression analyses were used to determine whether age or sex interacted with the level of stressors in predicting children's adjustment problems. There was no evidence that age interacted with stressors but there was a significant interaction effect for sex, indicating that boys were even more adversely affected by stressors than were girls (see Table 4).

DISCUSSION

To summarize, our findings showed that a number of everyday life stressors and certain life events were related to the number of behavioral, learning, and emotional problems among school-aged children. Children's adjustment was related to stressors in a variety of domains including mother's mental health, physical health, work situation, social networks, financial situation, and family characteristics. We totaled those stressors relating to mother's mental health and those relating to other environmental conditions and found that both types of stressors significantly predicted children's adjustment problems. Children's self-reported happiness in the parent-child relationship was not related to any of the individual stressors except for the stress their single mothers experienced over being single. While individual stressors were not predictive of children's happiness, the combined stressors relating to maternal physical and emotional health were predictive of a less happy relationship between parent and child. Thus, the mother's lack of emotional and physical well-being emerged as a type of stressor of central importance to the children in our sample.

The vulnerability of children to their mother's emotional health has been noted by other researchers (11, 12, 15, 19, 27, 29). When mothers are depressed or emotionally overwrought, their relationships with their children are likely to deteriorate. One study found that compared to women not suffering from depression, depressed mothers were less involved with and less affectionate towards their children, and less likely to meet their children's demands for attention and communication.[28] Our own observations of children and their mothers found that women who experienced more depressive symptoms were less responsive, less nurturing, and more punitive to their young children.[8] Since a supportive relationship between parent and child has been identified as an important buffer between stress and a child's maladjustment,[18] the emotional well-being of mothers played a critical role in a child's healthy development and adjustment.

We were somewhat surprised to find that most of the stressors relating to the mother's marital status and the quality of the marital relationship were not related to children's adjustment or their happiness in the parent-child relationship. For example, neither divorce nor living with a single parent mother was predictive of children's adjustment or happiness. Many other researchers have documented the profound negative impact on children of a conflicted marriage (7, 17, 29), yet we found only a marginally significant association between marital strain and behavioral problems ($p<.06$). Our measure of the quality of the marital relationship reflected the mother's degree of satisfaction with the relationship more than it tapped the amount of tension or lack of warmth in the relationship—dimensions which have been identified as being particularly stressful for children,[17] and this may account for the difference.

Presence of a "stepfather" was associated with more adjustment problems in our sample as has been noted for other samples (9, 13, 29). The presence of a stepfather may signify a number of other stressors that the child has had to contend with, specifically the loss of a father, adjustment to a new parental figure in the house, and conflicting loyalties between "new" fathers and "old" fathers. Several studies suggest that the school-aged child is particularly vulnerable to a parent's remarriage[13,26] because he/she is old enough to understand that relationships between parent and child have a permanence beyond time and place. In contrast, preschool children often accept the new stepparent as one of the family since their view of families is more concretely tied to the physical presence of who lives together.[7]

Other stressors that were related to children's adjustment problems included hospitalizations and serious accidents or illnesses (the latter only marginally so). It is not clear whether these events contribute to children's adjustment problems or are themselves consequences of stress. Some have argued that stress causes an increased physical vulnerability among children resulting in a higher rate of accidents.[1] However, intercorrelations among the different stressors for our sample indicated that neither serious accidents nor hospitalizations were consistently related to other life stressors, suggesting that they may be a distinct source of stress for children.

Maternal employment appeared to benefit both mother and child: employed women were generally less depressed than non-employed women and their children also had fewer behavioral problems. Not just any job, though, contributes to the well-being of mothers and children; rather, the quality of that employment is crucial. In a separate analysis of this same data base Tebbets found that the degree of inflexibility of the job was associated with greater stress and job dissatisfaction among working mothers.[22] In our analyses we found that children's behavior problems were associated with the level of job stressors reported by their mothers. These stressors included the unavailability of the mother while she was at work, the inflexibility of her schedule for attention to child-related matters, and the lack of paid vacation time.

Family income and money-related problems were both related to children's adjustment, but annual per capita income had no additional effect on children once other sources of stress were accounted for. Thus low income affects children's well-being by contributing to a stressful environment. Although low-income increases the risk of exposure to one or more stressful life conditions, our findings show that low-income children were no more vulnerable to the impact of the sum total of stressors than were the moderately low-income children included in our sample. In other words, there was no "buffering effect" of higher income, at least not in the low- to moderately low-income families in our study.

There did appear to be a somewhat increased vulnerability among boys to the impact of stressors. Other researchers have also found that boys and girls differ in their responses to life stressors (see: 5, 18, 25, 26, 29). Boys in particular appear more likely to respond to stress with behavioral, as opposed to neurotic problems.[16]

Finally, we think it is important to view children's reactions to stress in the context of their families. While we found a clearcut pattern of negative effects of stressors on children, particularly those stressors relating to maternal well-being, our research suggests that conspicuous life events and conditions explain even less of the variance in outcomes for children than they do for adults. In part this may reflect the fact that the study was originally designed to assess the impact of stressors on maternal mental health and therefore the interview was geared towards measuring those events and conditions believed to be most stressful to mothers. More likely, though, is the fact that school-aged children are buffered from the impact of life stressors in a variety of ways. Most important is the physical and emotional status of their mothers, but other factors, not included in our analysis are also significant, such as the supportiveness of the relationship between parent and child, the child's social networks outside the family, and the child's particular coping strategies. We will be better able to guage the impact of stress on children once we know the social and psychological context in which life stressors occur.

REFERENCES

1. Brown, G. W. & S. Davidson, Social class, psychiatric disorder of mother and accidents to children. *Lancet,* 1978, 1:378–381.
2. Earls, F., The impact of family stress on the behavior adjustment of preschool children. *Massachusetts Journal of Community Health,* 1980, 1:7–11.
3. Felner, R. O., A. Stolberg & E. L. Cowen, Crisis events and school mental health referral patterns of young children. *Journal of Consulting and Clinical Psychology,* 1975, 43:305–310.
4. Herzog, E. & C. Sudia, Children in fatherless families. In B. M. Caldwell & H. N. Ricciuti (Eds.), *Review of child development research, III: Child development and social policy.* Chicago: University of Chicago Press, 1973.
5. Hetherington, E. M., M. Cox & R. Cox, The aftermath of divorce. In J. H. Stevens & M. Mathews (Eds.), *Mother-child, father-child relationships.* Washington, DC: National Association for the Education of Young Children, 1978.
6. Langner, T., E. McCarthy, J. Gersten, O. Simcha-Fagan & J. Eisenberg, Predictors of child behavior and their implications for social policy. In R. G. Simmons (Ed.), *Research in community and mental health,* I. Greenwich: JAI Press, 1979.
7. Longfellow, C., Divorce in context: Its impact on children. In G. Levinger & O. Moles (Eds.), *Divorce and separation: context, causes and consequences.* New York: Basic Books, 1979.
8. Longfellow, C., P. Zelkowitz & E. Saunders, The quality of mother-child relationships. In D. Belle (Ed.), *Lives in stress: women and depression.* Beverly Hills: Sage Publications, 1982.
9. McCord, J., W. McCord & E. Thurber, Some effects of paternal absence on male children. *Journal of Abnormal and Social Psychology,* 1962, 64:361–369.
10. Radloff, L., The CES-D Scale: a self-report depression scale for research in

the general population. *Journal of Applied Psychological Measurement,* 1977, 1:385–401.
11. Rolf, J., The social and academic competence of children vulnerable to schizophrenia and other pathologies: current status. *Journal of Abnormal Psychology,* 1972, 80:225–243.
12. Rolf, J. & N. Garmezy, The school performance of children vulnerable to behavior pathology. In D. F. Ricks (Ed.), *Life history research in psycholpathology, III.* Minneapolis: University of Minnesota Press, 1974.
13. Rosenberg, M., *Society and the adolescent self-image.* Princeton: Princeton University Press, 1965.
14. Ross, H. & I. Sawhill, *Time of transition: the growth of families headed by women.* Washington, D.C.: Urban Institute, 1975.
15. Rutter, M., *Children of sick parents: an environmental and psychiatric study.* Institute of Psychiatry Maudsley Monograph No. 16, London: Oxford University Press, 1966.
16. ———, Sex differences in children's responses to family stress. In E. J. Anthony & C. Koupernik (Eds.), *The child in his family.* New York: John Wiley & Sons, 1970.
17. ———, Parent-child separation: psychological effects on the children. *Journal of Child Psychology and Psychiatry,* 1971, 12:233–260.
18. ———, Protective factors in children's responses to stress and disadvantage. In M. W. Kent & J. E. Rolf (Eds.), *Primary prevention of psycholpathology, III: Social competence in children.* Hanover: University Press of New England, 1979.
19. Rutter, M., J. Tizard & K. Whitmore. *Education, health and behavior.* New York: John Wiley & Sons, 1970.
20. Sandler, I. & T. Ramsey, Dimensional analysis of children's stressful life events. *American Journal of Community Psychology.* 1980, 8:285–302.
21. Swanson, G. W., The development of an instrument for rating child-parent relationships. *Social Forces,* 1950, 29:84–90.
22. Tebbets, R., Work, family, and mental health in the lives of low-income mothers. Paper presented at the Annual Meeting of American Psychological Association, Montreal, 1980.
23. Tehrune, K. W. & R. J. Pilie, *A review of the actual and expected consequences of family size.* Washington, D.C.: DHEW Publication No. 76–79, 1974.
24. Tuckman, J. & R. A. Regan, Intactness of the home and behavioral problems in children. *Journal of Child Psychology and Psychiatry,* 1966, 7:225–233.
25. Wallerstein, J. & J. Kelly, The effects of parental divorce: experiences of the preschool child. *Journal of the American Academy of Child Psychiatry,* 1975, 14:600–616.
26. ———, *Surviving the breakup: how children and parents cope with divorce.* New York: Basic Books, 1980.
27. Weintraub, S., J. B. Neale & D. Liebert, Teacher ratings of children

vulnerable to psychopathology. *American Journal of Orthopsychiatry,* 1975, 45:839–845.
28. Weissman, M. & E. Paykel, *The depressed woman.* Chicago: University of Chicago Press, 1974.
29. Werner, E. & R. Smith, *Vulnerable but invincible: a study of resilient children.* New York: McGraw-Hill, 1982.

CHAPTER 5

ENVIRONMENTAL CHANGE AND CHILDREN OF DIVORCE

Sharlene A. Wolchik, Ph.D., Bruce S. Fogas, B.A., and Irwin N. Sandler, Ph.D.

> *Divorce is a serious problem, and an increasing rate of divorce is predicted for the next decade. Given the potential of divorce to produce both transient and long-lasting adjustment problems, thorough examination of divorce and its effects is imperative for mental health professionals who work with children. In this chapter divorce is viewed not as a single event which children experience, but rather as a series of changes to which children must adapt. The literature concerning the effects of divorce is reviewed, with special emphasis given to social-environmental changes which occur during and after divorce. Changes occur in areas such as parenting, relationships with both parents, financial status, and practical aspects of the child's life. The methods which have been used to assess these changes and the problems associated with each of the approaches are discussed, and recommendations for future research are provided.*

During the past two decades, the number of children who have experienced parental divorce has tripled. In 1976, five out of every ten marriages ended in divorce[6] and in 1978, 4.5 million children were living with a divorced parent.[21] Although the rate of divorce is expected to increase more slowly in the current decade than in the previous one, it is estimated that by 1990, one-third of all children will have experienced parental divorce during childhood or adolescence.[21] Given the high rate of divorce, and the potential of this life transition to produce enduring negative effects, it is critical that we develop an understanding of what factors influence the effects of divorce on children. In this chapter, we will focus on the various social-environmental changes which children experience during and after the process of divorce.

In the first section, we will briefly review the literature on the effects of divorce on children's adjustment, and discuss divorce-related social-environmental changes which influence both behavioral and emotional adjustment. Methods of assessing these environmental changes and problems with these approaches will then be examined. We will then offer a conceptual framework which can be used to understand the effects of the social-environmental changes associated with divorce. This conceptual framework has been adapted from life-stress events research. The advantages of using a conceptual framework based on life events, and a methodology for implementing it, will also be discussed.

THE EFFECTS OF DIVORCE ON CHILDREN

What is the impact of the change in family structure from a two parent family to a single parent family? Although a few studies have reported no differences between children from intact and divorced families (see: 4, 30, 47, 53), the majority of studies in this area have demonstrated that several affective and behavioral problems are associated with divorce.

Depression, anger, self-blame, anxiety and low self-esteem frequently occur after divorce (see: 27, 28, 37, 39, 56, 58, 59). In addition, social interaction problems, noncompliance, aggression, and school difficulties occur more frequently among children of divorce than children from intact families (see: 18, 19, 27, 28, 37, 55, 56, 57, 58, 59). For some children, divorce produces mild or transient behavior problems, but for many others, this transition in family structure leads to enduring emotional and behavioral difficulties. For example, Wallerstein and Kelly reported that while thirty-four percent of the children in their "Children of Divorce Project" were psychologically healthy five years after participation in a brief intervention program, thirty-three percent were intensely unhappy.[59]

How can we understand the differential effects of divorce on children? If we conceptualize divorce as a series of social-environmental changes (changes in relationships with parents, changes in residence, changes in routines, etc.) rather than as a single event, [15,26] the impact of divorce may be seen as being due in large part to the different changes that occur in the lives of different children. Thus, an understanding of the differential effects of divorce needs to be based on an assessment of what changes occur, and how different children cope with the challenges presented by these changes. Prior research provides considerable evidence that a wide range of social-environmental factors can affect children's post-divorce adjustment.

SOCIAL-ENVIRONMENTAL FACTORS AFFECTING POST-DIVORCE CHILD ADJUSTMENT

Several aspects of the child's social environment have been identified as either facilitating or hindering post-divorce adjustment. Environmental factors which have been associated with better psychological adjustment to divorce include a continued, positive relationship with both the custodial[25,59] and noncustodial parent, (see: 25, 32, 59) parental encouragement to discuss divorce related issues,[33] and authoritative parenting by the custodial parent.[53] Other factors which have been shown to facilitate divorce adjustment include a psychologically healthy custodial parent,[27,59] agreement between parents on child rearing practices,[27] and contact with additional (non-parental) adult caretakers.[53] Environmental factors associated with more child adjustment problems following divorce include a high level of post-separation stress experienced by the mother,[39,55] a high level of parental conflict before and after divorce, (see: 20, 34, 39, 47) and a low level of available financial resources (see: 10, 20, 27, 30).

While these studies provide ample evidence concerning the impact of a wide range of divorce-related environmental changes on post-divorce adjustment, very few studies have examined the cumulative effect of such changes on the child's functioning. In order to maximize ecological validity in this area of research, it seems crucial for researchers to study the cumulative effect of these changes. Clearly the child's environment may change in many ways following a divorce. These changes may occur relatively quickly and require rapid adaptation on the part of the child, or they may occur more slowly, and require adaptation over a lengthy period of time. In either case, it is reasonable to believe that these demands of adaptation accumulate. For example, it should be more difficult for a child to adjust to a new school when he must also cope with a depressed mother and/or with arguments between parents.

Only two studies have examined the cumulative effect of divorce related changes on children's functioning. Stolberg and Anker examined the relationship between post-divorce adjustment and changes in family income, time spent with father, time spent with mother, and residence subsequent to separation.[55] High total change scores were associated with children's perceptions of being less able to control their world. Kurdek and Blisk studied the relationship between child adjustment and changes in the following areas: number of people living in the home, monthly income, hours each parent spends with the child, waking hours each parent spends in the child's home, and monthly rent or mortgage.[39] High degrees of change were negatively related to several indices of children's social and psychological adjustment.

We will return to the issue of assessing the cumulative effect of divorce-related environmental changes. Before returning to that critical issue, we will evaluate the methods which have been used to assess the social environment of children of divorce.

ASSESSMENT OF DIVORCE RELATED ENVIRONMENTAL CHANGE

Environmental changes that influence divorce adjustment have been studied using a variety of methods including interviews of parents, teacher report, rating scales, standardized personality measures, and behavioral observation. Typically, researchers have employed only one of these methods, but a few researchers such as Hetherington, Cox, and Cox[27,28] and Santrock & Warshak[53] have used a multimethod approach to assess post-divorce changes. In the next two sections, we will examine the various methods used to assess social-environmental changes after divorce and then discuss problems with these approaches.

Interviews

Several researchers have used interviews with parents to identify environmental changes which facilitate divorce adjustment. For example, Hess and Camara[25] interviewed both parents to assess the affective quality of parent-child relationships.[25] Interview data were summarized by two teams of raters and combined to form composite ratings of family process variables such as quality of mother-child and father-child relationships. These ratings had a median internal reliability of .79. Hess and Camara report a median inter-team reliability figure of .75 using the Spearman rho.[25] Jacobson used interviews with the custodial parent to examine the encouragement parents gave to children to discuss divorce related issues, and to examine the relationship between the noncustodial parent and the child.[32,33] In one of these studies,[32] custodial parents reported the amount of time that they and their ex-spouse spent in the child's presence, and the amount of time spent in activities with the child for a typical two week period prior to the separation, and for the two week period prior to the interview. Jacobson does not provide data on agreement between interviewers. In order to assess encouraging discussion about separation, Jacobson asked parents eight questions.[33] On the basis of their responses, a rating of the amount of parental attention given to the child to help him/her deal with separation was made on a five-point scale. Exact agreement between the ratings of the author and an independent observer occurred in eighty-four percent of the situations rated.

Wallerstein and Kelly employed clinical judgments made in the context of a brief intervention program to identify several social-environmental factors which facilitate divorce adjustment.[59] Psychological health of the custodial parent, quality of mother-child relationship, and consistency of visitation by the father were identified in this manner. Wallerstein and Kelly provide no information on agreement between clinicians.[59] Hetherington, Cox, and Cox assessed the degree of agreement on child rearing practices through structured interviews with each parent.[27] In this study, ratings of reports of agreement were made by two judges. Interjudge agreement for all data collected during the interviews averaged .82.

Interviews have also been employed to identify factors which hinder post-divorce adjustment. Examining conflict between parents, Rosen[47] interviewed the noncustodial parent while Fulton[20] used semi-structured interviews with either both parents or the custodial parent. Similarly, Jacobson asked parents eight questions such as "have you or your spouse physically attacked the other?" and used the sum of questions answered affirmatively as a measure of parental hostility.[34] Unfortunately, none of these authors provides data on agreement between interviewers.

Rating scales/Standardized measures

Several researchers have administered standardized inventories or tailor-made scales to parents or teachers in order to identify social-environmental changes which influence post-divorce adjustment. One important aspect of the child's social environment is the parents' behavior. Examining the effect of psychological health of the custodial parent, Hetherington, Cox, and Cox[27], and Kurdek, Blisk, and Siesky[40] employed the California Psychological Inventory[23] and the Adjective

Checklist.[24] Research has demonstrated that both of these inventories have adequate test-retest reliability and validity.[22,43]

Kurdek and Blisk have examined both conflict between parents and degree of post-separation stress experienced by the mother using tailor-made scales.[39] Degree of conflict was assessed using a five-point rating scale while the degree of stressfulness of twenty issues such as legal matters, financial status, and physical health was rated on a four-point scale. Cronbach's alpha for the summary score on this scale was .90.

Amount of environmental change has been assessed by both Kurdek and Blisk[39] and Strolberg and Anker.[55] Stolberg and Anker assessed the degree of life change experienced by mothers during the past six months using the total scores of the Recent Life Changes Questionnaire, the test-retest reliability of which has been demonstrated to be adequate.[46] These investigators also had mothers rate the changes experienced by their children since separation in the areas of income, time spent with mother, time spent with father, and residence. Similarly, Kurdek and Blisk collected pre- and post-separation information about the following areas: number of people living in the house, monthly income, hours per week each parent spends with the children, waking hours per week each parent spends in the child's home, and monthly rent or mortgage. Information about whether the family moved or sold their house was also obtained. Stolberg and Anker computed a total change score while Kurdek and Blisk standardized scores for each item and then computed a summary score. Kurdek and Blisk reported a Cronbach's alpha of .52.

Teachers have also provided information on social-environmental factors that are associated with post-divorce child adjustment problems. Both Felner, Farber, Ginter, Boike, and Cowen[17] and Felner, Ginter, Boike, and Cowen[18] used structured rating forms to assess divorce-related family problems such as economic difficulties, overprotective parents and parental rejection. These authors do not provide psychometric data for these rating forms.

Behavioral observation

Quality of discipline is the only social-environmental factor that has been examined using observational techniques. Santrock and Warshak[53] videotaped families for a ten minute period during which families were asked to plan an activity together and to discuss the main problems in the family.[53] Observers used nine-point scales to assess parental behaviors such as amount of control exerted over their child, attentiveness to the child, and confidence in themselves as parents. One fourth of the interactions were rated by two raters and the average interrater agreement was a Pearson product moment correlation of .78.

PROBLEMS IN ASSESSING DIVORCE RELATED ENVIRONMENTAL CHANGES

Several problems exist in the methods currently used to assess divorce related environmental change. These include insufficient attention to methodological concerns such as reliability and response distortion, a lack of attention to the child's perception of change, minimal attention to the cumulative effects of change, and a lack of focus on positive changes which may accompany divorce. We have also noted two more specific problems in the literature reviewed. A few researchers report relationships between changes associated with divorce and post-divorce child adjustment, but do not indicate how these changes were assessed (10, 30, 53). Other researchers have employed teacher reports to assess environmental change in the home.[17,18] However, the accuracy of this type of teacher report has not been established.

Psychometric and response bias issues

Several problems are present in assessing environmental changes through interviews. Perhaps the most central problem is the frequent lack of attention to the issue of interjudge agreement. Without demonstration that two observers would view the information obtained from a subject similarly, one cannot exclude the possibility that the interviewer's judgments reflect his/her own ideas about the relative importance of various environmental changes in the divorce process. Also, unless interviewers are provided with a standard set of questions, different interviewers may obtain different information about the presence or absence of specific changes.

Another critical issue concerns the reliance on the custodial parent to provide information about the noncustodial parent, a criticism which applies to the questionnaire method as well. Obviously, separation or divorce is a difficult period for all members of the family. Thus, the custodial parents' perceptions of their spouses' behaviors are likely to be distorted by their own psychological needs.

Although questionnaires provide a more objective means of assessing stressors than the interview method, rarely have investigators examined the psychometric properties of the scales they have constructed for their studies. When psychometric data is provided, it is limited to assessment of internal consistency. Attention to the stability of these measures is lacking.

Finally, researchers have not attended to the issue of response distortion. During the first year after divorce, parents and, in particular, mothers, experience depression, anxiety, rejection, and anger.[27] These feelings may increase the defensiveness of parents' responses to questions about their interactions with their children and about other aspects of their child's environment.

One advantage of behavioral observation is that it is less susceptible to the effects of distortion than either self report obtained through interviews or questionnaire methods. Nonetheless, reactivity to observation is a critical concern. Knowledge of assessment has been shown to influence parent-child interactions such that parents interact more positively with their children when they are aware of being observed.[61] It is unclear whether parental behavior under these conditions is representative of daily interactions with their child. Other disadvantages of behavioral observation include its expense and its lack of appropriateness for assessing many of the changes that occur subsequent to divorce (e.g., conflict between parents).

In the future, researchers need to attend to the issue of interobserver agreement when interviews are employed, and whenever possible, use standardized questionnaires with acceptable levels of internal and test-retest reliability. If a scale is devised for a particular study, concurrent demonstration of adequate psychometric properties is needed. Also, measures of response distortion, such as validity scales similar to those used in the Minnesota Multiphasic Personality Inventory or the Marlow-Crowne Social Desirability Scale[9] should be used. In addition, multiple informants (e.g., custodial parent, noncustodial parent, child) as well as multiple methods of assessing a particular environmental factor (e.g., assessing changes in parent-child interactions through questionnaires on parenting behavior and behavioral observation) would improve the quality of data on the environmental changes children experience during and after divorce.

The Child's Perceptions of Change

Although several researchers have argued that the child's viewpoint is critical in understanding the impact that divorce has on a child (see: 1, 38, 42), to date researchers have relied on significant others (e.g., parents, teachers) to describe the child's post-divorce environment. Attention to the child's perceptions is important for several reasons. First, since mothers are also in the process of adjusting to the change in family structure, their perceptions of their children's experiences may be distorted by their own psychological needs.[4,59] Recent research by Hingst suggests that parent and child perceptions of events during the divorce process differ significantly.[29] Differences occur regarding when the child was told about the divorce, who told the child about the divorce, and the type of statements which the mother made about the father after the divorce. Also, reliance on maternal reports of changes in the child's environment necessarily excludes changes of which the mother is not aware. Examples of these areas are the child's interactions with the noncustodial parent, and the child's relationships with the extended family of the noncustodial parent.

Cumulative Effects of Environmental Changes

All but two studies have examined the relationship between individual stressors and divorce adjustment. Furthermore, in the two studies which have examined cumulative change, a very limited number of changes were assessed. More specifically, Stolberg and Anker[55] studied change in four areas and Kurdek & Blisk[39] studied change in nine areas. Clearly, neither of these pairs of investigators attempted to include all of the significant changes which can occur during the divorce process. In order to understand the relationship between changes occurring during the divorce process and adjustment, attention to the impact of these changes in concert, and identification of those changes that are most significantly related to adjustment, are needed.

Study of a wide range of events is needed if we are to describe accurately the relationship between environmental change and child adjustment. A minimal criterion for assessing these changes is the content validity of the assessment instrument, or ensuring that a representative sample of changes that occur is assessed. The process of divorce is a complex one involving changes in nearly every area of functioning. Assessment of changes in the following areas seem critical:

(a) relationships with both parents, including qualitative and quantitative changes
(b) parental interactions, including arguments and more subtle expressions of hostility

(c) relationships with friends, and with the extended family of both parents
(d) practical aspects of living (e.g., financial status, residential changes and household responsibilities)
(e) social life of the custodial and noncustodial parents, including dating and remarriage

Positive changes

Research has focused primarily on the negative events which occur during the process of divorce. Examination of positive as well as negative changes may help us to understand why some children cope more effectively with this transition period than others. Although little empirical attention has been given to the study of how individuals adapt to positive events, recent research suggests that this kind of adaptation has important implications for happiness and psychological well-being.[60] The occurrence of positive events has been positively related to life satisfaction[5] and these events have been shown to buffer the relationship between negative events and depression.[8] Pertaining to divorce, examples of positive events include an increase in the time spent with fathers[27,59] and receiving more material objects from the noncustodial parent.[27] It is also conceivable that immediately following a divorce, there is less parental contact and thus fewer parental arguments for the child to observe. In the second year after the divorce there may also be an improvement in the parent's emotional well-being and a further decrease in the inter-parental conflict. All of these changes would be perceived as positive changes by the child.

INDIVIDUAL DIFFERENCES IN ADAPTING TO ENVIRONMENTAL CHANGES

Clearly, not all children react the same way to environmental change. Children may effect some environmental changes and actively interpret and react to the changes after they occur. Study of individual differences in interpretation of and reaction to divorce changes is an important area of research. While there is little research which has studied this area specifically, there is some evidence on the differential effects of divorce across different groups of children.

Several researchers such as Fulton, Kalter and Rembar, and Wallerstein and Kelly have reported marked differences in reactions to divorce across different age groups (see: 20, 36, 59). Preschoolers commonly experience nightmares, enuresis, eating disturbances, and self-blame, while academic problems, withdrawal and depression occur among school-age children (see: 37, 57, 59). Adolescents experience difficulties with independence and interpersonal relationships.[56,59] Researchers have also reported that older children exhibit better divorce adjustment than younger children.[40,41] Although several investigators have speculated that these age differences are due to developmental changes in a child's ability to infer the motives and feelings of the parents during divorce and to assess accurately his or her own role in the divorce process (see: 28, 42, 59), only recently has empirical support for this hypothesis been provided. Kurdek and his colleagues demonstrated a significant, positive relationship between interpersonal understanding and children's divorce adjustment.[40] While differences in reactions across age may be mediated by age-related variables such as interpersonal understanding, other factors may also play a role. For example, the extra-familial social support network of younger children may be smaller than that of older children. Alternatively, younger children may be less able to accept the extra-familial social support which is available to them. In either case, the buffering effect of social support on negative changes may differ for children of different ages.

Sex of child also influences divorce adjustment. Hetherington, Cox, and Cox reported that the negative effects of divorce were not only more pronounced in male than female preschoolers but were also more enduring.[27,28] Nearly all differences between girls from intact and divorced families had disappeared two years after divorce, but boys of divorced parents continued to play less maturely, felt more anxious, and had more difficulties with their peers than boys from intact families. Wallerstein and Kelly also report sex differences in adjustment to divorce.[59] Eighteen months after parental separation, boys exhibited more depression, felt more rejected by their fathers, were more opposed to the divorce, and felt more stressed within the family than girls. Studying children from six to eleven years old, Santrock and Warshak reported that both boys and girls exhibited more behavior problems when the opposite-sex parent had custody.[53] It thus appears that the interaction between sex of the child and sex of the custodial parent, and not just sex of the child, may be important in determining adjustment. Santrock and Warshak also suggest that children who live with the same sex parent may be better adjusted because they have more opportunities to learn appropriate sex-role behaviors, or because the parent is able to interact more effectively with a child of the same sex.

Psychological processes such as locus of control have also been implicated as affecting adjustment. Using the Nowicki-Strickland measure, Kurdek and his colleagues reported a significant relationship between internal locus of control and divorce adjustment, even after partialling out age of the child.[40] Other child variables which may moderate adjustment to divorce include temperament variables,[28] experiences with similar life transitions,[15] and child competencies such as self-esteem and tolerance for stress.

When we view divorce as a series of environmental changes, and the child as an active modifier of these experiences, gaining an understanding of the effects of divorce involves identification of the major and minor changes which occur within the context of divorce, as well as the characteristics of the child which moderate the impact of these changes.

A NEW APPROACH FOR STUDYING DIVORCE RELATED ENVIRONMENTAL CHANGES

Conceptual Framework

Divorce marks a transition period in which a child's family environment is changing. We, as well as other researchers, see this transition period as including a number of significant changes which have important effects on children's post-divorce adjustment.[15,38] Conceptually, three classes of variables need to be included in research on the effects of these changes: (a) the changes that occur; (b) individual characteristics that lead to differential coping with these changes; and, (c) social resources available to the child which assist coping with these changes. This conceptual framework is borrowed from life-stress events research[11,12] and much of the methodology developed in that area of research can be readily applied to study divorce changes and their impact on child adjustment.

Adapting Life Event Methodology To The Study Of Divorce

Research into life-stress has primarily focused on assessing the effects of major recent experiences (e.g., unemployment, family death, moving, etc.), and on physical and mental health results.[45,13] Parental divorce would be considered a stressful event from this framework and indeed is a single item on all existing life event scales for children (See: 7, 35, 44, 50). From our perspective, this model can be expanded so that divorce is viewed not as *an* event but as a life transition requiring adaptation to a series of environmental changes, and mastery of new tasks that occur as a result of these changes.[16]

By extending the life stress event methodology to focus on more specific, minor events which occur after divorce, we can identify the environmental changes involved in this life transition. Recently, the life stress event methodology has been expanded to describe the more minor life stressors of specific groups. For example, Sandler and Lakey[51] and Bauman, Sandler, and Braver[3] have tailor-made life event scales to assess the significant events that occur to university and community college students. The events on these scales were all empirically generated by asking students to identify experiences that had an important impact on them. The College Student Life Event Scale includes 112 events, such as a negative personal encounter with a professor, breaking up with a boyfriend or girlfriend, and a decline in course grades. The scale has been used successfully to predict student mental health problems.[49, 51]

Currently, we are in the process of developing a life event questionnaire which assesses the positive and negative changes that occur during the process of divorce. A form of the critical incident technique was used to identify a representative list of significant events that occur during the process of divorce. Key informants included psychologists involved in treating children of divorce, lawyers, divorced parents, and children who had experienced divorce. Each key informant was asked to identify positive and negative events that had an important impact on children during divorce. Members of the research team used these events to write non-overlapping items which described the events in a clear and unambiguous form. At this point, fifty-two items have been written describing divorce-related life changes. The items include the child's perception of change in parent discipline, parent mood and behavior, inter-parental conflict, and in the child's own physical and social environments.

A divorce-related life-event scale can be used to ask some very important research questions, including:

(a) *What factors influence the differential occurrence of divorce related events?* It is reasonable to propose that what happens during the process of divorce differs as a function of such variables as custody arrangement, financial resources of the parent or time since the divorce. Indeed, Hetherington, Cox, and Cox have described the first two years after divorce as a succession of significant changes in the family environment.[27] It may be that differences in children's adjustment to divorce over time or across different custody arrangements may be due in part to the occurrence of different events.

(b) *What is the cumulative impact of divorce related changes?* Life event methodology is traditionally used to assess the aggregate amount of a particular kind of experience which occurred in the recent past. The focus of this research has most often been on the total amount of environmental change[31] or the total amount of negative experiences.[54] It has been noted however that the methodology can be used to assess the aggregate amount of diverse other experiences (e.g., losses or entrances to the child's social field).[52] As reviewed above, divorce research has largely failed to examine the cumulative effects of divorce related changes. Life-event methodology allows us to assess the effects of the wide range of divorce related changes.

(c) *How is the effect of divorce related environmental changes moderated by coping abilities and social support?* The effects of changes undoubtedly differs across individuals. Kurdek and his colleagues, for example, reported that locus of control and internal reasoning ability correlated with more successful child post-divorce adjustment.[40] Similarly, the support children receive has been found to affect their adjustment to negative life events,[48] teenage pregnancy,[2] and poverty situations.[14] Using life event methodology, such moderator variable effects could be investigated as the statistical interaction between a life event score and either a personality characteristic or social support. Furthermore, research could investigate how coping with any particular experience might differ as a function of these variables.

Divorce is best viewed as a transition in family structure, involving a series of environmental changes which present new tasks for the child to master. For many children, this transition is a painful process which leads to emotional and behavioral difficulties. In order to help children cope effectively with parental divorce, and to understand differences in reactions to divorce, we must identify: (1) the specific changes that occur following divorce; (2) the individual characteristics that lead to differential coping with these changes; and (3) the social resources that are available to help a child cope with these changes.

To date, researchers have identified a number of social-environmental factors which either hinder or facilitate adjustment to divorce. However, several problems exist in much of this research. The most significant of these are: insufficient attention to methodological issues; a lack of attention to the child's perception of change; and insufficient attention to the impact of cumulative environmental changes. In future research, closer attention to these problems is necessary. We have proposed that by adapting the methodology used in the life-stress events research, we can enhance our understanding of the divorce process. With this methodology, the specific changes that occur following parental divorce can be identified, the impact of cumulative social-environmental change can be assessed and, more importantly, the personality characteristics and social resources that influence the child's adaptation to these changes can be studied.

REFERENCES

1. Anthony, E.J., Children at risk from divorce: a review. In E.J. Anthony and C. Koupernik (Eds.), *The child in his family,* III. New York: John Wiley & Sons, 1974, 461–477.
2. Barrera, M. Jr., Social support in adjusting to marital disruption: a network analysis. In B.H. Gottlieb (Ed.), *Social networks and social support.* Beverly Hills: Sage Publications, 1981, 69–96.
3. Baumann, D.J., I. Sandler & S. Braver, Use of life events as a method of needs assessment. Paper presented at the meeting of the American Psychological Association, Washington, D.C., 1982.
4. Berg, B. & R. Kelly, The measured self-esteem of children from broken, rejected, and accepted families. *Journal of Divorce,* 1979, 2: 363–370.
5. Block, M. & A. Zautra, Satisfaction and distress in a community: a test of the effects of life events. *American Journal of Community Psychology,* 1981, 9: 165–181.
6. Bloom, B.L., S.J. Asher & S.W. White, Marital disruption as a stressor: a review and analysis. *Psychological Bulletin,* 1978, 85, 4: 867–894.
7. Coddington, R.D., The significance of life events as etiological factors in the diseases of children: a survey of professional workers. *Journal of Psychosomatic Research,* 1972, 16: 7–18.
8. Cohen, S. & H.M. Hoberman, Positive events and social supports as buffers of life change stress: maximizing the prediction of health outcomes. Unpublished manuscript, 1981.
9. Crowne, D.P. & D. Marlowe, *The approval motive: studies in evaluative dependence.* New York: John Wiley & Sons, 1964.
10. Desimone-Luis, J., K. O'Mahoney & D. Hunt, Children of separation and divorce: factors influencing adjustment. *Journal of Divorce,* 1979, 3: 37–42.
11. Dohrenwend, B.S., Social stress and community psychology. *American Journal of Community Psychology,* 1978, 6: 1–15.
12. Dohrenwend, B.S. & B.P. Dohrenwend, *Stressful life events: their nature and effects.* New York: John Wiley & Sons, 1974.
13. ———, What is a stressful life event. In H. Selye (Ed.), *Selye's guide to stress research,* I. New York: Van Nostrand Reinhold, 1980, 1–20.
14. Felner, R.D., M.S. Aber, J. Primavera & A.M. Cauce, Adaptation and vulnerability in high risk adolescents: an examination of environmental mediators. *Journal of Community Psychology.* In press.

15. Felner, R.D., S.S. Farber & J. Primavera, Children of divorce, stressful life events and transitions: a framework for preventive efforts. In R.C. Price, R.F. Ketterer, B.C. Bader & T. Monahan (Eds.), *Prevention in Mental Health*, I. Beverly Hills: Sage Publications, 1980, 81–108.
16. ———Transitions and stressful life events: a model for primary prevention. In R.D. Felner, J.A. Jason, J.N. Moritsugu & S.S. Farber *Preventive psychology: theory, research and practice*. New York: Pergamon Press, in press.
17. Felner, R.D., S.S. Farber, M.A. Ginter, M.F. Boike and E.L. Cowen, Family stress and organization following parental divorce or death. *Journal of Divorce*, 1980, 4: 67–76.
18. Felner, R.D., M.A. Ginter, M.F. Boike & E.L. Cowen, Parental death or divorce and the school adjustment of young children. *American Journal of Community Psychology*, 1981, 2: 181-191.
19. Felner, R.D., A. Stolberg & E.L. Cowen, Crisis events and school mental health patterns of young children. *Journal of Consulting and Clinical Psychology*, 1975, 43: 305–310.
20. Fulton, J.A., Parental reports of children's post-divorce adjustment. *Journal of Social Issues*, 1979, 35: 126–139.
21. Glick, P.G., Children of divorced parents in demographic perspective. *Journal of Social Issues*, 1979, 35: 170–182.
22. Gough, H.G., The adjective checklist as a personality assessment research technique. *Psychological Reports*, 1960, 6: 107–122.
23. ———, *California psychological inventory manual*. Palo Alto: Consulting Psychologist Press, 1969.
24. ———, & A.B. Heilbrun, *The adjective checklist manual*. Palo Alto: Consulting Psychologist Press, 1965.
25. Hess, R.D. & K.A. Camara, Post-divorce family relations as mediating factors in the consequences of divorce for children. *Journal of Social Issues*, 1979, 35: 79–96.
26. Hetherington, E.M., Divorce: a child's perspective. *American Psychologist*, 1979, 34: 851–858.
27. Hetherington, E.M., M. Cox & R. Cox, The aftermath of divorce. In J.H. Steven, Jr. & M. Mathews (Eds.), *Mother-child, father-child relations*. Washington, D.C.: NAEYC, 1978, 149–176.
28. ———, Play and social interaction in children following divorce. *Journal of Social Issues*, 1979, 35: 26–49.
29. Hingst, A. Children and divorce: the child's view. *Journal of Clinical Child Psychology*, 1981, 3: 161–164.
30. Hodges, W.F., R.C. Weschler & C. Ballatine, Divorce and the preschool child: cumulative stress. *Journal of Divorce*, 1979, 3: 55–68.
31. Holmes, R.H. & R.H. Rahe, The social readjustment rating scale. *Journal of Psychosomatic Research*, 1967, 11: 213–218.
32. Jacobson, S.D., The impact of separation/divorce on children: I. Parent-child separation and child adjustment. *Journal of Divorce*, 1978, 1: 341–360.

33. ———, The impact of marital separation/divorce on children: II. Interparent hostility and child adjustment. *Journal of Divorce*, 1978, 2: 3–19.
34. ———, The impact of marital separation/divorce on children: III. Parent-child communication and child adjustment, and regression analysis of findings from overall study. *Journal of Divorce*, 1978, 2: 175–194.
35. Johnson, J.H., Life events as stressors in childhood and adolescence. In B. Lahey and A. Kazdin (Eds.), *Advances in Clinical Child Psychology*, V. New York: Plenum Publ. Co.. In press.
36. Kalter, N. & J. Rembar, The significance of a child's age at the time of parental divorce. *American Journal of Orthopsychiatry*, 1981, 5: 85–100.
37. Kelly, J.B. & J.S. Wallerstein, The effects of parental divorce: experiences of the child in early latency. *American Journal of Orthopsychiatry*, 1976, 46: 20–32.
38. Kurdek, L.A., An integrative perspective on children's divorce adjustment. *American Psychologist*, 1981, 36: 856–866.
39. Kurdek, L. A. & D. Blisk, Dimensions and correlates of mothers' divorce experiences. *Journal of Divorce*. In press.
40. Kurdek, L.A., D. Blisk & A.E. Siesky, Correlates of children's long-term adjustment to their parents' divorce. *Developmental Psychology*, 1981, 17: 565–579.
41. Kurdek, L.A. & A.E. Siesky, Children's perceptions of their parents' divorce. *Journal of Divorce*, 1980, 3: 339–378.
42. Longfellow, L.L., Divorce in context: its impact on children. In G. Levinger and O. Moles (Eds.), *Divorce and separation*. New York: Basic Books, 1979, 287–306.
43. Megargee, E.I., *The California psychological inventory handbook*. San Francisco: Jossey-Bass, Inc., Publ., 1972.
44. Newcomb, M.D., G.J. Huba & P.M. Bentler, A multidimensional assessment of stressful life events among adolescents: derivation and correlates. *Journal of Health and Social Behavior*, 1981, 22: 400–415.
45. Rabkin, J.E. & E.L. Streuning, Life events, stress and illness. *Science*, 1976, 194: 1013–1020.
46. Rahe, R., Epidemiological studies of life change and illness. *International Journal of Psychiatry in Medicine*, 1975, 6: 133–146.
47. Rosen, R., Some crucial issues concerning children of divorce. *Journal of Divorce*, 1979, 3, 1: 19–25.
48. Sandler, I.N., Social support resources, stress and maladjustment of poor children. *American Journal of Community Psychology*, 1980, 8: 41–52.
49. ———On buffers and boosters: Social support for negative and positive life events. In J. Glidewell (Chair), "Social support and quality of life in the community." Symposium presented at the meeting of the American Psychological Association, Los Angeles, 1981.
50. Sandler, I.N. & M. Block, Life stress and maladaptation of children. *American Journal of Community Psychology*, 1979, 7: 425–440.
51. Sandler, I.N. & B. Lakey, Locus of control as a stress moderator: the role of control perceptions and social support. *American Journal of Community*

Psychology, 1982, 10: 65–80.
52. Sandler, I.N. & T.B. Ramsey, Dimensional analysis of children's stressful life events. *American Journal of Community Psychology,* 1980, 8: 285–302.
53. Santrock, J.W. & R. Warshak, Father custody and social development in boys and girls. *Journal of Social Issues,* 1979, 2: 233–240.
54. Sarason, I.G., J.H. Johnson & J.M. Siegel, Assessing the impact of life changes: development of the life experiences survey. *Journal of Consulting and Clinical Psychology,* 1978, 46:932–946.
55. Stolberg, A.L. & T.M. Anker, Cognitive and behavioral changes in children resulting from parental divorce and consequent environmental changes. In press. *Journal of Divorce.*
56. Wallerstein, J.S. & J.B. Kelly, The effects of parental divorce: the adolescent experience. In E. J. Anthony & C. Koupernik (Eds.) *The child in his family,* III. New York: John Wiley & Sons, 1974, 479–505.
57. ———, The effects of parental divorce: experiences of the preschool child. *Journal of the American Academy of Child Psychiatry,* 1975, 14: 600–616.
58. ———, The effects of parental divorce: Experiences of the child in later latency. *American Journal of Orthopsychiatry,* 1976, 46: 256–269.
59. ———, *Surviving the breakup: how children and parents cope with divorce.* New York: Basic Books, 1980.
60. Zautra, A & J. Reich, Positive life events and reports of well-being: some useful distinctions. *American Journal of Community Psychology,* 1980, 8: 657–670.
61. Zeigob, L.E. & R. Forehand, Parent-child interactions: observer effects and social class influences. *Behavior Therapy,* 1978, 9: 118–123.

CHAPTER 6

MEASURING THE STRESSFULNESS OF A CHILD'S ENVIRONMENT

R. Dean Coddington, M. D.

> *In this chapter the problems associated with the measurement of environmental stressors are discussed in the context of describing the development of the Life Event Scale for Adolescents (LES-A) and the comparable scale for children (LES-C). These scales are shown to be reasonably reliable and valid for the purpose they are intended. The author suggests that they should be viewed as global measures, never as substitutes for careful case histories. Used as screening devices they can identify children at risk for the development of some form of maladaptive behavior but their predictive efficiency can be improved by adding a measure of the child's individual coping skills and his family and extrafamilial support systems.*

In an attempt to understand the whole person, Adolf Meyer advocated a systematic listing of life events, "the changes of habitat, of school entrance, graduations or changes, or failures; the various 'jobs'; the dates of possibly important births and deaths in the family and other fundamentally important environmental incidents."[29] This Life-Chart, as Meyer called it, may have been the first attempt to quantify environmental stressors; Meyer felt obligated to record positive as well as negative events. Generally speaking, psychiatrists have thought in terms of psychic trauma, focusing on negative rather than positive events, though regularly accepting positive events as traumatic in idiosyncratic cases; a man who experienced the loss of a parent soon after he had received some special award in second grade, might continue to associate positive recognition with a sense of loss. The uniqueness of everyone's Life-Chart, along with the respective mental associations attached to each experience, presents a real problem to those interested in measuring the stressfulness of the environment. Which events are sufficiently stressful to enough persons to be included on a list of events intended to measure environmental stressors?

In their empirical study of 3,000 medical records, Holmes and Rahe discovered that many events, positive as well as negative, had been recorded as occurring in the previous few months.[19] The most frequently recorded events were compiled into the Social Readjustment Rating Scale (SRRS), which has been widely used as a measure of environmental stress in studies involving adult subjects, despite some controversy regarding the weights attached to each event (see: 3, 26, 25) the degree of aversiveness of the events,[15,40] and the representativeness of the scale in terms of the entire domain of possible events.[12]

I, too, began with the fundamental assumption that positive, apparently desirable events are sometimes surprisingly traumatic, or so it would seem. I have known a beautiful fifteen-year-old girl who made a serious attempt at suicide after being nominated as queen of her high school, an eighteen-year-old boy who became chronically depressed after a successful bone marrow transplantation had cured him of leukemia, and others who seemed to be very much afraid of success. I will attempt to subject clinical experiences such as these to objective analysis.

In this discussion of the measurement of the stressfulness of a child's environment, I will first describe the development of the Life Event Scale for Adolescents (LES-A) and the comparable scale for children (LES-C). Then, following our effort to establish the reliability and validity of these instruments, I will examine the theoretical questions that have been raised.

DEVELOPMENT OF THE LES-A

Coddington[6] was the first to attempt the systematic measurement of environmental stress in children utilizing the methodology employed by Holmes and Rahe.[19] The rationale underlying the methodology was based on the psychophysical law described by Stevens,[35] who, with his co-workers, showed that the magnitude of the difference between two physical measurements was equal to the magnitude between two subjective estimates of the measurements. That is, difference between the intensity of two lights can be correctly estimated in terms of brightness: "this light is three times brighter than that one." This relationship between stimulus ratios and subjective ratios also holds between the intensity of sound and loudness, between physical distance and visual distance, and between physical length and visual length.[35] This human capacity was used by Holmes and Rahe[19] and Coddington[6] to determine the amount of readjustment required by the occurrence of various life events. Coddington used the birth of a sibling as a standard, with the arbitrarily assigned value of 500 units. Subjects were then asked to estimate other events relative to the standard. "If the birth of a sibling requires 500 units of readjustment on the part of an adolescent, how much readjustment is required by the marital separation of his parents?" This application of a psychophysical law to estimate the stressfulness of events—along with estimation by an appropriate sample of judges—establishes at least moderate construct validity of the resulting scale.

We selected as judges professionals who worked with children: teachers ($n = 131$) presumed to have had experience with children who had coped successfully, pediatricians ($n = 25$) who may have seen children who became physically ill following some event or series of events, and mental health workers ($n = 87$) associated with academic divisions of child psychiatry. They were asked to estimate the amount of readjustment necessitated by the occurrence of every event on each of several age-specific listings of events commonly considered important to children; some events were clearly positive and some negative, and some were within the child's control while others were not. The geometric mean value for each event was determined and the antilog divided by ten to arrive at final weights, after the method described by Masuda and Holmes.[27] Correlations between the three professional groups were all over .92 and estimates by those with over twenty years experience correlated very well with those provided by younger professionals.[6]

Life event data were then gathered from 3,500 normal children.[7] When their scores were plotted by age, a curve resulted (Figure 1) which can at once be recognized as paralleling the physical growth curve. This would seem to be further evidence of the scale's construct validity. Responses from the subjects of this investigation prompted some modification of the wording of ambiguous events, deletion of some and the addition of others. The study also led to the decision to query adolescent judges regarding their estimates of the readjustment required by an event.

A total of 368 adolescents attending community centers, recreation programs, schools and camps agreed to participate in a project in which the same psychophysical technique was used. A high degree of agreement between various subgroups of adolescents was demon-

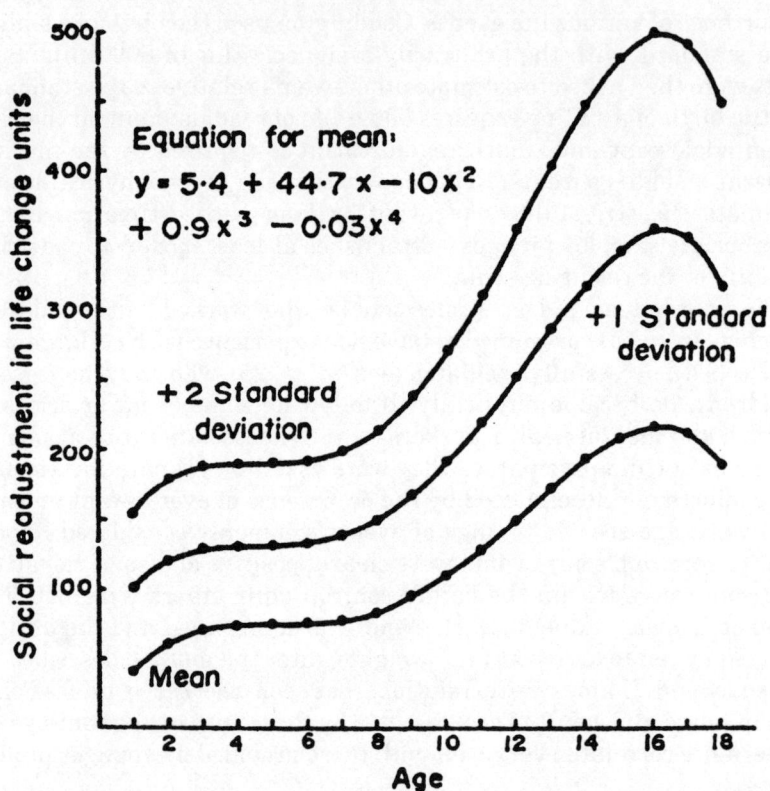

FIGURE 1
Social Readjustment Score by Age
N = 3526. (Coddington, 1972)

strated (Table 1) but the Pearson product-moment correlation with weights assigned by the previously studied professionals was only .37, although Spearman's rank order coefficient was .65 ($p < .001$). Neither age, race, sex, nor social class of the adolescents explained the differences.

The rating behavior of the adolescent judges was, however, quite distinct from that of the adults; adolescents used many more extreme values, sometimes in excess of 100,000. The frequency distribution of adolescents according to the number of extreme values assigned is presented in Table 2. Most used very high or low values for less than ten of the sixty items, but thirty-four percent deviated from their peers by assigning extreme values to more than a quarter of the items. A

TABLE 1

Pearson Product-Moment Correlation Coefficients Between Weights Assigned to Life Events by Various Adolescent Subgroups

Male ($n = 182$) vs Female ($n = 166$)	.95
Black ($n = 43$) vs White ($n = 306$)	.85
Under age 15 ($n = 114$) vs 15 & over ($n = 235$)	.95
First born ($n = 114$) vs Last born ($n = 123$)	.96
Experience with the event ($n = 25$) vs Lack of experience (44 events)	.67
Four 25% random samples	.92 to .96

Socioeconomic Class	I	II	III	IV	V
I ($n = 31$)	—	.85	.83	.84	.70
II ($n = 24$)		—	.95	.92	.79
III ($n = 66$)			—	.95	.86
IV ($n = 121$)				—	.87
V ($n = 37$)					—

Family Size	1-2	3-4	5-6	7+
1-2 Children ($n = 110$)	—	.95	.91	.91
3-4 Children ($n = 153$)		—	.93	.95
5-6 Children ($n = 43$)			—	.93
7+ Children ($n = 43$)				—

deviant score was computed for each subject. Multiple regression analysis with the deviant score as the dependent variable and age, sex, race, and social class as independent variables explained less than five percent of the variance of the deviant scores. Thus, it was concluded that the deviant score reflected an independent variable in the adolescent population.

A second multiple regression analysis was carried out separately for each event with the geometric mean as the dependent variable and age, sex, race, social class, the deviant score, and experience with the event as independent variables. The regression coefficient for the deviant score multiplied by the mean deviant score for all subjects was subtracted from the geometric mean in order to correct for this adolescent rating behavior. The correlation between adolescent and adult judges nearly doubled as a result of this correction, from .37 to .55 ($p <$

TABLE 2

Frequency Distribution of Adolescents by the Number of Events to Which They Assigned Weights of Zero or more than 2000

Number of Events	Number of Subjects	
	Absolute Frequency (%)	Cumulative Frequency (%)
0-3	33	33
4-6	10	43
7-9	10	53
10-13	5	58
14-17	8	66
>17	34	100

.001). Finally, data from all judges was combined by averaging, resulting in the Life Event Scale for Adolescents (LES-A) as it is currently used (Table 3).

Gersten and her group[15] suggested that undesirable events are more significant than the advent of desirable events. Though we believed otherwise on clinical grounds, we have routinely divided LES-A items into three subgroups, family events over which the child has little control, and extrafamilial events further subdivided into desirable and

TABLE 3

Life Events and Weights as They Appear on the Life Event Scale for Adolescents (LES-A)

The death of a parent	108
The death of a brother or sister	88
Divorce of your parents	70
Marital separation of your parents	62
The death of a grandparent	52
Hospitalization of a parent	52
Remarriage of a parent to a step-parent	51
Birth of a brother or sister	50
Hospitalization of a brother or sister	49

Loss of a job by your father or mother	46
Major increase in your parents' income	41
Major decrease in your parents' income	43
Start of a new problem between your parents	41
End of a problem between your parents	30
Change in father's job so he has less time home	35
A new adult moving into your home	34
Mother beginning to work outside the home	28
Being told you are very attractive by a friend	26
Going on the first date of your life	42
Finding a new dating partner	34
Breaking up with a boy/girl friend	39
Being told to break up with a boy/girl friend	35
Start of a new problem between you and your parents	43
End of a problem between you and your parents	35
Beginning the first year of senior high school	19
Move to a new school district	41
Failing a grade in school	47
Suspension from school	34
Graduating from high school	33
Being accepted at the college of your choice	39
Recognition for excelling in a sport or other activity	24
Getting your first driver's license	32
Being responsible for an automobile accident	36
Becoming an adult member of a church	25
Being invited to join a social organization	18
Being invited by a friend to break the law	21
Appearance in a juvenile court	31
Failing to achieve something you really wanted	32
Getting a summer job	35
Getting your first permanent job	40
Deciding to leave home	41
Being sent away from home	46
Being hospitalized for illness or injury	50
Death of a close friend	63
Becoming involved with drugs	45
Stopping the use of drugs	30
Finding an adult who really respects you	22
Getting pregnant or fathering a pregnancy Boys 61, Girls	88
Getting married	78
Outstanding personal achievement (special prize)	39

undesirable events. Since there are only two desirable family events on the LES-A, no subdivision was attempted.

The Life Event Scale for Children (LES-C) was similarly developed, but children were not solicited for their opinion due to the possible threat such an inquiry might invoke.

RELIABILITY

In discussing the issue of reliability of the SRRS, Sarason, de Monchaux and Hunt[33] state: "It is generally agreed that test-retest reliabilities of about .80 are reasonably adequate and that r's of .75 or below raise serious questions about the success with which the assessor is accomplishing his measurement task." Horowitz et al.[21] consider test-retest reliability correlations of .81 "quite high," but argue that since the reporting of whether or not a theoretical event occurred in a given time period should be precise, the correlation should be near unity, with any variation due to forgetting, deception, or inaccuracy in filling out the forms. The Horowitz group reported reliabilities of .82 and .71, respectively for a group of 27 psychiatric patients and a group of 20 non-patients, with a 6-week test-retest interval. Casey, Masuda, and Holmes[2] using a nine-month test-retest interval for a group of 54 resident physicians, reported correlations of .67 regarding events occurring over a 12 month period six years earlier, .64 for events occurring three years earlier, and .74 for events in the previous year. McDonald, Pugh, Gunderson, and Rahe[28] examined test-retest reliability with a six-month interval in Navy personnel and found correlations of .71 for events in the personal and social sphere, .69 for those in the world of work, .56 for marital relationships, and .09 for disciplinary conditions.

Though correlations of .70 only account for about 50% of the variance, it would seem that this is about as high as one can expect on a self-administered questionnaire. The higher correlations reported by Horowitz et al.[21] may be due to the fact that they used very small groups, making it possible to have research assistants or trained clerical personnel administer the instrument; they also used a very short test-retest interval.

The reliability of the LES-A was studied by asking 120 high school football players to complete the questionnaire and mail it in on three separate occasions, August 1980, December 1980, and July 1981. On each occasion they were to report events occurring between August 1979 and August 1980. Thirty-three boys complied with all three

TABLE 4
Life Events and Weights as They Appear on the Life Event Scale for Children (LES-C)

Event	Weight
The death of a parent	109
The death of a brother or sister	86
Divorce of your parents	73
Marital separation of your parents	66
The death of a grandparent	56
Hospitalization of a parent	52
Remarriage of a parent to a step-parent	53
Birth of a brother or sister	50
Hospitalization of a brother or sister	47
Loss of a job by your father or mother	37
Major increase in your parents' income	28
Major decrease in your parents' income	29
Start of a new problem between your parents	44
End of a problem between your parents	27
Change in father's job so he has less time home	39
A new adult moving into your home	41
Mother beginning to work outside the home	40
Being told you are very attractive by a friend	23
Beginning the first grade	20
Move to a new school district	35
Failing a grade in school	45
Suspension from school	30
Start of a new problem between you and your parents	43
End of a problem between you and your parents	34
Recognition for excelling in a sport or other activity	21
Appearance in juvenile court	33
Failing to achieve something you really wanted	28
Becoming an adult member of a church	21
Being invited to join a social organization	15
Death of a pet	40
Being hospitalized for illness or injury	53
Death of a close friend	52
Becoming involved with drugs	38
Stopping the use of drugs	23
Finding an adult who really respects you	20
Outstanding personal achievement (special prize)	34

requests. The results for the three test-retest intervals are tabulated in Table 5. Reliability of the LES-A seems to be inversely related to the length of time between testings, as one would expect.

TABLE 5

Pearson Product-Moment Correlation Coefficients with Three Test-Retest Intervals ($n = 33$)

	Test-Retest Interval		
	3 mo	7 mo	11 mo
Family event scores	.48*	.67**	.50**
Extrafamilial event scores	.69**	.68**	.56**
Desirable event scores	.68**	.62**	.37*
Undesirable event scores	.61**	.66**	.64**
Total LES-A scores	.69**	.67**	.56**

* $p < .02$
** $p < .002$

It is interesting to compare these results to test-retest studies of the IQ, as discussed by Hunt.[22] For teenagers and young adults the correlation is usually .89 when the retest is given immediately and .87 when the span between tests is 10 months. For younger groups, the stability is less. A more appropriate comparison can be made with the Personality Inventory for Children (PIC)[39] in which a mother is asked to provide information regarding her child. Two test-retest studies with intervals between testing of about two weeks and seven weeks resulted in correlations of .86 and .71, respectively. In comparison, our correlations of .69 with a three month span and .67 with a seven month interval would seem quite acceptable. It would seem prudent, however, to use more frequent data collection, requiring recall of three to six months, rather than of longer periods.

Table 6 indicates the results of an item analysis of the LES-A from the reports of sixty-three boys. Ten items seem unreliable, even though four of them appear quite objective (ex. death of a grandparent). Some respondents may have failed to read the directions carefully and may have reported events that occurred in the distant past rather than in the past year, as requested.

TABLE 6

LES-A Item Analysis (Pearson's r) with a Test-Retest Interval of Three Months ($n = 63$)

The death of a parent	1.00***
The death of a brother or sister	.99***
Divorce of your parents	1.00***
Marital separation of your parents	.65***
The death of a grandparent	.08
Hospitalization of a parent	.64***
Remarriage of a parent to a step-parent	1.00***
Birth of a brother or sister	.15
Hospitalization of a brother or sister	.56***
Loss of a job by your father or mother	.26*
Major increase in your parents' income	.18
Major decrease in your parents' income	.43***
Start of a new problem between your parents	.24*
End of a problem between your parents	.03
Change in father's job so he has less time at home	−.07
A new adult moving into your home	.14
Mother beginning to work outside the home	.53***
Being told you are very attractive by a friend	.69***
Going on the first date of your life	.56***
Finding a new dating partner	.55***
Breaking up with a boy/girl friend	.63***
Being told to break up with a boy/girl friend	.41***
Start of a new problem between you and your parents	.47***
End of a problem between you and your parents	.16
Beginning the first year of senior high school	.58***
Move to a new school district	.74***
Failing a grade in school	.42***
Suspension from school	.29**
Graduating from high school	1.00***
Being accepted at the college of your choice	−.05
Recognition for excelling in a sport or other activity	.22*
Getting your first driver's license	.43***
Being responsible for an automobile accident	.57***
Becoming an adult member of a church	.38***
Being invited to join a social organization	.39***
Being invited by a friend to break the law	.49***
Appearance in a juvenile court	.38***

Failing to achieve something you really wanted .64***
Getting a summer job .68***
Getting your first permanent job .55***
Deciding to leave home .20
Being sent away from home −.02
Death of a close friend .57***
Becoming involved with drugs .56***
Stopping the use of drugs .45***
Finding an adult who really respects you .55***
Getting pregnant or fathering a pregnancy 1.00***
Getting married 1.00***
Outstanding personal achievement (special prize) .38***

*$p < .05$; ** $p < .01$; *** $p < .001$

VALIDITY

Validity of Weighting Methodology

Two methods of estimating the stressfulness of events have been described recently. Van Houten and Golembiewski[36] developed the Life Event Inventory(LEI) in the course of an investigation into the causes of alcoholism and runaway behavior among adolescents. To determine item weights they utilized the Thurstone method[23] wherein a series of statements are sorted into twelve piles according to the relative degree to which they measure some attribute. Modification proved necessary for the adolescent judges, who became frustrated and sorted rather haphazardly when they had too many choices. Six piles were used, zero for nonstressful items and one to five for the amount of stressfulness associated with the item. The distribution of scaled values was plotted to find the median, and items with excessive interquartile ranges indicating great discrepancies between judges were dropped. The criterion sample consisted of 195 adolescents from five different U.S. locations. Their final list of 60 items included 18 similar enough to events on the LES-A to permit a valid comparison. The rank ordering of events was very similar (Spearman's $r = .77$, $p < .001$) and Pearson's r was .55 ($p < .01$).

Hart, Masuda, and Holmes,[17] working with weights derived by the psychophysical method and event frequency data, derived a formula in which the weight is expressed as a function of frequency:

$$\text{weight} = \text{constant} \left[\frac{1}{\text{frequency}} \right]^{0.5}$$

Frequency data from 748 adolescents were plotted against the weights used in the LES-A. The reciprocal of the frequency of each event was raised serially by a power of .01, ..., 2.0 and the correlation of the computed value and the LES-A weight determined. The best power function for our data was .05 making the formula:

$$\text{weight} = 151 + 179 \left[\frac{1}{\text{frequency}} \right]^{.05}$$

with the frequency expressed as the number of occurrences per 1,000 adolescents per year. Spearman's rank order correlation between weights for 52 events computed by this formula, compared to LES-A weights, was .50 ($p < .001$) and Pearson's r was .52 ($p < .001$).

The high correlation between weights derived by three independent methods can be viewed as cross-validation of each.

Content Validity

The representativeness of a life event list in relation to all the possible events that could occur was tested in a project involving 84 fourth graders and their parents.[10] The Life Event Scale for Children was administered 724 times, 345 times with children and 379 times with their parents. Other events that may have occurred but were not included on the LES-C were routinely solicited. Children reported only eight different additional events (e.g., "death of a great aunt," "ran winning touchdown in football," "appeared on TV regarding a nuclear power plant"); of the 378 events they reported, 370 (97%) were on the LES-C. Parents reported 555 events, 496 (89.4%) of which were on the LES-C. Examples of "other" events reported by parents are: "our house burned down," "an older child left home," "his dog was stolen," "mother broke up with boyfriend." Although 59 "other" events were reported, this was not the usual case. In 84.4% of the administrations of the LES-C to parents, no "other" events were added.

It would appear that the events included on the LES-C are fairly representative of those occurring in our sample population, indicating that there is reasonable content validity.

Concurrent Validity

Two members of the same family should report family events similarly, though a fourth source of error, individual perception, is introduced. It is equally clear that more personal extrafamilial events would be reported quite differently. Horowitz et al.[21] found considerable disagreement between couples living together, even in regard to such objective items as "hospitalization of a family member" and "birth or adoption of a child." (Correlation coefficients were not reported.)

The concurrent validity of the LES-A was tested by having the parents of thirty-three boys and the boys themselves report events that occurred during two different periods of time, August 1979 to August 1980, and December 1980 to July 1981. The results (Table 7) indicate agreement in respect to recent family events and desirable extrafamilial events, but disagreement over undesirable extrafamilial events. Perhaps the boys shared their successes but not their failures with their parents. Interrater reliability diminished markedly with time.

TABLE 7
Interrater Correlation Coefficients Between Adolescents and Their Parents ($n = 33$)

	Time Period Covered	
	Past 7 mo.	11-23 mo. ago
Family event scores	.57**	−.01
Extrafamilial event scores	.39*	.43*
Desirable event scores	.55**	.41*
Undesirable event scores	.10	.31
Total LES-A scores	.45*	.37*

* $p < .01$
** $p < .001$

Parent-child agreement using the LES-C has been studied on our fourth grade population, with the LES-C administered by a member of the research staff. As expected, children reported on the average relatively fewer family events than did their parents, 1.4 during the year compared to 2.0. The Pearson correlation to these data was .22 (p < .025). Children also reported fewer extrafamilial events, 3.0 compared to 3.9 (Pearson's $r = .27$, $< .01$). The average number of events reported by children as occurring during the year was 4.4, compared to the parental report of 5.9 (Pearson's $r = .30$, p < .005). The correlation coefficient between LES-C scores computed from data reported by children and their parents are .26, .27, and .27 for familial events, extrafamilial events, and total scores, respectively, all significant at the .01 level of confidence. Though significant, it is clear that young children and their parents are not in complete agreement regarding events that have occurred.

Concurrent validity clearly decreases with increasing disparity between ages, or, more correctly, with an increasing degree of individuality. Parents cannot be assumed to be accurate assessors of the stressfulness in their child's life.

Predictive Validity

The predictive validity of life event scales was also tested on the fourth grade population mentioned above.[10] A prospective cohort design was used, with the LES-C covering the first grading period, a measure of family supportiveness, and a measure of the child's intelligence (Comprehensive Tests of Basic Skills—CTBS)[1] as independent variables. The outcome variables, absenteeism and teachers' blind assessments of academic performance and classroom behavior, were recorded in each grading period throughout the remainder of the year. Children and their parents were queried separately regarding life events, and the two LES-C scores for the first grading period were average to determine HI (over 50) and LO groups. The HI CTBS group consisted of those children with standardized scores over the 40th percentile.

Academic problems did not occur any more often among children who had experienced more environmental stress, as compared to the control group (Table 8). Children in the second experimental cohort, those with below average achievement test scores, had an increased risk of academic problems, as one would expect. The same relative risks prevailed in the third cohort of children with high life event scores and below average aptitude.

Behavior problems did occur more often than expected in the high LES cohort (Table 9), but the difference reached statistical significance only in the second grading period, the period immediately following the occurrence of the events. Behavior problems did not occur more often in children of the LO CTBS cohort. However, in children in which both factors were present, the risk of behavior problems in every grading period was three times greater than the risk in the control group. Even though the number of behavior problems occurring in the high LES cohort did not reach statistical significance in the first (concurrent) grading period, 16 problems were reported in the first and second grading periods and only seven in the third and fourth. This

TABLE 8

Number of Children with Academic Problems by Grading Period and "Cause"

	n	Grading Period			
		1st	2nd	3rd	4th
HI LES, HI CTBS	22	5	4	2	2
LO LES, HI CTBS (controls)	23	4	5	2	1
Relative risk		1.31	.84	1.05	2.09
Chi square (1 df)		.2002	.0890	.0000	.3572
Significance		NS	NS	NS	NS
LO LES, LO CTBS	21	8	5	7	10
LO LES, HI CTBS (controls)	23	4	5	2	1
Relative risk		2.19	1.10	3.83	10.96
Chi square (1 df)		2.4304	.0207	4.0813	10.6515
Significance		NS	NS	<.05	<.005
HI LES, LO CTBS	18	5	7	7	6
LO LES, HI CTBS (controls)	23	4	5	2	1
Relative risk		1.60	1.53	4.47	7.67
Chi square (1 df)		.5770	1.3815	5.1929	5.8740
Significance		NS	NS	<.025	<.02

comparison, sixteen cases in the HI LES group compared to 6 in the control group, resulted in a Chi square of 4.8916 ($p < .05$). The effect of low CTBS scores was, on the other hand, evenly distributed throughout the year. These results are consistent with our expectation of an immediate adjustment required by the occurrence of life events and a long term, steady effect on classroom performance attributable to low aptitude.

The presence of a similar seasonal trend in the control group suggests the possibility that some of these children were also adjusting to events that occurred in the first grading period or perhaps in the preceding summer. One boy had a behavior problem and an academic

TABLE 9

Number of Children with Behavior Problems by Grading Period and "Causes"

		Grading Period			
	n	1st	2nd	3rd	4th
HI LES, HI CTBS	22	7	9	5	2
LO LES, HI CTBS (controls)	23	3	3	3	0
Relative risk		2.44	3.14	1.74	>2.09
Chi square (1 df)		2.2690	4.3697	.7363	2.0930
Significance		NS	<.05	NS	NS
LO LES, LO CTBS	21	6	5	4	5
LO LES, HI CTBS (controls)	23	3	3	3	0
Relative risk		2.19	1.83	1.46	>5.48
Chi square (1 df)		1.6180	.8821	.3341	6.1115
Significance		NS	NS	NS	<.02
HI LES, LO CTBS	18	9	9	7	8
LO LES, HI CTBS (controls)	23	3	3	3	0
Relative risk		3.83	3.83	2.98	>10.22
Chi square (1 df)		6.5442	6.5442	3.6291	12.7769
Significance		<.02	<.02	NS	<.001

problem in the first grading period, then performed well for the rest of the year. His mother had divorced a stepfather to whom he was closely attached three months before school started. His LES-C score for the summer was 125. Another boy had a very non-supportive family so that the LES-C score of thirty-nine may have exceeded his capacity to adjust without their added help. He had a behavior problem for the first three grading periods. These two boys and two others accounted for seven of the twelve academic problems (Table 8) and eight of the nine behavior problems (Table 9) experienced by children in the control group.

The data from the seven children in the high LES cohort that did not develop problems—false positives—were reexamined. One child had problems with absenteeism, having missed thirty days during the year. Four of the families had been classified as very supportive and one child was probably the brightest child in the entire group. Six false positives in the HI LES and LO CTBS cohort included another child who missed a lot of school, forty days, and two children from very supportive families.

The three cohorts, representing two "causes"—HI LES, LO CTBS, or a combination of the two—and the LO SUPPORT segment of the control group were assessed in terms of the proportion of academic problems that could be predicted by each of the "causes" (Figure 2). If one had the LES scores in the first two months of the academic year and nothing more, he could have picked up 45% of the children identified as having academic difficulty in the first grading period, half of those having problems in the second and third periods, and 42% in the last; if on the other hand, a teacher had only the previous year's achievement test scores, she could predict about 60% of the cases in the first semester and 80–85% in the second. If a teacher had both bits of information, she could predict 80–95% of the cases, and could further increase her prediction rate if she knew how supportive the family was.

Similar data regarding classroom behavior is presented in Figure 3. In this instance high LES scores are as predictive as the student's aptitude in the first, i.e., concurrent, grading period but are more predictive in the next two periods (65%). In the final period, aptitude assumes importance. Taken together, these two factors predict almost 85% of the behavior problems. If the teacher had the last bit of information, a measure of family supportiveness, her predictive success would reach 95%.

Thirty-two children (38%) developed serious problems, failing a grade, being "assigned" to fifth grade, or having academic, behavior, or absentee problems in at least three of the four grading periods. Life event scores over 50 would identify 20 of these children (62.5%) but would also identify 19 false positives; nine of these false positives had symptoms of one sort or another and only 10 had no problems. Below average aptitude carried the same risk, 20 (62.5%) with a serious problem, eight with some symptoms, and 11 false positives. Thus the LES-C administered during the first grading period is as accurate as the child's achievement test scores in predicting the development of a serious problem during the year. When one compares the cohort with both factors operating (HI LES, LO CTBS) with controls, the result is highly significant (Chi square = 12.6518, 1 df, $p < .001$).

Measuring the Stressfulness of Environment 115

FIGURE 2

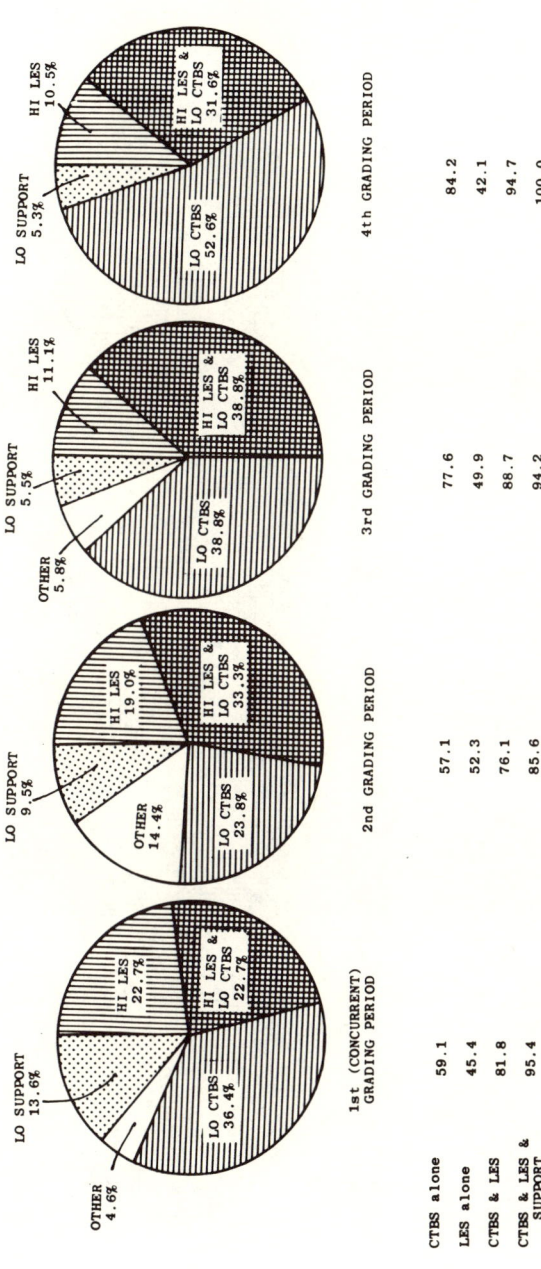

FIGURE 3

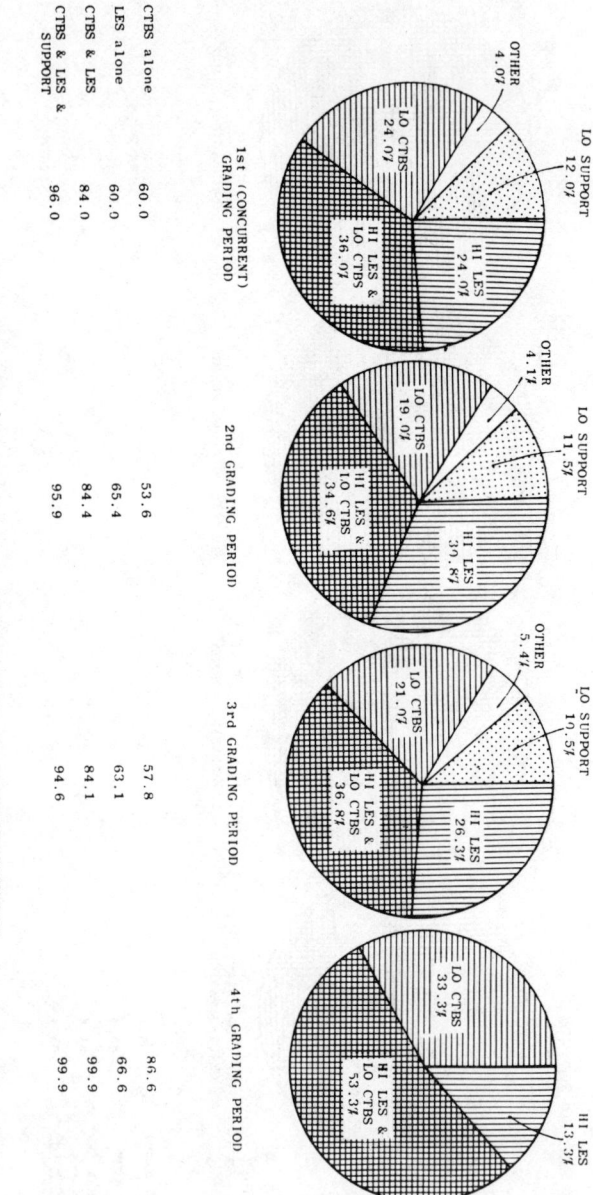

In order to evaluate more precisely the LES-C as a screening instrument, a third method was used. Any child who met any criterion of maladjustment, behaviorally, academically or by absenteeism, was identified as a "case" for that grading period. The predictive efficiency of the LES-C was computed and tested by means of the Kappa statistic.[14] Since the events that attribute to high LES-C scores preceed the maladaptive behavior, any association we find can be assumed to fit only one tail of the normal curve. The instrument's efficiency in the first grading period, i.e., the overall probability of a correct prediction, is .61 (Table 10), significant beyond the .025 level of confidence. The predictive validity is somewhat less in the second grading period, just reaching statistical significance. Though it appears that life events occurring in the first grading period are also predictive of maladaptive behavior in the last half of the year, one should use caution in interpreting the data, since other events are occurring as the year progresses. Ten children in the HI LES cohorts also had high scores in the second grading period, eleven in the third and eight in the fourth. One child had high scores all year long, while seven had high scores in three out of four grading periods.

TABLE 10

Number of Children Showing Signs of Maladaptation by Grading Period and LES-C Score

		Grading Period			
	n	1st	2nd	3rd	4th
HI LES	40	23	23	24	19
LO LES	41	15	16	15	12
Kappa		.22	.18	.24	.18
s.e.(k)		.11	.11	.11	.105
z		2.00	1.64	2.18	1.71
p (1 tail)		< .025	= .05	< .02	< .05

WEIGHTED VS. UNWEIGHTED SCORES

Gersten and associates[15] saw no particular advantage in using weighted scores since they found a correlation coefficient of .99 between a simple count of events and scores based on our originally reported weights. Rahe and Ransome[31] concur, reporting correlations of nearly .90 in large-scale Navy studies. Wildman[38] agreed that weighted scores have only a slight advantage over simple counts. Lloyd et al.[26] reported a correlation of .96, but found the weighted score to be a slightly better predictor of college grade point averages in the subsequent year. Furthermore, Lei and Skinner[25] argue that randomly assigned weights result in scores that are highly correlated with differentially weighted and unweighted scores. How can these divergent views be explained?

A partial answer becomes apparent when one realizes that most respondents will have experienced very few events, with the ones they have experienced being those more frequently occurring. In any population, a significant number (about 20%) will report no events; their life event scores will be zero regardless of methodology, and the correlation will be perfect. Likewise, a number of subjects will report the occurrence of either the same events, or events with similar weights, a situation that will also result in a perfect or near-perfect correlation. Lei and Skinner,[25] for instance, used a homogeneous population, 353 alcohol/drug abuse clients who had experienced many similar events. Judging from their item-analysis, many subjects reported "change in responsibilities at work," "change in living conditions," "revision of personal habits," "change in social activities," "change in financial state," "change in sleeping habits," and "change in eating habits," all of which were probably secondary to their illness. In children, the number of events is usually four to six per year, so there is not much opportunity for the development of a low correlation, unless someone experienced one or two rare events. These facts explain the occurrence of high correlations but shed little light on the desirability of weighted or unweighted scores.

This dilemma was tested in two of our projects, in both of which weighted scores proved superior.[8,10] Figure 4 shows data from 382 girls, 121 of whom were pregnant, with the regression line which resulted when weighted scores were plotted against simple scores. The same regression line was drawn in Figure 5 along with the data points for the 121 pregnant adolescents; most data points are located below the regression line indicating relatively higher weighted scores. The average weight for the events occurring to pregnant girls was higher than the average weight for non-pregnant girls, 52 and 36 respectively. (The event of pregnancy was, of course, excluded from these calculations). The mean event count was 19.7 for the non-pregnant girls and 22 for the pregnant girls (t = 1.81(381), $p < .05$). The respective mean weighted scores were, however, 99.55 and 104.88 (t = 3.28(381), $p < .001$). Simple event counts used in an attempt to screen adolescent girls for those at risk of pregnancy would

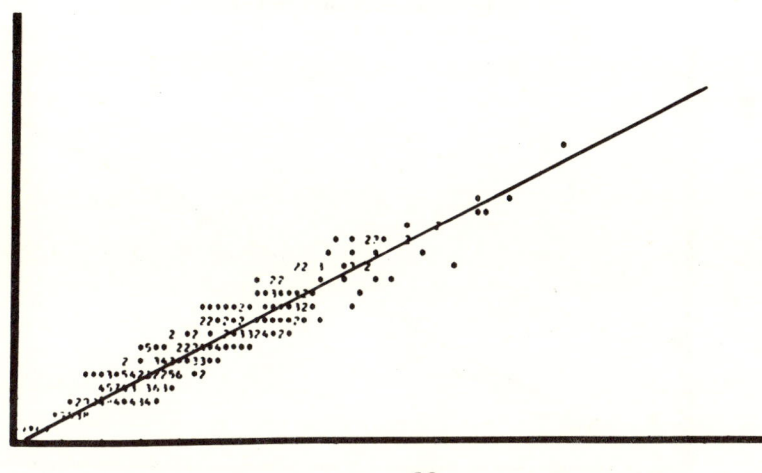

FIGURE 4
Weighted Scores (*x*-axis) versus Unweighted
(y-axis) for 382 Adolescent Girls
Pearson's *r* = .97

have a very low sensitivity, identifying only 13% of those who become pregnant, while weighted scores would pick up 29%, twice as good though still impractical.

The correlation between simple counts and weighted scores in the study of fourth grade children described above was very high, .96. However, an instrument based on the number of events occurring in the first grading period would increase the number of false negatives in the first two periods, lowering the predictive efficiency from .61 in the first grading period to .58 and in the second grading period to .57, neither of which is significantly better than chance.

If prediction is the research objective, weighted scores are preferable. Perhaps further work will support a compromise solution with all events involving loss of an object given a weight of, perhaps, 100, and other categorical groups of events assigned weights of 80, 60, 40, et cetera.

DESIRABILITY VS. UNDERSIRABILITY

The question of whether or not to pay due attention to desirable events has been considered by many authors, following Meyer's[29] assertion that one is *obligated* to include them in the attempt to

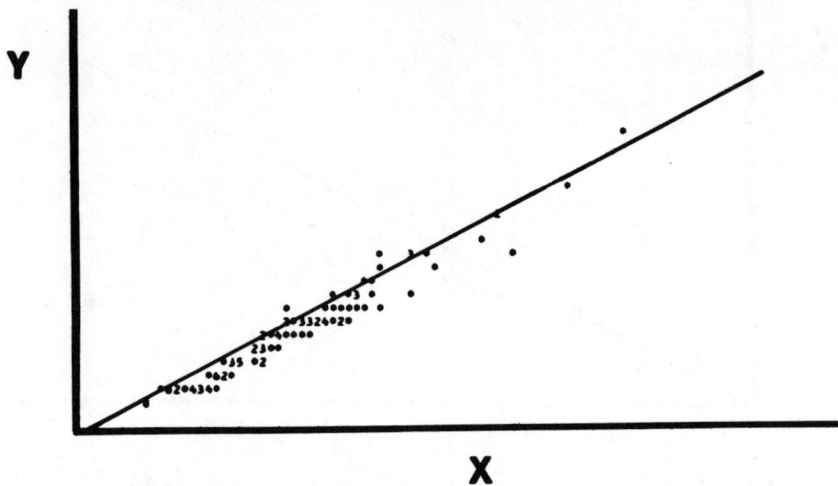

FIGURE 5
Weighted Scores (x-axis) versus Unweighted Scores
(y-axis) for 121 Pregnant Adolescents
The regression line is computed from the data
in Figure 4 rather than data shown here

understand the patient's health. Critics have said that Holmes and Rahe[19] based their decision to include positive events on an *assumption* of their importance when, in fact, Holmes had done considerable work with tubercular patients and arrived at his position through empirical research.[20] Nevertheless, Zeiss assessed the quality of the events on the SRRS and found an overall correlation of .69 with aversiveness ratings.[40] Thus, the SRRS is, in a general sense, a measure of traumatic or undesirable aspects of the environment, making the controversy rather academic.

The judges who originally estimated the weights used in the LES-A and LES-C assigned higher weights to the negative member of paired events, as, for instance, the start of a new problem as opposed to the end of a problem (Table 3 and 4), thereby making some allowance for undesirability. Moreover, our research supports the view that undesirable events have more impact than desirable events, contrary to our original clinically-based opinion. In the comparison of pregnant and non-pregnant adolescents, the pregnant girls had considerably higher undesirable event scores (t = 5.28(381), p < .0001) but equivalent desirable event scores. (Incidentally, the simple count of undesirable events did not distinguish the two groups.)

Sandler and Ramsay[32] suggest the development of subscores based on the qualitative differences and similarities of events, which they demonstrated with a factor analytic technique. Seven factors accounted for 63.6% of the variance. One must be cautious in applying the results of this excellent piece of work, however, because some of the factors included only three or four items. Larger groups of events are likely to produce more uniform results. Chiriboda and Dean also advocate subscores.[4] This concept has not yet been tested in respect to the LES-A.

ATTENTUATION OF STRESSFULNESS

At a recent meeting of the American Orthopsychiatric Association, Wallerstein[37] reported her findings on children of divorced parents, pointing out that the acute symptoms are usually relieved within a year. At the same meeting Krim and Wundheiler[24] asserted that the crisis phase following the loss of one's home or apartment by fire lasted three to four months. Horowitz et al.[21] showed, in the case of adult subjects, a definite decrease in the estimate of the stressfulness of an event when it was presumed to have occurred at some more distant point in time.

In an effort to better understand the attenuation of the effect of an event, we asked small groups of adolescents to estimate the amount of readjustment required by the occurrence of an event one week ago, one month ago, six months ago, and one year ago. Each group of ten to fifteen subjects were asked to consider only ten events in such detail. The curves depicted in Figure 6, expressed in terms of the percent of the initial value, were uniform for all events. Adolescents felt an event would only require half as much readjustment six months after its occurrence and thirty-five to forty percent after a year. We have, then, another argument for gathering life event data over a rather short period of time, say three to six months.

DEFENSE AGAINST STRESSFUL EVENTS

It is outside the scope of this chapter to review the research on coping mechanisms and social support systems. The measurement of the stressfulness of the child's environment, no matter how precise, can never be expected to account for a majority of the variance in the stimulus-illness relationship. Indeed, most of the studies report correlations around .30, accounting for only nine percent of the variance.

FIGURE 6

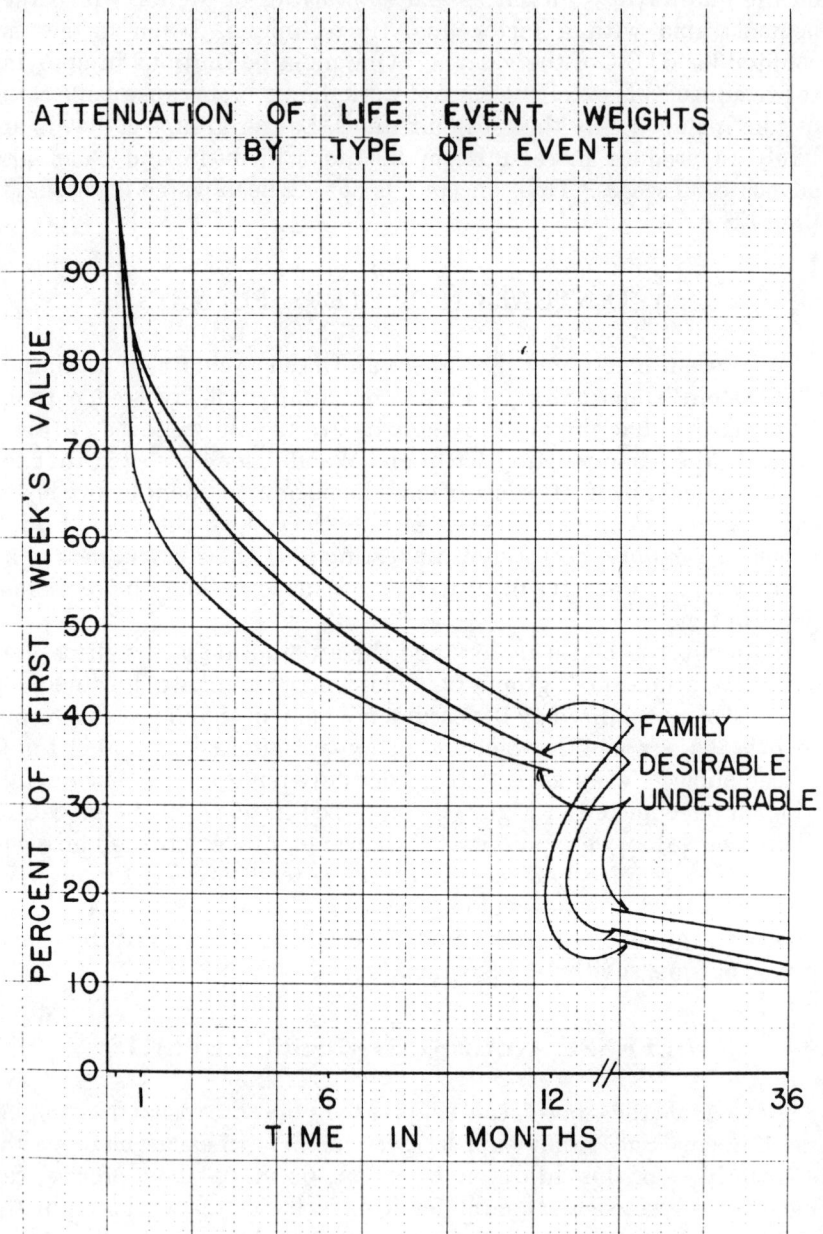

Defense and support systems must be included in the equation. Nuckolls, Cassel, and Kaplan[30] demonstrated this most adequately and Cobb[5] lucidly reviewed the point. In a clinic setting one is frequently nonplused at understanding how a child has done as well as he has under the circumstances. Intelligence helps, but is not universally successful. Family intactness helps, and so does the availability of extended family members. Peer groups, religious faith, and other social organizations can aid. Five out of eleven false positives in our fourth grade study—that is, children with high life event scores and no evidence of symptom formation had as their teacher the woman that the research team had identified in their own minds as the most sensitive. Did she prevent the development of problems?

We are working on a measure of family supportiveness,[11] but it would be premature to report any conclusions here. Suffice it to say that we have been impressed by what would appear on the surface to be an incredible lack of support in some families. Some families seem never to have time to discuss issues or problems. The family members go to work at odd and different hours, have their meals separately, and seem to have very different avocational and religious interests. Communication to any meaningful degree appears almost a catch-as-catch-can affair.

SUMMARY AND CONCLUSIONS

The development of the LES-A and LES-C have been described along with available data regarding their psychometric properties. They were designed to measure the stressfulness in a child's environment in a global way, never as a substitute for the individual evaluation of a child. They can be helpful in assessing children by simply calling attention to events the interviewer may have neglected to ask about, much as Adolf Meyer used his Life-Chart. A busy pediatrician might find the instruments quite useful, as long as he recognized the reliability and validity as being similar to those qualities of an electroencephalogram (EEG) rather than a WISC-R. The LES Score would call his attention to the occurrence of events, the effect of which would then require further exploration. Unlike an EEG, the LES is non-intrusive and can be administered frequently—ideally, every three months as a regular part of the child's health record. Data obtained in this manner would be sufficiently reliable and might, over several years, prove to be etiologically related to various illnesses (see: Heisel et al.[18]).

These measures can be economically administered to large groups and have been shown to have predictive validity. Is this predictive validity sufficiently strong to allow the identification, for instance, of teenagers who will abuse alcohol or drugs or those who are at risk of becoming a highway fatality? Duncan found an association between high LES-A scores and drug dependence.[13] There is also some support for a positive answer to the latter part of the question.[9] Though we have encouragement regarding this public health application of the LES-A, the answer to the question must be qualified, "no, not without some equally valid measure of family and extrafamilial support systems."

This is the direction in which future research should go. Rather than attempting to refine current measures of environmental stressfulness, an effort that will never result in an instrument psychometrically comparable to the WISC-R, we should try to increase their value by including other factors in the equation personal coping styles, family supportiveness, religiosity, and other support networks. We are on the right road, but have a way to go if we are to succeed in preventing the major effects of environmental stress.

REFERENCES

1. Borus, O.K., *The seventh mental measurements yearbook.* Highland Park: Gryphon Press, 1972.
2. Casey, R.L., M. Masuda & T.H. Holmes, Quantitative study of recall of life events. *Journal of Psychosomatic Research* 1967, 11: 239–247.
3. Chiriboda, D.A., Life event weighting systems: a comparative analysis. *Journal of Psychosomatic Research* 1977, 21: 415–422.
4. Chiriboda, D.A. & H. Dean, Dimensions of stress: perspectives from longitudinal study. *Journal of Psychosomatic Research* 1978, 22: 47–55.
5. Cobb, S., Social support as a moderator of life stress. *Psychosom. Med.* 1976, 38: 300–314.
6. Coddington, R.D., The significance of life events as etiologic factors in the diseases of children, I: A survey of professional workers. *Journal of Psychosomatic Research* 1972, 16: 7–18.
7. ———, The significance of life events as etiologic factors in the disease of children, II: A study of a normal population. *Journal of Psychosomatic Research* 1972, 16: 205–213.
8. ———, Life events associated with adolescent pregnancies. *Journal of Clinical Psychiatry,* 1979, 40: 180–185.
9. ———, The effect of life events on adolescent automobile accident rates. *Garyounis Medical Journal* 1980, 3: 51–54.
10. Coddington, R.D., M.M. Wallick & C.J. Larroque, Predicting maladaptive

behavior in children. Paper presented at the meeting of American Academy of Child Psychiatry, Washington, D.C. October, 1982.
11. ———Measuring family supportiveness. Paper presented at the meeting of the American Academy of Child Psychiatry, Washington, D.C., October, 1982.
12. Dohrenwend, B.P., Problems in defining and sampling the relevent population of stressful life events. In B.S. Dohrenwend and B.P. Dohrenwend (Eds.), *Stressful life events: their nature and effects.* New York: John Wiley & Sons, 1974.
13. Duncan, D.F., Stress and adolescent drug dependence: a brief report. *IRCS Med. Sc.: Psychol. & Psychiat: Social and Occup. Med.* 1976, 4: p. 381.
14. Fleiss, J.L., *Statistical methods for rates and proportions.* New York: John Wiley & Sons, 1973.
15. Gersten, J.C., T.S. Langner, J.G. Eisenberg & L. Orzeck, Child behavior and life events: undesirable or change per se? In B.S. Dohrenwend and B.P. Dohrenwend (Eds.), *Stressful life events: their nature and effects.* New York: John Wiley & Sons, 1974.
16. Grant I., H. Sweetwood, M.S. Gerst & J. Yager, Scaling procedures in life event research. *Journal of Psychosomatic Research* 1978, 22: 525–530.
17. Hart, C.A., M. Masuda & T.H. Holmes, *Life event magnitude judgements.* Presented at the meeting of the American Psychosomatic Society, Atlanta. 1978.
18. Heisel, J.S., S. Ream, R. Raitz, M. Rappaport & R.D. Coddington, The significance of life events as contributing factors in the diseases of children, III: A study of pediatric patients. *Journal of Pediatrics.* 1973, 83: 119–123.
19. Holmes, T.H. & R.H. Rahe, The social adjustment rating scale. *Journal of Psychosomatic Research* 1967, 11: 213–218.
20. Holmes, T.H., N.G. Hawkins, C.E. Bowerman, E.R. Clarke Jr. & J.R. Joffe, Psychosocial and psychophysiologic studies of tuberculosis. *Psychosomatic Medicine* 1957, 19: 134–143.
21. Horowitz, M., C. Schaefer, D. Hiroto, N. Wilner & B. Levin, Life event questionnaires for measuring presumptive stress. *Psychosomatic Medicine* 1977, 39: 413–431.
22. Hunt. J. M.V., *Intelligence and experience.* New York: Ronald Press Co., 1961.
23. Issac, S., & W.B. Michael, *Handbook on research and evaluation.* San Diego: EDMS Pub., 1975.
24. Krim, A. & L. Wundheiler, Families after fires. Paper presented at the meeting of the American Orthopsychiatric Association, San Francisco, 1982.
25. Lei, H., & H.A. Skinner, A psychometric study of life events and social readjustment. *Journal of Psychosomatic Research* 1980, 24: 57–65.
26. Lloyd, C., A.A. Alexander, D.G. Rice & N.S. Greenfield, Life events as predictors of academic performance. *Journal of Human Stress.* 1980, 6: 15–25.

27. Masuda, M. & T.H. Holmes, Magnitude estimations of social readjustments. *Journal of Psychosomatic Research* 1967, 11: 219–225.
28. McDonald, B.W., W.M. Pugh, E.K.E. Gunderson & R.H. Rahe, Reliability of life change cluster scores. *British Journal of Social & Clinical Psychology* 1972, 11: 407–409.
29. Meyer, A., 1919, The life chart and the obligation of specifying positive data in psychopathological diagnosis. In E.E. Winters (Ed.), *The collected papers of Adolf Meyer. Volume III, medical teaching.* Baltimore: The Johns Hopkins University Press, 1951, 52–56.
30. Nuckolls, K.B., J. Cassel & B.H. Kaplan, Psychosocial assets, life crises and the prognosis of pregnancy. *American Journal of Epidemiology.* 1976, 38: 300–314.
31. Rahe, R.H. & J.A. Ransome, Life changes and illness studies: past history and future directions. *Journal of Human Stress.* 1978, 4: 3–15.
32. Sandler, I.N. & T.B. Ramsay, Dimensional analysis of children's stressful life events. *American Journal of Community Psychology.* 1980, 8: 285–302.
33. Sarason, I.G., C. DeMonchaux & T. Hunt, Methodological issues in the assessment of life stress. In Levi, L. (Ed.), *Emotions, their parameters and measurement.* New York: Raven Press, Pub., 1975.
34. Sobel, R. & R. Underhill, Family disorganization and teenage auto accidents. *Journal of Safety Research.* 1976, 8: p. 8.
35. Stevens, S.S., On the psychophysical law. *Psychology Review.* 1957, 64: 153–181.
36. Van Houten, T. & G. Galemliewski, Adolescent life stress as a predictor of alcohol abuse and/or runaway behavior. Washington, D.C., National Youth Alternatives Project, 1978.
37. Wallerstein, J.S., Children of divorce: the tasks of the child in the divorcing family. Paper presented at the meeting of the American Orthopsychiatric Association, San Francisco, 1982.
38. Wildman, R.D., Life change with college grades as a role-performance variable. *Journal of Social Psychology.* 1978, 41: 34–36.
39. Wirt, R.D., D. Lachar, J.K. Klinedinst & P.S. Seat, *Multidimensional description of child personality, a manual for the personality inventory for children.* Western Psychological Services, 1977.
40. Zeiss, A.M., Averseness versus change in the assessment of life stress. *Journal of Psychosomatic Research* 1980, 24: 15–19.

CHAPTER 7

STRESS AND COMPETENCE

Bernard Brown, Ph. D.
and
Lilian Rosenbaum, Ph. D.

This chapter is concerned with experimental, clinical, and longitudinal study data that support the hypothesis that stress affects competence and intelligence. Children from families which function poorly and/or are exposed to high stressor levels develop inadequate skills that lead to suboptimal intellectual function. Stress management can improve competence and intelligence particularly through work to improve parents' coping skills and level of function.

INTRODUCTION

It is our hypothesis that stress affects competence and intelligence. This is a universal phenomenon equally applicable to a variety of populations. Our focus is on children who are at risk from acute and chronic stress.

In this chapter we define the terms *stressor* and *arousal,* describe the levels and kinds of stressors that impact on children and families and describe the factors that mediate stressor impact and stress coping skills. We review the literature on stress and test performance and evidence from longitudinal studies that stress affects intelligence. We then interpret our findings in terms of how the brain functions under stress and how family systems contribute to and are affected by stress. Finally, we briefly review stress management programs for children and families.

Note: The views and opinions expressed herein are those of the authors and do not necessarily represent those of the Department of Health and Human Services.

Along with the interaction of genetics, environment and experience in the shaping of physical, social, emotional and intellectual growth in children, we have added stress as a major determinant of intellectual development.

The basic hypothesis presented in this chapter, that stress affects intelligence and competence, was formulated by Lilian Rosenbaum on the basis of her clinical work in biofeedback, family therapy, and self-regulation. She arrived at the hypothesis by considerations that included Bowen's family systems theory,[5] MacLean's triune brain model,[69] and the effect of stress on cybernetic balance in the autonomic nervous system. Bernard Brown developed methods to test the hypothesis, employing data from longitudinal studies of child development and early intervention. He reviewed the stress and performance literature and developed the model of brain regression under stress.

Stress

Stress is a complex psychological and biological process that begins when an individual perceives potential harm or danger. For the purpose of this chapter we prefer to define a *stressor* as a stimulus or a situation that is perceived as potentially harmful or dangerous, and stress *arousal* as the internal psychophysiological response of an individual to a stressor. Stressors are often complex and they may derive from sources either outside or inside the body. Stressors act as a drain on physical or psychological resources when they trigger psychophysiological changes. These changes may be either acute or chronic and may be focused in specific bodily processes or may be general throughout the body.

Stressors induce psychophysiological effects upon individuals such as anxiety which is a transitory emotional state consisting of subjective feelings of fear and aggression, tension, apprehension, and worry. Stressors also produce changes in psychomotor performance, paying attention, problem solving, and social and emotional behavior. Stressors can change muscle tension, reaction time, heart rate and a great many other psychophysiological variables.

A person subjected to a stressor may be said to have increased arousal. The level of arousal is measured by physiological measures such as skin conductance, heart rate, and blood catecholamine levels.

The terms "stress" and "stressor" are interchangeable in the literature and in common usage, and we make no effort to redefine into strict categories of either stressor or stress when we cite the work of others.[1]

The essential stress phenomenon being considered is called the 'fight-or-flight response."[15] Humans, like other animals, react in a predictable way when stressful situations trigger an automatic survival response that has been part of our physiologic make-up for millions of years. But when real or imagined stressors persist, repeated "fight-or-flight" response can lead to chronic imbalance of the finely tuned control systems of the body as inability to return to homeostatic balance results in the breakdown of one or more of the control systems and in associated dysfunction.

The autonomic nervous system, made up of the sympathetic and parasympathetic nervous systems, is one of the major physiological components of the "fight-or-flight response." Under stress, there is usually heightened sympathetic activity. Two important indicators of this activity are increased electrodermal activity (increased sweat gland response) and decreased peripheral vascular flow with concomitant decrease in skin temperature. Other indicators of sympathetic activity include increases in heart rate, blood pressure, muscle tension, and respiration rate. In sympathetic activity the levels of epinephrine excreted into the blood by the endocrine system increase.

THE IMPACT OF STRESS ON CHILDREN

A vast number of studies show that stressors associated with family function, stressors in the schools and stressors in the community place children at heightened risk for social, emotional, physical, and intellectual dysfunction.

In reviewing the effect of stress on single mothers, Belle has made a strong case that traumatic life events, such as death and divorce in the family, have strong impact on women's mental health and child outcomes.[4] Beyond having to adjust to the stress of sporadic changes in life events, impoverished mothers are stressed by unchanging or only slowly changing conditions that their families must endure daily. Belle found that the various stressors and indicators of arousal level were highly correlated in her sample. This suggested that the stressors are additive and should not be considered in isolation from one another. One of the major stress effects of poor financial circumstances is that women who have responsibility for young children are more likely to become depressed.[12,92]

Belle, et al. found that the total number of life condition stressors experienced by impoverished single mothers was four times as great as that experienced in the general community.[4] There were large and significant correlations (.6–.7) between life condition stresses and such aspects of mental health as anxiety, a sense of mastery, self-esteem and depression.

Depression may be considered a mental disease, but the findings of Belle on stress-related depression are reminiscent of Adolph Meyer's statement that there are no mental diseases—only characteristic reaction patterns to stress. Vaillant found in his study of adults who rise above life circumstances that most mental illness is an inward struggle to adapt to life.[113] He claimed that increased stress in the lives of the mentally ill is a result of, and not a cause of, poor adaptation.

Stress is a serious problem in all children. The National Health Survey[85] found that, in a cross-sectional sample of 7,119 children of 6 to 11 years of age, parents had had trouble getting 22.1% of the children into bed and 12.2% of the children to sleep. Almost half of the children had unpleasant dreams. These problems remained essentially constant from age 6 to age 11. Over 4% of the children had difficulty getting along with other children and 2% stammered or stuttered. At age 6, 28.2% of the children were afraid of the dark; this declined to 17.4% by age 11. Thumbsucking decreased with age from 13.6% at age 5 to 6.2% at age 11. The number of children who were moderately tense or high strung increased from 40.7% to 48% by age 11. Over 50% showed occasional or frequent strong temper. There appears to be a pattern in American children of school age that stress increases with age as measured by parental reports of tension.

Other psychophysiological disorders in which stressors and high arousal levels affect cildren's health include ulcers, asthma, hypertension, allergy, and headaches.

There is a large body of evidence that stress is generated by psychosocial transitions, life events that change life circumstances—the individual's role at home and work or the structure of the family system.[95,98] These events include marriage, birth, death, starting school, retirement, divorce, and job loss. Another body of literature relating to life stress research in behavioral medicine has studied the effects of cumulative life change and of severe life events on the subsequent development of physical and mental illness in individuals. This literature includes the work of Rahe and his associates (see: 12, 24, 90, 91, 96, 97, 98). It describes the relationship between the intensity of change in a person's life over a period of time and the probability of onset of physical or mental illness. Rahe and associates[99] used the Holmes and Rahe Scale to show that severity of illness is related to the amount of life change of an individual in the preceding six months as well as to the increase of intensity of life change over its previous level.

Phillips performed a study of stress and anxiety in the public schools.[93] He found that socioeconomic background was an influential factor in children's response to school stress. Children who had a minority status appeared to be more stressed. Individual school practice influenced stressor and perceived stress levels. Phillips found a small but significant correlation between school anxiety and problem behavior in school children. School anxiety was correlated both with achievement and intelligence test scores, but weaker correlations were found in the case of middle class white children. He found that his prediciton of achievement had some loading on locus of control, academic self-perception, school anxiety, and coping style.

Prolonged exposure to a stressor is associated with decreases in performance and social behavior. Children living in noisy housing show greater impairment in auditory discrimination, puzzle solving, and reading ability compared to those who live in quieter housing.[34]

Life stress in children has been related to respiratory tract illness,[6] changes in the health status of chronically ill children,[3] accident frequency,[88] and adolescent depression.[44a]

Werner and Smith found that adolescents in Kauai who developed serious coping problems underwent stressful life events during their childhood with much greater frequency than adolescents without problems.[116] There were problems in family relationships, finances, and absence of parents. These adverse life events predicted delinquency and/or serious mental health problems by age eighteen. Prediction of serious coping problems was improved by including the family's socioeconomic status, mother's education, a history of severe perinatal stress, congenital defect, and marked handicap at age ten. These variables were key predictors of serious learning and behavior problems in childhood and adolescence, particularly for children from poor homes.

We have reviewed the literature of the past twenty years concerning the stressors that impinge on disadvantaged children and their families. At birth the disadvantaged child is at risk because of lack of maternal nutrition, prenatal and postnatal care and hospital delivery as well as early pregnancy, high parity, and short birth spacing. Disadvantaged children suffer from inadequate health care, stressful home conditions including large family size, and disordered, undisciplined schools. Disadvantaged families are at risk from domestic breakup, maternal depression, poor health (especially from stress-related disease), recurrent financial crises and disordered and uncontrollable life conditions (see: 4, 11, 12, 17, 22, 23, 33, 34, 37, 42, 50, 53, 58, 62, 86, 94, 100, 102).

STRESS AND TASK PERFORMANCE

In discussing our hypothesis that stress affects competence and intelligence we will refer to two kinds of performance on tests. The first kind is the performance of individuals on written tests which we call either achievement or in the case of IQ tests, intelligence. The second kind of performance is that observed in tests that life situations present which we call competence.

The literature clearly indicates that in addition to performance deficits associated with anxiety *prior* to test administration and to performance deficits deriving from concurrent stressors or from stress from the testing itself *during* test administration; there is also a performance deficit that takes place *after* stress that can adversely affect test performance. In addition, there are life conditions and life events that have long-term effects on performance.

A number of studies have dealt with the tendency under stress to reduce efficiency on complex performance tasks but to enhance efficiency on relatively simple tasks.[57] Mandler and Sarason,[74] Child[16] and Sarason, et al.[103] studied individual differences in vulnerability to failure stress. They have been concerned with the interference that takes place when anxiety is generated by expectation of failure and the anxiety in turn leads to defensive, task irrelevent response.

Tryon has reviewed the literature on test anxiety.[112] A significant negative relationship has been established between test anxiety and grade-point average and between test anxiety and various aptitude and achievement tests. The worry component of test anxiety correlates significantly and negatively with college grades. Anxiety is also related to intelligence and learning. Feldhusen and Klausmeier found that the correlation between the Manifest Anxiety Scale and intelligence as measured by the WISC varied as a function of WISC score.[29] The IQ scores of medium and low IQ children were more highly correlated with anxiety than those of the higher IQ children. Complex tasks increase anxiety.

Examination anxiety is a major source of high arousal. Becker, in a study of college students, found that pre-examination arousal was affected by the students' failure/success orientation including their level of aspiration, estimates of examination difficulty and their level of competence relative to others in their classrooms.[2] Preexamination behavior was also related to stress reaction (autonomic nervous system arousal, sleep loss), improper preparation, achievement motivation, and examination fear. Success-oriented students had fear levels that rose early and dropped before examinations but failure-oriented students had increasing fear gradients as the examination grew near.

There is evidence for an inverted-U relationship between stress and performance for relatively complex tasks. Hokanson and Burgess found that the level of task complexity showed an interaction with heart rate.[40] On low complexity tasks their high heart rate subjects showed superior performance but as task complexity increased the difference disappeared. It appears that the subjects with high heart rates were already operating at optimum arousal level and that further arousal placed them on the downward side of the inverted-U stress curve.

Doerr and Hokanson also found evidence for an inverted-U relationship for performance versus heart rate on a timed coding task in which frustration was administered.[23a] On a thermal regulation measure, time for vasodilation in the hand, Teichner & Youngling found an inverted-U shaped trend for performance on paired associate learning.[110] Fiske and Maddi summarized the research on the relationship of degree of arousal to level of performance on various tasks and reported general support for an inverted U-relationship.[31]

Lazarus et al., in a review of the literature on verbal performance under stress, found that stress impairs performance on relatively complex and difficult tasks but may improve it on relatively simple tasks.[61] Stressors involving fear of failure produced lower scores on: learning and recall of nonsense syllables; digit-symbol substitution; arithmetic; recognition of briefly exposed sentences; sentence formation; digit span and perceptual-motor performance such as card sorting and reaction time. Reaction time appears to lengthen with task complexity (see: 45, 46, 47, 48).

Lantz found that failure experience lowers Stanford-Binet scores in nine-year-old boys.[59] Tasks that required visual or rote memory were not affected, but those that required reasoning or thinking suffered a decrement.

Subjects asked to perform a continuous rotary-tracking task before, during, and after experiencing the stress of the human centrifuge performed best when galvanic skin resistance suggested moderate arousal.[105]

Arousal and performance were found to have an inverted-U relationship. Stennett measured heart rate under varying incentive conditions and found an inverted-U curve.[107] Eason measured EMG in trapezius, deltoid, biceps, and neck muscles and found an inverted-U relationship between tracking performance efficiency and target size.[25]

Experimenter effects concern a class of events in which test scores change as a result of the influence of the experimenter (or tester) on the subject. There are many studies that suggest that racial minorities may perceive a testing situation with fear and suspicion, verbal constriction, and strained and unnatural reactions, with the assumption of a facade of stupidity and low scoring in order to avoid personal threat.[52,104]

Perceived stress appears to depend on psychological sets and responses that individuals are more likely to bring into the testing situation than manufacture on the spot. They respond to tests and testing situations with learned patterns of stress reactivity. The patterns may vary among individuals and may reflect differences in autonomic nervous system conditioning, feelings of threat or worry regarding the symbolic meaning of the test or the testing situation, and coping skills that govern the management of complexity, frustration, information load, symbolic manipulation, and mobilization of resources. There are also individual patterns of maladaptive behavior such as anxiety, a sustained high level of autonomic activity after exposure to a stressor, and the use of a variety of such defense mechanisms as learned helplessness and avoidance behavior.[57]

Perceived stress also depends upon the nature of the task to be performed. As tasks get more complex and require greater degrees of coordination and integration of the nervous system, a given stressor level will affect task performance as if it were a stronger stressor.

Cohen, in reviewing the literature on the aftereffects of stress on performance and social behavior, cited evidence of post-stimulus aftereffects from noise, crowding, task load, electric shock, and bureaucratic harassment.[20] The aftereffects, which included impaired tolerance for frustration, reaction time, and proofreading accuracy, were more likely to occur following uncontrollable, rather than controllable stressors; i.e., perceived control ameliorated stress aftereffects. Behavior impairments in children included a decrease in helping other children, a decrease in the recognition of individual differences and an increase in agression.

In summary, the cognitive psychology literature suggests that stress affects individual performance on IQ tests through

test anxiety;

performance under stress;

stress aftereffects;
stressful life events and life conditions; and,
coping skills.

These stress variables combine to influence IQ test performance both in the immediate testing situation and developmentally as they interact with inherited traits environment and experience to shape the growth of intelligence.

LONGITUDINAL STUDIES RELATING TO STRESS AND COPING

Longitudinal studies are remarkably sensitive to the effects of stress and coping in children. Apparently, it takes many years for stressors to make impact on a child and for the child to develop his/her idiosyncratic styles of coping. These affect the rate at which the child grows, but the effects of changed growth rate require many years to be expressed in changed behavior, especially for the growth of intelligence.

McCall, et al., in a longitudinal study of patterns of IQ change with age, found that children in the Fels study who showed gains in IQ with age had parents who attempted to accelerate their children in intellectual tasks and took a moderate, rationally structured approach to discipline.[80] In contrast, children who showed declines in IQ with age had parents who were coercive, restrictive, punished bad behavior rather than rewarded good behavior and imposed severe punishment for misconduct. Preschool children who gained in IQ were independent and socially competitive.

Kellam, et al., performed a longitudinal study of a mental health program in twelve Woodlawn (Chicago) schools.[53] Using a teacher rating scale for social adaptation behavior, they showed that their measures of adjustment on five social task scales were significantly associated with scores on the Kuhlmann-Anderson IQ test at the end of the first grade and also in the third grade.

As an indication of the persistence of patterns of autonomic reactivity, type A behavior patterns found in adolescence carry over into adulthood.[79]

The NINCDS Collaborative Perinatal Project studied the impact of biological and social factors on intelligence.[8] They found relationships between IQ and family characteristics such as income, parental education, parental employment, mothers' marital status, and father presence in the home. IQ was related to the mother's perinatal characteristics such as parity, number of prenatal visits, and mother's hemoglobin level. Low birthweight, low head circumference, and disease states were negatively correlated with IQ.

We have examined the effects of stress on IQ in a sample of 4,154 of 41,540 seven-year-old children from the Collaborative Project. We developed a stress index which was a composite score of the number of medical/psychological problems found in a child. The variables were selected from the Collaborative Project data files collected in the 1960s. They included mother's marital status, employment, family configuration, history of illness, death, and divorce in the family, measures of autonomic function, achievement measures and physician-identified health disorders including vision, motor, speech and hearing problems. We found an inverted-U curve of performance on the WISC IQ test and its component subtests for IQ vs. stress level as measured by total number of problems per child.

For example, on the WISC Information subtest white middle-class children with three problems scored the equivalent of eight IQ points higher than those with no problems and thirteen points higher than those with ten problems. The Information, Block Design, and Coding subtests have the greatest sensitivity to stress and the Comprehension and Vocabulary subtests were the least sensitive. The inverted-U curve of the full-scale WISC IQ test was less pronounced than the curves of the subtests with only a seven-point difference between maximum performance level and the performance level under high stress. The curves of low-SES children were of the same inverted-U form but were peaked at lower stress levels suggesting higher arousal and stressor levels. Thus, we have shown that stress has a large effect on intelligence test scores.

Longitudinal studies of nutrition intervention have produced results similar to those of the longitudinal studies of behavioral intervention. McKay showed that an intensive combinaton of nutritional and educational interventions in Columbian preschool children can promote cognitive growth.[81] Barrett, Radke-Yarrow & Klein found that the INCAP nutritional and educational program in Guatemala resulted in behavior benefits apparently relating to adaptive behavior.[1]

Murphy and Moriarty found that IQ rose in children who displayed good coping skills and decreased in children who displayed poor ones.[83]

The Berkeley longitudinal data also showed that IQ in middle class children changes with coping skill.[38] Young middle class children, who develop adequate coping skills and defense mechanisms early, tend to carry them over into adolescence and adulthood. Appropriate coping is generally related to IQ acceleration and poor coping to IQ deceleration. Similar findings were reported by Werner and Smith.[116]

We have analyzed recent data from the Consortium for Longitudinal

Studies[19] and found stress-related effects on WISC-R subtests given to the followup sample of teenagers who had been in early intervention programs. The Block Design subtest of the WISC-R is well known for its sensitivity to stress.[87] The treatment group (N 1 422) scored 7.4 points higher (on the basis of 100 as normal) than the control goup (N 1 179). In contrast, on a relatively stress-free subtest, Picture Arrangement, the control group scored higher than the treatment group. Even so, both groups together scored lower on Block Design than on Picture Arrangement by eleven points. This suggests that both were impaired by stress-related factors, but that substantial school behavior improvements were made in the treatment group, probably through their learning of school related coping skills.

For each of the separate programs, Block Design scores of the treatment groups were higher than for the control groups. Moreover, except in one instance the control groups (who may have been slightly higher in SES) were higher on Picture Arrangement than the treatment groups.

These programs were found to have had dramatic impact on school stress as measured by grade retention, assignment to special education and environment. However, IQ had almost no relationship to any of the outcomes. Thus it may be that these early intervention programs which affected coping skills reduced arousal only in respect to a limited set of school and job functions.

This conjecture is in close agreement with the findings from the secondary analysis of data from the evaluation of the transition of Head Start children into the public schools. Cline et al., found that children who had been in Head Start showed remarkably higher ratings than children with no preschool experience in terms of being assertive, protecting their rights, and evidencing desire to have social contact with adults and other children.[17]

The impact of early intervention on Block Design subtest performance is of particular interest because of Jensen's claim that the WISC Block Design subtest is one of the best measures of Type II intelligence.[45] If the Consortium Block Design data are to be believed, then there are two alternative interpretations that would appear to apply depending on whether one hypothesizes genetic or stress-related causation of Block Design performance. If genetic causation is assumed, then one would have to conclude that the programs changed the children's genetic structures or so altered the environment that genetic expression was altered. On the other hand, from a stress and coping point of view the programs may have given the children coping skills that helped them manage their arousal levels and the endemic stressors in their homes and school.

The longitudinal studies provide a fascinating insight into how coping skills and cognitive factors affect response to stress. The partial amelioraton of competence through early intervention programs that teach school related skills appears to involve the learning of stress management skills. Despite this important impact, the children's IQs were not raised dramatically. We hypothesize that the key to the overall improvement of intellectual competence lies in dealing with family function as part of the general reduction of stressors in the child's environment.

FACTORS THAT MEDIATE STRESS

As is the case with other stressors, stressful life events have different impacts on individuals depending on mediating factors that include: (1) the characteristics of the stressful situation, (2) the individual's biological and psychological characteristics such as cognitive appraisal processes and (3) the nature of the social support systems available to the individual.[95]

The effects of exposure to stressors are likely to be reduced for those who are maturely connected to nuclear and extended families and for those who are tied into social networks and support systems.[5] Conversely, the effects of exposure to stressors are increased in cases of social isolation, social marginality (minority membership), and status inconsistency (e.g., incompatible social expectation for mothers and unmarried adolescents). Vaillant found that in his sample of achieving adults traumatic events rarely resulted in changes in individual lives.[113] He claimed that what counts is the interaction among choices of adaptive mechanisms and of sustained relations with other people.

Stressors have different effects depending on their magnitude, duration, rate of change, unpredictability, and novelty. An individual's perception of a stressor, its potential threat or challenge, is shaped by all of the above mediating factors which can affect both the nature of the stress reaction and subsequent coping behavior.

Werner and Smith have performed a major longitudinal study of the capacity of children to cope and overcome a home environment of extreme poverty and a series of stressful life events.[116] In their twenty-year study of the children of Kauai they found that one out of every five children developed serious behavior or learning problems at some time during the first two decades of their lives. Yet other children equally vulnerable to the same life stressors remained invincible and developed into competent and autonomous young adults "who worked well, played well, loved well, and expected well." Werner and Smith showed that it is the balance between risk factors, stressful life events, and protective factors within the child and the environment that accounts for the range of adaptive and maladaptive functioning. Several factors have an impact on this balance, including the stages of the life cycle, sex of the child, and the cultural context in which she grows up.

Werner and Smith described the coping patterns and sources of support among resilient children and youth. As infants, their mothers perceived them to be "very active" and "socially responsive." As toddlers they were observed to be autonomous and socially oriented; they also showed advanced self-help skills and adequate sensorimotor and language ability. In middle childhood the resilient children had adequate problem-solving and communications skills and their perceptual-motor development was appropriate to their age level. In late adolescence they had more internal locus of control, more positive self-concept, and more nurturant, responsible, and achievement-oriented attitudes toward life than those exposed to the same stressful life conditions who developed serious problems. As young men and women they had developed a sense of coherence in their lives and were able to draw on a number of informal sources of support. Peers (siblings, cousins, and friends) (35%), older friends (30%) including older relatives and parents of boy- or girlfriends were the primary sources of support for the majority of resilient youth (more so for girls than boys). Parents ranked next (25%), followed by ministers (11.5%) and teachers (11.5%, more for boys than for the resilient girls). Only a small proportion of the resilient children and youth had contacts with social, educational, or health service agencies during the first and second decades of their lives.[116]

The finding about the importance of informal sources of support is of particular interest as it fits into family systems theory and clinical practice data that functioning and coping can be altered by a variety of family systems interventions. Two such interventions are to decrease the emotional distance in the family and increase the responsible open contact by the persons at high risk with their nuclear and extended family systems.[5]

Lazarus developed models of cognitive techniques used by individuals to mediate the effects of stressors.[60] Such coping skills work together with other skills to control physiological response and determine the effect of a given stressor on the mind and the body. Meichenbaum has developed a cognitive behavior modification approach that includes stress inoculation training.[82]

Desensitization and "getting used to" stress is an important process that facilitates coping. Familiarization decreases the threat perceived in an unfamiliar stressor and contributes to cognitive mastery. The effect of exposure to manageable stress is resilience and mastery.[83]

STRESS AND BRAIN FUNCTION

Stressors rapidly and profoundly affect the higher mental functions. As Hughlings Jackson noted almost a century ago in the case of alcohol, the brain loses its function in inverse phylogenetic order. This has been shown to be true for low blood glucose (hypoglycemia) and low blood oxygen (hypoxia) as well. The higher centers such as the forelobes of the neocortex are the first to lose their function as alcohol concentration is increased; the lower motor function associated with the spinal cord maintains itself the longest. The behavior observed under stress appears to follow this order also.

Hypoxia is a well-studied type of stress that can help us to understand pathways through which stress affects the brain and behavior.[114] Hypoxia first affects the higher centers causing a blunting of the fine sensibilities, a decrease in voluntary coordination and attention, a loss of judgment and of self-criticism. There is often a mistaken sense of clarity and keeness of mind and frequently there is a fixity of purpose that may lead an individual into dangerous acts. There is a progressive regression to early function. In cases of extensive decortication, the subcortical centers can still carry out simpler responses to the same sensory input. When deprived of blood, the small pyramidal cells of the cerebrum will survive for only eight minutes. The medullary centers will survive for twenty to thirty minutes and the sympathetic ganglia will survive for an hour. In carbon monoxide asphyxia the cortex will survive for five minutes but the vasomotor and respiratory systems will survive for an hour.[36] Histologic changes under moderate hypoxia are first seen in the frontal lobe of the neocortex and then in the temporal lobe. The basal ganglia are less affected than the spinal cord and medulla.

The well-known tendency for individuals under stress to regress in inverse phylogenetic order suggested that a brain model based on phylogenetic development may be useful in describing how stress affects the brain. MacLean (see: 68, 69, 70, 71, 72, 73) has developed such a model, which he terms, "The Triune Brain," and we find that it helps explain and organize the research findings on how stress affects behavior. The model is compatible with the clinical observations of one of us (LR) in working with individuals and families under stress. MacLean's model is widely accepted and apt for our purpose of describing how stress affects the brain and hence behavior. We could have made an equivalent, though somewhat more awkward, statement using the findings on specific neurological responses to stress in specific parts of the brain. Moveover, while we are making anatomical distinctions, it should be borne in mind that the brain functions as a whole so that brain processes that are interactive cannot be pinpointed to particular anatomic sites. The sites are guides to explain relative imbalance in function.

The triune brain consists of three distinct anatomical and biochemical structures: the reptilian brain, the limbic system and the cerebral neocortex. The ancient reptilian core of the brain is concerned with routine (hunting, eating, sleeping) and ritual (courtship, territoriality, display). Its basic principle is: survival comes first. The reptilian brain is surrounded by a later structure, the limbic system. The limbic system reacts emotionally to events in the environment, flooding the body with hormones and coordinating with the reptilian brain to help it survive. The cerebral neocortex is the last part of the triune brain to evolve. It is the cortex of the limbic system and is the center for thought and knowledge. It interacts with and usually acts as a control over the emotional reactivity of the limbic system.

The brain stem reticular formation is activated during stress.[67] It is probably by this means that ideas or thoughts (presumably cortical events) can produce autonomic changes and alterations of muscular tone by downward discharge from cortex to reticular formation and then to the autonomic, motor, and sensory centers.[108]

The cerebral cortex coordinates external events and internal reactions to the events. The size and extent of the cortex has increased in history as animals ascended the phylogenetic scale. Reptiles adjust to external events using lower brain functions, not cortical connections. In birds the thalamus and basal ganglia coordinate the many forms of sensory input and give rise to instinctual reactions such as mating and nesting. In mammals the cerebral neocortex takes over many functions performed by the basal ganglia in lower species. The coordination of sensory information requires a more complex coordinating mechanism than the thalamus in order to effect desired motor responses. As seen phylogenetically, and ontogenetically as well, the brain's organization grows increasingly complex and its functional capability becomes increasingly differentiated, allowing finer, more complex perception and behavior. Thus the neocortex acts as the amplifier and prosthesis of the limbic system (see: 51, 89, 120).

There is a great deal of clinical and experimental evidence that various limbic system structures participate in the regulation of emotion.[36,38] The limbic system also appears to be involved in motivational functions that influence behavior in all learning situations but do not appear to be an integral part of the learning process itself. In lesion and stimulation studies, the components of the limbic system have been shown to influence learning.

The limbic system appears to be responsive to regulation by the cerebral neocortex. By ablation of the neocortex, some studies have shown that emotionality can be reduced presumably because excitatory signals to the subcortical emotion centers cease. If the amygdaloid complex or cingulate gyrus or hippocampus is also removed there is a striking increase in emotional reactivity.[36] In general, the neocortex appears to exert both excitatory and inhibitory influences on the limbic system. It regulates particular emotional variables and may be excitatory with respect to some targets and inhibitory with respect to others.[36]

After external events are relayed to the brain through the sensory pathways and the brain stem, they are interpreted by the neocortex and integrated by the limbic system. If a threat is perceived the hypothalamus emits catecholamines into the bloodstream that produce stress responses. There are also long-term stress effects from the endocrine system that pumps ACTH, a growth hormone and thyroid-stimulating hormone, into the blood stream. It appears that stress reactions to stimuli result from cognitive interpretation in the neocortex and emotional arousal in the limbic system.[28]

The triune brain is a finely balanced control system. Functionally, the triune brain is hierarchically organized in a manner very similar to Maslow's hierarchy of needs, with the reptilian brain tending to deal with lower needs and the cortex with highest needs.[77,78] Under stress, however, the balance of this finely tuned hierarchical control system is disrupted and the limbic system emotions with their biochemical sequelae increase in strength and interfere with normal neocortical function, in particular with performance on intellectual and psychomotor tasks. As stress and the resulting imbalances increase, the function and integration of the three brains decrease to earlier levels of function. There is, in addition, an increase in emotional reactivity as neocortical control over the limbic system is disrupted.

Lewis's studies of poverty cultures fit the picture of the triune brain disorganized by stress so that overreactivity in emotional areas (the limbic system) is the dominant mode of functioning.[63] Despite the harsh and brutalizing environment in the poor Puerto Rican families he studied, Lewis found that the families showed surprising fortitude, vitality, resilience, and ability to cope with problems that would have paralyzed many middle-class individuals. Yet they were subject to extreme impulsivity, uncontrolled rage and aggression, preoccupation with sex, and a deep need for love. There was an endemic lack of direction and lack of order as they submerged in a daily battle for survival. In a sense, there was effective coping, but it often took place at reptilian and limbic levels and rarely represented the response of an integrated brain coordinated with a fully functioning cerebral neocortex.

It is striking that those parts of the brain that are phylogenetically advanced and have the most complex coordinating and differentiating functions are the most susceptible to damage under severe stress. In particular, processes normally dealt with by the cerebral neocortex are under stress more often left to the automatic forces of the limbic system than when not under stress. These forces are toward togetherness and emotionality.[5] With enough stress, the individual does not have the choice to function primarily with neocortical control; the individual functions then primarily with limbic system control. This is less competent functioning and has been described as less intelligent functioning. The lower the degree of differentiation by the individual of his intellectual and emotional systems, the more likely that there is some functional impairment. This impairment may occur in social, emotional, physical, or intellectual functioning.

Although neocortical function regresses under stress to more emotional limbic system function, such behavior should not be thought of as necessarily inappropriate or dysfunctional. In moments of intimacy and sexual expression, for example, limbic behavior is quite appropriate. In situations of acute stress, such as a fire, it is often in the best interest of the individual to respond automatically. However, it is our hypothesis that in chronic or severe illness or in poverty, over a long period of time, people who learn to respond to stressors at a cortical level are more likely to function effectively with a wider, more differentiated coping style and show fewer indications of acute distress. Families and children who develop those skills that are often referred to as "cognitive ability" are more likely to be competent in all areas of their lives. In this view what has been termed "intelligence" is in part the application of competent stress management to those demands of modern industrial society and especially its educational systems that require sustained higher cortical function.

The phylogenetic development of brain function as described in the MacLean model parallels the ontogenetic development of function. IQ is at least in part a measure of development. As regression of intellectual function under stress takes place in inverse phylogenetic and ontogenetic order, the balance of integrated function shifts from the neocortex towards the limbic system and reptilian brain. We therefore expect that, as children regress to earlier levels of intellectual function under stress, they will function as if they had lower mental ages, i.e., they will appear to have lower IQ scores.

IQ AND FAMILY FUNCTIONING

The family is clearly the preeminent and major continuing influence on the child. Families under stress, such as those in poverty, tend to function poorly in terms of coping skills; e.g., separating intellectual from emotional issues. In terms of the triune brain model they cannot readily and by choice separate cortical from limbic system functioning. These individuals have difficulty defining their positions within the family and society and have difficulty learning to self-regulate behavior to cope with stress.[5] They also have to deal with high external stressors that add to their already high arousal levels. The combination of poor coping (low differentiation) and high arousal can lead to social, physical, and emotional impairment in parents and/or their children. This, in turn, can result in performance deficits in, for example, school tasks. Over a long period of time, as the child with a high arousal level performs suboptimally there will develop a generalized developmental lag. The immediate suboptimal performance may be transformed into a permanent deficit in IQ level, which reflects overall development.

This analysis suggests that the level of family functioning is a major determinant of IQ level. It follows that any attempt at intervention that does not result in a permanent change in the level of responsible family functioning or in the family's external stressor levels will not result in permanent gains in a child's IQ. Those early intervention programs that have been most successful in raising IQ's have been home and family based.[7] In contrast, early intervention programs aimed at early training in school related activities have produced large permanent gains in school related performance but have had relatively little impact on IQ.[10,19]

Developmental insults affecting the growth and level of intelligence appear to be the result of three epidemiological vectors that translate stress into dysfunction. These are: (1) high stressor levels, especially those associated with poverty and illness, which decrease ability to deal with daily stressors and complex tasks; (2) inadequate family function, which increases the incidence of stressful events and vulnerability to stress and (3) poor coping skills, which result in reduced self-management, social awareness and cortical control over emotion.

The impact of stress on intelligence can be observed along three developmental axes: On the performance axis, high arousal levels lead to reduced performance and skill acquisition. On the brain function axis, stressors and high arousal levels decrease cortical function and enhance emotionality and stereotyped behavior resulting in overall reduced capacity to function. On the learning axis, the various developmental influences of stress reduce learning, resulting in a cumulative deficit in knowledge and skills.

STRESS CAN BE REGULATED

The large body of literature on stress management and clinical practice clearly indicates its rapid and highly successful development. Stress management has assumed increasing prominence in the treatment of physical, emotional, and social disorders, in health enhancement, and maximizing human potential. Studies have decisively shown the cost effectiveness of psychophysiological self-regulation programs (see: 35, 75, 76, 121). Stress management has important and direct implications for institutions that deal with children for their efforts: (1) to enhance social competence in children; (2) to improve the capacity of their families to function effectively; and (3) to help teachers and other staff members to deal effectively with the pressures and stressors that impinge on them and indirectly upon the children in their care. For instance, a stress management program was shown to be highly successful in increasing achievement scores in fifth grade children in Clearwater, Florida schools.[27]

Biofeedback is the process that provides immediate and continuous information (through auditory or visual signals) of physiological responses of which we are ordinarily unaware. This information facilitates self-regulation. Biofeedback is now a major resource for medical and psychological treatment and for child development programs.[119] The efficacy of biofeedback for a variety of psychological and behavioral disorders has been investigated extensively (see: 13, 23, 30, 32, 101, 109, 118).

The biofeedback literature includes a variety of studies using biofeedback specifically for stress management in children, for instance in hyperactivity (see: 55, 56, 64, 66, 103) and asthma.[54] It has been shown that biofeedback training can improve examination performance of test-anxious college students.[18] In Butler's survey of the literature on biofeedback and related self-regulation techniques over 100 citations are specifically about children.[14]

IMPLICATIONS FOR COMPETENCE

On the basis of new data and a review of the literature we have put forward a body of evidence to support our hypothesis that stress affects intelligence.

We have presented evidence that many families are exposed to high stressor levels, both acute and chronic. Stress affects the level of anxiety, sense of mastery, self-esteem, depression, and general ability to function in the family which in turns shapes children's competence. Stressors influence performance both immediately and developmentally as they interact with genetics, environment, and experience to shape physical, social, emotional, and intellectual growth.

We have presented evidence that acute stressors disrupt the balance between cognitive and emotional function as highly differentiated thought decreases and the brain becomes emotionally overreactive. Children who experience chronic stressors, either real or perceived, show a long-term decline in intelligence if their coping skills are inadequate while children with appropriate coping skills rise in intelligence.

The hypothesis that stress affects competence implies a different set of interventions in dealing with dysfunction in children and families. Competence in functioning can be altered by modifying the degree of individual differentiation, the intensity, frequency, and predictability of the stressors, and/or the individual's response (arousal) to the stressors and processes of family function. These interventions can alter the present competence of the individual as well as presumably counter the transmission of suboptimal functioning across generations. These include education in family processes and/or therapy as well as training in a variety of self-regulation techniques such as biofeedback and stress management.[101] There are ways to increase the number of stress-resisting factors to protect children from unnecessary risk. We can intervene in schools and other organizations to insure that organizational processes do not lead to overreactivity in children and families. We can design curricula and materials that allow learning to take place at optimal levels of arousal. The goal is to facilitate the self-regulation of motivated individuals in order to maximize their responsibility for self, their identity, their integrity, and their coping capacity.

REFERENCE NOTE

Weigert, S. *Stress, Performance and the development of coping strategies in childhood* (Annotated bibliography). Washington, D.C.: Georgetown University, Family Center, Department of Psychiatry, 1982.

REFERENCES

1. Barrett, D. E., M. Radke-Yarrow & R. E. Klein, Chronic malnutrition and child behavior: effects of early calorie supplementation on socioemotional functioning at school age. In press. *Developmental Psychology*.
2. Becker, Peter., Fear reactions and achievement behavior of students approaching an examination. In Krohue, H. W. and L. Laux, (Eds.), *Achievement, Stress, and Anxiety*. Washington: Hemisphere, 1982.
3. Bedell, J. R., B. Giordani, J. L. Amour, J. Tavormina & T. Boll, Life stress and the psychological and medical adjustment of chronically ill children. *Journal of Psychosomatic Research*, 1977, 21: 237–242.
4. Belle, D., *Lives in stress: women and depression*. Beverly Hills: 1982.
5. Bowen, M., *Family therapy in clinical practice*. New York: Aronson, 1978.
6. Boyce, T. W., E. W. Jensen, J. C. Cassell, A. M. Collier, A. H. Smith & C. T. Raimey, Influence of life events and family routines on childhood respiratory tract illness. *Pediatrics*, 1977, 60: 609–615.
7. Bronfenbrenner, U., A report on longitudinal evaluations of preschool programs, II: Is early intervention effective? Washington, D.C.: U.S. DHEW Publication (OHD) 1974, 76–30025.
8. Broman, S. H., P. L. Nichols & W. A. Kennedy, *Preschool IQ: prenatal and early correlates*. Hillsdale: Erlbaum, 1975.
9. Broverman, D. M., E. L. Klaiber, W. Vogel & Y. Kobayaski, Short-term versus long-term effects of adrenal hormones on behavior. *Psychological Bulletin*, 1974, 81: 672–694.
10. Brown, B., *Found: long-term gains from early intervention*. Boulder: Westview Press, 1978.
11. ———*Growth retardation: a systems study of the educational problems of the disadvantaged child*. Unpublished Ph.D. dissertation. Washington, D.C.: American University, 1972.
12. Brown, G., M. Bhrolchain & T. Harris, Social class and psychiatric disturbance among women in an urban population. *Sociology*, 1975, 9, 2: 225–254.
13. Budzynski, T., Biofeedback in the treatment of vascular headache. *Biofeedback and Self-Regulation*, 1978, 3, 4: 409–34.

14. Butler, F. (Ed.), *Biofeedback: a survey of the literature.* New York: IFI/Plenum Press, 1978.
15. Cannon, J., *The wisdom of the body.* New York: Norton, 1932.
16. Child, I. L., Personality. In C. P. Stone & Q. McNemar (Eds.), *Annual Review of Psychology.* Stanford: Annual Reviews, 1954, 149–170.
17. Cline, M. G., J. R. Endahl & J. K. McBee, Executive summary of secondary analysis of the data from the evaluation of the transition of Head Start children into public schools. Contract No. DHHS/HDS 105–78–1303 Mod. #3 Washington, D.C.: Administration for Children, Youth and Families, 1981.
18. Collatz, F. A. & K. Gordon, Efficacy of EMG biofeedback training in improving examination performance of test anxious college students. *Consolidation and new dimensions: proceedings of the Biofeedback Society of America,* Eleventh Annual Meeting, 1980, 62–65.
19. Consortium for Longitudinal Studies. Lasting effects after preschool, Summary report. Washington, D.C.: Administration for Children, Youth and Families, 1979.
20. Cohen, S., Aftereffects of stress on human performance and social behavior: a review of research and theory. *Psychological Bulletin,* 1980, 88, 1: 82–108.
21. Deese, J., Skilled performance and conditions of stress. In R. Glaser (Ed.), *Training research and education.* Pittsburgh: University of Pittsburgh Press, 1962, 199–222.
22. Deutsch, M., I. Katz & A. R. Jensen, *Social class, race, and Psychological development.* New York: Holt, Rinehart and Winston, 1968.
23. Diamond, S. et al., Biofeedback in the treatment of vascular headache. *Biofeedback and Self-Regulation,* 1978, 3, 4, 385–408.
23a. Doerr, H. O. & J. E. Hokanson, A relation between heart rate and performance in children. *Journal of Personality and Social Psychology,* 1965, 2: 70–76.
24. Dohrenwend, B. S. & B. P. Dohrenwend, *Stressful life events: their nature and effects.* New York: John Wiley & Sons, 1974.
25. Eason, R. G., Relation between effort, tension level, skill, and performance efficiency in a perceptual-motor task. *Perceptual and Motor Skills,* 1963, 16: 297–317.
26. Easterbrook, J. A., The effect of emotion on cue utilization and the organization of behavior. *Psychological Review,* 1959, 66: 183–201.
27. Elligett, J. K., H. Danielson & M. Holland, A preliminary evaluation of the success imagery program in seven schools, 1980-1981. Clearwater, Florida: Pinellas County Schools, 1981, unpublished.
28. Everly, G. S. & R. Rosenfeld, *The nature and treatment of the stress response.* New York: Plenum, 1981.
29. Feldhusen, J. F. & H. J. Klausmeier, Anxiety, intelligence, and achievement in children of low, average, and high intelligence. *Child Development,* 1962, 33: 403–409.

30. Fernando, C. K. & J. V. Basmajian, Biofeedback in physical medicine and rehabilitation. *Biofeedback and Self-Regulation,* 1978, 3, 4, 435–55.
31. Fiske, D. W. & S. R. Maddi, *Functions of varied experience.* Homewood, Il: Dorsey Press, 1961, 17–56.
32. Fotopoulos, S. S. & W. P. Sunderland, Biofeedback in the treatment of psychophysiologic disorders. *Biofeedback and Self-Regulation,* 1978, 3, 4, 331–61.
33. Frost, J. L. & G. R. Hawkes, *The disadvantaged child: issues and innovations.* Boston and New York: Houghton Mifflin Company, 1966.
34. Glass, D. C. & J. E. Singer, *Urban stress: experiments on noise and social stressors.* New York: Academic Press, 1972.
35. Gonik, U., Cost effectiveness of biofeedback. Presented at the American Orthopsychiatry Association, Toronto, April 9, 1980.
36. Grossman, S. P., *Physiological psychology.* New York: John Wiley & Sons, 1967.
37. Grotberg, E. (Ed.), *Critical issues in research related to disadvantaged children.* Princeton: Educational Testing Service, 1969.
38. Haan, N., Proposed model of ego functioning: coping and defense mechanisms in relationship to I.Q. change. *Psychologial Monographs,* 1963, 77: 1–23.
39. Hess, W., *The functional organization of the diencephelon.* New York: Grune and Stratton, 1957.
40. Hokanson, J. E. & M. Burgess, Effects of physiological arousal level, frustration, and task complexity on performance. *Journal of Abnormal and Social Psychology,* 1964, 68: 698–702.
41. Hodge, G. K. & F. A. Collatz, Efficacy of EMG biofeedback training in improving examination performance of test anxious college students. *Proceedings of the Biofeedback Society of America.* Eleventh Annual Meeting, 1979.
42. Hollingshead, August B. & F. C. Redlich, *Social class and mental illness.* New York: John Wiley & Sons, 1958.
43. Holmes, T. H. & R. H. Rahe, The social readjustment rating scale. *Journal of Psychosomatic Research,* 1967, 11: 213–218.
44. Holmes, T. H. & M. Masuda, Life change and illness susceptibility. In B. S. Dohrenwend & B. P. Dohrenwend (Eds.), *Stressful life events: their nature and effects.* New York: John Wiley & Sons, 1974.
44a. Hudgens, R. W., Personal catastrophy and depression: a consideration of the subject with respect to medically ill adolescents, and a requiem for retrospective life event studies. In B. S. Dohrenwend and B. P. Dohrenwend (Eds.), *Stressful life events: their nature and effects.* New York: John Wiley & Sons, 1974.
45. Jensen, A. R., *Genetics and education.* New York: Harper & Row, 1972.
46. ———, *Bias in mental testing.* New York: The Free Press, 1980.
47. ———, Chronometric analysis of mental ability. *Journal of Social and Biological Structures,* 1980, 3: 103–122.

48. ———, Reaction time and intelligence. In M. J. Friendman, P. Das & N. O'Connor (Eds.), *Intelligence and Learning*. New York: Plenum, 1981.
49. Jensen, A. R. & E. Munro, Reaction time, movement time, and intelligence. *Intelligence*, 1979, 3: 121–126.
50. Kappelman, M. M., E. Luck & R. L. Garter, Profiles of the disadvantaged child with learning disorders. *American Journal of Diseases of Children*, 1971, 121: 371–379.
51. Kappers, C. U. A., G. C. Huber & E. C. Crosby, *Comparative anatomy of the nervous system of vertebrates*. New York: Hafner Publishing Company, 1960.
52. Katz, I., Factors influencing Negro performance in the desegregated school. In M. Deutsch, I. Katz & A. R. Jensen (Eds.), *Social class, race, and psychological development*. (Chapter 7). New York: Holt, Rinehart and Winston, 1963.
53. Kellam, S. G., J. D. Branch, K. C. Agrawal & M. E. Ensminger, *Mental health and going to school*. Chicago: University of Chicago Press, 1975.
54. Klein, L. N. et al., Biofeedback and group interaction as adjuncts to the medical management of asthma. The integration of biofeedback with other therapies. *Proceedings of the Biofeedback Society of America*, Twelfth Annual Meeting, 1981, 76–78.
55. Krasner, P. R. & S. Phillips, The control of hyperactivity in neurologically impaired children using a point system and stabilometer feedback. *Consolidation and New Dimensions: Proceedings of the Biofeedback Society of America*, Eleventh Annual Meeting, 1980, 76–78.
56. Krasner, P. R. et al., The use of EMG biofeedback procedures to deal with physical aggression and hyperactivity in mentally retarded individuals. *Proceedings of the Biofeedback Society of America*, Twelfth Annual Meeting, 1981, 175–78.
57. Krohne, H. W. & L. Laux, *Achievement, stress, and anxiety*. Washington, D.C.: Hemisphere, 1982.
58. Langner, T. S. & S. T. Michael, *Life stress and mental health*. New York: Free Press, 1963.
59. Lantz, B., Some dynamic aspects of success and failure. *Psychological Monographs*, 1945, 59 (1, Whole No. 271).
60. Lazarus, S., *Psychological stress and the coping process*. New York: McGraw-Hill, 1966.
61. Lazarus, R. S., J. Deese & S. F. Osler, The Effects of psychological stress upon performance. *Psychological Bulletin*, 1952, 49: 293–317.
62. Levi, L. (Ed.), *Society, stress and disease*, I. London: Oxford University Press, 1971.
63. Lewis, O., *La vida*. New York: Random House, 1965.
64. Linn, R. T. & J. K. Hodge, Use of EMG biofeedback training in increasing attention span and internalizing locus of control in hyperactive children. *Consolidation and New Dimensions: Proceedings of the Biofeedback Society of America*, Eleventh Annual Meeting, 1980, 81–884.

65. Londberg, U., In H. W. Krohne, & L. Laux, (Eds.), *Achievement, stress and anxiety.* Washington, D.C.: Hemisphere, 1982.
66. Loux, R. W. & M. L. Ascher, The effect of biofeedback-assisted relaxation upon the classroom behavior of hyperkinetic children. *Consolidation and New Dimensions: Proceedings of the Biofeedback Society of America,* Eleventh Annual Meeting, 1980, 85–86.
67. Magoun, H. W., *The waking brain.* Springfield: Charles C. Thomas, 1958.
68. MacLean, P. D., On the evolution of three mentalities. *Man-Environment Systems,* 1975, 5: 213–224.
69. ———, On the evolution of three mentalities. Revised in S. Arieti, & G. Chrzanowski (Eds.), *New dimensions in psychiatry: A world view,* II. New York: John Wiley & Sons, 1977.
70. ———, A mind of three minds: educating the triune brain. In *Education and The Brain.* Seventy-Seventh Yearbook, Part II. Chicago: The National Society for the Study of Education, 1978.
71. ———, Cerebral evolution and emotional process: new findings on the striatal complex. *Annals of the New York Academy of Science,* 1972, 193: 137–149.
72. ———, The brain's generation gap: Some human implications. *Zygon J. Relig. Sci.,* 1973a, 8: 113–127.
73. ———, A triune concept of the brain and behavior, Lecture I: Man's reptilian and limbic inheritance; Lecture II: Man's limbic brain and the psychoses; Lecture III: New trends in man's evolution. In T. Boag, & D. Campbell, (Eds.), The Hincks Memorial Lectures. Toronto: University of Toronto Press, 1973, 6–66.
74. Mandler, G. & S. B. Sarason, A study of anxiety and learning. *Journal of Abnormal and Social Psychology,* 1952, 47: 166–173.
75. Manuso, J., Stress and the relocating family. *The Equitable Relocating Service Newsletter,* 1980, First Quarter, 203.
76. Manuso, J. & K. Greenspan, Stress. In *Encyclopedia of Health & the Human Body* (Edited by the American Health Foundation). New York: Franklin Watts, 1977.
77. Maslow, A. H. "Higher" and "lower" needs. *Journal of Psychology.* 1948, 25: 433–436.
78. Maslow, A. H., *Motivation and personality.* New York: Flasper, 1954.
79. Mathews, K. A. & J. M. Siegel, The Type A behavior pattern in children and adolescents: assessment, development, and associated coronary-risk. In A. Baum & J. E. Singer, *Handbook of Psychology and Health.* Hillsdale: Erlbaum, 1982.
80. McCall, R. B., M. I. Appelbaum & P. S. Hogarty, Developmental changes in mental performance. *Monographs of the Society for Research in Child Development.* 1973, 38(3 Serial No. 150).
81. McKay, H. & A. McKay, The long-term effects of preschool nutritional health and educational attention. Paper given at the Eighteenth Interamerican Congress on Psychology, 1981.

82. Meichenbaum, Donald., *Cognitive behavior modification*. New York: Plenum Press, 1977.
83. Murphy, L. B. & A. E. Moriarty, *Vulnerability, coping and growth*. New Haven: Yale University Press, 1976.
84. National Center for Health Statistics, *Intellectual development of Children. Vital and Health Statistics*. Series 11, No. 110, Public Health Service. Washington, D.C.: Government Printing Office, 1971.
85. ———, *Parent ratings of behavioral patterns of children*. National Health Survey, Series 11, Number 108, 1971.
86. Newberger, E. H., C. M. Newberger & J. B. Richmond, Child health in America: Toward a rational public policy. *Health and Society,* 1976, 54, 3: 249–298.
87. Ogdon, D. P., *Psychodiagnostics and personality assessment: A handbook*. Los Angeles: Western Psychological Services, 1970.
88. Padilla, E. R., D. J. Rohsenow & A. B. Bergman, Predicting accident frequency in children. *Pediatrics,* 1976, 58: 223–226.
89. Papez, J. W., *Comparative neurology*. New York: Hafner, 1960.
90. Paykel, E. S., Recent life events and clinical depression. In E. K. E. Gunderson & R. H. Rahe (Eds.), *Life stress and illness*. Springfield: Charles C. Thomas, 1947a, 134–163.
91. ———, Life stress and psychiatric disorders: Applications of the clinical approach. In B. S. Dohrenwend & B. P. Dohrenwend (Eds.), *Stressful life events: Their nature and effects*. New York: John Wiley & Sons, 1947b, 135–150.
92. Pearlin, L. & J. Johnson, Marital status, life-strains and depression. *American Sociological Review,* 1977, 43: 704–715.
93. Phillips, B., *School stress and anxiety: theory, research, and intervention*. New York: Human Sciences Press, 1978.
94. Pless, I. B. & K. J. Roghmann, Chronic illness and its consequences: observations based on three epidemiologic surveys. 1971, *Pediatrics,* 79, 3: 351–359.
95. Rabkin, J. G. & E. L. Struening, Life events, stress and illness. *Science,* 1976, 194: 1013–1020.
96. Rahe, R. H., M. Meyer, M. Smith, G. Kjaer & T. H. Holmes, Social stress and illness onset. *Journal of Psychosomatic Research,* 1964, 8: 35–44.
97. Rahe, R. H., Life change measurement as a predictor of illnesses. *Proceedings of the Royal Society of Medicine,* 1968, 61: 1124–1126.
98. ———, Subjects' recent life changes and their near-future illness reports: a review. *Annals of Clinical Research,* 1972, 4: 393–397.
99. Rahe, R. H., L. K. Bennett, M. Romo, P. Siltanen, & R. J. Arthur, Subjects' recent life changes and coronary heart disease in Finland. *American Journal of Psychiatry,* 1973, 130: 1222–1226.
100. Roghmann, K. & R. J. Haggerty, Family stress and the use of health services. *International Journal of Epidemiology,* 1972, 1: 279–86.
101. Rosenbaum, L., et. al., Ongoing assessment: experience of a university biofeedback clinic. *Biofeedback and Self-regulation,* 1981, 6, 1: 103–112.

102. Rutter, M., Protective factors in children's response to stress and disadvantage. In M. W. Kent & J. E. Rolf (Eds.), *Primary prevention of psychopathology, III. Social Competence in children.* Hanover: University Press of New England, 1979.
103. Sandvick, R. W., Some differential effects of biofeedback assisted relaxation, training in reducing hyperactive behavior in children. The integration of biofeedback with other therapy. *Proceedings of the Biofeedback Society of America,* Twelfth Annual Meeting, 1981, p. 13.
103a. Sarason, S. B., K. S. Davidson, F. F. Lighthall, R. R. Waite & B. K. Ruebush, *Anxiety in elementary school children.* New York: John Wiley & Sons, 1960.
104. Sattler, J. M., Racial "experimenter effects" in experimentation, testing, interviewing, and psychotherapy. *Psychological Bulletin,* 1970, 73: 137–160.
105. Silverman, A. J., S. I. Cohen, & B. M. Shmavonian, Investigations of psychophysiologic relationships with skin resistance measures. *Journal of Psychosomatic Research,* 1959, 4: 65–87.
106. Singer, J. E., Traditions of stress research: integrative comments. In I. G. Sarason & A. D. Spielberger (Eds.), *Stress and Anxiety,* VII. Washington, D.C.: Hemisphere, 1980.
107. Stennett, R. G., The relationship of performance level to level of arousal. *Journal of Experimental Psychology,* 1957, 54: 54–61.
108. Sternbach, R. A., *Principles of psychophysiology.* New York: Academic Press, 1966.
109. Taub, E. & C. F. Stroebel, Biofeedback in the treatment of vasoconstrictive syndromes. *Biofeedback and Self-Regulation,* 1978, 3, 4: 363–373.
110. Teichner, W. H. & E. Youngling, Acclimatization, habituation, motivation and cold exposure. *Journal of Comparative Psysiological psychology,* 1962, 55: 322–336.
111. Teichner, Warren H., Interaction of behavioral and physiological stress reactions. *Psychological Review,* 1968, 75, 4: 271–291.
112. Tryon, G. S., The measurement and treatment of test anxiety. *Review of Educational Research,* 1980, 50: 343–372.
113. Vaillant, G. E., *Adaptation to life.* Boston: Little, Brown, 1977.
114. Van Liere, E. S. & J. C. Stickney. *Hypoxia.* Chicago: University of Chicago Press, 1963.
115. Wenger, Marion A. & Thomas D. Cullen, Studies of autonomic balance in children and adults. In N. J. Greenfield & R. A. Sternbach, *Handbook of Psychophysiology.* New York: Holt, Rinehart and Winston, 1972.
116. Werner, E. E. & R. S. Smith, Vulnerable but invincible. New York: McGraw-Hill, 1982.
117. White, B. L. & J. Watts, *Experience and environment: major influences on the development of the young child,* I. Englewood Cliffs: Prentice-Hall, 1973.
118. Whitehead, W. E., Biofeedback in the treatment of gastrointestinal disorders. *Biofeedback and Self-Regulation,* 1978, 3, 4: 375–378.

119. Winer, L., Biofeedback: a guide to the clinical. *American Journal Orthopsychiatry,* 1977, 47, 4: 626–38.
120. Woodburne, L. S., *The neural basis of behavior.* Columbus: Merrill, 1966.
121. Wright, C. R., Seeking a new medical horizon: towards a rational approach for reducing the contribution of psychosocial stress to illness behaviors. Unpublished Ph.D. Thesis, Union Graduate School-West, 1979.

PART II

CONTROLLING AND REDUCING STRESS IN CHILDREN

CHAPTER 8

TEACHING CHILDREN ABOUT STRESS

Joy N. Humphrey, M. S.

One of the first steps to successful stress reduction in children is to help children themselves understand something about the stress phenomenon. In this chapter the author presents a procedure for developing learning experiences for use with young children.

"Why does my heart beat faster when I get excited?" "Why do my hands sweat when I am afraid?" "Why do I breathe fast when something makes me mad?" Such questions from children tend to verify the fact that they know that something is going on in their bodies, although they are not necessarily aware that these conditions are reactions to stress.

It is interesting and important to recognize that the above questions are characterized by "Why?" This certainly should be expected because in recent years there has been a growing recognition of the fact that if people are going to be healthy they must obtain valid knowledge in health matters. The provision of such knowledge appears to be a very important function of the nation's schools. Because the schools are organized in such a way as to provide a climate for desirable learning, children can be placed in problem-solving situations and be taught *why* certain things are important. For example, if a child is required to eat foods that are "good" for him, but is never taught *why*, it is important that he be taught so that whenever he is away from the control of his parents he will not tend to choose foods entirely on the basis of what tastes best to him, but will take into account the needs of his body. Moreover, if he has never been taught what constitutes a good diet, it is not likely that he will know how to select one even if he should at last become aware of the importance of a good diet for vigorous health, weight control, and body efficiency. This same thinking can be applied to the subject matter of stress since it also requires that knowledge in matters pertaining to stress requires good teaching in a desirable educational setting.

It is well known that the stress concept is complicated and complex. How, then, does one attempt to develop such a complex concept with young children. At first glance this might appear almost impossible; nevertheless, serious attempts in this direction have been made by various individuals in relative recent years.

A concrete example of such an effort is the work undertaken by the coauthors of one of the selections in this volume—Charles and Elizabeth Stroebel. Their work has been found to be very useful in helping children understand the stress concept. The Stroebels' research with the *Quieting Reflex* in children (Kiddie QR: A Choice for Children, 1980, QR Institute, Wethersfield, Connecticut) is explored elsewhere in this volume.

A major thrust of the present chapter is to discuss in detail an approach developed by the present author and an associate (the editor of this volume) for the purpose of teaching children about stress.

PRELIMINARY CONSIDERATIONS

The late Dr. Hans Selye, who is often referred to as the "father of stress," was extremely influential in the development of many stress-related innovations. The germ of the idea for the project reported here actually originated with Dr. Selye. It came about during some correspondence with him about how teachers can cope with stress. This correspondence revealed that a major interest of his was in the area of developing informational materials that would bring the stress concept down to the level of understanding of young children.

The present author and her associate had published a number of children's books and in addition had conducted research in stress-related matters. Therefore, it seemed feasible to explore the possibility of preparing learning materials about stress for young children. Consequently, a meeting was arranged with Dr. Selye at the International Institute of Stress in Montreal to formulate plans to proceed with the project. At this conference it was decided that the material would be based on the principal behavioral implications of the code of behavior set forth in Dr. Selye's book, *Stress Without Distress*.

COLLECTION OF DATA

One of the first concerns was to determine how broad the concepts of stress would need to be for satisfactory internalization. This necessitated collection of data on stress-related experiences of children; that is, it was important to find out how definitive children would be when considering stressful situations as well as to ascertain their level of understanding about stress. This was accomplished by developing an inquiry instrument that involved a combination of free-response and projective type items. Following are some examples of the items along with some representative responses of children.

1. How do you feel when you do something nice for someone?
    "I feel nice myself and I feel happy."
    "I feel good and glad I did it."
    "A good feeling comes over my body."
    "I feel good and will do it again."
    "I feel happy and proud."
2. How do you feel before you take a test in school?
    "I get a funny feeling in my stomach."
    "I feel shaky or something scary."
    "I feel nervous and afraid I am going to fail."
    "I feel shaky, nervous and sick."
    "I feel like I might sweat or something."
3. How do you feel when you can't do something you want to do?
    "I get mad and I don't like it."
    "I feel like killing the person who said I couldn't do it."
    "I feel like screaming and throwing a fit."
    "I feel awful and if I can't do something I want to try to forget about it."
    "I feel let down."
4. I feel best when _____
    "I do something right."
    "I do something I always wanted to do."
    "I do something good or make somebody happy."
    "someone cares about me."
    "when I'm with my friends."
5. I feel worst when _____
    "I'm told I did bad."
    "report cards come out."
    "I've done something wrong."
    "I fail."
    "I work to do something and don't make it."
6. Sadness is _____
    "not feeling good."
    "being left out."
    "losing your best friend."
    "not being able to do what I want to do."
    "getting something you like taken away."

7. Happiness is _____
"being loved."
"when I learn something new."
"when school is out."
"when I get things my way."
"getting all my work done."

Data were collected on more than 100 children through this process and as a result sufficient information was provided to help determine the extent of the breadth of stress concepts as well as possibilities of internalization of the concepts. This information was also used in discussions with children to help them understand how and why their bodies responded in various ways during happy and unhappy situations.

PLAN FOR THE DEVELOPMENT OF STRESS CONCEPTS

The next step was the identification of concepts of stress and codes of behavior in *Stress Without Distress* that would be suitable for development with children and that could also be placed in a frame of reference to which they could relate.

With the above information at hand, the next step was to develop a thematic scenario to which children could relate. It was decided that this could best be accomplished by taking a central character (child) through an entire day with supporting characters in the form of parents, peers, a sibling, and a teacher. The environment included the home, school, and play time experiences. A story of approximately 1,500 words was developed in line with this scenario. The application of a standard readability formula placed the reading level of the story at seven years eight months with a two-month measurement error. (A total of twenty-seven picture clues and illustrations that accompany the text tend to reduce the readability level appreciably).

APPLICATION OF THE MATERIALS

The next undertaking was to try out the material with a large number of children from six to nine years. Because the reading level was too high for the children in the lower age range, the story was *read to* them. The purpose of the tryout was to determine the extent to which the children could understand the concepts as well as to evaluate their interest in the content.

The tryout was deemed successful, since teachers who observed the children indicated that they displayed considerable interest in the content as compared to other listening and reading materials. Some typical responses of teachers were:

1. "I feel that the story was well written; however, primary children's interest will always dwindle when there are no accompanying illustrations." (As mentioned previously, the story in final form is accompanied by twenty-seven picture clues and illustrations.)
2. "The children maintained an interest throughout the entire story and participated actively in the discussions that followed."
3. "The children seemed to understand and remember the events in the story."

The final step of the project was to have the material reproduced for widespread distribution to individuals who might wish to provide information for young children to help them have a better understanding of stress. To this end the project was produced by Kimbo Educational of Long Branch, New Jersey in 1980 under the title of *Helping Children Understand About Stress*. It consists of a long play recording (listening experience), ten books of the story, *Ted Learns About Stress* (reading experience), and a teacher's manual.

In summary, because the material for this stress-related story for children was scientifically selected, prepared, and tested, it might well be considered unique in the area of children's listening and reading material. To date, the results have been most satisfactory in terms of children's interest in the listening and reading content as well as their understanding of certain broad concepts of stress.

SOME PRINCIPLES TO APPLY TO HELP CHILDREN LEARN ABOUT STRESS

Obviously, there are no resolute standard procedures that are guaranteed to help children understand the stress concept. There are, however, certain general principles that may be applied by teachers and parents to help children gain a better understanding of the meaning of stress.

For purposes here the term *principle* is interpreted to mean *guide to action*. Thus, the following general principles for helping to teach children about stress should be considered as guidelines, but not necessarily in any particular order of importance. Moreover, it should be recognized that each principle is not a separate entity unto itself.

This means that all of the principles are in some way interrelated and interdependent upon each other.

1. *Personal health practices should be carefully observed.* This is an easy principle to accept, but sometimes it is a difficult one to implement. No one is against health, but not everyone abides by those practices that can help to maintain a suitable level of health. Parents should accept the major share of the responsibility for health practices of their children. In doing so, they can help to eliminate unacceptable health practices, relating such behavior to stress.

2. *There should be continuous self-evaluation.* The practice of constantly taking stock of one's activities can help to minimize many problems. This can be accomplished in part by taking a little time at the end of each day for an evaluation of the events that occurred during the day and reactions to those events. Setting aside this time period to review performance is not only important to the achievement of goals, but it is also important for remaining objective. Parents should consider this practice and attempt to guide their children in a direction that will help them understand why they may have become upset over an incident that happened during the day.

3. *Learn to recognize your own accomplishments.* One must learn to recognize his own accomplishments and praise himself for them, especially if such praise is not offered by others. This is generally known as "stroking" or "patting one's self on the back." In practicing this procedure teachers can develop positive attitudes and/or belief systems about their own accomplishments and thus reduce stress. The same can be said for parents as they try to instill this idea into the lives of their children.

4. *Learn to take one thing at a time.* This is concerned with time budgeting and procrastination. Teachers, parents and children are likely to put things off, and as a consequence, frustrations can build up as tasks pile up. There is a need to sort out those tasks in order of importance and attack them one at a time. Proper budgeting of time can help to alleviate procrastination, which in itself can be a stress-inducing factor. Budgeting of time can help to eliminate worries of time urgency and the feel of "too much to do in too short a time."

5. *Learn to take things less seriously.* This should not be interpreted to mean that teaching and parenting should not be taken seriously. It does mean that there can be a fine line between what is actually serious and what is not. Sometimes when people look back at a particular event, they may wonder how they could have become so excited about it. Those teachers who are able to see the humorous side in the classroom tend to look at a potentially stressful situation more

objectively, and this can assist in keeping stress levels low. This attitude can easily be conveyed to children.

6. *Do things for others.* Teachers and parents can sometimes take their minds off their own stressful conditions by offering to do something for other persons. Children should be taught to develop this concept early in life. When individuals are helpful to others in attempting to relieve them of stress, they will in turn tend to be relieved of stress. Much research tends to show that those persons who volunteer to help others often times get as much benefit from this practice as those they volunteer to help. In this regard, it has been clearly demonstrated that older children who have reading problems improve in their own reading ability when they assist younger children with these same problems.

7. *Talk things over with others.* Teachers and parents sometimes tend to keep things to themselves and may not be aware that others may be disturbed by the same things. Sometimes discussing something with a colleague or with a spouse can help one see things in a much different light. Children should be encouraged to talk things over with each other as well as with teachers, parents, and other friends.

8. *Stress should not be confused with challenge.* Recognizing that stress is a natural phenomenon of life is no doubt one of the first and most important steps in dealing with it. This is a concept that parents and teachers should make every effort to develop with children at an early age.

CHAPTER 9

THE INDIVIDUALITY PROFILE: A TOOL FOR PERSONALIZING STRESS MANAGEMENT

Barbara S. Kuczen, Ph.D.

Recognizing individuality means more than tolerating an isolated idiosyncrasy. It means systematically exploring the many easily overlooked facets of the child's personality that make the child unique and special. The child inherits a set of traits and characteristics that influence how he or she will respond to the environment, of which parents, teachers, and other adults are a significant part. Familiarity with the interacting forces in the child's life helps an adult understand what stresses the child, how he or she reacts, and what works best to keep stress under control. The Individuality Profile is suggested as instrumentation for collecting information to use for this purpose.

NATURE vs. NURTURE

Ask any adult about variations in children, and in one way or another you will be told, "Of course, all children are different!" The grandmother who satisfies her teenage granddaughter's taste for applesauce topped with ketchup; the teacher who seats the distractible first grader next to her desk; and the new mother who walks her fussy baby to sleep are all reacting to the individual differences in children. But recognizing individuality means more than tolerating an isolated

---

Note: The author wishes to thank Delacorte Press for granting permission to use certain materials from her book *Childhood Stress: Don't Let Your Child be a Victim,* Brunner/Manzel for granting use from Thomas and Chess in the adaptation of their work in *Temperament and Development,* and Prentice-Hall for use from Dunn and Dunn in the adaptation of their work in *How to Raise Independent and Professionally Successful Daughters.*

idiosyncrasy, such as an eight-year-old's attachment to an old baby blanket or a twelve-year-old's belief in the powers of a "lucky shirt." It means systematically exploring the many easily overlooked facets of the child's personality that make the child unique and special.

Every child has a matchless set of individual needs, skills, and characteristics that are distinctly personal, and no two children will ever have exactly the same blend. To truly understand a child, the adult must explore the intricacies of the child's individuality. The knowledge gained will be essential in the process of the adult helping the child to discover himself or herself. A profile of individuality enables adults to deal with a child based on singularity, rather than based on some "ideal average." The range of normal behavior for children at every age level is wide, and varies even among children in the same family. The often-cited "average child" does not exist. Even the noted Arnold Gesell and Louise Bates Ames, in the process of identifying general patterns of development, were struck by the differences in children—obvious from infancy.[1]

Newborns demonstrate behavior patterns that can vary widely. For example, one baby might sleep constantly, while another hardly ever naps and is extremely active. Some infants demand constant attention, while others seem to prefer less. In 1950, the White House Conference on Children and Youth stated:

> All who have had the opportunity of watching children of like ages have been impressed with the high degree of individuality which each one shows. Even as newborn infants they differ not only in such physical characteristics as weight and height, but also in the manner in which they react to events.[6]

In fact, women who have experienced more than one pregnancy often report, although unscientifically, that they can detect differences in their babies even before birth.

Experts have long weighed the comparative influence of nature vs. nurture in the total development of the child. The *constitutionalists* attribute individual differences to inborn traits, present at birth. The *environmentalists*, on the other hand, believe that individual differences are the result of the experiences that shape the child. Today, due in part to the work of such researchers as Chess, Thomas, and Birch, it is widely accepted that child development involves a complicated set of interactions between nature and nurture.[12] The child inherits a set of traits and characteristics that influences how the youngster will respond to the environment, of which parents, teachers, and other adults are a significant part. Familiarity with the interacting forces in the child's life helps an adult understand what stresses the child, how he or she reacts, and what works best to keep stress under control.

ACCEPTING INDIVIDUALITY

Every child is a marvelous composite of physical attributes and personality traits put together only once in eternity. Some characteristics, such as activity level or sensory threshold, appear to be inherited in the genetic package in much the same way as eye or hair color are transmitted. Other broader patterns of typical behavior, such as response to stress, are the result of a complex interactive process involving the child's basic temperament and the environment in which the child develops. Although everyone is constantly growing and changing, there seem to be certain qualities of behavior that remain more or less fixed, although certainly not immutable. The individuality profile can focus on the "givens" in the child's make-up and prevent the well-meaning adult from unwittingly contributing to a child's stress by working at odds with the child's individuality. Recognizing individuality does NOT mean adults should simply throw up their hands and allow children total freedom to "do their own thing." What it does is provide a source of information that must be considered in adult efforts to assist children to grow into productive, happy, coping adults.

It is impossible to consider coping without taking individuality into account, since stress, by definition, is generated when a stimulus in the environment is judged as being personally threatening. The importance of the individual's interpretation of potential stressors is illustrated in the case of two preschoolers at play. When a big dog approaches, one child becomes terrified and runs away, while the other is delighted and attempts to pet the animal. Once stress is generated, how a child reacts to it is also an individual matter. Jerry and Michael are both ten years old and excellent pianists. They even have the same piano teacher. Michael's performance, however, improves when he plays before a group, while Jerry goes blank and freezes when he is in a recital. Both examples suggest that analyzing and accepting the individuality that is bred from the interaction of inborn temperament and environmental conditioning can help an adult understand why a child is stressed, as well as the child's particular response. The individuality profile can better prepare us to guide children in tailoring coping strategies that work.

Failure to identify and accept a child's individuality generates stress that unnecessarily makes life more difficult for the child *and* adult.

Demands may be made that are impossible to meet, owing to the child's basic makeup. Sometimes adults are oblivious to the child's special needs. Consider children with learning disabilities, for example. In one study it was found that learning disabled boys are three times more likely to be arrested than their peers of similar age, race, and class. Those with parents in prestigious occupations or with parents who had completed high levels of education showed the greatest increases in delinquency, leading researchers to hypothesize that the stress of family expectations make failure a severe blow to self-image. As a result, the boys are more apt to respond to pressures from their delinquent friends, since their self-esteem is already low, and they wish to rebel against parents who fail to adjust to the special problems that are part of the child's individuality.[11] Many researchers have taken a close look at chronically ill[8] and mentally retarded[9] children and their families. They found it was difficult for the parents to accept a child's special circumstances. The parents often reacted with feelings of guilt, shame, blame, denial, and greater vulnerability to stress—feelings that were not only stressful to the parents but cast a shadow on the entire family.

A well-known commercial tells us that "you can't fool Mother Nature." Likewise, a child's individuality is undeniable, but adults sometimes do not like what they see, and therefore refuse to acknowledge certain components of it, or they exert efforts to get the child in step. Anyone who has spent time around children knows that some children are harder to deal with than others, but wishing that Bobby was more like his older brother or like you were as a child rarely serves any useful function. Recognition and acceptance of individuality is basic for helping children develop a coping system that really works for them. Individuality must be at the very core of adult interactions with children. Adults who are in tune with children's individuality usually find the levels of stress they experience in dealing with children are low, while the sheer joy of watching children naturally grow and mature is high.

Why Some Adults Do Not Accept Individuality

Individuality is a concept that receives a great deal of lip-service. Almost any adult, if questioned, will attest to the uniqueness of each and every child. However, in actual practice many adults seem to contradict their own firm belief in individuality by trying to change children, to make them fit a mold.

Universally, children are enchanting, appealing, refreshing, and simply magnificent. They are not perfect. Flawless children exist only in the minds of a few who have no children, but imagine what their children would be like if they did have them. Systematically compiling an individuality profile for a child will probably highlight areas of both strength and weakness. Mark Twain once wrote that "there is no sadder sight than a young pessimist." Adults must guard against contributing to a child's pessimism by overreacting to areas of weakness or difficulty. More weight should not be assigned to minor human frailties than is due. Instead, adults should help children maximize their innate human potential, rather than wasting time lamenting over what might have been. The child, as an individual, should be respected and guided in realistically assessing what can and should be expected from himself or herself. The child with a strong, positive self-image will grow in an atmosphere of freedom that encourages the child to begin the never-ending process of discovering new depths and dimensions of personal individuality.

Lack of sensitivity to a child's individuality can be explained in a number of ways. Following are ten of the more common adult misconceptions:

1. Kids Today Are Different. The world has changed drastically in one generation, with technological advances and modifications in lifestyle which impact on children. Nonetheless, it is not so much children that have changed, as it is childhood. The research findings of the Gesell Institute indicate that the major stages of growth and development, as well as the process of gaining maturity and independence, are still basically the same.[2] While it is true that children today are healthier, larger, and better informed, they are not radically different from children of the past. It is dangerous to make sweeping generalizations regarding children's level of sophistication. Adults who do so may discount their own valuable past experiences as an irrelevant source of information about childhood or have a tendency to expect more from today's children than was the norm thirty years ago.

2. Big Boys Don't Cry. Sex-role stereotypes, firmly anchored in tradition, threaten to diminish and compromise a child's individuality. The coping child has a good, strong self-image and does not sense subtle pressure to repress true emotions or to conform to molds that do not quite fit. The masculine stereotype, which forces men to be macho and prove it in sports, sex, work, and war, produces stress and anxiety. The feminine stereotype results in undue emphasis on appearance, lack of self-confidence, overdependence, and simultaneous fear of both success and failure. Coping requires the ability to

easily and rapidly adapt to changing situations. Allowing a child to explore the full range of his or her individuality helps the child become more versatile at handling stress. Historically repressed components of the male or female personality become acceptable, and the youngster is likely to grow into an adult who is equally adept at dealing with the stresses of a sick infant or a clogged plumbing pipe.

3. You'll Do It My Way! Some adults believe that there is one set of rules to follow in dealing with children. These adults reason that what worked with them when they were children, or what was effective with other children, will hold universally true. Rather than being viewed as an individual, the child is rigidly regarded as a miniature reflection of the parent.

4. I Go By The Book. Children today are under more pressure than ever. Books with titles like *How to Raise a Brighter Child,* or *Give Your Child a Superior Mind* focus attention on early achievement. Some adults lack self-confidence and look to experts to detail the easy steps to follow for creating a perfect child. Child care experts can provide valuable suggestions, but what works well with one child might be all wrong for another. When it comes to the individual child, the real experts are those adults who interact day-in and day-out with the youngster, especially the parents. There is no one formula guaranteed to work wonders, just as children are not totally shaped by adults. To make such assumptions ignores the importance of the child's biological blueprint.

5. It's My Duty As a Parent. Some parents feel personally responsible for their child's every action. If some aspect of the child's individuality is troublesome, the parent assumes the blame and resolves to alter the behavior. I am reminded of a mother who constantly berated her children for real, as well as imagined, shortcomings. When I suggested to her that she might be seriously damaging their self-image and esteem, the well-meaning woman was visibly shaken. She responded, "My common sense tells me what you're saying is true, but I always thought it was a parent's job to stay after a child." Parents do not create every problem, nor can they solve every one.

6. The Impossible Dream. It almost seems to be the "American Way" to believe that anything is possible, if you just set your mind to it. This philosophy has been transferred to guiding children, with some adults believing that any child is capable of truly extraordinary accomplishments if pushed hard enough. Children need self-confidence and faith in their own abilities. However, there is a realistic

limit beyond which a child cannot achieve. Adults who ignore individuality and create an inflated concept of what is actually possible are preparing the child for a painful fall—one that might permanently damage the child's self-concept. The challenge is to assist the child in maximizing the innate human potential.

7. I Want More For You. Some parents are determined that their children will have more than they ever had. Toward this end they begin making demands and prodding the child, sometimes with little regard for the youngster's needs, interests, and abilities. If the adults feels unfulfilled in life, the child might even provide a means for the parent to experience vicariously the success that has been missing.

8. We Have Standards. The justified concern over basic skills has resulted in testing for competence at every level, from the kindergarten through high school. More and more is being taught earlier and earlier. Research indicates this trend may not be a good idea. In the case of teaching preschoolers to read, for example, numerous reports show that there are no long term advantages to the practice.[14] In a few classrooms, the individual needs, skills, and interests of the students become secondary to passing criterion-referenced tests on schedule. The standardized end-product of education is all-important, rather than the individual student.

9. Super-parent. The state of the economy, women's liberation, and the large number of single-parent families have contributed to a dramatic increase in working parents. Time is one of their biggest problems, and as a result the myth of the super-parent has emerged. A super-parent somehow manages to always look terrific; gets enough exercise; keeps the house, yard, and family clothing spotless; serves regular, nutritious hot meals; remains active in school and civic matters; is a parenting expert; arranges to escape for romantic interludes; and still has time for self. The juggling it takes to try to live up to this model can generate lifestyle stress for everyone in the household. Parents often becomes so involved in their own stress that they have little energy or time left to devote to the child.[7] The parent loses sight of the child's individuality and current sources of stress.

10. Super-kid. Super-parents sometimes expect their children to be super-kids. They might think that a parent's love and good intentions are enough to sustain the child, who has an unlimited supply of strength and resiliency. The parents are so involved in merely making it through one day at a time, that they may try to ignore their own stresses, to push them into the background. If they use the

same technique with their children, they may fail to acknowledge important childhood stresses and deal with them—based on the child's individuality.

THE INDIVIDUALITY PROFILE

The pages that follow contain five separate checklists for determining a child's individuality profile. Although the checklists are by no means scientific, they are designed to focus adult attention on some areas which might not otherwise be considered. The *Individuality Profile* was originally developed for use with parents. In some cases, parents are specifically referred to in the profile. The Background Information and Interpretation are written in an informal manner so that parents and other adults can easily understand the information and apply it to their personal situations.

The complete profile contains five areas: (1) temperament; (2) modality preference; (3) learning style; (4) comparison of individuality; and (5) the coping road map.

Assessment 1 — Temperament

Background Information

How many times have you heard parents describe children with statements such as "She is as neat as a pin," "He is full of the devil," "Those two never stop moving," or "You could set a clock by that kid"? These remarks indicate that parents are aware of children's special characteristics. These basic differences in personality are the foundation upon which individuality is built, and are called *temperament*.

Temperament is usually thought of as a set of inborn dispositions toward a particular style of behavior. It is the inherited tendency of an individual's nature or makeup to respond to life in a distinctive manner and to attempt to seek out and organize environments that correspond to this temperament. For example, Ellen Henry has two daughters, Barbara and Carol. She often remarks that "Barbara is not happy unless she is in the middle of a three-ring circus. If there is no excitement going on, she will create some." On the other hand, when Ellen describes her other daughter she says: "Carol is just the opposite. She can be in the midst of a group of kids, and she will suddenly just quietly pick up and go off by herself to happily read or draw a picture." The difference in temperaments between these two sisters helps to explain their varying bahavior. Chess, Thomas, and Birch conducted careful research into the development of temperament and its affect on personality. They studied a number of children and found that as early as the first week of life infants demonstrate differences in temperament. Most of the children continued to exhibit many of the same styles of behavior as they grew older.[13] Problems arise when parents refuse to acknowledge the child's temperament and make impossible demands or try to overhaul the child. In some cases children experience prolonged stress caused by their parents' efforts to fight basic, natural tendencies or temperaments.

The following scale is a way to explore the elements of the child's temperament.[13] Some parents are fortunate to have amiable and good-natured children who make the job of parenting seem easy. Other Children are more difficult to raise. They are crabby, unpleasant, and present a real challenge for parents. Recognizing the differences in temperament can rid parents of nagging doubts such as "Johnny is such a handful, I must have done something wrong." There is nothing abnormal about any of the behaviors presented. Difficult children don't automatically face a life of doom, especially if parents take their special traits into consideration. Chess, Thomas and Birch have suggested that parents accept their children's temperament as a "given," and work with it—rather than against it.

The nine categories that Chess and her fellow researchers have identified in their study of temperament follow. Accompanying each category are five statements that describe behavior. Read each statement and decide if it applies "almost never" to the child, "sometimes," or "almost always." Circle your choice, based on the way you think the child compares to other children of the same age.

Interpretation

The nine types of behavior you just rated make up the child's temperament, which is one ingredient in the child's life—not the entire recipe. Happiness and adjustment can be realized if the parent and child work with the raw material that they have, rather than wishing it were different or trying to alter it.

Contrary to some common beliefs children cannot be molded like clay. They enter life with their basic temperament, and although the process of growth and development will be accompanied by some change, adults are better off to adapt to the child's personality, instead of trying to modify it.

The combination of traits makes some children more difficult to raise than others. High activity level, irregularity, rejection, slow adaptabil-

ACTIVITY LEVEL

	Almost Never	Sometimes	Almost Always
My child has difficulty sitting still, even for reasonable periods of time.	0	1	2
My child squirms and wiggles at the dinner table, while I am helping with homework, in the car, or at the movies.	0	1	2
At regular intervals my child needs physical activity as an outlet for excess energy.	0	1	2
My child prefers play that involves movement, such as playing ball or running, to quiet play such as coloring.	0	1	2
My child moves rapidly and likes to run rather than walk.	0	1	2

Record your child's total score. ____

Plot your child's score on the line below.

```
0                    5                          10
```
Low activity level	Moderate activity level	High activity level

REGULARITY

	Almost Never	Sometimes	Almost Always
My child goes to sleep and awakens at the same time each day (within the half hour).	0	1	2
My child gets hungry at about the same time each day.	0	1	2
My child has a bowel movement at about the same time each day.	0	1	2
My child sleeps about the same number of hours each night.	0	1	2
My child eats about the same amount of food each day.	0	1	2

Record your child's total score. ____

Plot your child's score on the line below.

```
0                    5                          10
```
Irregular	Variable	Regular

The Individuality Profile

APPROACH/WITHDRAWAL

	Almost Never	Some- times	Almost Always
My child likes to perform in front of others.	0	1	2
My child is outgoing when it comes to meeting new people.	0	1	2
My child enjoys jumping into new activities and new situations rather than holding back at the sidelines.	0	1	2
My child prefers new toys or clothes to old, familiar ones.	0	1	2
My child enjoys trying new foods or experiencing new surroundings.	0	1	2

Record your child's total score. ___

Plot your child's score on the line below.

0	5	10
Rejects and withdraws	Variable	Accepting and approachable

ADAPTABILITY

	Almost Never	Some- times	Almost Always
My child learns to like food that was once disliked.	0	1	2
My child easily "makes himself/herself at home" in new surroundings by easily adapting to the new life-style or set of rules that apply.	0	1	2
After a break in routine such as a trip or school vacation, my child easily gets back into the routine.	0	1	2
My child gets over attacks of shyness very rapidly.	0	1	2
My child changes the rules or format for games and play.	0	1	2

Record your child's total score. ___

Plot your child's score on the line below.

0	5	10
Slow to adapt	Moderate rate of adapting	Quick to adapt

SENSORY THRESHOLD

	Almost Never	Sometimes	Almost Always
My child is conscious of odors and comments on pleasant and unpleasant smells.	0	1	2
My child is sensitive to temperature and apt to complain that a room is too hot or too cold, or that food is not the right temperature.	0	1	2
My child cries easily when suffering a minor cut or bruise.	0	1	2
My child is sensitive to noise and apt to complain about loud music, bells, or alarms.	0	1	2
My child complains when clothing is too tight, itchy, ill-fitting, or if it becomes dirty or damp.	0	1	2

Record your child's total score. ___

Plot your child's score on the line below.

```
0                    5                              10
```

| High threshold (responds to major changes in environment) | Moderate threshold | Low threshold (responds to slight changes in environment) |

POSITIVE/NEGATIVE MOOD

	Almost Never	Sometimes	Almost Always
My child laughs, smiles, and seems to be having a good time.	0	1	2
When my child is upset, it is easy to comfort the child.	0	1	2
My child takes losing a game in stride, without upset.	0	1	2
My child avoids arguments or becoming upset when not given own way.	0	1	2
My child tends to tell me about the good things that happen, avoiding complaints and criticism.	0	1	2

Record your child's total score. ___

Plot your child's score on the line below.

```
0                    5                              10
```

| Negative mood | Variable mood | Positive mood |

The Individuality Profile

INTENSITY OF REACTION

	Almost Never	Sometimes	Almost Always
My child shows emotions with facial expressions, body language, or verbal intonations.	0	1	2
It is obvious when my child is under stress.	0	1	2
My child gets enthusiastic and excited when telling a story.	0	1	2
My child reacts immediately and vigorously when the child feels rights have been violated.	0	1	2
My child reacts with enthusiasm and excitement to special events, trips, or visitors—rather than taking things "cooly."	0	1	2

Record your child's total score. ___
Plot your child's score on the line below.

0	5	10
Low-intensity reactions	Moderate-intensity reactions	High-intensity reactions

DISTRACTIBILITY

	Almost Never	Sometimes	Almost Always
My child's concentration is easily broken by noises, other children, or whispering.	0	1	2
If my child is set on one particular toy or activity, it is easy to substitute another.	0	1	2
If my child is in a bad mood, it is easy to snap the child out of it.	0	1	2
If someone tries to interrupt while I am explaining something to my child, the child loses attention.	0	1	2
When the child is involved in a task, the child responds quickly when told it is time to stop and drops everything.	0	1	2

Record your child's total score. ___
Plot your child's score on the line below.

0	5	10
Hard to distract	Moderately distractible	Easy to distract

ATTENTION SPAN/PERSISTENCE

	Almost Never	Sometimes	Almost Always
When my child is interrupted, the child does not go back to the same activity.	0	1	2
When my child is learning something new, the child is easily frustrated and wants to do something else.	0	1	2
If I am too busy to answer a question, the child goes away and does not come back later for the answer.	0	1	2
My child dislikes doing the same thing for a long period of time and doesn't finish what is started.	0	1	2
If my child has difficulty with something, the child looks for immediate assistance, rather than trying to figure it out.	0	1	2

Record your child's total score. ___
Plot your child's score on the line below.

0	5	10
Long attention span	Moderate attention span	Short attention span

ity, low sensory threshold, negative mood, high-intensity reactions, distractibility, and short attention span are among the characteristics often associated with the difficult child. These elements of the personality can produce friction between adult and child if the adult does not accept them and work toward helping the child adjust. On the other hand, even parents with children who are classified as easy to rear are often not satisfied. Take the example of Sharon Rush, who was very adaptable and had a sunny disposition. Her mother was concerned and told her she was "easy pickins." Sharon was often stressed by her mother's insistence that she become more assertive. For her part, the mother experienced guilt, doubt, and a sense of failure at not raising a better adjusted child.

Another child, Linda Washington, was extremely active and highly distractible. Her parents were deeply committed to this difficult child's successful adjustment and never expected overnight success. They were patient when she was fidgety or flighty. They didn't blame themselves or some mistake they made when she was an infant. Little by little they helped Linda understand and adapt to life's rules, routines and natural consequences—always letting her know they supported, accepted and loved her.

You can avoid putting yourself and your child under stress by understanding the temperamental tendencies. While you may not be able to change the fact that the child is prone to be slow to adapt or highly irregular, it is possible to help the child acknowledge these characteristics and actively work to form good habits and self-discipline. While a child's personality will always have the predisposition toward certain types of behavior, it can often be controlled.

Assessment 2 — Modality Preference

Background Information

Have you ever noticed the different ways people absorb information? For example, when given an important set of directions, one person might say, "Wait a minute, I want to write that down," while another asks: "Would you mind saying that again? I want to be sure I have it straight." In the first case the individual prefers to rely on sight for processing facts. In the second case hearing is the choice. Perhaps you fall apart trying to follow a set of step-by-step directions for assembling a new toy. You just can't "see" how it all goes together unless a visual diagram is provided. Each situation illustrates the importance of modality. Modality refers to the way we process information. There are three basic modalities: (1) visual (sight), (2) auditory (hearing) and (3) kinesthetic (body movement).

Research shows that approximately one third of elementary school children are strongest in visual modality; about one third have mixed modality, which means they are equally strong in two or more areas; one fourth possess auditory strength. Most children are capable of learning through the kinesthetic sense; however, they are seldom provided this opportunity in the traditional school situation. Younger children are generally more auditorily inclined. In the later grades many begin to develop more visual potential, and by adulthood substantial numbers of people have mixed modality.

The implications of modality preference for learning and learning-related stress are clear. Children with mixed modality, or strength in all three areas, have a definite advantage. They can pick up information no matter how it is presented. For children with strength in only one area the struggle to understand often generates stress. Their difficulties do not stem from lack of intelligence, but from the incongruence between their method for learning and others' methods of teaching. If you are basically a visual person, chances are you will teach the child in a visual way. That is fine *if* the child has visual-modality strength. If not, the child may face an unnecessary stumbling block. When you find yourself saying, "I must have told you that a hundred times," or "I showed you that over and over," it is time to stop and think. If your child has not learned after being "told a hundred times," or "shown over and over," maybe it is time to change the technique which has been proven ineffective. The following short questionnaire will provide a very rough indication of a child's modality strengths. Select the choice that best fits the child. In a few cases, you may find it necessary to mark more than one. If a statement is not applicable at this time, try to judge how the child reacted in the past or would react in the future. If you are uncertain how to respond, ask the child.

Interpretation

This assessment gives you a crude indication of a child's preference of modality. Perhaps the child's strength is clearly in one area, or scattered almost equally among the three areas. Don't be surprised if you found you checked a large number of kinesthetic responses. Most children enjoy learning by doing and like lots of "hands on" experiences, although it may not be their strongest area. Unfortunately, many parents and teachers do not take advantage of this natural tendency. If a child would prefer to grow a pencillium mold on bread, rather than read about it, why not make greater use of the kinesthetic modality?

Modality is another component of a child's total individuality. Stress can be minimized and learning maximized when you take it into account. To get the best indication of a child's modality strength, watch the child in action, discuss the matter with his or her teacher, and experiment by presenting information in the various modalities.

Assessment 3 — Learning Style

Background Information

Few children learn in exactly the same way. A child's individuality dictates a particular learning style, which consists of a number of interrelated characteristics. Once you recognize the conditions that promote the child's learning, you can boost effectiveness by providing the environment and materials that fit. I am certain you can recall frustrating times when you were trying to study for an important test and were disturbed by noise, poor lighting, or icy feet. Throughout

MODALITY STRENGTH

When it is time to play indoors, my child prefers	A. listening to the radio, records, or tapes. K. "doing" something, such as coloring or assembling a model. V. watching television.
My child most likes to see his/her good work noted by	A. hearing himself/herself praised in glowing terms. K. receiving a handshake, slap on the back, or hug and kiss. V. seeing good work on display around the house or stuck on the refrigerator.
My child would probably learn best how to cut a valentine heart if I	A. explained it verbally. K. stood over the child as he/she attempted the first heart and guided the actual cutting. V. showed the child a sample.
If I were selecting a gift to bring home for my child, the gift my child would most enjoy would be	A. a musical toy. K. a coloring book. V. a decorative item to hang in the child's room.
My child would probably best learn a new board game by	A. listening to an explanation of the game. K. jumping right in and learning while playing. V. watching others play the game.
My child would be most excited if the classroom teacher planned	A. a new listening corner with tapes and records. K. a "hands on" experience, such as an experiment. V. a movie.
If my child entered a room filled with debris, and heard a telephone ringing and couldn't find it, my child would try to locate the phone by	A. listening for the ring. K. moving items around and groping for the phone. V. trying to spot the phone.

The most effective way to teach my child a new skill would probably be to	A. buy a set of taped lessons. K. enroll the child in lessons. V. buy a book on the subject.
If my child wanted to learn more about insects, the child would probably	A. ask questions. K. catch some. V. get a book on the subject.
If my child had three social studies assignments, the first one the child would probably do is	A. ask older residents about the history of the community. K. make a model of a building in the community out of a cardboard box. V. read the article about communities in the children's magazine.

Total number of A. (auditory) responses: ____
Total number of K. (kinesthetic) responses: ____
Total number of V. (visual) responses: ____

childhood, you were developing a gradual awareness of your learning style.

The next assessment is designed to help focus on a child's learning style, but more importantly, it is intended to help the adult to help the child understand it.

Following is a learning style survey to conduct with the child.[4] The procedure is informal, and you will probably want to ask the child to elaborate on some of the answers, or even to add questions of your own. Its major purpose is to heighten adult and child sensitivity to learning style. Some questions do not apply to younger children.

Interpretation

The implications of a child's responses to the above questions are relatively obvious. For example, if the child indicates a preference for studying alone, it makes little sense to suggest that a friend come over for a study session. Answers dealing with the best time of day to learn, location for study, temperature preference, noise level, movement requirements, and eating habits clearly suggest the ideal setting for the child's learning.

However, many children and parents never consider what the opti-

LEARNING STYLES

Social

Do you learn better alone, with one friend, or in a group?

When you are studying, do you like to have adults help, be available to help, or leave you alone?

Time Rhythm

Do you learn best early in the morning, right before lunch, after lunch, after school, or right before bedtime?

Does it take you a long time to really feel awake in the morning?

Do you sometimes have trouble staying awake after lunch or dinner?

Do you like to get up early?

If you stay up late, do you feel "foggy" the next day?

Location

Where is the best place for you to study? (Examples—at a desk, in bed, at the library, on the floor.)

Do you like to study in a room with bright or dim lights?

Temperature

Do you think you feel cold or hot more often than other people?

Do you like a room to be a little on the warm side or a little on the cool side?

Auditory Stimuli

Can you study if you hear a radio or television in the background?

Are you distracted if you hear people talking or other children playing?

Do you like to study with music playing? If so, what kind of music?

Would you rather study alone, in a quiet room?

Movement

Do you find it hard to sit still while studying for a long time and need a lot of breaks?

Do you like to leave your studies to go see what is going on, get a drink, or change room or position?

Do you like to keep at your work until it is done?

Eating Habits

Do you like to eat, chew gum, or have a drink while you are learning?

Do you overeat, or chew your fingernails or a pencil when you are nervous?

Do you have trouble eating when you are nervous?

Motivation

Are good grades important to you?

Do you think your grades are really important to your teacher and parents?

Do you think getting a good education is one of the most important things in life?

Do you think reading is important for more things in life than just school?

Is it more important for you to get good grades to please adults or to please yourself?

Do you like school?

Do you let things go to the last minute?

Do you feel responsible for your learning? Does it bother you when you don't do well, are late, or don't finish an assignment?

Do you like solving your own problems or do you prefer being told exactly what is expected and how to do it?

Do you get upset easily when you are learning?

Do you like to learn and find out, even when you aren't in school and don't have to?

Do you have trouble concentrating? Do you find you daydream a lot?

Does it bother you when someone criticizes you?

Do you usually try to do your very best?

Anxiety

Do you think you worry more about school or tests than the other children?

Do you feel "shaky" when the teacher asks you to read aloud, get up in front of the class, or write on the board?

Do you ever have bad dreams about school or learning, such as making the teacher mad because you don't know your lessons or having a "surprise" test?

mal conditions should be. Study is a hit-or-miss proposition. The learning style survey calls attention to these factors. While the home environment can be structured to correspond to the learning style, the school tends to be a more fixed environment. If a child functions best in an atmosphere of little structure, an open classroom, in which a hundred or more students share a large open space with no walls, could be ideal. However, the child who has a short attention span, is distractible, and requires fixed routines and structure, as well as a low noise level, would probably fall apart in such an environment. Or, if the child learns best in the afternoon, the common practice of teaching reading in the morning may not be the best approach in his or her case.

If you think that there is a wide difference between your child's learning style and the school's style, discuss the matter with the teacher. In some cases, adjustments can be made. For example, if your child is distractible, the teacher might be able to arrange to move the child from the open classroom to a traditional classroom. Or provide a quiet corner or "office" by surrounding three sides of the student's desk with a large cardboard box. If you find that the conditions can not be modified, you may want to look into other schools, or make whatever adjustments are possible.

There are two other areas of the survey to bear in mind. The first deals with motivation. The child's answers will provide some insight into the level of motivation. If you found the level low, perhaps the learning experience is not stimulating enough or doesn't offer enough chances for success. A thorough examination of the problem is justified. The second area examines anxiety. Studies show that most children who perform under low levels of anxiety do better or difficult tasks than highly anxious children. Therefore, it is important to keep this type of stress under control. Take time to discuss the problem with the child and develop a plan for personal stress management.

Winston Churchill once said, "Personally, I'm always ready to learn, although I do not always like being taught." Use the result of the survey to maximize learning and you will help provide the child with a precious endowment—the love of learning.

Assessment 4 — Comparison of Individuality

Can You Mix Oil and Water?

In the process of analyzing the child's individuality you most likely found yourself examining your own, making comparisons between yourself and the child. Adult personalities, too, must be taken into account in the adult/child relationship. The noted lawyer Clarence Darrow once observed, "The first half of our lives is ruined by our parents, and the second half by our children." Unfortunately, there can be an element of truth to his statement. Great contrasts between the parent and child in temperament, modality preference, or learning style can be stress-producing for everyone concerned. Therefore, individuality cannot be considered in isolation. Many parents face a real dilemma. Firmly committed to both their own and their child's individuality, they find that each must be provided for within the context of the other. Following are some illustrations of this point.

CASE 1   Fran and Mark Blake have one son, Joseph. Mr. and Mrs. Blake love a change. They like to eat supper seated on the floor Japanese-style, camp out in the backyard, or have surprise visitors. Their son feels more comfortable with a fixed routine. He likes to awaken at the same time, eat at the same hour each day, and follow a general pattern. The older Blakes' quest for something different has resulted in three moves in the past eight years. Fran and Mark have enjoyed the experiences of living in Manhattan, Denver, and San Francisco. However, since their last move, Joseph is noticeably more anxious than ever before. This condition is interfering with his schoolwork and social life.

Fran and Mark are highly adaptable and not overly concerned with regularity. Joseph, on the other hand, is not. His parents' frequent adaptation demands may be the source of the child's stress.

CASE 2   Edward Rymes is a self-made man. His parents were poor and uneducated, and from the time Ed was seven years old, he worked hard for everything he got. At sixteen he held a full-time job to help support his family and earned top marks in school. He worked his way through college, set records in track, and won tennis championships. He graduated with honors and went on to law school. Edward Rymes believes that anything worth doing is not only worth doing well, but is worth doing better than anyone else. His son Claude has always been a good student, even making the honor roll on a few occasions. The teachers report that he is cooperative and has many friends. Claude enjoys baseball and football. When his father told him that if he didn't make better grades he would never get into law school, Claude replied "So what?" Lately, Ed has been riding the boy more than ever, and the teachers report that Claude seems to have quit trying.

The root of problem between Ed and Claude Rymes is a difference in their levels of aspiration. Ed is competitive, while Claude is cooperative. This fact is demonstrated in their respective choices in sport—Ed electing tennis and track, his son prefering team sports. The conflict between the two has produced a stressful situation, in which Claude has stopped trying in school out of the frustration of never being able to please his father, or perhaps merely to rebel.

CASE 3 Marta Lyons loves her twelve-year-old daughter Paula, but the two just cannot seem to get along. Marta is a widow, and she has managed to work herself into an excellent job in her company. She never trusts anything to chance, especially when it comes to her daughter. People who know Marta say she is in perfect control of her life. Paula is much like her mother. She is a leader and serves as class president and a teacher's assistant at Sunday school. She usually takes command of games and play activities with her friends. When a counselor recently asked Paula why she had disobeyed her mother and sneaked into an R-rated movie, Paula responded: "I did it because Mom told me not to. I really didn't want to see that dumb picture. I am just sick and tired of her telling me everything to do. She won't even let me pick my own clothes or friends."

Marta and Paula both share an extreme desire to control. This strong personality trait results in constant friction, in which Paula will often buy some item she doesn't even want or do something she doesn't want to do, simply to prove that she is in control.

CASE 4 Karen Carmichael is convinced there is something wrong with her three-year-old Amy. The child awakes to the slightest noise, refuses to eat most foods, and cries vigorously when only slightly injured. This child is not her first, and she can't figure out why Amy has been so difficult since birth.

There is nothing wrong with Amy. She merely has a different sensory threshold than Karen's other children. She is more sensitive to sound, taste, and pain. Karen apparently does not share this sensitivity and hasn't been able to recognize it, so far.

These cases reveal that individual differences can be powerful stressors. In some cases, the wide variation in personalities between parent and child is the source of strain, while in others the close similarity creates tension. Admittedly, there are no simple solutions. However, in each situation there is a lack of understanding and tolerance. If the parents recognized and accepted their children's basic temperament, as well as their own, they would take the first big step toward adjusting to the problems. The Blakes, realizing their son is not highly adaptable, might stick to a slightly more fixed routine when the child is involved. When an unusual circumstance or move puts Joseph under stress, they can provide coping assistance by avoiding additional disruption, offering extra warmth and security, and helping the boy develop a coping strategy.

Ed Rymes needs to acknowledge the differences in levels of aspiration and competitiveness between himself and his son. Although it might be difficult to accept, Ed should realize that his son will probably never share his drive. While there is no need for Ed to change, neither is it imperative that Claude change. Ed should tolerate and respect his son's individuality. In situations like this one, professional counseling is often useful.

Marta and Paula Lyons should both learn to compromise. Once they identify the components of their personalities that cause the friction between them, they can make progress. This case is another that might best be handled by a family therapist.

Karen Carmichael's problem is the easiest to solve. Hopefully, Amy's pediatrician or a more experienced parent will set her straight.

Following is the final assessment, a comparison of individuality exercise. This scale is designed to compare how the adult and child match on twenty individuality factors. Read each pair of traits. Start at the point in the middle of the line, which is the average or neutral position. Decide how close you fall to either extreme of behavior listed, as compared to how close the child would be plotted. Use two different colored pencils—one color for you, one for the child. For example, on the first item if you feel you are about average when it comes to disposition, you would place a mark somewhere near the midline. If you feel your child is very moody, you would place a second, different colored mark near the end of the line where it says, "Moody Disposition." Remember, this assessment tool is designed to compare differences and similarities, rather than to assign a precise value. If you or the child do not lean toward either extreme, your marks should be close to the midpoint. The greater the strength of the characteristic listed, the closer the mark should be placed to the extreme, or endpoint.

COMPARISON OF INDIVIDUALITY

Even disposition	Moody disposition	
		Curious — Indifferent
Follower	Leader	
		Originator — Imitator
Prefers teamwork	Prefers individual effort	
		Doer — Thinker
Easily distracted	High concentration	
		Low level of aspiration — High level of aspiration
Easily frustrated	High tolerance	
		Low achiever — High achiever
Quits or withdraws	Persistent	
		Low response to threat of punishment — High response to threat of punishment
Impulsive	Contemplative	
		Low response to promise of reward — High response to promise of reward
Irregular (schedule or routines)	Regular (schedule or routines)	
		Broad range of interests — Narrow range of interests
Prefers loose structure	Prefers tight structure	
		Organizes thoughts and concepts into broad categories — Organizes thoughts and concepts into narrow categories
Avoids responsibility	Assumes responsibility	
		Extroverted — Introverted

Interpretation

After you have completed the comparison exercise, look at the range of differences between you and your child for each set of traits. In some cases you might be at opposite ends of the continuum, while in others you are probably quite close. In either case, ask yourself if the wide variation or close similarity is contributing to stress in your relationship.

If the answer is yes, everyone concerned needs to work jointly at developing a coping strategy. Belief in the uniqueness of each and every individual results in a live-and-let-live attitude.

Assessment 5 — The Coping Road Map

Background Information

In *The Widening World of Childhood,* Dr. Lois Murphy of the Menninger Foundation writes that children have individual ways of coping with stress which can play a significant role in their adjustment and development.[10] A child's individuality has a lot to do with how the child copes, and it must be considered in all efforts to guide children in engineering more effective strategies.

In general, the child who has a positive, realistic self-image and receives support both at home and school is better able to handle the routine stresses of childhood than a child growing up with a poor self-concept in an atmosphere marked by insecurity.

The more fortunate child gains confidence from the knowledge that when the going gets really tough, there is always someone to help. Concern, love, and wisdom are available, and unreasonable coping demands are not made. When the child is successful in handling a stressful situation, adults are there to notice and provide a pat on the back. As childhood progresses, the youngster becomes more and more confident in coping with stress.

Individual coping strategies vary among children, and there is usually more than one successful means for dealing with a stressful situation. Vulnerability to stress also differs, even in the same child over a brief period of time. A number of variables help to determine the extent of a child's reaction to a potentially stressful occurrence, including status of current health and level of stress present when a new stressor is introduced.

Overlooking or glossing over the child's problem with attitudes such as, "It's only a stage the child is going through," or "Don't worry about

The Individuality Profile

it, everything will be fine," assumes that the adult's lack of concern for the problem can be automatically transferred to the distressed child. A few moments of retrospection in which the adult recalls childhood will probably rekindle memories of problems which seemed major to you, but rather minor to the adults in your life. Maybe they thought the worries were silly or cute, or didn't recognize them at all, but to you they were a serious source of anxiety. The following checklist will help identify the coping strategies the child typically takes when faced with stress (see pp. 192–93).

Interpretation

If you checked statement number 1, you probably checked few, if any, of the others. The remaining sixteen descriptions all indicate that the child is using maladjustive coping strategies. You can help the child adjust more easily and quickly to stress by:
> Reassuring the child that the stressful situation does not signal the end of the world. The problem can be solved.
> Discussing the ineffective coping strategy being used, in light of the child's better perspective on the problem.
> Developing an effective coping strategy, based on individuality.

An example of maladjustive coping might be the child who is overwhelmed by having fallen desperately behind in homework, with the enormousness of the job ahead too much to face. The child uses coping strategy number 9—collaborating with others who are suffering with a similar problem. He or she suddenly prefers the company of underachievers and poor students. You can help the child to understand the components of temperament that led to the problem in the first place. Then, considering learning style and modality preference, work with the child to break the pile of work down into small chunks, so he or she sees a realistic possibility for progress.

Prolonged exposure to stress or maladjusted behavior that goes unchanged is demoralizing. The adult goal is certainly not the elimination of all stress from childhood. Stress is an important part of growing up and learning to survive in the real world. Coping with childhood stress is the best training for handling adult stress.[5] However, when stress is non-stop, or the child is in over his or her head, intervention is necessary. An important part of understanding the child is recognizing what coping strategies the child typically uses. If the child is quick to move onto the course of adjustment, and stress serves as a stimulating force leading to positive problem solving and improved performance, the adult has little cause for concern. The child

READ YOUR CHILD'S COPING ROAD MAP

____ 1. My child seems energized by a stressful situation and usually jumps right in to start finding effective solutions for adapting to the stress.

____ 2. My child reacts to stress by trying to avoid the particular problem or to avoid stressful situations altogether.

____ 3. My child becomes isolated during stress.

____ 4. My child tries to hide true feelings during stress by faking the appearance of being tough, silly, angry, or happy.

____ 5. My child builds mountains out of mole hills by magnifying the seriousness of the perceived threat, which in turn amplifies the stress reaction.

____ 6. My child introduces additional, irrelevant stressors to the stressful situation. When stressed, the child becomes upset about other problems which are totally unrelated and usually not worth worrying about.

____ 7. My child reacts to stress by trying to control others with temper tantrums or by bullying children.

____ 8. My child becomes overly dependent on others to handle stressful situations instead of personally coping with them. The child looks to others to "do something," stop fights, or run interference. The child thinks everyone should understand when stress is a problem and render kid-glove treatment.

____ 9. My child collaborates with others who are suffering from similar maladjustive coping processes, thinking that there is safety in numbers. For example, rather than handling problems at school the child joins with other children who are having similar difficulties, and everyone tells each other that "school is for the birds, anyway."

____ 10. My child simply gives up the fight. For example, if the child is experiencing stress associated with personality conflicts, the child becomes docile and just goes along with the other person.

____ 11. My child reacts to stress with aggressive behavior and physically, verbally, or emotionally tries to hurt or insult others.

_____ 12. My child tries to hide the fact that stress is a problem by cheating or lying about it.

_____ 13. My child blames others for generating the stress, and therefore feels somehow less responsible for dealing with it.

_____ 14. My child reacts to stress by going blank or becoming unable to function.

_____ 15. My child relies on rules, regulations, or highly traditional means for coping with stress, demonstrating a reluctance to try creative, fresh solutions.

_____ 16. My child withdraws from the reality of stress in any of the following ways: overeating, daydreaming, excessive reading or television viewing, reverting to babyish behavior, use of alcohol or drugs, avoiding friends, or illness—real or imagined.

_____ 17. My child tries to disguise inadequate coping ability with boasts, daredevil stunts, or fantastic claims of skill or ability.

might often recognize when stress is a problem and ask for help. On the other hand, some children are prone to maladjustive coping techniques. Instead of attempting to protect the child from stress, adults should be involved in facilitating adjustment by offering whatever support and guidance is needed to redirect maladjusted coping behavior. Initially, the child may not recognize that help is needed, that the adult has something of value to offer, or that inability to cope is not synonymous with failure. It can be difficult to approach a child who has chosen isolation. However, once children recognize that adults are willing and able to offer valuable assistance, they more readily seek it. Optimal results are possible when the child seeks this aid without hesitation, before stress is out of control. With a little adult intervention, childhood stress need not result in devastation, but can play an important part in the child's development.

REFERENCES

1. Ames, L. B., C. Gillespie, J. Haines & L. Ilg, *The Gesell Institutes's child from one to six.* New York: Harper & Row, 1979.
2. Ibid.
3. Chess, S. & J. Whitbread, *Daughters.* Garden City: Doubleday, 1978.

4. Dunn, R. & K. Dunn, *How to raise independent and professionally successful daughters.* Englewood Cliffs: Prentice–Hall, 1977.
5. Elder, G.H., Historical change in life patterns and personality. In *Life span development and behavior, II.* New York: Academic Press, 1979, 118–159.
6. Johnson, A. M., & S. A. Szurek, The genesis of anti–social acting–out in children and adults. *Psychoanalytic Quarterly,* 1952, 21,323.
7. Keating, K. How work is affecting American families. *Better Homes and Gardens,* February, 1982, p. 19.
8. Kubler–Ross, E., *On death and dying.* New York: Macmillan, 1969.
9. Miller, L., Toward a greater understanding of the parents of the mentally retarded child. *The Journal of Pediatrics,* 1968, 73:699–705.
10. Murphy,L. & Associates, *The widening world of childhood.* New York: Basic Books, 1962.
11. Study reported in *Psychology Today,* May, 1982, p. 74.
12. Thomas, A. & S. Chess, *Temperament and Development.* New York: Brunner/Mazel, 1977.
13. Ibid.
14. Wenar, C., *Personality development from infancy to adulthood.* Boston: Houghton Mifflin, 1971.

CHAPTER 10

DEALING WITH EMOTIONAL STRESS IN CHILDHOOD

James H. Humphrey, Ed. D.

> *In considering childhood emotional stress the author discusses factors concerning emotional development, emotional needs of children, and opportunites for emotional development in the home and school environment. A rating scale is presented for use of the parent and/or teacher as a means of evaluating influences of the environment on emotional stress.*

Emotional stress can be brought about by the stimulus of any of the emotional patterns. For example, the emotional pattern of anger can be stimulated by such factors as the thwarting of one's wishes or a number of cumulative irritations. Response to such stimuli can be either *impulsive* or *inhibited*. An impulsive expression of anger is one that is directed against a person or an object, while the inhibited expressions are kept under control and may be manifested by such overt behavior as skin flushing.

Generally speaking, emotional patterns can be placed into the two broad categories of *pleasant* emotions and *unpleasant* emotions. Pleasant emotional patterns include such things as joy, affection, happiness, and love in the broad sense, while included among the unpleasant emotional patterns are anger, sorrow, jealousy, fear, and worry—an imaginary form of fear.

It is interesting to note that a good proportion of the literature is devoted to emotions that are unpleasant. It has been found that in most basic psychology books much more space is given to such emotional patterns as fear, hate, and guilt, than to such pleasant emotions as love, sympathy, and contentment.

At one time or another all children manifest emotional behavior as well as ordinary behavior. Differences in the structure of the organism and in the environment will largely govern the degree to which each individual child expresses emotional behavior. Moreover, it has been suggested that the pleasantness or unpleasantness of an emotion seems to be determined by its strength or intensity, by the nature of the situation arousing it, and by the way the child perceives or interprets the situation.

The ancient Greeks identified emotions with certain organs of the body. For example, in general, sorrow was expressed from the heart (a broken heart), jealousy was associated with the liver, hate with the gall bladder, and anger with the spleen. In regard to the latter we sometimes hear the expression "wreaking the spleen" on someone. This historical reference is made because in modern times we take into account certain conduits between the emotions and the body. These are by way of the nervous system and the endocrine system. That part of the nervous system principally concerned with the emotions is the *autonomic* nervous system which controls functions such as the heartbeat, blood pressure, and digestion. When there is a stimulus of any of the emotional patterns, these two systems activate; by way of illustration, if the emotional pattern of fear is stimulated, the heartbeat accelerates, breathing is more rapid, and the blood pressure is likely to rise. Energy fuel is discharged into the blood from storage in the liver, which causes the blood sugar level to rise. These, along with other bodily functions, serve to prepare a person for coping with the condition caused by the fear.

Dealing with childhood emotions implies that sympathetic guidance should be provided in meeting anxieties, joys, and sorrows and that help should be given in developing aspirations and security. In order to attempt to reach this objective, we might well consider emotions from a standpoint of the growing child maturing emotionally.

For purposes of this discussion *maturity* will be considered as concerned with a state of *readiness* on the part of the organism. The term is most frequently used in connection with age relationships. For example, it may be said that "Johnny is mature for six years of age," Simply stated, *emotional maturity* is the process of acting one's age.

Generally speaking, emotional maturity will be achieved through a gradual accumulation of mild and pleasant emotions. Emotional *immaturity* indicates that unpleasant emotions have accumulated too rapidly for the child to absorb. One of the important factors in this regard is the process of *adjustment,* which can be described as the process of finding and adopting modes of behavior suitable to the environment, or to changes in the environment.

The child's world involves a sequence of experiences that are characterized by the necessity for him to adjust. Consequently, it may be said that "normal" behavior is the result of successful adjustment, and abnormal behavior results from unsuccessful adjustment. The degree of adjustment that the child achieves depends upon how adequately he is able to satisfy his basic needs and to fulfill his desires within the framework of his environment and the pattern of ways dictated by society.

For purposes here, *stress* will be considered as any factor acting internally or externally that renders adaptation difficult and that induces increased effort on the part of a person to maintain a state of equilibrium within himself and with his external environment.

When stress is induced as a result of the child's not being able to meet his needs (basic demands) and satisfy his desires (wants or wishes), *frustration* or *conflict* result. Frustration occurs when a need is not met, and conflict results when: (1) choices must be made between nearly equally attractive alternatives, or (2) when basic emotional forces oppose one another. In an emotionally healthy person, the degree of frustration is ordinarily in proportion to the intensity of the need or desire. That is, he will objectively observe and evaluate the situation to ascertain whether a solution is possible and, if so, what solution would best enable him to achieve the fulfillment of his needs or his desires.

Every person has a *zone of tolerance* or limits for emotional stress within which he normally operates. If the stress becomes considerably greater than the tolerance level or if the individual has not learned to cope with his problems and objectively and intelligently solve them, some degree of maladjustment can possibly result.

In order to counteract some of the above problems and to be able to pursue a sensible course in helping children become more emotionally mature, there are certain factors concerned with emotional development of children that need to be taken into account. Some of these factors are the subject of the ensuing discussion.

FACTORS CONCERNING EMOTIONAL DEVELOPMENT

Some of the factors concerned with emotional development of children that need to be considered are: (1) characteristics of childhood emotionality; (2) emotional arousals and reactions; and (3) factors that influence emotionality.

Characteristics of Childhood Emotionality

Ordinarily, the emotions of children are not long lasting.

A child's emotions may last for a few minutes and then terminate rather abruptly. The child gets it "out of his system," so to speak, by expressing it outwardly. In contrast, some adult emotions may be long and drawn out. As children get older, expressing the emotions by overt action is encumbered by certain social restraints. This is to say that what might be socially acceptable at one age level is not necessarily so at another. This may be a reason for some children developing *moods*, which in a sense are states of emotion drawn out over a period of time and expressed slowly. Typical moods of childhood may be "sulking" due to restraint of anger, being "jumpy" from repressed fear, and becoming "humorous" from controlled joy or happiness.

The emotions of children are likely to be intense

This might be confusing to some adults who do not understand child behavior; that is, they may not be able to see why a child would react rather violently to a situation that to them might appear insignificant.

The emotions of children are subject to rapid change

A child is capable of shifting rapidly from laughing to crying or from anger to joy. Although the reason for this is not definitely known, it might be that there is not as much depth of feeling among children as there is among adults. In addition, it could be due to lack of experience that children have had, as well as their state of intellectual development. We do know that young children have a short attention span that could cause them to change rapidly from one kind of emotion to another.

The emotions of children can appear with a high degree of frequency

As children get older they manage to develop the ability to adjust to situations that previously would have caused an emotional reaction. This is probably due to the child's acquiring more experience with various kinds of emotional situations. Perhaps a child learns through experience what is socially acceptable and what is socially unacceptable. This is particularly true if the child is reprimanded in some way following a violent emotional reaction. For this reason, the child may try to confront situations in ways that do not involve an emotional response.

Children differ in their emotional responses

One child confronted with a situation that instills fear may run away from the immediate environment. Another may hide behind his mother. Still another might just stand there and cry. Different reactions of children to emotional situations are probably due to a host of factors. Included among these may be past experiences with a certain kind of emotional situation, willingness of parents and other adults to help children become independent, and family relationships in general.

Strength of children's emotions are subject to change

At some age levels certain kinds of emotions may be weak and later become stronger. Conversely, with some children emotions that were strong may tend to decline. For example, small children may be timid among strangers, but later when they see that there is nothing to fear, the timidity is likely to wane.

Emotional Arousals and Reactions

If we are to understand the emotions of children, we need to take into account those factors of emotional arousal and how children might be expected to react to them. Many different kinds of emotional patterns have been identified. For purposes here we have arbitrarily selected for discussion the emotional states of fear, worry, anger, jealously and joy.

Fear

It is possible that is is not necessarily the arousal itself but rather the way something is presented that determines whether there will be a fear reaction. For example, if a child is trying to perform a stunt and the discussion is in terms of "if you do it that way you will break your neck," it is possible a fear response will occur. This is one of the many reasons for using a positive approach in dealing with children.

A child may react to fear by withdrawing. With very young children this may be in the form of crying or breath holding. With a child under three years of age and in some older children as well, the "ostrich" approach may be used; that is, he may hide his face in order to get away from it. As children get older, these forms of reactions may decrease or cease altogether because of social pressures. For instance, it may be considered "sissy" to cry, especially among boys. (The validity of this kind of thinking is of course open to question.)

Worry

This might be considered an imaginary form of fear, and it can be a fear not aroused directly from the child's environment. Worry can be aroused by imagining a situation that could possibly arise; that is, a child could worry about not being able to perform well in a certain activity. Since worries are likely to be caused by imaginary rather than real conditions, they are not likely to be found in abundance among very young children. Perhaps the reason for this is that they have not reached a stage of intellectual development at which they might imagine certain things that could cause worry. While children will respond to worry in different ways, certain manifestations such as nail biting may be symptomatic of this condition.

Anger

This emotional response tends to occur more frequently than that of fear. This is probably because there are more conditions that incite anger. In addition, some children quickly learn that anger may get attention that otherwise would not be forthcoming. It is likely that as children get older they may show more anger responses than fear responses because they soon see that there is not much to fear.

Anger is caused by many factors, one of which is interference with movements the child wants to execute. This interference can come from others or by the child's own limitations in ability and physical development.

Because of individual differences in children, there is a wide variation in anger responses. As mentioned previously, these responses are either *impulsive* or *inhibited*. In impulsive responses, the child manifests an overt action either toward another person or an object that caused the anger. For instance, a child who collides with a door might take out the anger by kicking or hitting the door. (This form of child behavior is also sometimes manifested by some "adults.") Inhibited responses are likely to be kept under control, and as children mature emotionally, they acquire more ability to control their anger.

Jealousy

This response usually occurs when a child feels a threat of loss of affection. Many psychologists believe that jealousy is closely related to anger. Because of this, the child may build up resentment against another person. Jealousy can be devastating in childhood, and every effort should be made to avoid it.

Jealousy is concerned with social interaction that involves persons the child likes. These individuals can be parents, siblings, teachers, and peers. There are various ways in which the child may respond. These include: (1) being aggressive toward the one of whom one is jealous or possibly toward others as well; (2) withdrawing from the person whose affections he thinks have been lost; and (3) possible development of an "I don't care" attitude.

In some cases children will not respond in any of the above ways. They might try to excel over the person of whom they are jealous or they might tend to do things to impress the person whose affections they thought had been lost.

Joy

This pleasant emotion is one for which we strive because it is so important in maintaining emotional stability. Causes of joy differ from one age level to another and from one child to another at the same age level. This is to say that what might be a joyful situation for one person might not necessarily be so for another.

Joy is expressed in various ways, but the most common are laughing and smiling, the latter being a restrained form of laughter. Some people respond to joy with a state of relaxation. This is difficult to detect because it has little or no overt manifestation. Nevertheless, it may be noticed when one compares it with body tension caused by unpleasant emotion.

Factors That Influence Emotionality

If we can consider that a child is emotionally fit when his emotions are properly controlled and he is becoming emotionally mature, then emotional fitness is dependent to a certain extent upon certain factors that influence emotionality in childhood. The following is a descriptive list of some of these factors.

Fatigue

There are two types of fatigue, *acute* and *chronic*. Acute fatigue is a natural outcome of sustained severe exertion. It is due to physical factors such as the accumulation of the by-products of muscular exertion in the blood and to excessive *oxygen debt*—the ability of the body to take in as much oxygen as is being consumed by the muscular work. Psychological considerations may also be important in acute fatigue. That is, an individual who becomes bored with his work and who becomes preoccupied with the discomfort involved will become "fatigued" much sooner than if he is highly motivated to do the same work, is not bored, and does not think about the discomfort.

Chronic fatigue refers to fatigue that lasts over extended periods, in contrast to acute fatigue, which tends to be followed by a recovery phase and restoration to "normal" within a more or less brief period of time. Chronic fatigue may be due to any or a variety of medical conditions ranging from a disease such as tuberculosis to malnutrition. (Such conditions are the concern of the physician who, incidentally, should evaluate all cases of chronic fatigue in order to assure that a disease condition is not responsible). It may also be due to psychological factors such as extreme boredom and/or worry of having to do what one does not wish to do over an extended period.

Fatigue predisposes children to irritability; consequently, actions are taken to ward it off, such as having rest periods or, in the case of the nursery school, fruit juice periods. In this particular regard, some studies show that the hungrier a child is, the more prone he may be to outbursts of anger.

Inferior health status

The same thing holds true here as in the case of fatigue. Temporary poor health, such as colds and the like, tends to make children irritable. There are studies that show that there are fewer emotional outbursts among healthy than unhealthy children.

Intelligence

Studies tend to show that, on the average, children of low intellectual levels have less emotional control than children with higher levels of intelligence. This may be because there may be less frustration if a child is intelligent enough to figure things out. The reverse could also be true because children with high level intelligence are better able to perceive things that would be likely to arouse emotions.

Social environment

In a social environment where such things as quarreling and unrest exist, a child is predisposed to unpleasant emotional conditions. Likewise, school schedules that are too crowded can cause undue emotional excitation among children.

Family relationships

There are a variety of conditions concerned with family relationships that can influence childhood emotionality. Among others, these include: (1) parental neglect; (2) overanxious parents; and, (3) overprotective parents.

Aspiration levels

It can make for an emotionally unstable situation if parent expectations are beyond a child's ability. In addition, children who have not been made aware of their own limitations may set goals too high and as a result have too many failures.

All of these factors can have a negative influence on childhood emotionality, and thus, possibly induce emotional stress. Therefore, efforts should be made as far as possible to eliminate the negative aspects of these factors. Those that cannot be completely eliminated should at least be kept under control.

EMOTIONAL NEEDS OF CHILDREN

It is a very difficult matter to identify specific components of emotional fitness. Therefore, in the absence of such definitive components, we need to look in other directions in our efforts to help children maintain satisfactory levels of emotional fitness. Emotional maturity, and hence, emotional fitness, could be expressed in terms of the fulfillment of certain emotional needs. These needs can be reflected in the developmental characteristics of growing children. A number of emotional characteristics are identified in the following lists at some of the different age levels. These lists of emotional characteristics have been developed through a documentary analysis of more than a score of sources that have appeared in the literature in recent years. It should be understood that these characteristics are suggestive of the behavior patterns of the so-called normal child. This implies that, if a child does not conform to these characteristics, it should not be interpreted to mean that he or she is seriously deviating from the normal. In other words, it should be recognized that each child progresses at his or her own rate and that there will be much overlapping of the characteristics for each of the age levels.

Five-Year-Old Children

1. Seldom show jealousy toward younger siblings.
2. Usually see only one way to do something.
3. Usually see only one answer to a question.
4. Inclined not to change plans in the middle of an activity, but would rather begin over.
5. May fear being deprived of mother.

6. Some definite personality traits evidenced.
7. Learning to get along better, but still may resort to quarreling and fighting.
8. Like to be trusted with errands.
9. Enjoy performing simple tasks.
10. Want to please and do what is expected of them.
11. Are beginning to sense right and wrong in terms of specific situations.

Six-Year-Old Children

1. Restless and may have difficulty in making decisions.
2. Emotional pattern of anger may be difficult to control at times.
3. Behavior patterns may often be explosive and unpredictable.
4. Jealous toward siblings at times; at other times take pride in siblings.
5. Greatly excited by anything new.
6. Behavior becomes susceptible to shifts in direction, inwardly motivated, and outwardly stimulated.
7. May be self-assertive and dramatic.

Seven-Year-Old Children

1. Curiosity and creative desires may condition responses.
2. May find it difficult to take criticism from adults.
3. Want to be more independent.
4. Reaching for new experiences and trying to relate to enlarged world.
5. Overanxious to reach goals set by parents and teachers.
6. Critical of self and sensitive to failure.
7. Emotional patterns of anger are more controlled.
8. Becoming less impulsive and boisterous in actions than at six.

Eight-Year-Old Children

1. Dislike taking much criticism from adults.
2. Can give and take criticism in own group.
3. May develop enemies.
4. Do not like to be treated as children.
5. Have a marked sense of humor.

6. First impulse is to blame others.
7. Becoming more realistic and want to find out for themselves.

Nine-Year-Old Children

1. May sometimes be outspoken and critical of adults they know, although they have a genuine fondness for them.
2. Respond best to adults who treat them as individuals and approach them in an adult way.
3. Like recognition for what they have done and respond well to deserved praise.
4. Likely to be backward about public recognition, but like private praise.
5. Developing sympathy and loyalty to others.
6. Do not mind criticism or punishment if they think it is fair, but are indignant if they think it is unfair.
7. Disdainful of danger to and safety of self, which may be a result of increasing interest in activities involving challenges and adventure.

It should be obvious that the above emotional characteristics reflect some of the emotional needs of children at the different age levels. These characteristics should be taken into account if we expect to meet with success in meeting such needs of children.

GUIDELINES FOR EMOTIONAL DEVELOPMENT OF CHILDREN

It is imperative to set forth some guidelines for emotional development if we are to meet with any degree of success in our attempts to provide for emotional development of children. The reason for this is to assure, at least to some extent, that our efforts in attaining optimum emotional development will be based upon a scientific approach. These guidelines might well take the form of valid *concepts of emotional development*. This approach enables us to give serious consideration to what is known about how children grow and develop. The following list of concepts of emotional development with certain implications for the school and/or home environment is submitted with this general idea in mind.

1. *An emotional response may be brought about by a goal's being furthered or thwarted.* The teacher or parent should make a very serious effort to assure successful experiences in the school or home for every child. In the school setting this can be accomplished in part by

attempting to provide for individual differences within given school experiences. The school or home setting should be such that each child derives a feeling of personal worth through making some sort of positive contribution.

2. *Self-realization experiences should be constructive.* The opportunity for creative experiences that afford the child a chance for self-realization should be inherent in both home and school. Teachers might well consider planning with children to see that all school activities are meeting their needs and, as a result, involve constructive experiences.

3. *Emotional responses increase as the development of the child brings greater awareness and the ability to remember the past and to anticipate the future.* In the school setting the teacher can remind the children of their past pleasant emotional responses with words of praise. This could encourage children to repeat such responses later in similar situations and thus provide a better learning situation.

4. *As the child develops, the emotional reactions tend to become less violent and more discriminating.* A well planned program of school experiences and wholesome home activities should be such that it provides for release of aggression in a socially acceptable manner.

5. *Emotional reactions tend to increase beyond normal expectancy toward the constructive or destructive reactions on the balance of furthering or hindering experiences of the child.* For some children the confidence they need to be able to face the problems of life may come through physical expression. Therefore, experiences such as active play in the home surroundings and good physical education programs in the schools have tremendous potential to help contribute toward a solid base of total development.

6. *Depending on certain factors, a child's own feelings may be accepted or rejected by the individual.* Children's school and home experiences should make them feel good and have confidence in themselves. Satisfactory self-concept is closely related to body control; physical activity oriented experiences might be considered as one of the best ways of contributing to it. Therefore, it is important to consider those kinds of experiences for your children that will provide them with the opportunity for a certain degree of freedom of movement.

OPPORTUNITIES FOR EMOTIONAL DEVELOPMENT IN THE HOME AND SCHOOL ENVIRONMENT

The school and home have the potential to provide for emotional stability. The extent to which this actually occurs is dependent primarily on the kind of emotional climate provided by the teacher and the parent in the school and home. For this reason, it appears pertinent to examine some of the potential opportunities that exist for emotional development in both the school and home situations. It should be borne in mind that these opportunities will not accrue automatically, but that both teachers and parents need to work constantly to try to make such conditions a reality.

1. *Release of aggression in a socially acceptable manner.* This appears to be an outstanding way in which school activities such as physical education can help to make children more secure and emotionally stable. For example, kicking a ball in a game of kickball, batting a softball, or engaging in a combative stunt can afford a socially acceptable way of releasing aggression. The same can be said for a home environment where parents provide their children with a wholesome recreation and active play opportunities.

2. *Inhibition of direct response of unpleasant emotions.* This statement does not necessarily mean that feelings concerned with such unpleasant emotions as fear and anger should be completely restrained. On the contrary the interpretation should be that such feelings can take place less frequently in a wholesome school and home environment. This means that opportunities should be provided to relieve tension rather than to aggravate it.

3. *Promotion of pleasant emotions.* Perhaps there is too much concern with suppressing unpleasant emotions and not enough attention given to promoting pleasant ones. This means that the school and home should provide a range of activities by which all children can succeed. Thus, all children, regardless of ability, should be afforded the opportunity for success, at least most of the time.

4. *Recognition of one's abilities and limitations.* It has already been mentioned that a wide range of activities should provide an opportunity for success for all. This should make it easier in the school setting to provide for individual differences of children so that all of them can progress within the limits of their own skill and ability.

5. *Understanding about the ability and achievements of others.* In the school experience emphasis can be placed upon achievements of the group, along with the function of each individual in the group. Team play and group effort is important in most school situation.

6. *Being able to make a mistake without being ostracized.* In the school setting this requires that the teacher serve as a catalyst that helps children understand the idea of trial and error. Emphasis can be placed on *trying* and on the fact that one can learn not only from his own mistakes but also from the mistakes of others.

This discussion has included just a few examples of the numerous opportunities to help provide for emotional development in the school and home environment. The resourceful and creative teacher or parent should be able to expand this list manyfold.

IMPLICATIONS OF RESEARCH IN EMOTIONAL BEHAVIOR OF CHILDREN

Over the years, attempts have been made to study various aspects of childhood emotions. A recent undertaking by the National Institute of Education provides some information that might be useful.[1]

The purpose of this report was to provide preschool and early elementary school teachers with a summary of current psychological research concerned with the social development of young children. In submitting the report, the authors noted that caution should prevail with reference to basic research and practical implications. In this regard, the following suggestions are submitted:

1. What seems "true" at one point often becomes "false" when new information becomes available or when new theories change the interpretation of the old findings.

2. Substantial problems arise in any attempt to formulate practical suggestions for professionals in one discipline based on research findings from another discipline.

3. Throughout the report, recommendations for teachers have been derived from logical extensions of experimental findings and classroom adaptations of experimental procedures.

4. Some of the proposed procedures may prove unworkable in the classroom, even though they may make sense from a psychological perspective.

5. When evaluating potential applications of psychological findings, it is important to remember that psychological research is usually designed to derive probability statements about the behavior of groups of people.

6. Individual teachers may work better with a procedure that is, on the average, less effective.

The following is a list of generalizations derived from the findings of the study of *aggression* in children, and accompanied by possible general implications for the school or home environment. These implications are suggestive only, and the reader will no doubt be able to draw his or her own implications and make practical applications that apply to particular situations.

1. *Children rewarded for aggression learn that aggression pays off.*

This generalization is concerned with the extent to which a teacher or parent uses praise for achievement. The teacher must be able to discern quickly whether success was due more to aggressive behavior than skill or ability. The important thing here is the extent of aggressive behavior. Certainly a teacher should not thwart enthusiasm. It is sometimes difficult to determine whether an act was due to genuine enthusiasm or to overt, undesirable, aggressive behavior.

2. *Children involved in constructive activities may be less likely to behave aggressively.* In the school setting, this implies that lessons should be well-planned so that time is spent on constructive learning activities. When this is accomplished, it will be more likely that desirable and worthwhile learning will take place.

3. *Children who have alternative responses readily available are less likely to resort to aggression to get what they want.* This is concerned essentially with teacher-child or parent-child relationships. While the school environment generally involves group situations, there are many "one-on-one" opportunities between teacher and child. (This situation pertains as well to the home environment if a parent is willing to spend time on these one-on-one relationships). This gives the teacher a chance to verbalize to the child the kind of behavior that is expected under certain conditions. For example, a child who *asks* for an object such as a ball is more likely to receive cooperation. A child who *grabs* an object is more likely to elicit retaliatory aggression. Teaching reinforcement can increase children's use of nonaggressive solutions to interpersonal problems.

The teacher should be ready to intervene in a potentially aggressive situation before aggression occurs, encouraging children to use nonaggressive methods to solve conflicts. The teacher can provide verbal alternatives for those children who do not think of them. For example, "I am playing with this now," or, "You can ask him to trade with you."

4. *Children imitate behavior of people they like, and they often adopt a teacher's behavior.* Teachers are more likely to be a model adopted by children than would be the case with most other adults, sometimes including parents. One of the reasons is that many children like to try to please their teachers and tend to make serious efforts to do so. Of course it is helpful if a teacher is nonaggressive in his or her own behavior.

5. *Cooperation may be incompatible with aggression.* This could be interpreted to mean that a teacher or parent should consistently attend to and reinforce all cooperative behavior. Children consistently reinforced for cooperative behavior are likely to increase cooperative interactions while simultaneously decreasing aggressive behavior.

EVALUATING INFLUENCES OF THE ENVIRONMENT ON EMOTIONAL DEVELOPMENT

What we are essentially concerned with here is how an individual teacher or parent can make some sort of valid evaluation of the extent to which the school or home environment contributes to emotional development. This means that the teacher or parent should make some attempt to assess school and home experiences with reference to whether or not these experiences are providing for emotional maturity.

One approach would be to refer back to the list of opportunities for emotional development in the school and home environment suggested previously. These opportunities have been converted into a rating scale as follows and may be used by a teacher and/or parent.

1. The school/home experiences provide for release of aggression in a socially acceptable manner.
    - 4 most of the time
    - 3 some of the time
    - 2 occasionally
    - 1 infrequently
2. The school/home experiences provide for inhibition of direct response to unpleasant emotions.
    - 4 most of the time
    - 3 some of the time
    - 2 occasionally
    - 1 infrequently
3. The school/home experiences provide for promotion of pleasant emotions.
    - 4 most of the time
    - 3 some of the time
    - 2 occasionally
    - 1 infrequently
4. The school/home experiences provide for recognition of one's abilities and limitations.
    - 4 most of the time
    - 3 some of the time
    - 2 occasionally
    - 1 infrequently
5. The school/home experiences provide for an understanding about the ability and achievement of others
    - 4 most of the time
    - 3 some of the time
    - 2 occasionally
    - 1 infrequently

6. The school/home experiences provide for being able to make a mistake without being ostracized.
   4 most of the time
   3 some of the time
   2 occasionally
   1 infrequently

If a teacher or parent makes these ratings objectively and conscientiously, a reasonably good procedure for evaluation is provided. Ratings can be made periodically to see if positive changes appear to be taking place. Ratings can be made for a single experience, a group of experiences, or for the total school or home environment. This procedure can help the teacher or parent identify the extent to which school or home experiences and/or conditions under which the experiences take place are contributing to emotional development, and thus to the control of emotional stress.

REFERENCE

1. Roedell, W., R. G. Slaby & H. B. Robinson, *Social Development in Young Children: a Report for Teachers.* Washington, D.C.: National Institute of Education, January, 1976.

CHAPTER 11

USE OF SYSTEMATIC DESENSITIZATION IN THE TREATMENT OF CHILDREN'S FEARS

D'Ann Whitehead, Ph. D.
Mariela Shirley, Ph. D.
and
C. Eugene Walker, Ph. D.

It is clear from research and clinical examples that various treatment modalities including systematic desensitization based on imagery, in-vivo desensitization, shaping, cognitive strategies, and modeling all show considerable promise in the treatment of children's fears. Adaptations of traditional imagery based systematic desensitization appear to be more useful, in general, due to developmental considerations discussed in this chapter. However, for children with severe fears and phobias, imagery may be very useful as a starting point. Clearly, much more research is needed to establish the best methods to treat various degrees of fear in children of different developmental levels. In the meantime, clinicians will have to tailor the methods available, in a trial and error manner, for patients with whom they work. Psychotherapy remains largely an art.

INTRODUCTION

Fear is generally defined as a normal and specific reaction to a genuine threat, which is present at the moment. Anxiety is usually defined as a more generalized reaction to a vague sense of threat in absence of a specific or realistic dangerous object. However, the terms are often used loosely and almost interchangeably. When fearful or anxious, individuals experience unpleasant changes in overt behavior, subjective feelings (including thoughts), and physiological activity.

Fears are common among children, particularly early in childhood.[36] Examples of such fears are fear of dogs, insects, the dark, ghosts, and going to school. Childhood fears sometimes appear to be unexplainable and children have marked individual differences in susceptability to fear. However, there is evidence that children display a definite tendency to learn their parents' fears through identification with the parents or simply by observing the parents engage in fearful behavior.[63] For example, if during a storm a child observes a parent being fearful, the child is likely to develop a similar fear and fear response pattern. On the other hand, many childhood fears are a function of direct contact or experience with frightening events (e.g., if the child were attacked by a dog). Parental warnings, without the parent necessarily being fearful of such, about certain objects or events (e.g., watch out for strangers, stay away from fires) may also lead to the development of fears in children. Kazdin reports that occasionally fears become extremely intense and fail to decrease over time. Further, these "intense fears" may interfere with daily functioning.[36]

Several theoretical models have been advanced to explain the development and maintenance of fears. (For an excellent and detailed discussion of these the reader is referred to Reference 24).

LEARNING PRINCIPLES AND FEAR

Behavioral explanations of the development and maintenance of fears are based on learning principles. Basically it is assumed that all behavior, and thus the individual's fear responses, are learned from the environment. Three paradigms by which such learning takes place have been proposed: respondent conditioning, operant conditioning, and the two-factor theory of learning.[24]

Respondent Conditioning

Let us consider respondent conditioning first. If a neutral stimulus is presented simultaneously with presentation of a fear provoking stimulus, the neutral stimulus will become a conditioned stimulus for fear. Thus, on subsequent occasions, the previously neutral stimulus will evoke a fear response. A famous experiment by Watson and Raynor[79] illustrates this process. In the experiment, a child learned to fear a white rat. Initially, the child, Little Albert, was shown the white rat for which he showed no fear. While the child was paying attention to the rat, he was frightened by a loud sound (striking a steel bar with a hammer held a safe distance behind the child's head). Following several repetitions of this, the child was noticed to be afraid of the rat. The original neutral stimulus (rat), therefore, became a conditioned stimulus to elicit fear. It was later noticed that the child generalized this fear to other "furry" objects (e.g., his mother's fur neckpiece). Watson and Raynor whimsically noted that a dynamically oriented child psychologist examining this child might produce many speculations as to the origin of the fear, but almost certainly would not state in his or her report that the child was obviously frightened by striking a steel bar behind his head as a white rat was placed in front of him—yet that is how the fear was produced.

Operant Conditioning

Operant conditioning can account for the development of fear or the basis of reinforcement via the environmental contingencies that follow a fear response. For example, the child's fear of the dark may lead to much social reinforcement in terms of parental attention (including bedtime stories, snacks, and so forth) at bed time. Similarly, a fear of bugs or dirt may make it "impossible" for the child to help pull weeds in the garden.

Two-Factor Theory

The two-factor theory was proposed by Mowrer.[57] Both respondent and operant conditioning are embodied in this conceptualization. According to this theory, fears first develop via respondent conditioning and are maintained via operant conditioning. Initially, a neutral stimulus is paired with a fear provoking stimulus and the neutral stimulus becomes a conditioned fear stimulus. The individual then engages in behavior which enables him or her to escape or avoid the conditioned fear stimulus. If such maneuevers are successful, they decrease the level of experienced anxiety or fear. This fear reduction serves to reinforce the behaviors that were instrumental in reducing the fear. For example, if a child is taking a bath and gets water in his nose, he may then develop a fear of baths. In order to reduce the fear and anxiety, he may hide until just before bed time, fall asleep in the living room, or throw a tantrum when told to take a bath. The anxiety reduction experienced by avoiding the bath reinforces continued avoidance of baths.

PHOBIC DISORDERS

If a fear becomes sufficiently extreme and irrational it may be referred to as a phobia. The essential feature of phobic disorders is a persistent and irrational fear of a specific object, activity, or situation that results in a compelling desire to avoid the dreaded object, activity, or situation. The fear is recognized by the individual as excessive or unreasonable in proportion to the actual dangerousness of the object, activity, or situation.[2] The phobic individual may display agitation, depression, and ritualistic behavior (characterized by obsessiveness/compulsiveness, and excessive rumination, and "checking.") Thus, if fearful of germs, he may go about searching the house to be sure it is free of such; may spend a great deal of time thinking about germs and disease; and, may repetitiously spray the house with disinfectant. Such behaviors can pose a significant problem to effective functioning in daily living.

ADULT ATTITUDES TOWARD CHILDREN'S FEARS

Children's fears often tend not to be taken seriously by adults. Adults generally hold the belief that children's fears "will pass" or that they will "grow out of them." However, it has been found that this may not always be the case, and that without treatment many fears may be maintained through adulthood.[56] Many treatment methods have been used in the treatment of fears and phobias. These treatment modalities include modeling, systematic desensitization, response prevention techniques (e.g., flooding and implosive therapy), relaxation training, and biofeedback, among many others. The focus of the present chapter is on the use of systematic desensitization in the treatment of fears and phobias.

SYSTEMATIC DESENSITIZATION

Behavior therapy procedures for phobias tend to be based on the model of classical conditioning. In this model, two processes are presumed to reduce avoidance and decrease anxiety. In the first, counterconditioning, the anxiety response is paired with a response deemed to be antagonistic to anxiety (e.g., muscle relaxation). In the second, extinction, the anxiety response is continuously elicited but not reinforced. Systematic desensitization involves the gradual substitution of a favorable (relaxed) response which is incompatible with an unfavorable (tense) response to a stimulus.[43] This therapeutic technique is aimed at the alleviation of maladaptive anxiety and involves the pairing of relaxation with imagined scenes highlighting situations the individual has indicated elicit anxiety.[69] It is thought that, if the individual learns to relax while imagining the anxiety provoking scenes, the anxiety response will extinguish and real life situations will not elicit the high levels of anxiety previously experienced. As a result, there will be no need for the patient to engage in avoidance behavior.

Therapists have viewed systematic desensitization as useful in the treatment of rational and irrational fears. This behavior change technique has been used in the treatment of a wide variety of phobias such as fear of open spaces (agoraphobia), flying, water, death, injections, snakes, insects, test anxiety, heights, and many others. The first explicit use of desensitization was reported by Mary Cover Jones in 1924.[31] She described the successful elimination of the fear of rabbits in a male child. Her procedure involved bringing the feared object into the child's presence in a gradual manner while the child was eating. It was assumed that a decrease in anxiety would occur because of the pairing of eating (a relaxing activity) with the presentation of a rabbit.

In the more modern application of these procedures, Wolpe envisions the task of the therapist as one who teaches the individual a response or behavior which competes with and decreases sympathetic nervous system activity.[82] Behaviors characterized by parasympathetic nervous system activity (e.g., relaxation) were deemed ideal in terms of inhibiting sympathetic nervous system activity (anxiety). The rationale presented to the patient generally consists of some explanation of how fears can be produced as a result of traumatic conditioning along with a discussion about how systematic desensitization using relaxation will eliminate the fear response. For example, Wolpe's classic description of the process begins as follows:

> I want to give you some idea of the nature of your disturbances and of the means we shall adopt to overcome them. Your trouble is basically that you react with fear too often or too strongly. You may say that the word "fear" is not a correct label for some or any of your disturbed feelings. You may feel that "anxiety" or "tension" or "disturbance" or "distress" is a better word, or the feelings may be so unusual that no words can describe them. Even so, fear is the root emotion, but various factors may modify the physiological responses that produce the fearful feeling. Not all fear is undesirable. In some circumstances it is an entirely reasonable and even useful response. You would not come for treatment if your fears were only of such things as poisonous

snakes or an actual threat of losing all your money on the stock exchange. But if you are afraid of going in a lift or of walking in a street or of entering a room full of people, then you are afraid in situations in which there is no actual danger. Such fears are useless fears. Nevertheless they do not exist for nothing. Always, definite circumstances have brought these useless fears into being. These circumstances vary greatly in detail but they have a common central core which I shall illustrate by means of a simple example.

A young child goes into his mother's kitchen, puts his hand on the big black stove and burns himself. At that moment he experiences pain and fear and makes a movement of withdrawal. A lasting aftereffect of this experience is that on subsequent occasions when the child enters the kitchen and sees the stove, he reacts with fear and with an impulse to keep away from it. In other words, he has now learned a reaction of fear and avoidance of a dangerous object. This, of course, is desirable.

But another, seemingly odd reaction may also be observed. Suppose that in the bedroom of the child's mother there is a large black chest of drawers. It may now be noticed that the child is also afraid of this chest of drawers, just because, in common with the stove, it has the characteristics of largeness and blackness. The resemblance has thus made the child uselessly afraid of a harmless object. Even in this limited example the disadvantages of such a useless fear may readily be seen. First, merely to experience unnecessarily the unpleasant emotion of fear is undesirable. Then, if the chest of drawers should happen to be in the child's path, he has to make a detour. Finally, if his mother keeps candy in one of the drawers this is no longer accessible to him.

This example is a model of the learning of all useless or neurotic fears. Whenever a person is subjected to an intensely fearful experience or to a fearful chronic situation, he is liable to become conditioned to react with fear whenever subsequently, in actually benign circumstances, he encounters things or stimuli smaller to any that were closely associated with the situation of fear. Here is an example: A young women came to see me, primarily because she was inexplicably terrified of her employer. It turned out that she had had an extraordinarily cruel father of whom she had been rightly afraid. By the principle of resemblance I have described, she had become afraid of practically all other people too, and her special fear of her boss was due to the fact that he had certain mannerisms strongly reminiscent of her father.

Following this, he proceeds to show how systematic desensitization will be used to do away with the unnecessary fear.

Next, the therapist and the patient set up a hierarchy of scenes which the patient indicates are anxiety-arousing. The hierarchy generally focuses on one type of fear only. It consists of a graded series of situations or scenes which the patient will later imagine while in a state of relaxation. The items in the hierarchy are rank ordered, from high to low, according to the degree of anxiety or fear they produce.

Following the development of an appropriate hierarchy, the individual is asked to imagine the least anxiety-arousing item in the hierarcy. Opinion varies as to the recommended length of exposure per scene. Paul[61] recommended ten seconds, whereas Ross and Proctor[70] recommend a longer exposure of thirty seconds. Walker, et al.[77] recommend two or three seconds the first time or two that the scene is presented, gradually increasing to fifteen to twenty seconds on subsequent presentations. Following each presentation of a given scene, the patient rates the degree of anxiety using a Subjective Units of Disturbance Scale (SUDS) on which a value of zero is given to the most relaxed the person has been in his or her life and 100 is the value given to the most anxious he or she has ever been.

Each scene is repeated over and over by the therapist until the patient can imagine it with little or no anxiety (SUDS scene of less than 10). The therapist then proceeds to the next higher item on the hierarchy until all items are covered. As items are desensitized in imagined scenes, the patient is given homework assignments to do the items on the hierarchy in real life. This completes the process of desensitization and insures that it will generalize to real life situations. Often, several different hierarchies will be employed in the treatment of a given patient. Full, step by step procedures for use of systematic desensitization are presented by Walker, et al.[77]

The experimental literature supporting the efficacy of systematic desensitization with adults is considerable. The technique has repeatedly been found to be useful with phobias as well as other anxiety-based disorders (see 35, 61, 83).

It has frequently been pointed out that systematic desensitization is a complex treatment involving several components. For example, considerations entering into the effectiveness of desensitization are cognitive variables,[7,17] social reinforcement,[14] and subjects' expectations regarding success (see 4, 8, 47).

ADAPTATIONS OF SYSTEMATIC DESENSITIZATION FOR USE WITH CHILDREN

In order to employ systematic desensitization in the treatment of children, certain considerations must be taken into account. Some of these considerations have to do with cognitive development in children. For example, Piaget states that developmentally, imagery is thought to first occur in late infancy, when "deferred imitation" takes place.[3] Mental imagery apparently cannot occur before this time. In "deferred imitation" the child is able to distinguish a mental image from the actual event it represents. However, Piaget says that the image is very specific to the event it is imitating and is concrete rather than conceptual. Therefore, it is questionable whether four and five years olds can manipulate imagery in the ways required for systematic desensitization. Brunner also states that the younger child may be able to attend to only a limited number of characteristics of the stimulus because of his or her stage of development.[10]

It may be that using other procedures, in place of imagining scenes, is best for these children. For example, in-vivo desensitization can be used; the child can use toys to play out a hierarchy of feared situations; or, the child can be allowed to draw the feared scenes.

Anticipatory imagery[64] develops at about age seven to eight. The imagery allows for manipulation of the mental representation so that it can be moved about in space or changed in form. It is plausible that seven and eight year olds could use systematic desensitization effectively. However, few studies using traditional systematic desensitization have been done with children under ten years of age. With many children, reinforcement may also be necessary to motivate the child to attempt and then practice visualizing.

Elliott and Ozolins state in their review of the literature that the concrete images that young children (below age seven or eight) use have a very high degree of affect associated with them.[16] This means that the therapist must be cautious in the use of imagery of an aversive nature, due to the possibility that the child might imagine such an aversive scene as to experience further trauma rather than treatment.

Children also frequently create unintended aversive stimuli through misunderstanding or exaggeration. Therapists can avoid problems in this area by choosing their words carefully and constantly observing the child's non verbal behavior. It is also important to verbally check with the child periodically to see what he or she is imagining.

Finally, Rimm and Masters state that the therapist must determine that the individual is capable of learning relaxation strategies and relaxing in a relatively short period of time.[68,79] Again, cognitively, children may have difficulty learning relaxation strategies if they are presented as they would be to an adult. Rewards may need to be given to the child for following the relaxation procedures and then practicing on a daily basis. Additionally, it may be helpful for the child to be taught relaxation techniques in his or her own language. For example, instead of being told to tense his or her leg muscles, the therapist could say, "pretend your legs are a bridge of thick wood. Imagine that a car has to get over the bridge. Make your legs stiff and strong so that the car won't fall in the water. Now the car has gone over the bridge and your legs become the water. Let your legs go limp and float like water, feeling cool and relaxed." Elliott has developed such a stategy for teaching breathing techniques to children undergoing painful medical procedures.[16] Children are taught to pump their bodies up like a tire and then pretend someone punched a hole in the tire and the air is leaking out as the tire becomes flat. Children are told to make a hissing noise as they exhale.

Lazarus and Abramovitz developed a technique originally intended for use exclusively with children.[42] This was in response to their observation that children sometimes had difficulty learning and using relaxation techniques. The technique, called "emotive imagery," replaces relaxation as the anxiety inhibiting response in systematic desensitization. It is meant to arouse feelings of bravery, pride, and assertiveness in the child. Like systematic desensitization a graduated hierarchy of the patient's fears is developed. However, instead of imagining the scene concurrent with relaxing, the child is guided (by the therapist) in imagery of the feared scene with credible events woven around his or her favorite hero. The following is an example of Lazarus's[41] use of emotive imagery with a school phobic child.

> Imagine that Batman and Robin have asked you to assist them in catching a criminal. They lend you a special wrist radio so that they can contact you whenever necessary. Nobody must know the secret, that you are actually helping Batman and Robin to solve a crime right in your own school. Batman says to you, "Peter, I have placed a secret message in your school locker. When you get to school tomorrow morning, go to your locker as soon as possible and read the message. Then destroy it!!! Of course you don't want to tell Batman and Robin about your fears, so you go to school the next morning and head straight for your locker. Picture yourself going to school. As you ride toward the school in the bus, you are wondering what the message will say. You get into the school yard, get out of the bus, and you walk slowly to your locker. You don't want to rush there because you don't want to make anyone suspicious.
>
> You open your locker and there you see a slip of green paper. It has the emblem of a bat on it and you know who the sender is. You slip it into your pocket, and some of your friends come up and talk to you. As soon as you manage to do so without being seen, you read the message from Batman and Robin. It says, "We will signal you on your wrist radio during your first recess. Over and out!" You wonder what

Batman and Robin will want you to do next. You carry on with your work. The nasty teacher who left the school comes back into the classroom. You look at him, but you can't let that bother you. Bigger things are at stake. What will Batman and Robin ask you to do?

It is clear that simply because a technique is effective with adults does *not* mean that it can be used in an identical manner with children and be expected to have the same results. Factors such as the child's cognitive development, age and sex may make adaptations, such as the above necessary. In the following section we will review the use of systematic desensitization in a variety of contexts.

SYSTEMATIC DESENSITIZATION IN THE CLASSROOM

Children may exhibit various fears and anxieties in the classroom setting ranging from mild anticipatory anxiety, to test anxiety, and even school phobia. Teachers are frequently faced with the child who is fearful of some situation in school, particularly the young child who is entering school for the first time. Although they may not realize it, teachers frequently use desensitization procedures with their students on the first few days of school. Assuming that chidren being each school year with some sort of mild anxiety or apprehension, teachers desensitize their students to the routine of school by starting the first few days off slowly with many "fun" get-acquainted and get-organized types of activities and little demanding work. Day by day, more challenging activities are added until the child is carrying a full class load.

Many variations of systematic desensitization have been used by researchers in the school setting. Applications for dealing with test anxieties and school phobia will be reviewed here, followed by a discussion of implications for the use of systematic desensitization in the classroom.

Test Anxiety

Test anxiety can be defined as apprehension by the student, directly related to the situation of test taking, which prevents optimal performance.[66] Although volumes of research have been published on test anxiety among college students, relatively little has been done with younger subjects. Traditional systematic desensitization, in-vivo desensitization, and some combination of the two have been examined in the research literature.

Barabasz divided eighty seven fifth and sixth grade students into High Test Anxious and Low Test Anxious groups on the basis of galvanic skin responses (GSR).[5] Galvanic skin resistance is known to increase during relaxation.

The groups were exposed to systematic desensitization for five consecutive days which included relaxation training for two days followed by a test anxiety hierarchy which was introduced over the next three days. Subjects were asked to imagine themselves in fifteen situations ranging from a presumably low anxiety situation (e. g., "Picture yourself sitting in front of a fireplace on a cold winter's day") to a high anxiety situation for test-anxious subjects (e. g., "Picture yourself taking a difficult examination that determines whether you pass or fail.")

Results indicated that High Test Anxious subjects taught systematic desensitization exhibited significantly lower anxiety scores, as measured by galvanic skin resistance, than High Test Anxious controls. No significant difference was found between Low Test Anxious experimental and Low Test Anxious Control Groups. In other words, systematic desensitization, presented to both groups together, helped the high test-anxious students and did not impair the low test-anxious students. This finding is significant as related to implementation of systematic desensitization in the classroom, in that there is no indication that low test anxious students need be segregated from the treatment intervention. In another study Deffenbacher and Kemper treated high test-anxious eleven to thirteen year olds with a test anxiety hierarchy.[15] Results showed that those subjects who received treatment significantly improved their grade point average while control subjects showed no improvement.

Leal and his associates compared systematic desensitization to cognitive modification with thirty test-anxious high school students.[44] Anxiety level was initially determined by three self-report measures. Subjects were subsequently exposed to one of three conditions: (1) systematic desensitization, which consisted of deep muscle relaxation paired with presentation of imaginary anxiety provoking situations; (2) cognitive modification, where subjects learned to recognize their emotional arousal level, label inappropriate responses, and replace self-defeating thoughts with more realistic, positive ones; or (3) waiting list control, where subjects simply participated in pre and post testing under simulated stress conditions.

Results indicated that systematic desensitization was significantly more effective than cognitive modification or waiting list control on test performance, while cognitive modification was more effective on one of the self report measures. The authors of this study felt that the superiority of systematic desensitization on performance measures of test anxiety must be interpreted cautiously, however. Although the gain for the systematic desensitization group was the only statistically significant result, the "relative gain in terms of within-group variability" was greater for the cognitive modification group. Therefore, no strong conclusions could be drawn.

Little and Jackson studied thirty-four seventh and eighth grade students who had scored in the upper quartile on the Test Anxiety Scale for Children (TASC) and within the two middle quartiles of the General Anxiety Scale for Children (GASC).[48] These subjects were randomly assigned to one of five conditions: (1) relaxation training; (2) attentional training (which involved training subjects to focus absolute attention on tasks while working on them, filmed modeling of students overcoming their test anxiety, and intensive practice); (3) attentional training plus relaxation training; (4) placebo-expectancy, (which involved task practice without instructions to attend fully to the tasks); (5) no treatment control, (in which subjects were informed that the program was filled and they could obtain treatment at a later date). Although this study did not use traditional systematic desensitization procedures, desensitization was used in vivo through relaxation and alteration of ongoing cognitions during the actual test-taking event.

Results indicated a statistically significant decrease both in test anxiety and general anxiety for those subjects exposed to the combination of attentional training plus relaxation. None of the other conditions was effective in reducing anxiety. The authors hypothesized that the combination treatment was the only one which addressed both the emotionally (effective and physiological responses) and worry (cognitions) components of test anxiety and thus was the only successful intervention.

Andrews examined a combination of treatments as well.[1] In this study "underachieving anxious" children fifteen to eighteen years old with above-average IQ were randomly assigned to one of three conditions: (1) client centered counseling; (2) individual systematic desensitization plus time-in-therapy contingent on classroom attendance and completed homework; or (3) control group. A significant decrease in level of anxiety was demonstrated only in the desensitization group, as measured by self report measures. No groups showed an improvement in grade point average. Again, because the desensitization group also included operant contingencies, it is difficult to determine what factors results in decreased test anxiety.

Mann examined several treatments, including modeling, with test-anxious seventh and eighth graders.[51] Subjects were randomly assigned to one of the following groups: (1) imitation of modeled responses in which the therapist used systematic desensitization with another test-anxious subject; (2) observation of the model without imitation; (3) observation of the model during the presentation and visualization of the hierarchy without relaxation; and (4) control group. Both a reading test and an anxiety scale showed equivalent improvements in all three treatment groups immediately after treatment and one month later. Control subjects treated later replicated the results. It is surprising that such varied treatments yielded similar results.

Johnson and associates compared group desensitization to speech practice with students who had demonstrated speech anxiety on a test.[30] Both treatment groups showed a significant decrease in anxiety as measured by a speech anxiety questionnaire completed one week following treatment. This decrease was not evident in the control group. Results are difficult to interpret due to intervening variables. It is difficult to determine whether treatment or attention and encouragement from the therapist alone was responsible for improvement, since the control group had no contact with the therapist.

Over the past ten years, many dissertations have addressed the treatment of test anxiety through systematic desensitization (see: 20, 21, 22, 26, 27, 37, 40, 73, 80). One study[21] worked with nine to ten year olds; however, the majority dealt with slightly older subjects, mostly fifth grade through high school. Traditional systematic desensitization was used in every study. Dependent measures varied somewhat; however, most studies used both an anxiety scale and an aptitude test. Overall, for those studies that found systematic desensitization successful, statistically significant improvement was observed only on anxiety scales. No difference was seen in test performance of subjects treated with systematic desensitization.[22,73] Many times other treatments such as relaxation alone,[26] focusing instructions[27], or vicarious systematic desensitization[37] were as effective as systematic desensitization in relieving anxiety. Only three studies reported follow-up (see 21, 27, 51) and control groups were generally "no treatment" rather than "placebo" groups. These factors present some obvious obstacles to determining the effectiveness of systematic desensitization in the treatment of children's test anxiety.

Since most schools do not have enough psychologists available to routinely expose all test anxious students to desensitization procedures, Barabasz explored the feasibility of training classroom teachers to use systematic desensitization with their test-anxious students.[5]

Teachers of fifth, sixth, and seventh grade students attended a one hour seminar on test anxiety followed by training sessions in the desensitization of test anxiety given on four consecutive days immediately prior to the experimental period. Training included theoretical background, review and discussion of an audiotape of relaxation instructions, and role play utilizing relaxation instructions and procedures for facilitating visualization from the test anxiety hierarchy. The hierarchy consisted of twenty nine items ranging from 0—"Picture yourself at the beach in the sun just relaxing and the thought briefly crosses your mind that you will return to school in two whole months" to 29—"You read the test instructions and begin working through the test questions." Students participated in the desensitization program in their regular homeroom settings, taught by their homeroom teachers, for five consecutive days.

Results indicated that administration of a systematic desensitization program by trained classroom teachers resulted in a significant decrease in test anxiety, measured by galvanic skin response, for high test-anxious subjects as compared to controls. Similarly, low test-anxious subjects displayed a tendency toward lowered anxiety responses, although results for them were not statistically significant. Pre-post California Achievement Reading Comprehension subtest scores of high-anxious students who participated in the program also demonstrated significant improvement. No significant changes were found for subjects in other groups.

Several research design problems have plagued research on systematic desensitization for test anxiety in children. For example, few authors indicated exactly how test-anxious their subjects were. The average length of treatment in these studies was five sessions, which may be sufficient for very mildly anxious subjects but not for moderately to severely test anxious children. The dependent measures used in many of the studies were questionable. Validity of anxiety tests used was not discussed in any published study. Only one author, Barabasz, used physiological measures of anxiety.[5] A variety of instruments have been used in different studies to measure test performance, again with no explanation of why a particular instrument was chosen. Finally, very few studies did any follow-up and for those that did, follow-up was quite limited, generally no more than four to five weeks after treatment.

With the aforementioned difficulties, it is not an easy matter to come to solid conclusions concerning the effectiveness of systematic desensitization for test anxiety. However, some trends were evident in the research. Systematic desensitization does appear to be effective in reducing subjectively and objectively measured test anxiety levels in children. However, this reduction in test anxiety does not necessarily mean an improvement in actual academic test performance. This question needs to be addressed more carefully in future research. It is possible that many of the subjects employed were anxious in test situations but not so phobic that their performance deteriorated. Thus, the desensitization made them more comfortable in test situations, but no change in performance was possible. A study with more carefully selected students who were demonstrating underachievement due to test anxiety would be very interesting.

School Phobia

School phobia is a fairly common and a very serious problem. There are many factors which may contribute to a child's consistent absence from school. Not surprisingly, there are also many and varied psychological treatments for school phobia. Desensitization techniques which have been used to treat school phobia include systematic desensitization, in-vivo desensitization, and emotive imagery. Many times a combination of these approaches has beed used. Most research in this area is in the form of case studies.

The first reported case of systematic desensitization for treatment of school phobia was by Lazarus.[43] He noted that some children may have difficulty experiencing anxiety to imaginal stimuli and therefore must be presented with the actual feared object or situations to become desensitized. Following his suggestion, the majority of research in this area has used some form of in-vivo as opposed to traditional systematic desensitization techniques.

Miller treated a ten-year-old boy who had ceased attending school eight weeks prior, following criticism by his teacher in front of his peers.[55] The child also displayed a fear of separation from his mother, an inability to fall asleep at night, and nocturnal enuresis. Treatment included training in deep muscle relaxation for thirty minute sessions, once weekly. Relaxation responses were reinforced with both candy and verbal praise. Response hierarchies were developed for imagined separation from mother and school situations. The subject reported a fear of dying in the night as well, which was handled by telephone calls where the frightened child called the therapist who then encouraged the child to forget his fears and fall asleep. After six weeks, the phone calls ceased and the child reported no fear of dying. In addition, his enuresis gradually ceased. Following completion of desensitization to the imaginal scenes, the child agreed to gradually return to the classroom. He was told to use relaxation exercises in-vivo if he felt overwhelmed with anxiety. By the fifth week of school following reentry, the child was attending school on a full-time basis. Follow-up at three months and 18 months revealed no new problems and maintenance of behavior changes.

Phillips and Wolpe used a combination of desensitization procedures with a twelve-year-old boy who had previously been treated for two years with psychoanalysis and was described by his psychiatrist as the worst case of phobia he had ever seen.[63] These authors felt that the child's problem was more one of severe separation anxiety and obsessive compulsive disorder than school phobia. Therefore, treatment was addressed more to those symptoms. Standard desensitization utilizing imagery was used in conjunction with in-vivo desensitization. Imagined hierarchies included separation from parents, past traumatic events, waiting at home without his parents, and anticipation of danger for the father. The authors reported that this was an extremely slow and tedious process, the child sometimes requiring forty nine presentations to reach an anxiety level of zero. In the present case, the fact that the father was an alcoholic and the mother agoraphobic, resulted in the treatment spanning a two-year period of eighty-eight sessions, with two sessions per week.

During treatment, the child received points, which could be traded for rewards, for practicing relaxation multiple times per day. More points could be earned for relaxation during more anxiety provoking situations (e. g., relaxation when both parents were home = one point, relaxation when his father was traveling toward home and unreachable by phone = ten points). In-vivo practice occurred both in the biweekly therapy sessions and at home. Again, points could be earned as the child achieved the steps. An in-vivo school program was also instituted. The child returned to school, which was facilitated by gradual exposure, relaxation exercises, his mother's presence at school, and pleasant imagery (e. g., he imagined riding his mini-bike in a field). He was also required to phone his father daily from school and report that he was doing well and his father was to reinforce the statements with verbal praise.

Six months following initiation of treatment, the child was spending full days in school alone. At the end of the treatment no anxiety regarding school or separation from his parents was reported.

Vander Ploeg reported the case of a fourteen-year-old boy with school phobia and an excessive urge to urinate.[76] The author hypothesized that the following chain of events was operating: school stimuli →anxiety→urge to urinate→anxiety→stronger urge to urinate→avoid school. He chose to work directly with anxiety to school stimuli. The child was first taught muscle relaxation; next the therapist used repeated treatments involving thirty seconds of guided imagery describing an easy hour at school followed immediately by thirty seconds of discussions of the child sailing his boat (a very pleasurable activity for the child). The therapist reported that the child's anxiety subsided each time the competing responses occurred (e. g., talking about the sailboat). After fifteen session over five weeks, the patient displayed difficulty feeling anxiety with imagined school stimuli, and in-vivo desensitization was begun. The boy gradually increased his time at school and decreased anxiety while there by practicing the distracting stories and telling himself he could resist the urge to urinate. At one month and eighteen month follow-ups, no complaints were reported, and the child was attending school regularly.

Barabasz treated nineteen middle and high school students with systematic desensitization.[6] All of the students had been truant from school and "school phobia was considered to be a significant element of each subject's disorder." This study is unique in that it examined systematic desensitization in the treatment of more than one subject. However, it is questionable whether the students treated were actually school-phobics. Barabasz used two types of systematic desensitization: one group was exposed to traditional desensitization where hierarchy construction was carefully planned; the other group was exposed to a procedure in which a hierarchy was used but no special attention was given to its construction or presentation. Barabasz found, using physiological recordings of anxiety, that a carefully planned hierarchy was important for these subjects to achieve relief of anxiety.

The present authors have often clinically used a type of in-vivo desensitization with good success. In this procedure the child is taught to relax and go to school first thing in the morning to pick up homework assignments. He then goes home to work. After a few days of this, the child is required to stay at school for the first period of classes. After a few days he stays for the second class, then the third and so on until he is there for the whole day. Unfortunately, we have not had the opportunity to conduct research on this program.

It is interesting to note that virtually all of the reports on the treatment of school phobia by systematic desensitization are case reports. This is probably due to the fact that the more common treatment of school phobia involves putting the child back in school at once, which amounts to a type of flooding or implosive therapy. These approaches are generally very successful, making other approaches unnecessary except in extreme cases.

There are some problems with research methodology in case studies which should be mentioned. Case studies lack comparative data from treatment and control subjects. Since almost any intervention (or none at all) might seem to work for a given case, it is difficult to know whether the treatment would work for additional cases in the future. Also, it is generally not possible in such situations to determine what the effective elements of the treatment were because there was only one subject who received all of the treatments (and case studies generally employ multiple component treatment programs). On the other hand, case studies have a great deal to offer. They are very useful as pilot experiments in new areas of treatment or in the use of new techniques. Case studies also explore details about the subject and the treatment which might be lost in a group study. Further, there are increasingly sophisticated research designs and procedures for statistical analysis becoming available that reduce some of the problems noted above, making the case study a much more valuable tool.[36] In the present situation, the only conclusion to be drawn is that several case studies suggest that systematic desensitization may be a useful treatment for school phobia. However, much more research is needed.

Most of the research described in this chapter thus far has dealt with children aged ten and older. It would be of considerable interest to explore the use of these techniques with younger children to emperically determine at what age a child is cognitively sophisticated enough to use systematic desensitization effectively.

SYSTEMATIC DESENSITIZATION IN MEDICAL SETTINGS

In the last ten years published research on the use of traditional systematic desensitization with children in medical settings has been relatively scarce. However, numerous applications are possible, some of which will be reviewed here.

Systematic Desensitization in the Treatment of Medical Conditions

Systematic desensitization has been used as an anxiety reducing measure with children who have asthma and motion sickness. With these conditions, anxiety can exacerbate symptoms. Children probably do not develop asthma simply due to anxiety. However, increasing anxiety and fear, particularly during an asthma attack can result in increased severity of the attack even to the point of admission to an intensive care unit.

Some comparisons have been made between systematic desensitization and relaxation as an adjunctive treatment of asthma, finding the former to be slightly more effective.[18]

In another study, Miklich and associates compared systematic desensitization to no treatment with nineteen severe to moderately asthmatic children.[54] Following treatment there was a significant difference between treatment and no treatment groups' Forced Expiratory Volume (FEV). Additionally, at follow-up, the treatment group had reduced maintenance medications and appeared to be experiencing more stable symptoms. However, other measures, such as number of hospitalizations and subject reports, showed no difference between the two groups.

Saunders used systematic desensitization in the treatment of a thirteen-year-old male who had displayed symptoms of motion sickness (nausea, vomiting) since the age of six months.[71] An assumption was made that the boy had a physiological imbalance during infancy which had produced the motion sickness and that the onset of symptoms had gradually evoked anxiety which exacerbated or produced the symptoms he was now experiencing. Treatment involved relaxation training, in-vivo desensitization and systematic desensitization done concurrently. Hierarchy items included, such items as "the night before a ride across town with his parents" (minimally anxiety provoking) to "feeling slightly nauseous while riding in a car on a long trip" (maximally anxiety provoking). Treatment lasted eleven sessions over a four-month period. Improvement was almost immediate, with the patient reporting only one feeling of nausea and no vomiting throughout the treatment phase and a nineteen month follow-up. During this time, he took many car rides and medication was not used at any time.

Systematic Desensitization in Treatment of Fear of Medical Procedures and Settings

Desensitization has been used in the treatment of children's dental fears, however, little research has been published in this area. Treatment of children's dental fears is important not only because it eliminates any immediate problems, but also because it prevents future adult fearful dental behavior and neglect of dental health. Machen and Johnson, in a well-controlled study, obtained positive results with both desensitization and modeling groups.[50] Thirty-one children, three to five years old, who had never been to the dentist were assigned to control, desensitization, or modeling groups. Desensitization consisted of explanation and exposure to a hierarchy of dental situations. Modeling consisted of viewing an eleven minute videotape of a child demonstrating positive behavior during dental treatment and being verbally reinforced by the dentist. The modeling condition was used as a treatment because children naturally learn much of their behavior through imitation. Additionally, modeling has been repeatedly demonstrated to be effective in decreasing fear in adults and children. These researchers found that neither of the treatments affected children's behavior during the first dental visit (consisting of examination, prophylaxis and radiographs). However, children who received treatment did demonstrate significantly less negative behavior than controls at the second and third visits in which dental caries were treated. There was no significant difference between behavior of the two treatment groups.

Melamed and associates studied effectiveness of modeling alone on 16 black children, ages five to eleven years, with no previous dental visits.[52] Treatment was similar to Machen and Johnson's modeling condition;[50] however, a more comprehensive assessment including physiological measurement and maternal anxiety was completed. In addition, the control group viewed a film unrelated to the dental situation, making the two conditions more similar. No significant differences were found between modeling and control groups during prophylaxis or examination. However, during treatment of the carious tooth, the modeling group showed significantly lower disruptive behavior than the control group.

Follow-up was not addressed in any of the dental studies. Generalization of effect should be explored. Equally important to explore is similar treatment of children who initially demonstrate moderate to severe fear of the dental situation. Such children are likely to display increasingly more disruptive behaviors when in the dental office unless treatment interventions are implemented.

Wallick described desensitization with a two-year-old child who was extremeful fearful of physicians.[78] This was not traditional systematic desensitization in that no relaxation was used and a hierarchy was not constructed. However, the child and her therapist played out the feared situation with blocks and dolls followed by one-month, one-year and two-year follow-ups. At termination of therapy and all follow-ups, the child displayed no fear of medical settings.

Melamed and Siegel, in another well controlled study, investigated effects of modeling on reduction of anxiety in children facing hospitalization and surgery.[53] They studied sixty children, ages four to twelve, who had no prior history of hospitalizations and were scheduled for either tonsillectomies, urinary-genital tract surgery, or hernia surgery. Length of hospital stay for these children ranged from two to three days. Anxiety was measured by parental reports, physiological measures, observer ratings and self-reports. Children were assigned to either control or modeling groups. One hour prior to admission, children in the modeling condition group observed a sixteen minute film of a seven-year-old white male hospitalized for a hernia operation. It depicted the various events most children encounter from admission to discharge. Children in the control group viewed a film of similar length but unrelated in content to hospitalization. Both children later received preoperative instruction from the hospital staff, a standard procedure at the hospital.

Results indicated that experimental subjects who had observed the modeling film showed fewer anxiety-related behaviors, lower sweat gland activity, and fewer self-reported medical concerns than control subjects at preoperative and postoperative assessments. A four-week post hospital examination demonstrated generalization as group differences on all measures of anxiety were maintained.

Yule reported a case of a sixteen-year-old boy with a long history of phobia to the sight or mention of blood.[85] The patient was taught to use relaxation and a hierarchy of blood related situations was developed. In-vivo desensitization was used as well. The boy fainted during the third session as his blood was drawn. However, desensitization was continued and the procedure was later repeated, with no negative effects. Treatment lasted five sessions. Follow-up at two and a half months and again at five years revealed no problems.

Jay and associates completed a limited N design study examining effects of a package of behavioral techniques on coping behavior in children receiving bone marrow aspirations and lumbar puncture.[29] Included in the package was a form of desensitization in which the child practiced the medical procedures, using the actual medical instruments on a doll. This was followed by pretend practice on the therapist and the therapist's pretending to practice the procedure on the child. Modeling was obviously a part of this technique. As the child was pretending to receive the procedure and during the actual procedure, he was instructed to breathe deeply, blow himself up like a tire and breathe out with a hissing sound. Emotive imagery was also encouraged. Initial results using these techniques, with children who are seen as poor copers, have been promising. Significant and often drastic reductions in screaming, flailing, and so forth have been observed in the children. These researchers are currently involved in studying these behavior techniques more fully with a larger subject group.

Implications for Further Research

As can be seen from these suggestive reports, there is much opportunity for the use of systematic desensitization in medical settings. Recent research, however, has focused more on modeling, distraction, and cognitive strategies. Nevertheless, systematic desensitization can be useful, particularly with those children who demonstrate severe fears. There are problems with the research in this area, as in others. Case studies, which represent almost half of the research in the area, have the built-in methodological flaws discussed earlier. Additionally, it is difficult to measure behavioral distress in pediatric patients. Katz, Kellerman, and Siegel[33] as well as Elliott[16] have developed a behavior rating scale completed by observers during painful medical procedures. Such scales, in addition to physiological measures of anxiety, will aid in determining children's distress level and thus the impact of treatments such as systematic desensitization. Finally, the nature of the problems and professional ethics often require research designs that are fully justified on humane grounds, but which violate statistical assumptions and confound results.

SYSTEMATIC DESENSITIZATION IN THE TREATMENT OF VARIOUS OTHER FEARS

Many times parents desensitize their children to a feared object or situation. For example, upon going to the beach for the first time, some children are afraid of the water. Parents may help the child alleviate fear of the water by encouraging the child to play near the water for awhile, followed by putting a foot in the water, wading in the water to the ankles, then knees and thighs, and finally swimming. Another example is fear of the dark which many children experience. Parents may allow their child to sleep with a light on in the room for several nights, followed by turning out the light in the room but leaving one on in an adjacent room with the door open, then on successive nights closing the door progressively more, and finally, when the fear has been eliminated, encouraging sleeping with the light off and the door closed.

In this section various childhood fears will be discussed. However, most of these fears are serious enough to warrant clinical intervention. Included will be elective mutism, fear of the dark and nightmares, water, snakes, loud noises, heights, shyness/withdrawal and multiple phobias.

Treatment of Elective Mutism

Elective mutism refers to a child's refusal to speak in absence of any organic factors which would render him unable to speak. The electively mute child almost always displays a normal pattern of speech development and speaks to some people, usually those in his immediate family, but not to others. The present authors recently treated a child who talked to his toys and pets when alone but would not speak if he was aware that another person was within hearing range. Often, mutism results from abuse or following a significant traumatic experience.

Croghan and Crowen described two different groups of elective mutes: one for whom mutism is a manipulative attempt to gain attention or some other reward, and one for whom speaking in front of others has become an extremely anxiety provoking event.[12] They suggest that treatment should differ, depending on which group the child fits into. Their suggestion does merit attention, and perhaps would lead to successful results more quickly. However, no other work published in the last ten years made such a distinction in type of elective mutism. Children who are electively mute are frequently not brought to the attention of professionals until they enter school and refuse to participate in verbal classroom activities. Many of these children are bilingual.[12]

Scott used desensitization with a seven-year-old girl who had never spoken outside her immediate family.[72] Since the child would speak into a tape recorder, the therapist spend eight trials having the child speak into it, with the therapist returning and listening to the tape recording while the child remained present. In trials nine to nineteen, the therapist gradually left the door between her and the child open (the therapist always being out of sight). Trials twenty to thirty four consisted of the therapist moving into view and towards the child until she was directly opposite her, followed by trials thirty five to forty where the child (speaking into a microphone) responded to the therapist's taped questions. From trial forty on, the child had to respond directly to the therapist. This was followed by a question and answer game of "I Spy." The patient first answered the questions (which were in a "yes" or "no" format) and then was expected to ask them. Once this game was played openly with the therapist, generalization was begun, introducing other adults into the game, first in the presence of the therapist, and later with the child alone. Finally, the child's response was generalized to the classroom, in the presence of seven children and the teacher. The entire process lasted four weeks.

A three-month follow-up revealed that the patient was verbally interacting more at home in the presence of relatives and strangers. At school she was making requests of the teacher and answering questions in front of the entire class. Speech continued to be limited with children in her class, although it had improved. The author felt that this child would probably always remain shy, as was her entire family. Although desensitization was apparently the treatment variable which resulted in the child's speech, the author did note that the child's positive and close relationship with the therapist added to therapeutic success. The relationship was developed in therapy sessions prior to the implementation of desensitization.

Croghan and Craven reported using systematic desensitization successfully with an eight-year-old girl who spoke only to her step-father, mother, and younger brother.[16] She was taught relaxation techniques and she herself prepared, in writing, a hierarchy of anxiety provoking speech situations. Lowest on the hierarchy was "talking to two teachers, without students present," while highest was "talking in front of everyone, explaining math on the board in front of the class." Treatment lasted for eleven sessions over a two-month period. Homework imagery of the hierarchy was given in addition to session practice.

Improvement was immediate and continued unabated. The patient spoke to all teachers and students in the regular classroom. Follow-up one year later revealed treatment gains were maintained in spite of family crises. Results this striking, achieved within such a short period of time, are notable, especially since this child had been previously treated over a four-year period with various interventions, primarily behavioral, without success. The authors noted that success may have been even more rapid had they used stimulus fading (e. g., initially allowing family members the patient spoke with into the treatment and gradually having them present for shorter and shorter periods of time until they were eventually absent).

Rosbury used in-vivo desensitization with an eleven-year-old girl who had been mute for six years.[67] For eight months preceding implementation of desensitization, two therapeutic treatments were used unsuccessfully: (1) Play therapy and (2) behavior therapy in which language imitation was positively reinforced. This child spoke to her immediate family, but would decrease her verbal behavior as her proximity to other people increased. Treatment consisted of a hierarchy where she was to read sentences describing enjoyable activities printed on cards, in a "normal" tone of voice for three consecutive days to her father. As a reward for reading all the cards, she was allowed to participate in one of the activities of her choice, which she had read.

Movement up the hierarchy involved speaking, with the father present, in closer proximity to the school and other people and finally to others outside the family in the absence of her father. The hierarchy consisted of fifteen steps and treatment lasted 140 sessions (one per day).

Treatment was successful, although with each new step up the hierarchy, the child's voice decreased in volume and then increased over successive days. In addition, unexpected intrusions (school bus, other children, adults) inhibited her speech until the final stages of the program. Finally, near the end of treatment, the child spontaneously generalized her speech response to other adults, and the other children. The authors hypothesized that improvement might have been even more rapid had there been more than one reward given to the child daily. Long term follow-up was not possible, because the child was burned severely and had to be hospitalized for two months.

Lowenstein treated twenty one electively mute children ages three to eight with in-vivo desensitization.[49] Unfortunately, there was no control group and treatment varied with each child. Treatment ranged from two to twenty one weekly sessions, each lasting forty five minutes and consisted of a stimulus fading procedure whereby: (1) the child first spoke to a "catalyst" (someone the child had a close relationship with and spoke freely to) in the presence of a psychologist; (2) the child then transferred this by speaking to the psychologist in the presence of the "catalyst"; (3) this was followed by the psychologist speaking to the child as the "catalyst" gradually removed herself from the room; and (4) the psychologist became the "catalyst," thus relating to other people the words the child spoke to him.

With this treatment, three children continued to be mute, seven had "some speech" and eleven were "very much improved." A seven-year follow-up showed two children with no speech, six with "some speech" and thirteen with "very much improved to normal speech." The author did not operationally define what "some speech" meant in terms of number of verbalizations or to whom. This author noted, as have others, that he felt the relationship with the therapist was an important variable. Finally, he pointed out that at least half of the children in the study had failed to re-learn speech using "psychotherapy" previous to desensitization.

Treatment of Fear of the Dark and Nightmares

Fear of the dark and nightmares are common in children. Parents tend to accept such fears as a stage in the child's development which will be outgrown. However, occasionally these fears intensify and linger, sometimes for years. A child's extreme fear of the dark can result in family tension and conflict. For these reasons, fear of the dark is a significant problem for which effective treatment is often sought. Several studies will be reviewed here, from those examining normal to extreme fears. All use some variation of traditional systematic desensitization techniques.

Cavior and Dentsch used desensitization with a sixteen year old inmate of a state correctional facility for juvenile offenders.[11] The patient had a recurrent dream (approximately once per week) in which he saw his father killing his mother. He would awaken in a highly anxious and fearful state and could not resume sleeping. Treatment consisted of a standard relaxation procedure used with a hierarchy of twelve steps. The subject was asked to go through the relaxation sequence only once at the beginning of the session, and later in the session, on becoming anxious, the therapist would instruct him that he was still very relaxed. This differs from standard procedure. The patient was told to practice desensitization twice daily. After three sessions, the patient reported that the dream had recurred but he handled it, and was able to fall asleep again. Therapy was terminated. Follow-up interviews at one, two, and six months revealed that the boy was still experiencing the dreams, but without the associated anxiety. The author noted that this was an inexpensive, efficient, effective technique which would be particularly beneficial in institutional settings, where nightmares are a frequent complaint.

Leitenberg and Callahan studied fourteen mild to moderately fearful children, ages four to six.[45] All parents of subjects felt their child's fear of the dark was a minor problem which they would outgrow with age. Children were either assigned to an experimental or control group. Experimental subjects received treatment which consisted of: (1) gradual and repeated practice in remaining in a darkened room alone; (2) reinforcement (choice of a "prize") of any gains in time spent in the room; (3) feedback of progress through use of a visual "thermometer"; and (4) instructions designed to evoke expectations of gradual success. Children in the control group experienced only pre- and posttreatment evaluations where they were asked to remain in the darkened room until they became afraid, at which time they could leave the room. Children who received treatment improved dramatically and significantly in their ability to remain in the dark. Control group children showed no such improvement.

Kelley studied forty pre-schoolers with mild to moderate fear of darkness.[38] Subjects were placed in either (1) no treatment control, (2) play placebo, (3) play desensitization, (4) play desensitization with non-contingent reinforcement, or (5) play desensitization with contingent reinforcement. No relaxation was used in this study. The four treatment groups received three one-half hour therapy sessions, over a period of three weeks. A fifteen-step hierarchy was used with desensitization groups. Following treatment, none of the groups showed significant decreases in fear of darkness on either self-report or behavioral measures. However, there was a significant effect as a result of instruction. Those subjects who were told to remain longer in the dark room demonstrated increased endurance for the dark. For some, this was a dramatic increase. Behavioral and self-report measures both showed improvement in these subjects. This study appears to demonstrate that young children who experience moderate fear of the dark may respond better to direct instruction from adults to remain in the dark than they would to a systematic, detailed therapy program. Such findings may also explain the results of Leitenberg and Callahan's study.[45] Such instruction does provide maximal contact with the feared stimulus and finally extinction of the feared response. However, these results probably cannot be generalized to other fears or more extreme fear of the dark.

Kanfer, Karoly, and Newman, in a well controlled investigation, studied the effects of training children to use verbal responses to increase tolerance to darkness.[32] Three types of mediating responses were used with forty-five subjects, five to six years old. Again, children with severe fears of the dark were eliminated from the study. Group one, the competence group, was taught to use sentences emphasizing the child's active control (e. g., "when you are in the dark you know you can turn on the light when you feel like it"). Another group, the stimulus group, was taught to use sentences focusing on reducing the aversive components of the darkened room (e. g., "the dark is the best place to go to sleep and have good dreams"). Finally, the control group was taught to use neutral sentences (e. g., "Mary took a lamb to school one morning"). Children were placed in a darkened room and their duration of time spent in the room as well as the degree of illumination they chose for the room was measured. Results showed that differential training significantly influenced both duration in the darkened room and intensity choice. The competence group demonstrated generally superior coping than did either the stimulus or control groups. The authors speculated about different reasons for the superiority of the competence group. They concluded that what is clear from these findings is that, "positive self-descriptions involving active coping with a stressful situation were more effective in enhancing tolerance than the rehearsal of statements focusing on the positive elements of the dark."

Graziano and Mooney studied thirty-three families of children ages six to twelve with severe nighttime fears of long duration (two years or more).[25] The procedure used was very different from traditional systematic desensitization. Children were told to (1) lie down and relax their muscles (no systematic progressive muscle relaxation was used), (2) imagine a pleasant scene of their choosing, and (3) say their "special" words (e. g., "I am brave and I can take care of myself when I am in the dark"). They were to practice these exercises each evening with their parents. Bravery tokens could be earned by children, depending on how successfully they practiced.

After three weeks of practice, with parents as therapists, children's fear in the treatment group was significantly less than control children's on parents' measures of frequency, duration of event, family disruption, and seriousness. Effects did not generalize to other fears or to overall social adjustment, meaning treatment was very specific to the fear. Two, six and twelve month follow-ups showed that children in the treatment group maintained or continued to increase the improvement they had shown at post treatment assessment (two children relapsed at six months, but then had improved at twelve months). The control group was provided with the same treatment package after posttreatment assessment. They achieved success rates similar to the original treatment group. Thus, this was a highly effective and efficient treatment. It resulted not only in improvement for the children, but for the families, who had previously experienced long standing problems.

Jackson and King desensitized a five-and-one-half-year-old boy to extreme fear of the dark using emotive imagery.[28] A nineteen-step hierarchy was used and the boy was asked to imagine he was Batman's special agent. He was given a "torch" (a flashlight) which he could turn on for one minute should he be afraid. The hierarchy was spread over four sessions. Following treatment, the child was free of fear episodes and slept through the night. Follow-up at one, two, three, fifteen and eighteen months revealed that treatment gains were maintained.

Treatment of Water Fear

Three studies from research published in the past ten years were found on fear of water. Only one study used children who were extremely fearful and none used relaxation training in their treatment package.

Pomerantz and associates used in-vivo desensitization to treat a four-year-old's water phobia.[65] This child would scream and run about uncontrollably when he heard bath water. The desensitization procedure was performed by the mother, who was trained and supervised by a paraprofessional. Thirty-minute sessions were performed in the child's bathroom. The hierarchy steps ranged from the child, fully clothed and playing with a toy on the bathroom floor to undressing the child as the tub was filling with water, and putting him in the tub with the toys in it. (Before entering the bathroom the child was rewarded with a soft drink). If any anxiety was observed (whimpering, clinging to mother, crying), the session was terminated. After eleven treatment days, the child's fear of water had been eliminated. Follow-up at two and six months showed maintenance of treatment gains.

Ultee, Griffinson and Schellekens studied twenty-four children, ages five to ten, whose parents or swimming teachers described as having fear of water.[74] Children were divided into one of three groups: (1) four sessions of imagery desensitization followed by four sessions of in-vivo desensitization; (2) eight sessions of in-vivo desensitization only; (3) no treatment control. Both experimental groups used hierachies. After four sessions, the in-vivo only group showed significantly greater improvement than either of the other groups. There was no significant difference between the imagery/in-vivo group and the control group. After eight sessions, the in-vivo only group was still significantly superior to the control group, but not the imagery/in-vivo group (whose last four sessions had consisted of in-vivo desensitization). Results indicated that in-vivo desensitization is superior overall. It may be that subjects did not profit from imagery desensitization because of their mild to moderate fear level and/or level of cognitive development. Extremely fearful children in some cases might have difficulty handling the in-vivo situation immediately, making it necessary to first use imagery.

Imagery desensitization is used primarily for convenience (it is easier to work with words and images in the office than to go out into the community to find proper exposure) and for stimuli that are too threatening for the person to confront in real life, or that do not occur often enough to permit treatment to proceed without delay. However, even when imagery desensitization is used, the process is not complete until the patient confronts the stimulus in real life. As was mentioned earlier, the patient is often given homework assignments to do the things that previously were anxiety provoking. Thus, in-vivo desensitization is crucial in either case.

Lewis, in a very well designed study, examined the effect of modeling, in-vivo desensitization, and a combination of the two on water fear in forty male children ages five to twelve.[16] A behavior rating scale was used at pre-, post-treatment, and follow-up to measure water avoidance behaviors. Children in the modeling group viewed an eight minute film of three black males, ages seven, ten, and eleven performing swimming activities. A coping strategy was used whereby the models appeared to be somewhat frightened initially, but became progressively more confident. Each child in the in-vivo group spent ten minutes in the pool with an adult who encouraged him to attempt a hierarchy of tasks. Praise was given for all activities attempted and the adult physically assisted each child if necessary. The combination group viewed the film, immediately followed by the activities experienced by the in-vivo group. Allowances were made to eliminate any effects that experimenter contact or film viewing alone might have on the subjects. Results demonstrated that the combination of modeling and in-vivo desensitization was the most effective in reducing water avoidance behaviors. All treatment groups demonstrated improvement over the control group. However, modeling alone was the least effective treatment. Follow-up was done to assess stability of effects. Only twenty-five subjects were available to be evaluated. However, these children, who had received a brief period of swimming instruction, demonstrated not only maintenance of the original behavioral changes, but additional improvement in their water fear and in swimming abilities. The author suggested that other studies, which have demonstrated modeling to be a highly successful form of treatment, may actually have utilized more of a combination approach than modeling alone. It may be that the in-vivo participation factor, rather than viewing of the model, is the more important element in reducing children's fears.

Treatment of Snake Fear

Many times when people think of phobias, they immediately think of fear of snakes. Fear of snakes is common in both adults and children. Fortunately, most people do not encounter snakes on a regular basis.

Murphy and Bootzion examined effectiveness of active versus passive contact desensitization on snake fear of seventy-five children in first through third grade.[58] Contact desensitization employs modeling, graduated exposure to and interaction with the feared object, and physical assistance from the therapist in performing the feared behavior. Children were assigned to either active participation (where the child performed each of the feared steps immediately after the model performed them), passive participation (where the child remained stationary as the therapist approached him with the snake and molded the snake's body so it touched the child's hands), or no treatment control group. Results showed that both treatment procedures were significantly more effective in eliminating fear of snakes as compared to the control group. Active participation was not superior to passive participation. The authors concluded that in-vivo desensitization is such a powerful and effective technique that the type of subject participation is irrelevant.

Kornhaber and Schroeder studied effects of different types of models on forty second and third grade girls who demonstrated behavioral fear of snakes.[39] Subjects were assigned to one of five groups: (1) fearless adult modeling (models appeared unafraid and showed no reluctance in performing the task); (2) fearful adult modeling (adult models expressed apprehension and reluctance in performing the task); (3) fearless child modeling (fearless children performing the tasks); (4) fearful child modeling (apprehensive child models); and (5) no treatment control. Results indicated that level of fear expressed by the model was unimportant but model similarity in terms of age was important. Modeling by young girls was more effective in diminishing avoidance behavior in elementary-school-aged girls.

Treatment of Fear of Loud Noises, Heights, and Shyness/Withdrawal

Several studies have been published in recent years which examined effects of desensitization and/or modeling on various other fears including fear of loud noises, fear of heights, and shyness/withdrawal in children.

Wish, Hasazi and Jurgela used a procedure they called automated direct deconditioning with an eleven-year-old boy who feared loud noises.[81] Treatment consisted of relaxation in a darkened room in the boy's home followed by "listening to a tape recording in which feared sounds were systematically superimposed upon selections of his favorite music." The boy's parents reinforced his participation. After eight days (twenty four sessions) the child no longer displayed any fear of noises.

Croghan and Musante treated a seven-year-old boy with a fear of skyscrapers.[13] In-vivo desensitization was combined with some playing in the presence of the feared object. Following six sessions, the child displayed little fear of tall buildings. Three months, and again one year later, the child maintained therapeutic gains.

Three studies have examined modeling used with direct shaping procedures in treatment of shyness in children. In shaping procedures, the child receives some type of reward (e.g., praise, attention, tokens) for approximating the desired behavior, which in this case was interaction with others. Both O'Connor[64] and Walker and Hops[77] found that shaping was effective. In the O'Connor study, shaping was as effective as modeling. Evers and Schwartz found that shaping did not add to success of the modeling procedure.[19]

Treatment of Multiple Phobias

Some children exhibit fear of more than one object or situation. These children often have extreme fears which severely limit their everyday functioning. Two case studies will be discussed here, one involving a more traditional systematic desensitization approach and the other an adaptation.

Van Hasselt and associates treated an eleven-year-old whose primary fears were blood, heights, and test taking.[75] Responses on motoric, cognitive, and physiological measures were recorded, before, during, and after treatment. Treatment included traditional relaxation training, practiced twice daily, and hierarchies consisting of twelve to fifteen steps for each feared stimulus. Hierarchies were completed in four to six sessions each. Primary focus was maintained on one hierarchy at a time. Results showed impressive changes on motoric (e.g., ladder climb for height) and cognitive (self-report) measure of fear. Physiological functioning (heart rate and pulse volume) showed improvement as well, though not as dramatic. One, four, and six month follow-ups showed maintenance of most of the gains. As was hoped, treatment effects generalized to situations outside the treatment sessions.

Bornstein and Knapp treated a twelve-year-old boy who had fears of separation, travel, and illness.[9] They used Goldfried's adaptation of systematic desensitization. Goldfried views systematic desensitization as an active, cognitive approach to anxiety reduction.[23] He, therefore, stresses that patients maintain the stressful image and cope with it while relaxing, rather than eliminating the fearful image upon experiencing anxiety. Goldfried adds that hierarchies can include diverse situations, rather than systematically dealing only with the feared object. He strongly favors in-vivo desensitization.

Treatment for this patient involved construction of three separate hierarchies, ranging from ten to twenty-five items administered randomly. Two treatment sessions (one per week) were required to complete each hierarchy to the point of the patient's reporting no anxiety as he "coped" with the image. Results showed the treatment package to be highly effective. Number of fear related verbalizations for all fears significantly decreased. One year later, fearful verbalizations had decreased even more. Fear Survey Scores showed a similar substantial decrease, maintained at follow-up. Behaviorally, the patient showed much improvement, attending school regularly, interacting appropriately with peers, and engaging in extracurricular activities. Relaxation alone did not result in behavioral change.

From the discussion in this chapter it can be seen that systematic desensitization has been used successfully with children displaying a variety of fears. Adaptations are sometimes necessary to deal with the fact that the child's attention span or level of cognitive ability are not adequate for reliance on traditional imagery based desensitization. However, in-vivo desensitization appears to work quite effectively. Modeling also appears to add significantly to the treatment process.

REFERENCES

1. Andrews, W. R., Behavioral and client-centered counseling of high school underachievers. *Journal of Counseling Psychology,* 1971, 18: 93–96.
2. American Psychiatric Association, Diagnostic and statistical manual of mental disorders (3rd Ed.).
3. Baldwin, A. L., *Theories of child development.* New York: John Wiley & Sons, 1968.
4. Bandura, A., Self-efficacy: toward a unifying theory of behavioral change. *Psychological Review,* 1977, 84: 191–215.
5. Barabasz, A. F., Group desensitization of test anxiety in elementary school. *Journal of Psychology,* 1973, 83, 2: 295–301.
6. Barabasz, A. F., Classroom teachers as paraprofessional therapists in group systematic desensitization of test anxiety. *Psychiatry,* 1975, 38, 4: 388–392.
7. Beck, A. T., *Cognitive therapy and the emotional disorders.* New York: International Universities Press, 1976.
8. Birn, M., & T. Wilson, Treatment of phobic disorders using cognitive and exposure methods: a self-efficacy analysis. *Journal of Consulting and Clinical Psychology,* 1981, 49: 886–899.
9. Bornstein, P. H. & M. Knapp, Self-control desensitization with a multiphobic boy: a multiple baseline design. *Journal of Behavior Therapy and Experimental Psychiatry,* 1981, 12, 3: 281–285.
10. Bruner, J., Image and symbol in development of magnitude and order. In J. F. Rosenblitz & W. Allinsmith (Eds), *The causes of behavior: Readings in Child Development and Educational Psychology.* Boston: Allyn & Bacon, Inc., 1969.

11. Cavior, N. & A. M. Deutsch, Systematic desensitization to reduce dream-induced anxiety. *Journal of Nervous and Mental Disease,* 1975, 161, 6: 433–435.
12. Croghan, L. M. & R. Craven, Elective mutism: learning from the analysis of a successful case history. *Journal of Pediatric Psychology,* 1982, 7, 1: 85–93.
13. Croghan, L. M. & G. J. Musante, The elimination of a boy's high-building phobia by in-vivo desensitization and game playing. *Journal of Behavior Therapy and Experimental Psychology,* 1975, 6, 1: 87–88.
14. Davison, G. C. & G. T. Wilson, Processes of fear-reduction in systematic desensitization: cognitive and social reinforcement factors in humans. *Behavior Therapy,* 1973, 4: 1–21.
15. Deffenbacher, J. L. & C. Kemper, Counseling test anxious sixth graders. *Elementary School Guidance and Counseling,* 1974, 9: 22–29.
16. Elliott, C. H. & M. Ozolins, Use of imagery and imagination in treatment of children. In C. E. Walker & M. Roberts (Eds.), *Handbook of child clinical psychology.* New York: John Wiley & Sons. In press.
17. Ellis, A., *Reason and emotion in psychotherapy.* New York: Lyle Stuart, 1962.
18. Erskine-Milliss, J. & M. Schonell, Relaxation therapy in asthma: a critical review. *Psychosomatic Medicine,* 1981, 43: 365–372.
19. Evers, W. L. & J. C. Schwartz, Modifying social withdrawal in preschoolers: the effects of filmed modeling and teacher praise. *Journal of Abnormal Child Psychiatry,* 1973, 1: 248–256.
20. Fitzsimmons, G. W., Group desensitization of test anxiety: the contribution of therapeutic homework assignments, *Dissertation Abstracts International,* 1975, 35, 9-A: 5922–5923.
21. Freedenberg, R. A., Effects of systematic desensitization and attention training on anxiety and performance of nine and ten year old children. *Dissertation Abstracts International,* 1975, 35, 9-B: p. 4649.
22. Gavalas, N., Group systematic desensitization with test anxious ninth grade students of differing locus of control orientations. *Dissertation Abstracts International,* 1977, 38, 1-A: p. 171.
23. Goldfried, M. R. & G. C. Davison, *Clinical behavior therapy.* New York: Holt, Rinehart and Winston, 1976.
24. Graziano, A. M., I. S. DeGiovanni & K. A. Garcia, Behavioral treatment of children's fears: a review. *Psychological Bulletin,* 1979, 86, 4: 804–830.
25. Graziano, A. M. & K. L. Mooney, Family self-control instruction for children's nightime fear reduction. *Journal of Consulting and Clinical Psychology,* 1980, 48, 2: 206–213.
26. Haskins, D. L., Desensitization of test anxiety in junior high school students. *Dissertation Abstracts International,* 1973, 33, 12-B: p. 6079.
27. Hyman, J. R., Systematic desensitization of mathematics anxiety in high school students: the role of mediating responses, imagery, emotionality and expectancy. *Dissertation Abstracts International,* 1974, 34, 11-B: 5680–5681.

28. Jackson, H. J. & N. J. King, The emotive imagery treatment of a child trauma-induced phobia. *Journal of Behavior Therapy and Experimental Psychiatry*, 1981, 12, 4: 325–328.
29. Jay, S. M., et al., Reduction of distress in pediatric cancer patients undergoing painful medical procedures using behavior therapy techniques. Unpublished manuscript, Oklahoma University, 1982.
30. Johnson, T., et al., Systematic desensitization and assertive training in the treatment of speech anxiety in middle-school students. *Psychology in the School*, 1971, 8: 263–267.
31. Jones, M. C., The elimination of children's fears. *Journal of Experimental Psychology*, 1924, 7: 382–390.
32. Kanfer, F. H., P. Karoly & A. Newman, Reduction of children's fears of the dark by competence-related and situational threat-related verbal case. *Journal of Consulting and Clinical Psychology*, 1975, 43: 251–258.
33. Katz, E. R., J. Kellerman & S. E. Siefel, Behavioral distress in children with cancer undergoing medical procedures: Developmental considerations. *Journal of Consulting and Clinical Psychology*, 1980, 48, 3: 356–365.
34. Kazdin, A. E., Advances in child behavior therapy: applications and Implications. *American Psychologist*, 1979, 34: 981–987.
35. Kazdin, A. E. & L. A. Wilcoxon, Systematic desensitization and nonspecific treatment effects: a methodological evaluation. *Psychological Bulletin*, 1976, 83: 729–758.
36. Kazdin, A. E., *Research design in clinical psychology*. New York: Harper & Row, 1980.
37. Keller, A. H., Vicarious versus imaginal stimuli in group systematic desensitization of test anxiety. *Dissertation Abstracts International*, 1975, 36, 6-A: p. 3515.
38. Kelley, C. K., Play desensitization of fear and darkness in preschool children. *Behavior Research and Therapy*, 1976, 14, 1: 79–81.
39. Kornhaber, R. C. & H. E. Schroeder, Importance of model similarity on extinction of avoidance behavior in children. *Journal of Consulting and Clinical Psychology*, 1975, 43: 601–607.
40. Lautin, D. J., The effects of systematic desensitization on test anxiety, general anxiety and attitude toward school among fifth grade pupils, *Dissertation Abstracts International*, 1973, 34, 4-A: 1619–1620.
41. Lazarus, A. A., *In the mind's eye*. New York: Rawson Associates, 1977.
42. Lazarus, A. A. & A. Abramovitz, The use of emotive therapy in the treatment of children's phobias. *Journal of Mental Science*, 1962, 108: 191–195.
43. Lazarus, A. A., The elimination of children's phobias by deconditioning. In H. J. Eylenck (Ed.), *Behavior Therapy in the Neuroses*. New York: Pergammon Press, 1960.
44. Leal, L. L., et al., Cognitive modification and systematic desensitization with test anxious high school students. *Journal of Counseling Psychology*, 1981, 28, 6: 525–528.

45. Leitenberg, H. & E. J. Callahan, Reinforced practice and reduction of different kinds of fears in adults and children. *Behavior Research and Therapy,* 1973, 11: 19–30.
46. Lewis, J., A comparison of behavior therapy techniques in the reduction of fearful avoidance behavior. *Behavior Therapy,* 1974: 648–655.
47. Lick, J. & R. Bootzin, Expectancy factors in the treatment of fear: methodological and theoretical issues. *Psychological Bulletin,* 1975, 82: 917–931.
48. Little, S. & B. Jackson, The treatment of test anxiety through attentional and relaxation training. *Psychotherapy: Theory, Research and Practice,* 1974, 11, 2: 175–178.
49. Lowenstein, L. F., The result of twenty-one elective mute cases. *Acta Paedopsychiatrica,* 1979, 45, 1: 17–23.
50. Machen, J. B. & R. Johnson, Desensitization, model learning, and the dental behavior of children. *Journal of Dental Research,* 1974, 53: 83–87.
51. Mann, J., Vicarious desensitization of test anxiety through observation of videotaped treatment. *Journal of Counseling Psychology,* 1972, 19: 1–7.
52. Melamed, B. G., et al., Reduction of fear-related dental management problems using filmed modeling. *Journal of the American Dental Association,* 1975, 90: 822–826.
53. Melamed, B. G. & L. Siegel, Reduction of anxiety in children facing hospitalization and surgery by use of filmed modeling. *Journal of Consulting and Clinical Psychology,* 1975, 43: 511–521.
54. Miklich, D. R., et al., The clinical utility of behavior therapy as an adjunctive treatment for asthma. *The Journal of Allergy and Clinical Immunology,* 1977, 60: 285–294.
55. Miller, P. M., The use of visual imagery and muscle relaxation in the counter-conditioning of a phobic child: a case study. *Journal of Nervous and Mental Disease,* 1972, 154, 6: 457–460.
56. Miller, L. C., et al., Factor structure of childhood fears. *Journal of Consulting and Clinical Psychology,* 1972, 39: 264–268.
57. Mowrer, O. H., A stimulus-response analysis of anxiety and its role as a reinforcing agent. *Psychological Review,* 1939, 46: 553–565.
58. Murphy, C. M. & R. R. Bootzin, Active and passive participation in the contact desensitization of snake fear in children. *Behavior Therapy,* 1973, 4, 2: 203–211.
59. Mussen, P. H., J. J. Conger & J. Kagan, *Child development and personality,* (4th edition). New York: Harper and Row, 1974.
60. O'Connor, R. D., Relative efficacy of modeling, shaping, and the combined procedures for modification of social withdrawal. *Journal of Abnormal Psychology,* 1972, 79: 327–334.
61. Paul, G. L., Outcome of systematic desensitization, I: background procedures, and controlled reports of individual treatment. In C. M. Franks, (Ed.), *Behavior Therapy: Appraisal and Status.* New York: McGraw-Hill, 1969.

62. ———, Outcome of systematic desensitization, II: controlled investigations of individual treatment, technique variation, and current status. In C. M. Franks, (Ed.) *Behavior Therapy: Appraisal and Status.* New York: McGraw-Hill, 1969.
63. Phillips, D. & J. Wolpe, Multiple behavior techniques in severe separation anxiety of a twelve-year-old. *Journal of Behavior Therapy and Experimental Psychiatry,* 1981, 12, 4: 329–332.
64. Piaget, J. & B. Inhelder, *Mental imagery in the child.* New York: Basic Books, 1971.
65. Pomerantz, P. B., et al., The in-vivo elimination of a child's water phobia by a paraprofessional at home. *Journal of Behavior Therapy and Experimental Psychiatry,* 1977, 8, 4: 417–421.
66. Prout, H. T. & J. R. Harvey, Applications of desensitization procedures for school-related problems: a review. *Psychology in the Schools,* 1978, 15, 4: 533–541.
67. Rosbury, W. C., Behavioral treatment of selective mutism: a case report. *Journal of Behavior Therapy and Experimental Psychiatry,* 1974, 5, 1: 103–104.
68. Rimm, D. C. & J. C. Masters, *Behavior therapy: techniques and empirical findings.* New York: Academic Press, Inc., 1974.
69. ———, *Behavior therapy: Techniques and empirical findings,* 2nd ed. New York: Academic Press, Inc., 1979.
70. Ross, S. M. & S. Proctor, Frequency and duration of hierarchy item exposure in systematic desensitization analogue. *Behavior Research and Therapy,* 1973, 11: 303–312.
71. Saunders, D. G., A case of motion sickness treated by systematic desensitization and in-vivo relaxation. *Journal of Behavior Therapy and Experimental Psychiatry,* 1976, 7, 4: 381–382.
72. Scott, E., A desensitization programme for the treatment of mutism in a seven-year-old girl: a case report. *Journal of Child Psychology and Psychiatry and Allied Disciplines,* 1977, 18, 3: 263–270.
73. Thomas, R. J., The effects of three methods on test anxiety and the achievement test performance of elementary students: providing test-taking information test-wiseness training, and systematic desensitization. *Dissertation Abstracts International,* 1977, 37, 9-A: 5717–5718.
74. Ultee, C. A., et al., The reduction of anxiety in children: a comparison of the effects of systematic desensitization in vitro and systematic desensitization in-vivo. *Behaviour Research and Therapy,* 1982, 20, 1: 61–67.
75. Van Hasselt, V. B., et al., Tripartite assessment of the effects of systematic desensitization in a multi-phobic child: an experimental analysis. *Journal of Behavior Therapy and Experimental Psychiatry,* 1979, 10, 1: 51–55.
76. Van Der Ploeg, H. M., Treatment of frequency of urination by stories competing with anxiety. *Journal of Behavior Therapy and Experimental Psychiatry,* 1975, 6, 2: 165–166.
77. Walker, H. M. & H. Hops, Group and individual reinforcement contingen-

cies in the modification of social withdrawal. In L. A. Hamerlyorck, L. Mandy, and E. Mash (Eds.), *Behavior change: methodology concepts and practice.* Champaign: Research Press, 1973.
78. Wallick, M. M., Desensitization therapy with a fearful two-year-old. *American Journal of Psychiatry,* 1979, 136, 10: 1325–1326.
79. Watson, J. B. & R. Rayner, Conditioned emotional reactions. *Journal of Experimental Psychology,* 1920, 3: 1–14.
80. Wilson, R. N., Group desensitization of test anxiety in fifth and sixth grade students. *Dissertation Abstracts International,* 1975, 35, 12-A, P + 1: 7734–7735.
81. Wish, P. A., J. E. Hasazi & A. R. Jurgela, Automated direct deconditioning of a childhood phobia. *Journal of Behavior Therapy and Experimental Psychiatry,* 1973, 4, 3: 279–293.
82. Wolpe, J., *Psychotherapy by reciprocal inhibition.* Stanford: Stanford University Press, 1958.
83. Wolpe, J., *The practice of behavior therapy,* (2nd edition). Oxford: Pergamon, 1973.
84. Yorkston, N. J., et al., Verbal desensitization in bronchial asthma. *Journal of Psychomatic Research,* 1974, 18: 371–376.
85. Yule, W. & P. Fernando, Blood phobia—beware. *Behavior Research and Therapy,* 1980, 18, 6: 587–590.

CHAPTER 12

THE QUIETING REFLEX: A PSYCHOPHYSIOLOGIC APPROACH FOR HELPING CHILDREN DEAL WITH HEALTHY AND UNHEALTHY STRESS

Elizabeth L. Stroebel, M.Ed., M.S.
and
Charles F. Stroebel, Ph.D., M.D.

The Quieting Reflex concept was discovered in 1974 as an outgrowth of an attempt to use biofeedback to treat stress disorders in an outpatient clinic population ranging from age seven to seventy. Younger patients acquired body safety skills with ease, which older patients found increasingly more difficult with age, particularly in transferring skills from the controlled clinic setting to the real world with its inevitable stresses and worries. Controlled studies have demonstrated that the Quieting Reflex program is remarkably effective in classroom and clinical settings. In this chapter the authors go into detail with regard to the theory and application of this self-regulation technique for children.

INTRODUCTION

The metamorphosis of an egg into a caterpillar, to a cocoon, to a butterfly is an awesome phenomenon because it is relatively rapid; maturity is achieved in a few weeks and it can proceed full circle in complete view of the observer. The changes occurring within a child are equally cataclysmic, but are cloaked by a deceptive surface appearance of a "cute miniature person." Many adults are prone to expect, first: that given food, support and time, this miniature adult will grow up; and, second: that there is little reason to expect significant variation and marked individual differences in the speed and nature of the developmental process. Individuals specializing in child development, however, universally recognize that under the observable superficial behavior, the "still waters" of this engaging miniature adult run very deep indeed and on many levels—symbolic, physiological, emotional, mental.

Historically, age has been assigned as an index of developmental readiness of children to satisfy the need to systematize and reference, a simplistic trap which is changing as developmental research continues. Particularly deceptive is the fact that most children develop remarkable language skills without awareness of a single rule of grammar, but until their brain's developmental processes are ready, many children experience trouble in learning how to code their speech abilities into reading, writing, and spelling, and in developing an adequate language for communicating emotions and feelings. These children become emotionally frustrated, unaware of what is wrong, and experience stress which may surface as antisocial behavior, such as withdrawal or acting-out. Evidence of physiological stress generally begins to appear as children experience the pressures of structured educational settings and the competitive milieu of their peer world.

In language study, children learn about the rules of grammatical construction and in their science classes they observe the physical laws of nature. The consequences of misusing either, whether it be social ineptness or physical danger, are generally clear. It is incongruous that any less importance should be placed upon learning about the interaction of emotional and physiologic principles that govern man, as well as the consequences of ignoring their impact on health. These physiological body laws, their warning signs, and the body's safety mechanisms for optimal functioning include the following: (1) the fight-or-flight emergency-alarm response; (2) the resistance and exhaustion phases of the General Adaptation Syndrome; and, (3) the faulty bracing of dysponetic effort.

It is remarkable how many children are capable of understanding these complicated physiologic laws and how they can translate the principles involved into metaphors and analogies compatible with the framework of a child's point of view! This revelation stems from a virtually universal finding in the application of a technique known as biofeedback to help individuals overcome stress disorders; namely, children seem to learn self-regulation of body safety mechanisms for dealing with stress much more rapidly than do adults. This was particularly apparent in early applications of the Quieting Reflex.

THE QUIETING REFLEX

The Quieting Reflex concept was discovered in 1974 as an outgrowth of an attempt to use biofeedback to treat stress disorders (estimated to be up to seventy percent of all medical complaints) in an outpatient clinic population ranging from age seven to seventy.[8] Younger patients acquired body safety skills with ease, which older patients found increasingly more difficult with age, particularly in transferring skills from the controlled clinic setting to the real world with its inevitable stresses and worries.

Initially, the six-second Quieting Reflex (QR) was designed to help adults not "just relax," but to automatically adjust arousal levels up or down to meet the actual stress at hand. After six months' practice, QR remarkably improved their ability to avoid and lessen stress illnesses, often without the assistance of the biofeedback instrumentation. Because the biofeedback instruments would be cumbersome and expensive in a classroom or at home, we wondered about the alternative of teaching children the six-second Quieting Reflex technique without equipment, speculating on teaching at an early age before the ravages of stress illness set in the four Rs, namely, reading, 'riting, 'rithmetic, and QR.

This early experience with children led to the hypothesis that the Quieting Reflex, like the emergency response, is an inborn trait. Studies are currently being conducted to determine if this is indeed so. Young children seem to adapt happily, with very few stress-related problems, until they encounter the discipline, confinement, and pressure of parental expectations that accompany starting school at the age of five or six. This observation lends credence to the idea that the Quieting Reflex is inherent at birth and is only extinguished or overwhelmed as children encounter the frequent arousal and stress levels of classroom and peer-pressure life. When children do begin to experience such tension, their physiological responses are often identical to those of adults, except that children have fewer choices than adults in avoiding stressful situations.

The hypothesis that the Quieting Reflex is a counterbalancing safety mechanism to the emergency reflex is illustrated in Figure 1. The six steps of the initial six seconds of the emergency reflex, as shown in Figure 2, namely, sympathetic nervous system outflow, secretion of adrenaline, increase in tension in the facial muscles, a catch or hold in the breathing pattern, constriction in blood flow to the hands, feet, and intestines, and a clenching of the jaws are exactly counteracted by the

FIGURE 1

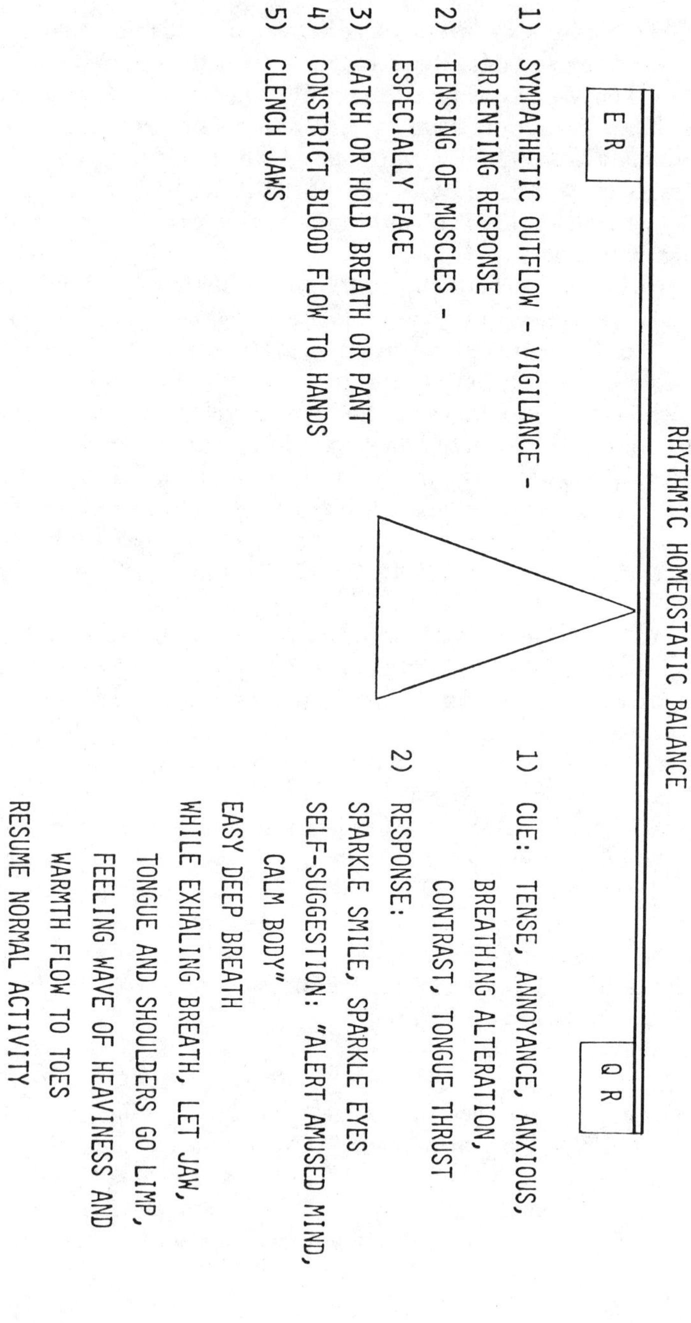

RHYTHMIC HOMEOSTATIC BALANCE

[E R] ◁ [Q R]

1) SYMPATHETIC OUTFLOW - VIGILANCE - ORIENTING RESPONSE
2) TENSING OF MUSCLES - ESPECIALLY FACE
3) CATCH OR HOLD BREATH OR PANT
4) CONSTRICT BLOOD FLOW TO HANDS
5) CLENCH JAWS

1) CUE: TENSE, ANNOYANCE, ANXIOUS, BREATHING ALTERATION, CONTRAST, TONGUE THRUST
2) RESPONSE:
SPARKLE SMILE, SPARKLE EYES
SELF-SUGGESTION: "ALERT AMUSED MIND, CALM BODY"
EASY DEEP BREATH
WHILE EXHALING BREATH, LET JAW, TONGUE AND SHOULDERS GO LIMP, FEELING WAVE OF HEAVINESS AND WARMTH FLOW TO TOES
RESUME NORMAL ACTIVITY

FIGURE 2

HOW Q R INTERRUPTS THE STRESS SEQUENCE

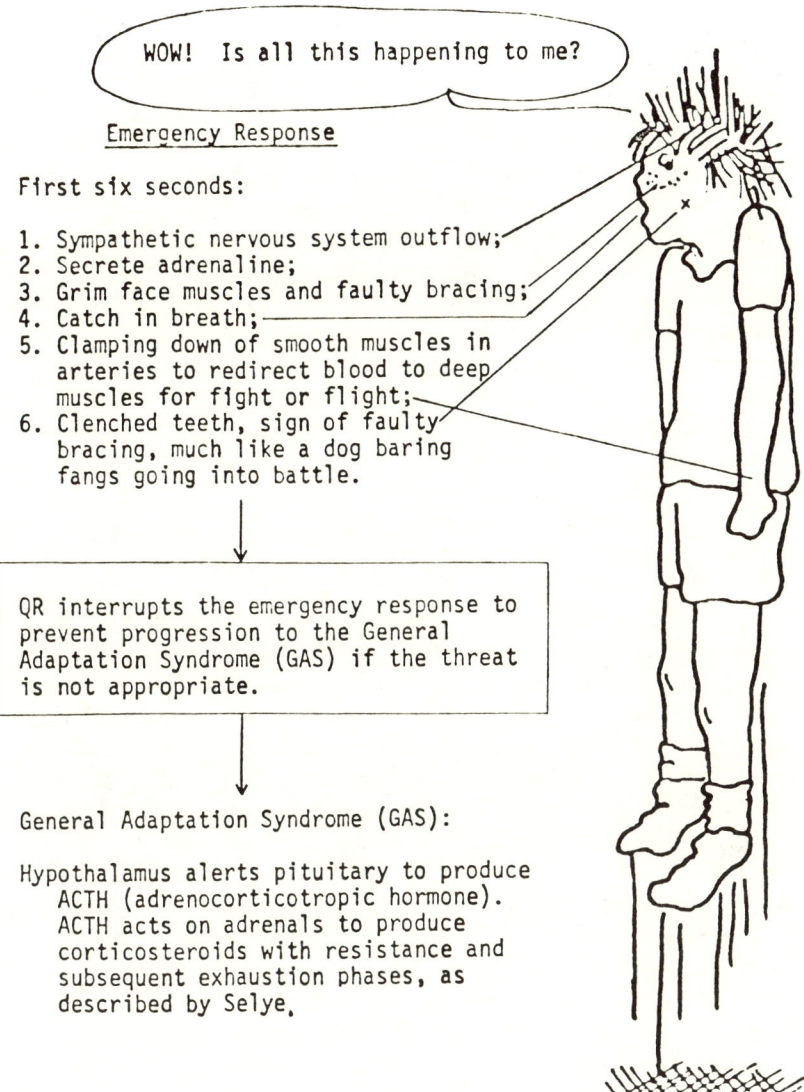

Emergency Response

First six seconds:

1. Sympathetic nervous system outflow;
2. Secrete adrenaline;
3. Grim face muscles and faulty bracing;
4. Catch in breath;
5. Clamping down of smooth muscles in arteries to redirect blood to deep muscles for fight or flight;
6. Clenched teeth, sign of faulty bracing, much like a dog baring fangs going into battle.

QR interrupts the emergency response to prevent progression to the General Adaptation Syndrome (GAS) if the threat is not appropriate.

General Adaptation Syndrome (GAS):

Hypothalamus alerts pituitary to produce ACTH (adrenocorticotropic hormone). ACTH acts on adrenals to produce corticosteroids with resistance and subsequent exhaustion phases, as described by Selye.

steps of the Quieting Reflex. The Quieting Reflex introduces a six-second pause in the initial steps of the overall stress reaction of the body to permit finer and finer levels of discrimination as to whether or not body arousal is truly appropriate for dealing with the perceived threat at the moment. The Quieting Reflex concept involves the following principles, namely: (1), increased discrimination of arousal cues and faulty muscle bracing (dysponesis); (2), easy abdominal breathing, and elements of progressive relaxation; (3), autogenic training; (4), and rational emotive therapy. All are directed to achieving an inner balance of the body which prominent physiologists like Neal Miller and others have called adaptive homeostasis.[10] By performing a QR during the initial six seconds of the stress sequence, both children and adults learn to pause for six seconds with an alert mind-calm body, proceeding with the subsequent stages of stress physiology only if a true physical emergency exists. In application with well over a million adults under professional supervision since 1974, the Quieting Reflex has proven to be of significant value in managing stress problems in approximately eighty percent of the population, and has become popularized in book form as *QR: The Quieting Reflex*.[15]

The children's version of this program, called *Kiddie QR*, and a subsequent professional program for adolescents, divide the adult QR technique into sixteen brief, four- to seven-minute experiential exercises, easily integrated into classroom use or dental and pediatric settings without significant interruption of the ongoing routine.[14] The children's program uses child-oriented images and metaphors to accomplish some of the identical objectives as the adult program, namely, developing a hierarchy of behavior lasting approximately six seconds which is incompatible with inappropriate activation of the emergency response.

In the children's program, QR is presented as a constant friend who lives inside the child's body, along with many other symbolically named body characters. Some of these characters, referred to as bothersome friends like "Rigid Robot" and "Fighty Fists", represent faulty bracing states seen in tense children. Understanding the rationale and then experiencing skill exercises in "Body Bike Cycle" and "Grouchy Head" helps youngsters deal with tendencies of hyperactivity. Many other body characters represent helpful elements of the QR training. The program emphasizes to the child that he can choose the appropriate body friends for the situation at hand and gives him a new way of communicating his emotions and feelings which has previously been overlooked by the educational and health communities in their devotion to teaching the traditional basics of reading, writing, arithmetic, and health maintenance.

The concept of "Breathing Pores" in the bottoms of the feet in the adult program is taught to children as "Magic Breathing Holes" to help elicit sensations of flowing heaviness and warmth within the body, relaxing skeletal muscles and smooth muscles. Discrimination of facial tension and practice of the jaw drop is accomplished by an imaginary "Magic Jaw String" tied to the chin that can be used to slowly pull the jaw down and up. The little ones learn about the temporomandibular joint, which is located in the face just in front of the ears where the jaw articulates with the skull and is a focal point of tension in the early phases of the emergency fight-or-flight response. Children learn to explore tension in this region, referring to it as "Mr. TMJ", and go on 'finger trips' with this body friend to locate it and discuss its role in health and stress. They learn the words "dysponesis" and "homeostasis"—the former as faulty bracing and the latter described as "My Very Own Good Feeling Self." They love to use these big words in the hope that an adult will ask "What does that mean?" Then they go on to describe it in their own terms with sophistication and reassurance. The children also go on a "D and W" or on a "dysponesis watch" when they're riding in a car. They look out the window and see adult drivers exhibiting passing-gear emergency responses as they sit in traffic, frustrated and clenching the steering wheels of their cars while gritting their teeth. The children often giggle and say that if people were doing their QR they would not be so tense.

QR teaches children to pause and discriminate body arousal states. They learn that they have a choice and the control to interrupt the fight-or-flight response and shift body gears before difficult tasks, unpleasant situations or fights overtake their bodies. Because many children think that adults do not worry about the things that they do, they are also taught that fears and worries are normal. They learn that it is all right to have worries, but also that their sixteen "body friends" can help them deal with these worries. With these friends, the children learn how to build a "healthy, happy body." They develop coping strategies to integrate negative stressful aspects of their lives with positive stresses experienced by all healthy individuals and particularly in children, who encounter developmental milestones in their lives which are truly a cataclysmic metamorphosis that adults tend to take for granted. The QR experiences, language, and body friends provide a new set of emotional and feeling communication skills that children can share and healthfully explore the enormous tasks of developmental socialization required of them as they adapt to a complex and oftentimes confusing adult world.

ADAPTIVE HOMEOSTASIS

"All systems go" is the twentieth century space-age jargon for the historic concept of Adaptive Homeostasis. The famous physiologist Walter Cannon introduced this term to describe the body's intrinsic inner balance, which in kiddie terms is "my very own good feeling self"—a state in which there is harmonious integration of body and mind. Normally, homeostasis functions without our awareness, much like an airplane flying on automatic pilot. When the airline pilot pulls the switch for automatic pilot, he hands over his voluntary controls, so to speak, to the aircraft's automatic devices. The pilot is still in control of the craft but in a *passive way*. He is in absolute command of the activities important to the safety and progress of the airplane, but the automatic mechanisms built into the airplane act involuntarily for the pilot.

Similarly, many aspects of the body's systems (circulatory, cardiovascular, immune, and others) and the body's organs (heart, lungs, liver, others) normally function involuntarily or on automatic pilot without direct interference, except in instances of malfunction, when the body may experience sensations of pain or discomfort. There are other systems and organs (skeletal muscles, vocal cords, and the muscles which move the eyes, facial expressions and the diaphragm) that are normally under voluntary control.

Children are fascinated by the body's automatic pilot mechanism and feel reassured by the body's safety features for wellness as well as reliability. There is an enormous sense of relief to know that their breath is always there, and that blood continues to flow, even during sleep. What if, instead, every minute detail of each system and organ would not operate without the conscious voluntary direction of each move? You wouldn't have time to do anything because every second of your life would literally be consumed with directing the complicated processes of the central nervous system, cardiovascular function, hormonal release, enzyme activities, digestive function, neurological and musculature activities.

It is educational and enjoyable for the older children to imagine how busy they would be trying to regulate just a very few of the hundreds of body functions that occur automatically 24 hours a day when they are asleep or awake:

—When to open and close each of your four heart valves in proper sequence.
—When to secrete hydrochloric acid for digestion.
—When to regulate blood pressure for lying or standing.
—When to order your liver to switch from storing glucose to dispensing blood sugar for energy.
—And dozens upon dozens of other operations.

If this conscious brain had to worry about controlling all of the intricate inner machinery of the body, they would not be able to carry out the unique aspects of human functioning such as reading, writing, driving a car, listening to music, conversation, or playing games. To carry this example to an extreme, they would not be able to go to sleep.

Dr. Neal Miller of The Rockefeller University, an authority on the mechanisms of adaptive homeostasis, marvels at the body's ability to readjust, adapt, and to restore balance. He often asks his audiences to consider how fascinating it would be for us to be able to somehow measure the number of times a day our bodies automatically achieve homeostasis, that is, automatically readjust or adapt to restore balance when we become unbalanced due to excessive or inappropriate stresses. The number would be in the billions. He concludes: "The human body, including the brain, has a wonderful capacity to recover from a great variety of infections, physical injuries, and psychological traumas."[10]

MIND/BODY INTEGRATION

Children and adults alike confuse the common experiences in daily life of being "psyched" and "hyped." The expression "psyched up" generally implies a heightened mental state which may be likened to a positive enthusiastic state of healthy stress (eustress) or simple healthy excitement. The expression "hyped up" implies an excessive degree of body arousal, suggestive of non-productive energy. Because of the pressures of daily living it is easy to confuse these states and assume that both reactions are part of ongoing healthy behavior. For good health and development, it is essential to have access to the full spectrum of our emotional and physical reactions, to be aware of the subtleties in states or shifts in arousal level that are natural and that make us wonderfully unique.

A fairly simple illustration to help children grasp the complex idea of mind/body integration is the comparison between the interaction of emotional and physiological reaction in their bodies and the construction and operation of a toy car.

Car Frame	Bones
Radiator	Blood
Carburator, Exhaust	Lungs
Pumps	Heart
Headlights	Eyes
Tires	Feet
Windows	Mouth/Breath
Brakes/Power	Muscles
Gasoline	Stress Hormones
Battery	Energy Source
Accelerator/Speedometer	Emotions

This comparison helps children to conceptualize how the emotional arousal level mechanisms in the brain trigger off physiological reactions within the body.

In order for their toy race car to perform well, they must control the speed, check out the car and the track for problems, and keep an alert mind and calm body to keep the car functioning at optimal performance. Crucial is balancing moments of lower speed with moments of heightened acceleration through shifting into the appropriate speed gear. Similarly, they learn that their body functions much like the mechanism and operation of a car and that their emotions act as the control center in their body frame, just as the accelerator pedal acts as the speed control in the car. And as in the car race, they recognize that signaling mechanisms ready the body systems and organs to *gear up* to a higher arousal state when their emotional gas pedal or stress hormones alert their brain to do so and when to *gear down* when their emotions signal the brain to slow down or lower the arousal.

It is important to emphasize the healthy aspect of these unique body mechanisms. There are appropriate times to use our passing gear: for playing tag, racing on our bikes, jumping up and down for joy when we are happy. Passing gear is a body safety feature for emergencies too—when we are late for dinner and want to 'step on the gas' so as to run quickly home, or for more serious problems when we need to move away from real danger. Within the discussion, children can talk about why it would not usually be appropriate or safe to use our passing gear in the house where we might break something or hurt ourselves or while we are trying to do our school work and the "wiggle" gear would interfere with mental performance.

"QR and My Body Bike Cycle" is an experiential exercise in shifting body gears through learning to discriminate among the physiologic changes that can be observed and felt. For example, the children can observe changes in their breathing pattern, in feeling their heart rate accelerate as well as experiment with overt muscles tensing. They experiment with arousal states by exploring appropriate and inappropriate 'body speeds,' by learning how to balance the emotions that accompany stressful situations with comfortable emotions and unstressful situations. In general they learn that unnecessary wear and tear on the body diminishes performance and creativity. This exercise lends itself nicely to show physically how 'hyper' or Type A tendencies are similar to keeping the body in passing gear all the time. The experiential work coupled with discussion is an avenue of communication that makes sense to children and is a way to talk about the consequences of these long-term patterns in a positive non-threatening framework so that the child need not become fearful or feel guilt.

The analogy of the car and the body helps a child visualize mind/body integration. Here is an appropriate place in your discussion to talk about how our emotions trigger off uncomfortable body sensations such as butterflies in the stomach, or a pounding heart, or the scary uneasy feelings that we experience without understanding their origins. All of the elements in the QR program are especially useful for children who display hyperactive behavior tendencies and who need a means to understand their body arousal state which is disquieting to them. By becoming aware of the mind/body integration concept, they can acquire practical skills and ways to discriminate their emotional and physiological speed and then how to adjust their mental and physical arousal levels for the task at hand.[11]

BODY AROUSAL

Our arousal level of combined mental and physical activity is often referred to as one's "body arousal state." Arousal theory, however, involves very complex aspects of physiology and behavior. Despite controversy there is fairly consistent agreement that, in order to maintain healthy episodes of *higher* arousal (not inappropriate high arousal), the body must be balanced by episodes of *lower* arousal, (not inappropriate low arousal). Popular misconceptions in the literature confuse these states by interchanging the use and meaning of low and high with lower and higher.

To clarify this point, figure 3 illustrates mental tension levels, running from low to high on the vertical scale, coupled with body tension levels running from low to high on the horizontal scale. Low levels of both mental and body tension generally are accompanied by

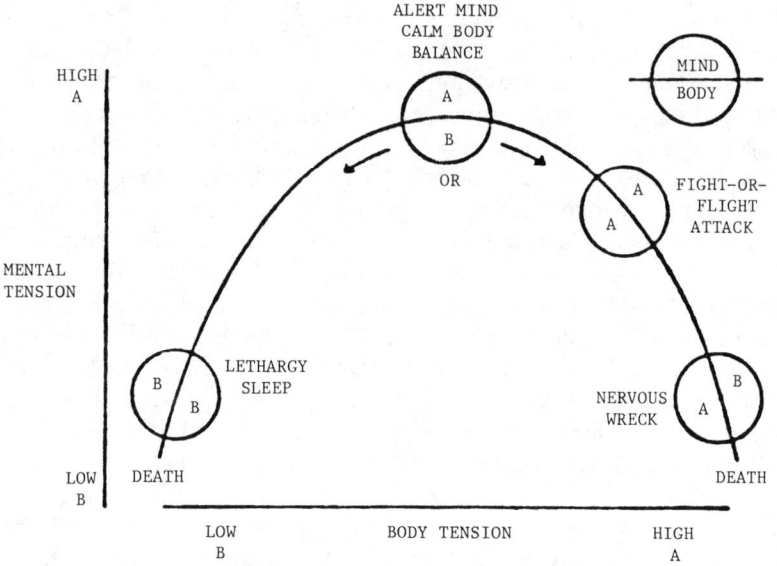

FIGURE 3

feelings of lethargy. Frequently overlooked and misunderstood is that the state of low mental arousal may be accompanied by nervous exhaustion and muscle tension, characteristically associated with high body arousal. As the figure indicates, states of moderately high levels of both mental and body arousal tend to be associated with hyperkinetic and/or relatively spontaneous attack behaviors.

In summary, the inverted 'U' relationship in the figure of either too low or too high a level of body arousal is incompatible with a healthy life style.

Elementary aspects of body arousal states are taught in Element 14, "My Body Bike Cycle," where children learn that sustained periods of low (inadequate) or high (excessive) arousal are incompatible with wellness behavior habits. The lethargic child lacks pep, feelings of spontaneity of excitement over even the simple joys of life and even in overt emotional arousal during episodes of trouble. He is often labeled as lazy and/or as having a 'bad' attitudinal problem or is described as being emotionally flat. Conversely, the child with 'hyper tendencies' seems to lack control over his restless and random activity. He is likely to be labeled as a behavior problem child. In both instances, the emotional and physical fatigue associated with each state interferes with the child's ability to concentrate so as to complete necessary or fun tasks, or to feel a sense of control.

The Quieting Reflex: A Psychophysiologic Approach

Paradoxically, both the lethargic and "hyper" child experience similar muscle tension. The outward posture of the inactive child may appear limp and in general project an attitude of hopeless/helplessness; yet deceptively the smooth muscles that line the blood vessels of the body, most of the gastrointestinal tract including the stomach, intestines, and air passageways of the lungs, may be unduly tense, producing sensations of discomfort and significantly altering mental functioning without conscious awareness. The outward posture of the hyper child may suggest "body rigidity in motion." Skeletal muscle activation leads to bracing muscles, including the diaphragm, and hence holding the breath and clenching the jaws. The smooth muscle contraction produces similar discomfort as described in the lethargic child. Both types of children may experience coldness in the extremities, caused by the constriction of blood flow to the hands and the feet.

The effects of the constriction of blood flow and ways to induce vasodilation are the base of the sequential exercises in Elements 9, 10, and 11 - "Fighty Fists," "Finger Balloons," and "Octopus"; these are among the favorite body friends of children using the QR program. The bothersome friend, "Fighty Fists" introduces the child to the tensing or bracing mechanism of the emergency response as it causes specific discomfort in the fingers, hands, and wrists. As the child experiments with his "Fighty Fists" through discriminating muscle tension states, detecting skin discoloration and the generally tense appearance of the knuckles, he then sees what appears to be specific tension spots within his fist, casually generalizes to other areas of his body such as the entire arm, shoulder and neck muscles as well as within the chest cavity. This inappropriate bracing of the fist and related areas alters his normal breathing pattern.

The physiological objectives introduced by "Finger Balloon" and "Octopus" help the child experience sensations of heaviness associated with relaxation of skeletal muscles and the sensations of flowing warmth associated with the relaxation of the smooth muscles located in the blood vessels, lungs, and gastrointestinal tract. The combination of Elements 9, 10, and 11 provides a physiological rationale as well as an understanding of how thoughts and feelings and muscle tension are related.

TYPE A BEHAVIOR

The idea of Type A behavior, as defined by Friedman and Rosenman, is a crucial concept that has forced scientists to think about stress and its consequences for the body.[4] The long-term studies of Hunter,

Berenson, and colleagues of early Type A coronary-prone behavior patterns indicate that some correlation exists between psychosocial factors and cardiovascular risk in children and adolescents.[6] These Type A behavior patterns, whether they be primary or secondary to the conditions described by these researchers, are introduced in the QR program through a bothersome body friend called "The Hurrier I Go," a metaphor for the Type A person as characterized in figure 4. A group of children were looking at this figure and discussing 'wiggly bodies' and 'passing gear.' We asked them what might happen if they kept their sneakers on the move all of the time like this fellow in the picture. One child quickly replied, "My shoes get untied and I fall." We asked, "Do you tie them?" He said, "No, I can't stop."

FIGURE 4

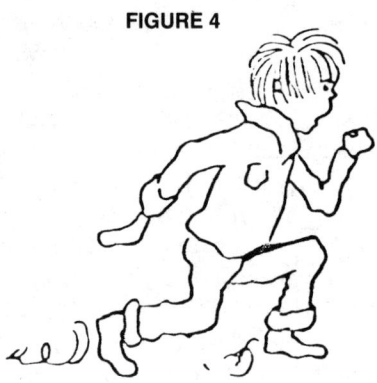

The Hurrier I Go

What a marvelous description of the emotional and physiological dilemma of the Type A personality, a description that children can understand and associate with the mechanisms of the car-body analogy previously discussed. In the various QR exercises (elements) of the program that deal specifically with body arousal, we emphasize that trying, succeeding, and failing are normal. Emotional growth is dependent upon exploring possibilities and recognizing limitations. However, the child learns how he can unconsciously teach his body to override appropriate arousal states until excessive arousal becomes a way of life without his being aware of it. Whether the Type A behavior characteristic is genetic in origin or acquired as a learned pattern of behavior, it apparently carries over into adulthood.

Beginning with the pre-school years through parental and educational pressures, most of us have been taught that the way to achieve in our complicated, high-pressured world is to try hard, harder, and then harder still. This is what is termed the Western work ethic and is a remarkably powerful motivating force for using our brains, sometimes at the expense of our health in what may encourage Type A behavior. The suggestion of "you can do it if you try hard" strategy is usually a well-intended message of encouragement and belief in the youngster's ability to succeed. However, in a daily world that measures personal success by effort, the "try harder" philosophy may be self-defeating in creating dysponetic, faulty bracing efforts.

Just as the "try hard" message fails, so does the "don't worry, just relax" strategy. Children do worry and become more tense when they fail to achieve this 'downer' state. Since most children have an innate zest, curiosity, and wonderment in discovering what the world is all about, the "just relax" message seems incompatible with their physical and emotional growth.

The little body of "The Hurrier I Go" is momentarily in a hurry—the "trying too hard passing gear." The slightly grim facial expression gives the appearance that he's under emotional pressure, whether real or imagined, to get somewhere quickly. Beneath his clothing you can be fairly certain that his body's insides are geared up for emergency speed. Physiological monitoring instruments would show a change in breathing, increased heart rate, increased sweat gland activity, tightened facial muscles, increased body muscle tension in general, and numerous other "unconscious" physiological responses. In addition, he usually does not notice details in his environment. Operating under a pressured sense of time urgency, he experiences a loss of focused alertness which actually serves as a withdrawal defense.

Passing gear, then, is a high arousal state. It is healthy and absolutely normal to shift your body into passing gear for emergencies, for spirited moods, for appropriate times when a 'psyched up' body and mind is useful and fun. Heightened arousal shifts occur during momentary anger, fear, and crying states as well. Passing gear is a safety mechanism but should only be evoked for the appropriate reasons.

Always in the discussion of this figure, some child will say, "But I love to run!" Of course, running is fun. It is natural for a child to run home for supper if he is late, or to run away from danger. Racing and running for the sake of racing and running in play is healthy and very normal for bodies engaged in positive physical activity which expends pent-up energy. There is something wonderful and exciting to see an active child engaged in invigorating play, just as it is to see adults joining in marathons, running, taking walks, or participating in sports activities.

What is the difference, then, between our little friend "The Hurrier I Go" and the healthy activity of the children and adults we just described? Figure 5 indicates arousal-tension-level index. To maintain health, episodes of higher arousal need to be balanced by periods of lower arousal. This state is termed "adaptive homeostasis," that is, balanced arousal within limits.

The stress problems of modern man develop from the tendency to overactivate the sympathetic branch of the nervous system as a defense against whatever is threatening. The ability to perceive a threat and simultaneously activate our body defense is a magnificent safety device in face of real danger. This concept is illustrated by the solid line in figure 5 which represents shifting balance into an appropriate state for the task at hand as it shifts from high to lower arousal. The dotted line indicates a state in which the sympathetic high arousal system is overactivated and remains there, failing to return to a state of balance.

It is important to emphasize that every physiological action within the body should be followed by reaction (analogous to Newton's Third Law—for every action there is an opposite *and equal* reaction). This process is a safety feature for health but endangers our wellness when

FIGURE 5

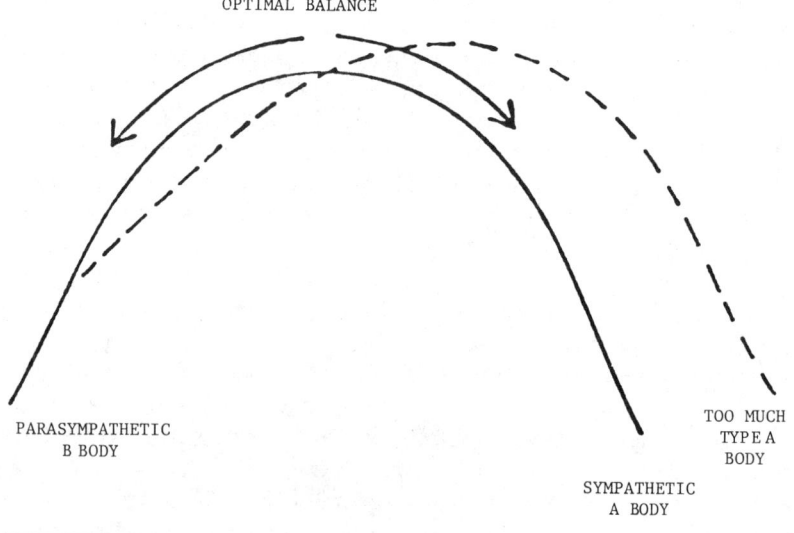

the recovery period for reaction to a normal balance is prolonged. Many individuals recognize, at a common sense level, their tendency to overrespond. They assume that "downer" techniques should solve the problem, which accounts for the widespread popularity of medications, "relaxation," and passive meditation techniques. Unfortunately, the 'downer' techniques serve a one-dimensional emphasis, as shown in figure 5 as a flattened line reducing mental alertness.

The QR is not a relaxation technique; rather, it teaches arousal shifting. It is crucial to teach a child to recognize when his body and mind are in 'passing gear' and *how* to shift his body gears down and out of emergency gear. If you ask a child who is prone to Type A behavior tendencies, "Why are you running so fast?", the response might well be, "I'm not running." The important point to be made here is that children and adults are frequently unaware that their body is in passing gear, that they are inappropriately "running," and that "The Hurrier I Go" becomes a pattern common to their lifestyle.

The first step in teaching a child how to shift his body gears begins with teaching him discrimination of body states through body scans and through tensing and releasing exercises, calling upon sensory awareness techniques.[7] The second step is to help him examine what in his lifestyle encourages this "Hurrier I Go" behavior and under what conditions it surfaces. The third step is to effect an appropriate change in his physiological reaction to the identifiable stressors. QR permits an alert mind to shift into the best body gear, from passing to amused coasting, to deal with the stress at hand. It does not interfere with an emergency response when it is warranted. Indeed, because Kiddie QR prevents the waste of energy through excessive stress responses to the pressures of ordinary living, one can react with more power and vigor to a real physical threat.

SIGNALING SYSTEMS

The body musculature is designed to maintain healthy balance between parts; however, the musculature takes its cue for action from a central signaling system in the brain that does not have the screening process to signal muscles that one stressful event is minor or another one is major. The signal is the same and the body reacts the same. In all elements of the Kiddie QR, the child is taught to discriminate between situations that require full emergency body power and those that do not. For example, in observing children setting up dominoes, you may overhear statements such as "don't anyone move."

Without training, these children have learned one half of the message. It is important to lower the body arousal to complete the game, but their strategy of freezing the body undoes the purpose.

As activation of the emergency response is experience, the body swings into a complex set of hormonal and neurological interactions with muscles. For some children the sensations from muscle strain seem to localize in the gut area (nervous stomach); in others, in the cardiovascular system (changes in heartbeat rate, or tight sensations), the respiratory system (changes in breathing paatterns) or in the skin (sweat).

We know that our nervous system influences all muscle activity. However, germane to maintaining homeostatic balance is the question of what parts do our musculature and body control systems play in our day to day stress? We asked a child "how do you think your muscles work?" and the child's answer was fairly characteristic of the way children look at muscle activities, "they get messages that tell them to go up and down, in and out, all around." This five-year old's answer is reasonably accurate.

The muscles may be viewed as biological motors which receive signals from our nervous system or messages from hormones traveling in the bloodstream. The children are introduced to two major types of muscle groups in the body—skeletal muscles and smooth muscles. It would seem that the concept of skeletal muscles is easier for children to grasp than smooth muscles. The skeletal muscles operate quickly and are under the voluntary control of our "thinking brain." Children can learn that skeletal muscles move their eyes, vocal cords, and their skeletons. Smooth muscles operate more slowly and are under less voluntary control. However, in the QR exercises, children are introduced to smooth muscle activity as internal body muscle friends who are there to help with heart functions, stomach functions, etc. They learn that the smooth muscles manage the inner machinery of their body of which they have little awareness unless it malfunctions and produces signs of pain. These smooth muscles line the blood vessels of the body, most of the gastrointestinal tract (including the stomach and the intestines), air passageways of the lungs, and are also associated with glands and hormone activity.

Teachers easily spot tense children via their emotional expressions of frustration, anger, crying accompanying tight, rigid little bodies. There is an increasing concern over the number of children who show signs of stress either in acting out behavior, a maladaptive form of tension release, or withdrawal, an unhealthy internalization of unreleased tension. In either case, the most long-term devastating body effect is muscle bracing that interferes with the healthy function of all organ systems and eventually is a major contributor to illness. Patterns of chronic muscle tension are closely associated with a person's attitude toward life and his responses to emotional upset.

FAULTY BRACING

One of the most significant, but still widely unrecognized contributions to the understanding of the physiology of stress has been made by George Whatmore, M.D. of the University of Washington with his concept of dysponesis, more commonly called faulty bracing or "trying too hard."[17]

Faulty bracing is a term for a physiological condition of shortened muscle fibers and constricted blood flow to the muscles. Whatmore's research has shown that inappropriate or too much faulty bracing cramps the organ systems in our bodies and causes irregular function. As an example of this, Roger, age nine, feels that the world is a scary place. To protect himself, he maintains a rigid body posture. This produces a constant state of skeletal muscle tension which also squeezes down blood flow to the muscles. He develops writer's cramp, which can be seen in his knuckles and fist. Roger develops stomach upsets and head tension.

All of us have been taught since we were very young that we could accomplish our goals in life by trying hard, harder, harder. However, when a malfunction begins to develop in our inner body systems, this mental effort of trying hard, harder, harder, sends bracing signals to our musculature, which oftentimes intensifies the problem or makes the pain worse. Through the QR approach children learn which emotional and physiological states and reactions are unnatural and unhealthy, When the reaction is consistently inappropriate for the situation, the child recognizes that his body is thrown into a physiological state of hyper-readiness or emotional bracing:

Dysponesis hits the spot
Makes your muscles tight, that rots!
Loosen up and just let go
Watch your body, brains just flow.

This little jingle may offend some adult sensitivities, but it was created by a group of inner-city children to conceptualize their way of translating a highly sophisticated physiological concept into language that was meaningful to them.

A child can create a stress reaction or emergency response because of a distortion in his perception of a situation or of others around or in his wavering sense of confidence, all resulting in what Whatmore calls faulty mental bracing. The reasons for a child's distortion in his perception of what he can and cannot do involves complex psychological dynamics including ego strength, self-image, fear of rejection, expectation vs. ability, previous experience, manipulation tactics, etc. Whatever the motivation behind the distortion, the child gets caught up in a physiological body reaction that further prevents performance.

Another bracing posture is related to what Whatmore calls *performing effort*. These efforts are learned muscle bracing patterns that relate to motor skills and performance.

As you watch the very young child try to manipulate a crayon, bear in mind that complex processes of mind and motor coordination are involved that simultaneously involve muscle integration with emotion (determination, frustration, etc.). As the child tries to manipulate his fingers, hands, and arms, the hard contact with the crayon may be rigid in a tight grip. As he begins to manage the crayon with greater success, the muscle tension usually lessens and less obvious bracing or gripping effort is noticeable.

The similar hand and forearm bracing effort is noticeable in older children experiencing stress from various origins as they are involved in writing tasks. An overt clue that a youngster is experiencing difficulty of some sort can be seen in the rigidity of his fingers and hands as he grips his pencil. The harder he mentally tries the more intense the hand grip becomes.

How this bracing affects the well-being of each child in the long term will depend upon many variables, perhaps genetic, behavior patterns, stamina, and ego strength. Children especially are more vulnerable to setting up bracing patterns in contrast to adults who are likely to be in a position to express, and even scream out what they dread. Generally, an adult has negotiating power and can initiate change. For the child, however, very little liberty exists. The only alternative for some is to internalize the situation and in doing so maintaining high level body tension. The QR exercises help the youngster to release these kinds of bracing tensions. Physiological measurement indicates that a sensation of heaviness is experienced with relaxed skeletal muscle. Similarly, sensations of flowing warmth are associated with relaxation of the smooth muscle located in the blood vessels, lungs, and gastrointestinal tract.

Early in life QR can teach children how to shift up or shift down the emotional and physical body gears to interrupt faulty bracing patterns or to prevent the onset of inappropriate and unhealthy bracing postures. The experiential exercises of the program allow children to learn a productive way to use their muscles for positive healthy body tensions that foster healthy achievement and wholesome lifestyle.

BRACING FOR WORRISOME EVENTS

Individuals adopt unconscious bracing postures as survival maneuvers. For example, a child who is yelled at consistently when he comes in from out-of-doors, might consciously prepare for the verbal assault by protectively bracing his body for the dreaded event, even though no physical threat is present. His body assumes a fixed position, hands clenched, shoulders tightened, face grim. The dreaded event triggers off an emergency response within the body. Over the course of time, this emotional and muscular defense can become so natural a reaction that it assumes a normal tendency in the child's behavior. Unconsciously, this reaction pattern carries over to other situations unrelated to coming in from play time. The child may react in the same way when he enters a classroom. Thus, at a very young age, he begins to unconsciously throw his body into an alert state at inappropriate times, when no real danger is present.

The hormones are released from a variety of organs and are transmitted via the bloodstream to various target areas where their effect is to increase or decrease acitivity. A delightful and important explanation of hormonal activity is introduced in Bedford's concept of "stress and tiger juice."[2] The association of the body chemicals (involved in arousal and their effect on body stress) and tiger juice helps the child to visualize chemical movement and its positive and negative power within the body.

When either skeletal or smooth muscles are under undue tension, they send signals to the brain via the nervous system which may significantly alter the child's mental functioning without his conscious awareness. For example, if the muscles lining the air passages in the lungs are exposed to an allergenic substance they may constrict, increasing the rate of breathing and causing an uncomfortable mental sensation. The child can learn that a muscle spasm means that the nervous system has lost momentary control of muscle activity and that the muscle is operating in a reflexive nature. A common example of this is the overconstriction of the smooth muscles of the arteries in the body which frequently produces a sensation of cold hands or cold feet. In this instance, it is easy for the child to conceptualize this problem by working with his body friends, "Fighty Fist," "Finger Balloon," and

"Octopus," which can assist the child in understanding that constriction in his hands is similar to the constriction that occurs inside his body. This is especially useful to help the child understand how the smooth muscles lining the lower gastrointestinal tract will create feelings of cramping and sensations of pain. It also helps the child to understand how excessive contraction of skeletal muscles covering the skull may be the basis for the feeling of pain or tension experienced as a headache.

Bracing is a safety feature of the fight-or-flight response. During an emergency response, your body chooses its line of defense—to run away or to stay and fight. Sometimes bracing is a positive, protective mechanism. You physiologically put your body on guard in order to carry out your reaction to the emergency situation at hand.

Many times little children are unaware of how much they are bracing, ranging from such simple acts as a slightly clenched fist, a tightly held pencil, or a tightened jaw, to the generalized tense, rigid posture of their bothersome friend, "Rigid Robot."

BRACING FOR THE IMAGINARY

Youngsters experience realistic as well as imaginary worries that are characteristic of their age and developmental stage. However, when the imagined worry becomes exaggerated, the child's emotional state evokes excessive muscle bracing, which can expend enormous emotional and physiological energies and can result in illness or fatigue. They may experience odd bodily sensations that they do not really understand which, in turn, intensify emotions of fear, panic or anger. In combination, all of these factors result in a vicious cycle of emotional and physical dysponetic effort.

BRACING FOR THE DREADS

Body bracing can be a physiological indication of "the dreads," which children may not be able to talk about very well or even recognize. If you observe the child who dreads going to school, or one who dreads the dark, you will notice individual posture differences and even defense strategies peculiar to that child, as well as some general similarities, but the physiological internal bracing of the skeletal and smooth muscles will be the same.

Children are not formally taught that outward appearance, the way they stand, look, sit, or walk, may reveal much about what is going on inside them. Kiddie QR can provide the desire and the means for them to learn that body movements and facial expressions can give off clues as to how they feel about themselves, their sense of worth within specific environs, and their attitude toward those around them.

Part of the experiential exercises in the exercise "QR and Grouchy Face," graphically presented in figure 6, helps a child to focus on outward body signs of tension by looking at this picture. Clearly, the Grouchy Body mouth, set jaw, tightened cheekbones, set eyes, tightened forehead, tilting of the neck, and tense shoulders reveal faulty bracing. This caricature illustrates how the internal emotional state affects the mind, which in turn affects the muscles.

As the children look at this grouchy face, they realize that, in order to change the facial expressions and body posture, the child in the picture needs to shift emotional gears in order to shift the physiological gears for lessening muscle tension.

The specific elements of the QR teach the child to recognize his "dreads," to cue into how his internal body reacts once these discriminations are made. Whatever the dread associated with a task, such as doing homework, cleaning the room, walking in the dark, he can choose whether to upset his internal body or to do his QR, which will

FIGURE 6

Grouchy Body

assist him through his dreads. QR does not excuse him from the responsibility of the task; it makes it less unpleasant.

CONCLUSION

As the emphasis and focus in health care changes, Marigold Edwards raises a crucial question for educators regarding self-regulation techniques for children. In the National Education Association report on health care in the 1980s, she asks: "What can the average classroom teacher do? Time is limited. The curriculum is already crowded. No money is available for equipment. The teacher has no special training." Edwards concludes that one answer to these pressing problems is teaching the Quieting Reflex as a coping skill for life.[3]

Teaching self-regulation skills in the classroom raises concerns for their suitability for school use. Although contemporary educators are aware of and concerned about stress management, many "relaxation" programs have been rejected by schools because they do not work well in the classroom. In addition, some stress management programs for use in schools seem to threaten the belief structure of many families. Some forms of meditation, for example, are opposed by parent groups because members believe they represent a religious position other than their own. QR, as a quick, scientifically based technique that can be used "at the scene of the crime" of stress, surmounts these difficulties. It does not involve psychotherapy or infringe on parental beliefs.

Controlled studies have demonstrated that QR is remarkably effective in classroom and clinical settings. The Mesa, Arizona school system was the first major school district to pioneer the QR program as early as 1979. The significance of this project under the direction of Dr. Richard Duncan, director of psychological services, lies in his early recognition that the effectiveness of any program must involve psychological services, prevention services, the superintendency, regular and special education teachers as well as parents. Since this project began, over 850 school districts are addressing the stress needs of their staff and students. In addition, there is appropriate application for the Head Start and day care centers.

The program has been adapted successfully for the youngster with special needs to include the emotionally handicapped and physically impaired. Noteworthy is the work of Lenord Silverstein with cerebral palsy children and adults.[13]

Medical researcher and child psychiatrist Enrique Huerta, M.D.,

Cleveland Clinic Foundation, acknowledges the need to integrate self-regulation techniques as a useful way for staff, children, and parents to deal with hospital stressors. He contends that improved methods of treatment should become available for disorders in which physical and emotional factors interact to perpetuate the illness.[5] For example, biofeedback therapy has direct application to the treatment of anorexia nervosa, where the therapy focuses on increased awareness of inner stimuli and increased sense of positive control.[9]

Other children at risk are those who experience separation issues such as divorce or foster home placement. Attorney Donald J. Cantor and child psychiatrist James C. Black (Hartford, Conecticut) are currently examining the feasibility of such program use within the framework of the youth services divisions and the court system, a formidable and valuable task.

The QR program is not a panacea for all stress needs. However, whatever program is used with children two factors must be considered or the program will most likely fail in the long term.[1] These factors are compliance and transfer of training. Compliance in Kiddie language means "sticking to what you are doing." Programs that impose time restrictions for best results or "drop out" activity have low compliance. Children drift away from the technique. Teaching techniques must be built into the program to ensure transfer of training. Core transference techniques mean carry over effect. Many potentially good programs fail to be implemented because they lack this vital component.[16] The QR is a life long coping skill that goes with you and the child from the place of learning, whether at home or in school, to be used at the moment of stress anytime, anyplace. You do not need the therapist or teacher to be present to guide you through the motion. Once the response is learned, practice makes it automatic, a skill that stays with you forever. This is what is involved in transfer of training.

Much of our personality and temperament is influenced by past experiences, education, and environment in general, but Hans Selye points out that man is not locked into fate.

Teaching QR to children as a lifelong coping strategy may indeed change their "fate." Incorporating this health technique into their daily routine will most certainly affect the quality of their lives. How marvelous if prevention or health awareness were as significant a part of early childhood education as the three Rs. By teaching children positive, enjoyable ways to maintain wellness, you will give them a precious gift indeed—a chance to avoid or minimize the killer, stress-related disorders of our generation.[12] QR cannot eliminate stress in their lives, but it does teach children to appreciate happy, healthy stresses and to gain self-mastery over the effects of unhealthy stress on their bodies.

REFERENCES

1. Adler, C. S. & S. M. Adler, Biofeedback and psychotherapy for the treatment of headache. *Headache,* 1976: 16.
2. Bedford, S., *Stress and tiger juice.* Chico: Scott Pub., 1980.
3. Edwards, M., *Stress management, health education in the 1980's.* Washington, D. C.: National Education Association, 1981.
4. Friedman, M. & R. H. Rosenman, *Type A Behavior and your heart.* Greenwich: Fawcett Crest, 1974.
5. Huerta, E., Group therapy for anorexia nervosa. In M. Gross. (Ed.), *Anorexia Nervosa.* Lexington: Collamore Press, 1982.
6. Hunter, S., et al., *Type A Coronary-Prone Behavior Pattern and cardiovascular risk factor variables in children and adolescents.* New York: Pergamon Press, Inc., 1982.
7. Jencks, B., *Your body: biofeedback at its best.* Chicago: Nelson-Hall, 1977.
8. Kaplan, H. I., Treatment of psychomatic disorders. *Comprehensive textbook of psychiatry, III.* Baltimore: Williams and Wilkins, 1980.
9. McKee, M., J. F. Kiffer, Clinical biofeedback therapy in the treatment of anorexia nervosa. In M. Gross (Ed.), *Anorexia Nervosa* Lexington: Collamore Press, 1982.
10. Miller, E., Behavioral medicine biofeedback and homeostasis: new applications of learning. *Psychiatric Annals,* 1981: 11.
11. Peper, E., et al. (Eds.), *Mind/Body Integration.* New York: Plenum Press, 1979.
12. Setterlend, S., *Techniques of tension control: a survey of methods and research focused on children, youth and school.* University of Karlstad, Sweden, 1982.
13. Silverstein, L., Personal communication. United Cerebral Palsy Treatment and Rehabilitation Center, Roosevelt, Long Island, New York.
14. Stroebel, E. L. & Charles F. Stroebel, *The Kiddie QR: a choice for children,* QR Institute, Connecticut, 1980.
15. Stroebel, C. F., *QR The Quieting Reflex: A six-second technique for coping with stress, anytime, anywhere.* New York: G. P. Putnam's Sons, 1982.
16. Stroebel, C. F. & Bernard C. Glueck, Optimizing compliance with behavioral medicine therapies. In J. H. Masserman (Ed.), *Current psychiatric therapies,* 1981, 20.
17. Whatmore, G. B. & D. R. Kohli, *The Physiopathology and Treatment of Functional Disorders.* New York: Grune and Stratton, 1974.

CHAPTER 13

USE OF BIOFEEDBACK RELAXATION PROCEDURES WITH LEARNING DISABLED CHILDREN

John L. Carter, Ph. D.
and
Harold Russel, Ph. D.

> *During the past several years the authors of this chapter have been involved in developing an EMG biofeedback relaxation training program for learning-disabled children. This chapter describes their theories, procedures they have developed, the results, and cautions based upon their experience with training over 600 children. Generally, the findings indicate significant gains in reading, spelling, verbal IQ, attention span, behavioral self control, and self-concept.*

This chapter will describe our theories, our research methodology, and some of our results in the application of biofeedback-based relaxation training for over 600 children. This is intended as an overview of our work during the past six years and should not be interpreted as a review of the literature; however, when applicable, evidence from the literature will be cited and discussed.

Our research primarily involves the idea that learning is most effective when the child or adult is physically relaxed and mentally attentive to the material being presented. For many learning-disabled children and adolescents, attending school daily and performing poorly results in their experiencing a psychophysiological response called the "fight or flight reaction". When an individual, child or adult, feels physically or psychologically threatened, a characteristic pattern of arousal occurs automatically to prepare that individual for dealing with this threat. The pattern usually includes, but is not limited to, heightened muscle tension, more rapid breathing, increased heart beat, increased cerebral and large muscle blood flow, decreased peripheral blood flow, decreased stomach blood flow, and a decrease of digestive action.

This mighty rush of internal activity designed for self-protection is inappropriate in most of the child's world. Neither running nor fighting is an acceptable response, so there is no easy way for this heightened internal level of arousal to dissipate except over a period of time. If this threat or stress persists, the child continues to have difficulty in learning, and a chronically high and fluctuating internal activity level will be maintained. This is usually accompanied by heightened levels of anxiety. Sheer has reported that learning-disabled children show much more automatic liability and inability to focus attention on relevant stimuli than do normal controls.[28]

The magnitude of the problem is indicated by reports that from fifteen to twenty percent of children of normal intelligence are functioning poorly in academic learning tasks. In the United States there are an estimated 8 million learning-disabled children, and boys outnumber girls approximately ten to one.[26] Harrower[21] reported that over seventy-five percent of juvenile delinquents were poor readers and Hammer[19] reported that sixty-seven percent of adolescent school under achievers were learning disabled.

This inability to perform adequately for a long period of time is stressful and produces anxiety in children. This anxiety has a negative effect on a variety of learning tasks including reading, spelling, and arithmetic. The psychological effects of chronic early school failure are readily observed. A vicious cycle is started in which poor performance generates criticism which results in the development of a poor self-concept which in turn lowers motivation and interests that result in lowered performance. Combs and Taylor found that even a mild degree of threat not only raises anxiety but impairs performance on intellectual tasks.[14] Further, McMillan reported that failing learners tend to perceive even neutral events as failures and this lowers their sense of self-worth.[25]

BIOFEEDBACK RATIONALE

The possibility of teaching direct control over this autonomic "fight or flight" response is relatively new. During the past ten to fifteen years biofeedback training has been developed as a means of teaching the individual to control his or her psychophysiological response to particular stressors. Biofeedback assisted treatment has been reported successful in control of migraine headaches,[16] muscle tension headaches,[5] and in the control of pain in burned children.[27] During the past few years exploratory work using small numbers of children has suggested clearly that children can learn control over their bodies with immediate clinical application in the enhancement of academic learning.

Biofeedback is the obtaining of immediate information about the current state of biological processes. If you are ill and take your temperature you are using one major ingredient of biofeedback—gaining information.

Relatively recent advances in electronics technology allow instruments continually to monitor even minute changes in certain body functions. These continuous changes can be observed on a meter. For example, temperature changes of one-hundredth of a degree or muscle tension changes of one-millionth of a volt can be detected and observed. Biofeedback, then, is the utilization of sophisticated electronic instruments to detect physiological changes, thus enabling a person to learn to control them.

Research results have indicated that with practice most individuals can learn to reduce muscular tension, to increase fingertip temperature, to alter brain waves, and even to slow heart rate.

Learning to control one or more of these functions is called biofeedback training. The final objective of such training is the ability to attain the desired bodily changes voluntarily without the instruments. This can only be done through practice. As with learning any other skill, consistent guided practice makes for more efficiency. Consequently, biofeedback training requires continuous and active participation by an individual in learning how voluntarily to control the required bodily function.

During the past few years research results have demonstrated that biofeedback procedures are especially effective in helping people learn to control stress—their body's reaction to various pressures. Most of this work has been done with adults. Relatively little research has been reported on the effects of biofeedback with children in an educational setting.

BIOFEEDBACK RESEARCH

General Background

Many kinds of handicapped children labeled minimally brain injured, learning disabled, educable retarded, and emotionally disturbed show excessive muscular tension while attempting to do desk work at school. In fact, one of the levels of reading recognized by reading specialists is called the "frustration level."[2] The child's voice becomes more highly pitched and strained, and he uses more repetitions and hesitations as he characteristically begins to squeeze his fist around the book. The entire muscular system becomes involved and quite rigid.

The neuromuscular efficiency in the movements used in handwriting appears to be significantly impaired with many children with learning problems. Whether this excessive tension is physiologically or emotionally based seems to be of little importance. These children squeeze their pencil, press their paper, purse their lips and otherwise use an inordinate amount of energy and concentration when trying to do written school work. While writing, their entire body becomes rigid and consequently their progress is slow and laborious. It simply should not take that much muscle energy and effort to write. Finally, the results of such extreme effort are usually not rewarded. The children may even be punished because of the poor quality or slow speed of their written work. This increases the stress level, and the children are often required to do extra drill or practice in what for them is a tedious and difficult task. These children could be described as "having an A or B in their head and an F in their hand."

Pilot Investigation

Some educators and psychologists have developed special sensorimotor training activities designed to enhance eye-hand coordination abilities (see: 1, 18, 23). Rather than looking directly at the poor motor coordination and trying to remedy it, we tried to develop a system of more efficient use of muscular energy while writing and doing other kinds of school work. With this in mind, we engaged in a series of research projects focusing on muscular biofeedback based relaxation training.

A pilot study was conducted using four boys diagnosed as learning disabled.[10] Electromyographic (EMG) biofeedback training was used. This involved placing electrodes on the flexor muscle of the preferred writing forearm. As the muscle became more relaxed the child heard a tone of decreasing volume. The child was asked to "turn off" the tone by relaxing. The training sessions were conducted for ten weeks, two times per week for one hour. Ten minutes of individual muscle relaxation feedback training was given during each session. The other fifty minutes of each session were used for guided handwriting practice. In addition, there were homework assignments including listening to prerecorded relaxation instructions three times per week.

During this ten week training period the boys gained nearly seven months in reading and spelling as measured by the Wide Range Achievement Test. In addition, and perhaps more importantly, teachers and parents spontaneously reported behavior changes of greater self-control, less impulsiveness, less distractability, fewer careless errors, and generally a greater degree of conscientiousness in school. As hoped, both handwriting quality and speed also increased markedly. Although a statistical analysis was not conducted, the gains appeared to be much more than would be expected during a ten week time interval.

Muscle Tension (EMG) Reduction Research

The pilot study justified a more detailed investigation of self-control and academic gains following biofeedback muscle relaxation training.[11] Accordingly, a group of children, fifteen boys and one girl, who were identified as learning disabled, were selected to form the experimental group. Twelve boys and two girls formed the comparison group.

The biofeedback relaxation training program was similar to that in the pilot study. The sixteen children in the experimental group were further divided into two groups of eight children for treatment. Each group met for one hour twice a week. First they entered a classroom and began the pre-determined handwriting practice. Once settled and working, the children were taken one at a time to the biofeedback room where they were given ten minutes of biofeedback muscle tension reduction training. No reinforcement or reward system was used other than what may have been intrinsic to the situation. Homework assignments included listening to a ten-minute pre-recorded relaxation audio tape followed by completion of a one-page handwriting exercise. This was done three times a week for the six week program. A comparison group of sixteen learning disabled children was identified and received the same pre- and post-experimental tests.

The results indicated a significant forty-nine percent decrease in muscle tension level. More importantly, the children in the two experimental groups gained significantly over the comparison group on the two measures of reading and spelling. Significant gains over the comparison groups were also made on the Bender Gestalt Test using the Koppitz scoring system.[24] The IQ on the Slosson Intelligence Test also increased significantly more than that of the comparison children, as did auditory memory. Handwriting legibility and speed also increased, as was expected. It should be noted that handwriting practice was the only area of academic treatment. Immediately following the training, group interviews were conducted with the children in the experimental group as well as with their parents. This was done in order to further adjust and refine the program.

As the results of this program became known in the area, many parents and educators began referring children, especially those with handwriting problems, and impulse and attention difficulties. During the next four years, this training procedure has been used with over 600 children.[7] Consequently, all of the children seen were not necessarily diagnosed as learning disabled. Many were described as "non-diagnosed." However, the same test data were obtained on all children, regardless of classification. All of the children were having consistent and long term difficulties in school. Essentially the same results were obtained. Approximately eighty-five percent of the children trained have made the gains shown in Table 1.

TABLE 1

Gains Made by Children Receiving Training

Test	Amount of Gain
Wide Range Achievement Test	
Reading	.71 year
Spelling	.65 year
Arithmetic	no gain
Slosson Intelligence Test	7.0 points
Gray Oral Reading Test	.67 year
Bender Gestalt	Significant decrease in errors
Tennesse Self Concept Scale	
Total	Significant increase
Self Criticism	Significant decrease
Cassell Behavior Rating	Significant increase

These results can be attributed to the muscle relaxation intervention training. Children in the experimental groups learned to cope more effectively in school. The children did not learn the academic information during the biofeedback relaxation training. Instead, previously learned material was found to be more easily accessible for application. The children became less tense and gained more control over their tension and increased in self confidence.

For eighty-five percent of the children, as muscle tension levels decreased, improvements in verbal facility, memory, reading, spelling, handwriting, self-control, and self-concept increased. Further analysis of the data revealed that older children (over 10½ years) tended to make more gains on basic academic skills, such as reading, spelling, and handwriting. The younger children (under 10½ years) tended to gain more in academic prerequisite skills of attention, memory, and coordination.

Throughout the investigations, teachers and parents consistently remarked on improved behavior in the classroom and at home. In order to get quantifiable information about these changes in behavior the Child Behavior Rating Scale was administered to the mothers.[12] Positive significant gains were obtained on all subscales and on the Total Adjustment Scale.

If the child was in fact controlling his behavior more positively and this change in performance was being recognized, then the possibility arose that perhaps his self-concept would be enhanced. To explore this possibility, the Tennessee Self Concept Scale was administered before and after subsequent training programs.[9] The results were as expected. Highly significant improvements were obtained on the total Self-Esteem scale as well as on each of the subtests. Apparently, the children began to think more positively about themselves, began developing a higher level of self-confidence and were less critical of themselves.

Figure 1 shows an example of the improvement in handwriting legibility during the six-week training program. These improvements were observed at school and maintained for six months. Systematic long range follow up at that time was not possible due to lack of funds.

THE EXISTING TRAINING PROGRAM

Our program involves working with small groups of children. At present we find it most efficient to work with five or six children at a time. The children enter one room and begin copying a paragraph written on the chalkboard. While they are doing this, we observe and attempt to change a number of poor writing habits. For example, many children copy only one letter or word at a time, constantly glancing at the board and looking back at their paper to do so. For those who copy one letter at a time, we get them to look at the board and visualize and spell an entire word at a time. For those who copy only one or two words, we get them to increase their vision span and read and copy a phrase or sentence at a time. We also observe and attempt to lightly correct posture and pencil grip. This is important as many children

FIGURE 1
Example of Handwriting Improvement

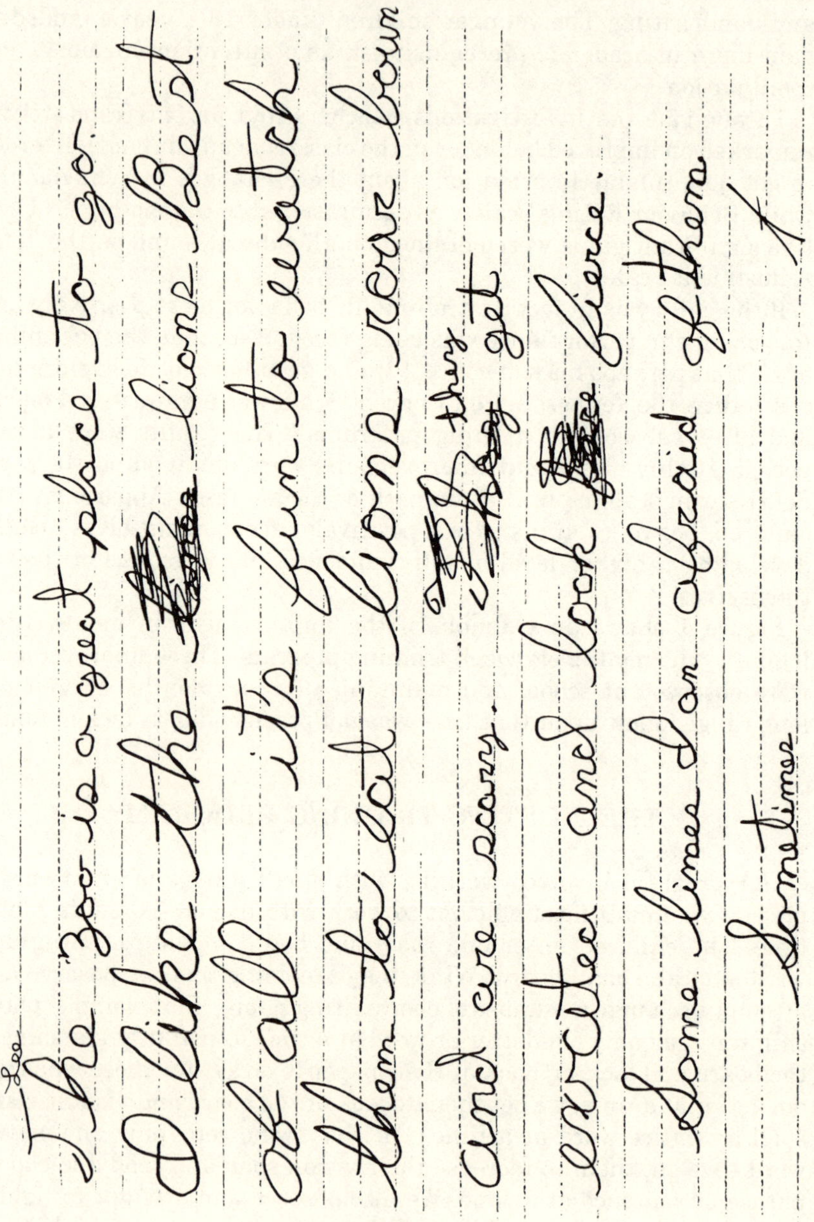

The Zoo is a great place to go. I like the ~~lions~~ lions best of all. It's fun to watch them to eat lions roar ~~they~~ ~~they~~ get excited and look ~~~~ fierce. Sometimes I am afraid of them. Sometimes and are scary.

Too

☺ yeah
you really tried this
time.

Robert ran around roar-
ing like a tiger. Ron told
Robert to roar some more.
Ron and Robert raced
around the room. Ron
heard the roaring and ran
in. Ron and Robert roar-
ed some more. Roaring
belongs in
the zoo.

simply grasp their pencil too tightly for the smooth fluid movements required for handwriting. When the paragraph is completed worksheet exercises are made available. These worksheets incude exercise or activities which are found in most penmanship workbooks. There are letters and words to trace and copy. The idea is to supervise their copying a good penmanship model. Once all the children are settled and busy with their handwriting exercises, one child at a time is taken to the biofeedback room and attached to the EMG biofeedback equipment. The equipment is arranged so that every two minutes a visual display is presented of the average muscle tension level for that period. The goal is to have each successive presentation lower than the one before. Children sit on bean bags and attempt to decrease muscular tension. As this is done, a tone becomes softer and softer. If tension increases, the tone becomes louder. The ten minutes of training are made up of five, two-minute readings which are displayed and recorded. After that, they are unhooked and returned to the handwriting room to finish their handwriting exercises for the rest of the one-hour period. They do this twice a week for six weeks.

In addition, we have developed a series of six pre-recorded relaxation tapes for the children to take home for their home practice. The first tape is designed after Jacobsen and involves tensing and then relaxing various muscle groups.[22] This is to help make the children aware of their own muscular tensions and to learn how it feels to release these tensions. The following sequence is taken from the first pre-recorded audio tape. We ask the children to tense for five seconds and then to relax and feel the tensions leaving for ten seconds.

1) Squeeze your eyes shut—tightly—hold it, relax
2) Push your lips together, very tightly—hold it—relax
3) Press your tongue to the roof of your mouth—hold it—relax
4) Shrug your shoulder up toward your ears—hold it—relax—feel the tensions leaving.
5) With both hands make a fist as tight as you can—feel the tension building—relax. Feel the tension leaving.
6) Make a fist with your right hand. Notice the difference between your tense right hand and your relaxed left. Relax your right hand.
7) Make a fist with your left hand. Feel the left hand getting tense while your right hand is relaxing—relax your left hand.
8) Pull your stomach way in toward your backbone—hold it—relax—feel the tensions leaving.
9) Push your knees together—hard—hold it. Relax.
10) Pull your toes toward your knees, way up. Hold it, hold it, relax. Feel the tensions leaving your legs.

11) Point your toes. Hold it—relax.
12) Now tighten every muscle in your body—hold it—relax your entire body. Let your entire body get very limp—relaxed and comfortable.

When this is completed, breathing instructions are presented. The children are asked to breathe in through their nose and out through their mouth. We ask them to do this naturally and rhythmically. Each time they breathe out, they are reminded to let themselves get just a little more limp, a little more relaxed, and a little more comfortable.

The second tape deals with passive relaxation. In this tape the children are asked to think about the same groups of muscles in the same sequences one at a time and to let those muscles relax even more. These first two tapes are followed by four other pre-recorded tapes which focus more on visual imagery. A full transcript of one of the imagery tapes is included.

After the children listen to the ten-minute relaxation tape, they are instructed to complete one page of handwriting exercises. They are asked to do this home practice three days a week. This gives them a total of five sessions of relaxation and handwriting practice each week.

FLOAT RIDE

The following narrative is presented in a soft, slow and soothing voice giving the children plenty of time to listen, absorb and passively follow the directions. The dashes represent pauses. Soft music is in the background.

FLOAT RIDE

Now, get in a very comfortable position _____
Close your eyes, and try to relax your body _____
Think about your breathing _____
Breathe in _____ Breathe out _____
Breathe in through your nose, and out through your mouth _____
Now take a deep breath, hold it _____
and let it out slowly _____
Feel yourself sinking deeper and deeper into the chair _____
You're beginning to feel very comfortable and relaxed _____
Today we're going to take a ride on a float in the Gulf. We each have a float and it needs to be blown up _____
So first thing we do is blow them up. Take your float and blow into it, by taking deep breaths and exhaling into the float _____

You will need to blow into your float at least ten times _____
So now, take a very deep breath and, slowly exhale into your float ____
Each time you breathe out, let your body become more and more relaxed _____
Each breath should let you feel really good inside _____
Now that our floats are blown up, we'll walk down to the water.
The sun is very bright, and it feels warm on your skin _____
The sand feels warm and cushy and soft against our feet _____
As we get closer to the water we can smell the salty air _____
We can hear the waves _____ of the ocean as they hit the beach ____
The water is closer now and the sand begins to get a little cooler _____
The sun is shining on us, and we feel good _____
We will pause for a few moments now to feel the sun and the sand beneath our feet _____
We are now at the edge of the water and we get on our floats _____
The floats feel very comfortable and secure _____
The air is warm and the water is cool _____
We are slowly floating away from shore on our floats and we feel very relaxed _____
There are seagulls in the sky and we open our eyes to watch them fly by us _____
The water is warm and we feel it with our hands and our legs _____
The water is moving our floats away from the beach and we feel very comfortable and safe _____
As the waves pass under us, the floats move slowly up, and slowly down _____
We move with the floats—up, and down _____ up, and down _____ very slowly _____
We feel as if we were being rocked to sleep _____
The water is pushing us up and down _____ up, and down.
We feel very relaxed and comfortable _____
As the waves are passing under us, they begin to pull us closer and closer to the beach _____
For just a few more seconds we can ride on our float without having to touch the sand _____
The sun is warming our bodies, and the float ride is relaxing our bodies and our minds _____
The floats touch the sand and we must get our bodies to move again ____
So for a few seconds, bring yourself back to alertness and get off the floats _____
The sand feels warm against our feet once more and we feel very good inside and outside _____

The air is warm and is drying our bodies quickly as we slowly walk away from the water _____
Now we let the air out of the floats, and with each gust of wind escaping from the float we let it relax our bodies _____
Now we have finished with the ride and with the floats and must return to the room _____
As I count backward from five to one, slowly bring yourself back to being alert and relaxed _____
5 _____
4 _____ Begin to feel more alert and allow energy to flow into your body _____
3 _____ Move your arms and legs _____
2 _____ Wiggle your fingers and your toes _____ open your eyes
1 _____ Sit up, stretch and feel alert and good all over

RESEARCH SPONSORED BY THE BUREAU OF THE EDUCATION OF THE HANDICAPPED

Because of our positive results with 300 children, we were awarded a research contract by the Bureau of the Education of the Handicapped.[13] This was a three-year project designed to develop and test a workable system for implementing a biofeedback relaxation training program in the public schools.

The purpose of the first year was to determine which of the four treatments (biofeedback, relaxation tapes, home practice, or handwriting exercises or combinations of treatments) were the most effective with learning-disabled children. A secondary objective was to evaluate the effectiveness of the training by ages of the children.

Learning-disabled children were selected from three age ranges: 7½ to 9½ to 11½ to 13½. Four children were randomly assigned to one of the eleven treatment by age groups making a total of 132. Four children from the control group were also assigned to each of the three age groups.

All subjects were administered the following battery of tests:
    Slosson Intelligence Test (SIT)
    Peabody Individual Achievement Test (PIAT)
    Gray Oral Reading Test (GORT)
    Bender Motor Gestalt Test (Bender)
    Auditory Memory
    Penmanship Evaluation

These are essentially the same measures used in our earlier investigations. The training of the children was conducted in the schools by graduate psychology students.

Table 2 shows that biofeedback treatment was the most significant training factor for eight of the eleven criterion gains and added significantly to two other measures. Listening to the pre-recorded relaxation tapes produced the best gains in reading comprehension and biofeedback significantly added to the gains. Listening to the relaxation tapes was a significant additional factor for three other variables: math, spelling and total achievement on the PIAT. Either biofeedback or listening to the relaxation tapes was a significant contributor to the gains on all measures but the Bender, which was not significantly altered.

Age, sex, and IQ were not significant contributors to any of the criterion measures, while handwriting practice was the most significant factor in increased penmanship quality. Biofeedback-based relaxation training, however, significantly added to this improvement.

TABLE 2

Changes in Criterion Measures Attributed to Training Variable.

Dependent/Criterion Measures	Training Variables
SIT IQ:	
Peabody Individual Achievement Test	*Bio.*, Writ., Tapes, Sex, IQ
Math:	*Bio., Tapes,* Writ., Sex, IQ
Read Rec:	*Bio.*, Sex, Tapes, IQ, Writ.
Read Comp:	*Tapes, Bio.*, Sex, Writ., IQ
Spell:	*Bio., Tapes,* Writ., Sex, IQ
Info:	*Bio.*, Sex, Tapes, Writ., IQ
Total:	*Blo., Tapes,* Writ., IQ, Sex
Gray Oral Reading Test	*Bio.*, Tapes, Writ., Sex, IQ
Bender Motor Gestalt	Writ., Sex, Bio., Tapes, IQ
Auditory Memory	*Bio., Writ.*, IQ, Tapes, Sex
Penmanship	*Writ., Bio.*, Sex, Tapes, IQ

Note: For each criterion measure the training variables that contributes to the change are listed in descending order of magnitude. If the first training variable resulted in a significant change on the criterion test, it is italicized. As each succeeding variable adds significantly to the change, it is also italicized.

These results are very consistent with those obtained in the earlier studies. Muscle relaxing biofeedback training and listening to prerecorded relaxation tapes, especially in combination, enhanced general attention levels, verbal facility, coordination ability and the basic academic abilities of reading, spelling, arithmetic, and handwriting quality.

Second and Third year

The primary goal of the second year of the project was to determine if teachers or other educators could be taught to deliver the same biofeedback relaxation program to learning disabled children in their schools. Twelve teachers were given about twenty hours of small group training in how to present the program. The training was then given by the teachers to children enrolled in their classes for the learning disabled. The children received one hour of training in their classroom, two days per week for eight weeks.

A "placebo group" of sixty learning disabled children was also established. These children received an amount of individual time equal to that of the children in the experimental group but they played educational games. This group was included in order to evaluate the possible artifact of individual or small group attention which the experimental children received. The same teachers trained both the placebo groups and the experimental groups in order to counteract possible teacher effects. As usual, a control group was utilized. These children were only identified and received the pre and post battery of tests.

The results indicate that the children in the experimental group did make gains over those in the placebo and control groups, but these gains were not as dramatic as those in our previous investigations. Children who received training by advanced graduate students in the university diagnostic center made significantly greater gains than those children trained by their teachers in their school classroom. The children made greater gains when the teachers used relaxation tapes than they did when the teachers used biofeedback training.

It is clear that the teachers never became comfortable with the biofeedback instruments. They remained worried and preoccupied with the instruments and procedures, at times almost forgetting the children they were training. Apparently, the teachers do not have the appropriate background or training in delivering individual clinical services which seems to be an intergral part of the biofeedback training process.

The teachers did quite well, however, in assisting the children in listening to the relaxation tapes. It is felt that this was more consistent with the teachers' training and experience.

Another facet of this investigation was to perform follow-up testing of the children trained during the first year. The purpose was to determine the extent to which the positive changes were stable over time. With this in mind, a fifty percent random sample of the 132 children trained during the first year was selected and tested. The results indicate that the most viable treatments, biofeedback, and pre-recorded relaxation tapes, also yielded the most stable results. Although the differences between those children receiving biofeedback and taped relaxation exercises and the children not receiving the training is still significant, the magnitude of those differences is not as great. Possibly, periodic refresher training would stop this regression and maintain the positive results over time. Perhaps, the periodic incorporation of systematic relaxation training in the curricula of learning disabled children is a solution to reducing their stress due to inefficient learning.

The third year of the project is just beginning. The purpose is to develop a self-contained instructional package to teach relaxation procedures to learning disabled children. Two levels of training are envisioned. They are:
1) Train teachers how to effectively incorporate the use of pre-recorded relaxation exercises with their children.
2) Train school psychologists and counselors how to utilize muscle tension reduction biofeedback procedures with selected children in need of more intensive training.

Muscle Tension and Reading

Concurrently with the above investigations, an attempt was made to relate muscular tension levels to reading levels. Educators have long recognized a frustration reading level in children (see: 3, 20, 29). Since reading scores were significantly enhanced through muscle relaxation training, the possibility was considered that muscular tension could be related to reading levels in "disabled" readers. To explore this possible relationship, 11 boys who were enrolled in the university remedial reading program were used as subjects. The mean age was 10.3 years and all scored average with a mean SIT IQ of 103.2. All were two or more years behind in reading level. For each boy, the independent, instructional, and frustration reading levels were obtained on the Silvaroli Classroom Reading Inventory.[29]

The boys were taken, one at a time, and EMG electrodes were

attached to the flexor muscles of the preferred forearm. Each child received a two minute orientation to the instrument and was then asked to relax for two minutes in order to obtain a baseline level. Following this, the child was then asked to read orally selections at his predetermined independent instructional and frustration levels. Very little increase in muscular tension was found between baseline and independent reading levels. Somewhat more tension was found between independent and instructional levels. A very significant increase was found in muscular tensions between the instructional and frustration levels.

This preliminary investigation suggests that EMG biofeedback measurement of skeletal muscle tension levels may be developed into a reliable index of physiological stress while reading. The next step in our investigations will be to institute remedial reading while the youngster is attached to the EMG biofeedback equipment. Then, we will attempt to teach them to read while maintaining a relaxed state.

ELECTROENCEPHALOGRAPHIC BIOFEEDBACK (EEG)

The studies that we have discussed involved decreasing muscle tensions with subsequent increases in self-control and academic proficiency. Throughout the investigations, we observed that the learning disabled children tended to improve in the verbal areas of reading, spelling, auditory memory, and IQ. Arithmetic test scores were not changed for reasons that were not clear to us.

An examination of our records indicated that the bulk of the learning-disabled children showed a significant verbal-performance discrepancy on the Wechsler Intelligence Scale for Children—Revised.

From our clinic files we selected the records of fifty children who showed at least a fifteen-point discrepancy between verbal and performance IQs. Half of the records chosen were those of children with verbal low and performance high IQs. The other half were of children with higher verbal scores. Surprisingly, learning-disabled children who scored fifteen points or lower on the Verbal Scale than on the Performance Scale tended to have lower reading achievement scores than arithmetic achievement scores. Just as interestingly, children with higher Performance Scale IQs had higher arithmetic than reading achievement test scores, an observation which is not widely known or reported.

There is an increasing body of literature that suggests that the right and left hemispheres of the brain differ in the functions they perform.

The left hemisphere deals primarily with verbal, logical, and sequential thinking while the right hemisphere deals more with spatial, holistic thinking processes. Most of our instructions during muscle relaxation training were verbal—i.e., listening to audio tapes and copying words.

Our speculation was that the muscle relaxation training which was primarily verbal influenced left hemisphere activity more than right hemisphere activity. With this in mind, we initiated a second pilot investigation.[8] The purpose was to explore the effects of systematic left hemisphere training in producing alpha waves (8-13 Hz) or beta (13-28 Hz) activity. The theory was that in the normally functioning child the left hemisphere shifts as needed from the resting state, alpha activity, to the active attending beta state. Some children may have difficulty in making this shift. Children who perform poorly on verbal, logical, and sequential tasks as compared with their higher ability to perform tasks involving spatial and holistic processing would be expected to have difficulty in shifting back and forth between alpha and beta.

Our theory was that if learning-disabled boys were selected on the basis of their having a verbal IQ significantly below their performance IQ, and given sufficient training in switching from alpha or beta activity in their left hemisphere, their verbal abilities would improve. We speculated that the result would be a decrease in their verbal-performance discrepancy scores.[26]

Four elementary school-age learning-disabled children with at least a fifteen-point verbal-performance discrepancy were recommended by their counselor for the investigation. Through an error, only three of the boys had the lower verbal IQ while the fourth had a lower performance IQ score. Since a commitment had been made and as a possible check on our theory, we decided to administer the same training to all four boys. All were of average full scale IQ and were right handed.

Each child received the same individual training in thirty-minute sessions two times per week for eight weeks. Electrodes were placed on the left temporal lobe (T3) and left occipital (01) with the ground at the left frontal (Fp1) position. Each child was then asked to produce high levels of alpha activity for a five minute period. Then, they were asked to produce high levels of beta activity for five minutes. These tasks were alternated for the thirty-minute session. To assist in the production of alpha the experimenter asked the child to let himself "sort of drift" and daydream in order to relax. As alpha production increased, a tone was heard indicating the presence of alpha activity. For the production of beta waves, the experimenter asked the child "to put on your thinking cap" and answer simple questions such as, "name some things you can put in your pocket" or repeat the following, "F-R-Q," etc. The questions were easy and designed to elicit sustained attention. As beta activity increased, a tone was heard by the child. The task of keeping the tone on remained the same although the frequency range of the instrument was changed. Each child was also asked to practice relaxing at home twice a week for fifteen minutes. They were provided the same pre-recorded audio cassette relaxation tapes used in the muscle relaxation studies.

The results indicated a twelve-point increase in verbal IQ in the three verbal IQ low boys as was anticipated. The performance IQ showed no change. The one high verbal IQ boy showed no IQ changes. It is theorized that his verbal ability (left hemisphere) was already at an effective level and right hemisphere training was not given.

These pilot results suggested the necessity of further studies by enlarging the number of children in the experimental group and including right as well as left hemisphere training. Table 3 summarizes our research design. Ten subjects who were verbal IQ low were randomly placed into either the left or right hemisphere training group, while ten children with low performance IQs were also randomly placed into one of the two training groups. All children were right-handed, ranged in age from nine through eleven, had a verbal-performance IQ discrepancy of at least twenty points, and were selected from classes for learning-disabled children.

TABLE 3

Summary of Mean IQ Difference and Gain Scores for all Groups

IQ Discrepancy		Pre	Po	Gain		Pre	Po	Gain
Verbal Low	V:	80.4	92.4	12.0	V:	79.0	82.4	3.4
	P:	106.2	104.2	2	P:	97.4	102.0	4.6
	DIF:	25.8	11.8	14.0	DIF:	18.4	19.6	+1.2
		Pre	Po	Gain		Pre	Po	Gain
Performance Low	V:	103.8	105.6	1.8	V:	98.8	99.8	1.0
	P:	84.0	88.4	4.4	P:	77.2	85.6	8.4
	DIF:	19.8	17.2	2.6	DIF:	21.6	14.2	7.4
		LEFT				RIGHT		
				TRAINING HEMISPHERE				

The training procedures were derived from the earlier investigation. Each child received individual thirty-minute training sessions two times per week for eight weeks. Those receiving right hemisphere training had the electrodes placed at 02, T4 and the ground at Fp2. Left hemisphere placement was the same as in the previous study, 01, T3, and Fp1. Once attached to the equipment each child was asked to produce high levels of alpha for five minutes and then to shift to high levels of beta activity for five minutes. This was continually alternated during the thirty-minute sessions. The children were assisted in their training in the same way as in the pilot study. Also, as in the previous investigation, each child was asked to listen to pre-recorded relaxation tapes three times a week.

Table 2 summarizes the results as well as the experimental design. The findings support our theory of specific treatment effects. The low verbal IQ children receiving left hemisphere training gained a significant twelve points in verbal IQ and only two on performance IQ. As predicted, the low performance IQ children gained eight performance IQ points with right hemisphere training. No gains were made by the low performance IQ children who received left hemisphere training or by the low verbal IQ children who received right hemisphere training.

We were concerned that gains by the low performance IQ children receiving right hemisphere training were not as great as the gains made by low verbal children receiving left hemisphere training. All instructions were verbal and there was no training dealing with visualization, quantification, or organization. We concluded that the training was not as directly facilitative to right hemisphere functions as it was to left hemisphere functions.

These results are consistent with the results obtained by Cunningham with verbal-performance I.Q. discrepant learning disabled children.[15] He trained some subjects to increase right hemisphere activity and decrease left hemisphere activity and decrease left hemisphere EEG frequency. This resulted in increased arithmetic scores. Other children were trained in increase left hemisphere activity and decrease that of the right hemisphere. These children improved in reading comprehension. He concluded that EEG feedback training produced changes in arousal level and that there was a relationship between left hemisphere and training susceptibility in low verbal IQ children.

The implication is clear that there may be a specific hemispheric relationship with intellectual abilities and that specific effects can be elicited by specific training of specific kinds of children. The treatment must match the child.

The literature indicates that one diagnostic sign of learning disability in children is a significant verbal-performance IQ discrepancy. This is consistent with Barbara Brown's statement that "training to alter EEG contributions of these mental activities should alter the intuitive-analytic relationships towards a more balanced or more useful state. Imbalances between the two types of cognitive styles may be the cause of certain learning disabilities."[4]

It is conjectured that one means of assisting many learning-disabled children may be to work to decrease the verbal-performance discrepancy, if one exists. When the two hemispheres function equally well, the child may learn more efficiently. This specific hemispheric training may well be dealing with a basic source of learning disability rather than with the observable symptom of poor academic progress.

The next step in our investigative sequence is to determine the immediate and long range effects of specific hemispheric training upon schoolroom performance and self-control.

CAUTIONS

Although there is mounting research evidence that biofeedback relaxation training for learning-disabled children can be an effective treatment, the amount of the scientific art is very new. This is especially true when considering applications in the public schools. Much more research must be conducted in the laboratory as well as in the schools before any type of biofeedback should be incorporated on a large scale. To date, most of school-applied investigations have dealt with muscle-relaxation biofeedback. Not only are many of the studies limited, but there has been little attempt to compare the effectiveness of different biofeedback modalities. Questions such as, distribution of practice, locations of electrode placements, type of feedback signal, number of training sessions, criteria for reaching training levels, and child characteristics, have not been systematically investigated.

Answers to these major questions as well as others just as important must be obtained before wholesale educational application is made. We are attempting to address a number of these questions, but we cannot hope to address all or even most.

Very little work in the schools has utilized temperature feedback, skin conductance feedback, or EEG feedback. Most investigations have taken place in university research centers in areas of interest to the investigator rather than with research that is concerned directly with the needs of the children. Many current published reports concern the treatment of a single child or of a few children. That the techniques used can be effectively applied to larger groups of children is uncertain until further investigations are made.

Another concern deals with expectations. Many people seem to demand a quick remedy or an immediate solution to problems. If these are not forthcoming the treatment is dropped, even precipitously. Our experience in the schools indicates that when a child was referred we were often asked by the teacher after the first session how he had improved. Or, after the first session the teacher indicated that the training has not been effective. It takes time and practice for the child to learn the biofeedback task. Then, more time is required for the child to be in the relaxed state to produce the desired behavioral changes. Learning biofeedback relaxation is a skill analogous to learning to ride a bicycle. There are levels of skill attainment related to the amount of practice. Some children learn more quickly and to greater degrees of skill than do others.

A much greater concern to us is the uncritical acceptance of the biofeedback instrument per se. As the term "biofeedback" gains popularity and becomes more of a buzzword, there may well be a stampede for the boxes as a quick and easy answer. This can only lead to disappointment. The effectiveness of biofeedback does not reside in the instrumentation but in the clinical abilities of the trainer. For example, Fahrion reported on the great variation in the effectiveness of biofeedback trainers.[17] He indicated that successful results depends upon warm rapport between the trainer and the subject. Our investigations revealed similar results. In general, our teachers received more than twenty hours of EMG biofeedback training but few were comfortable in the situation. Consequently, they did not obtain the desired results using the biofeedback equipment. The teachers, however, were able to administer the pre-recorded audio relaxation tape portion of the program with good results. This application was more consistent with their experience.

This leads us to a final concern. If biofeedback relaxation training is beneficial, who should deliver the training? We feel that there should be levels of training depending upon the needs of each individual child. The first level is teachers working with small groups of children who apparently can profit from relaxation support with audio tapes. All children do not need this! The next level would be for children who require more intensive training. This level could be conducted by counselors or school psychologists who have received special training in biofeedback. Finally, a third level would involve highly trained and experienced clinicians. Children in need of more intensive assistance who were not responsive to training at level two could be referred to level three.

We feel strongly that biofeedback training of any modality, temperature, EMG, skin conductance, or EEG is a clinical tool to be used by well-trained and experienced clinicians.

Biofeedback relaxation training of many children presenting school-related learning problems looms on the horizon as a potentially valuable ancillary service. Our studies clearly show that a large percentage of learning-disabled children can learn to reduce their internal arousal levels. This is accompanied by a broad spectrum of positive behavioral changes, including better self control, improved academic performance, and increased self-esteem. Continued research, however, is required to determine the most effective use of this tool.

REFERENCES

1. Barsh, R.H., Achieving perceptual-motor efficiency. *Special child publications.* Seattle: 1967.
2. Betts, E.A., *Foundations of reading instruction.* New York: American Book Co., 1957, p. 451.
3. ———, *Foundations of reading instruction.* New York: American Book Co., 1957.
4. Brown, B., *Stress and the art of biofeedback.* New York: Bantam Books, 1977, p.215.
5. Budzynski, T., Biofeedback in the treatment of muscle contraction (tension) headache. *Biofeedback and Self-Regulation,*1978, 3: 409-434.
6. Carter, J.L. & H.L. Russell, EEG Alpha and Beta Training for learning disabled boys with intellectual verbal-performance IQ discrepancies. Unpublished manuscript, 1982.
7. ———, Application of biofeedback/relaxation training to exceptional children. Paper presented to the 12th annual meeting of the Biofeedback Society of America, Chicago, 1981.
8. ———, Changes in verbal-performance IQ discrepancy scores after left hemisphere EEG frequency control training: a pilot report. *American Journal of Clinical Biofeedback,* 1981, 40: 66-67.
9. ———,Use of biofeedback/relaxation procedures with learning disabled children. Paper presented to the Eleventh annual conference of the Biofeedback Society of America, Colorado Springs, 1980.
10. ———, Biofeedback and academic attainment of L.D. children. *Academic Therapy,* 1980, 15: 483-486.
11. ———, Gains in learning disabled children after biofeedback relaxation training. Proceedings of the Biofeedback Society of America, Tenth annual conference, 1979.

12. ——Application of biofeedback/relaxation training in special education. Paper presented to the First World Congress on Future Special Education, Stirling, Scotland, June, 1978.
13. Carter, J.L., Application of biofeedback relaxation procedures to handicapped children. BEH, Department of Education, Grant NO. G008001608.
14. Coombs, A.W. & C. Taylor, The effects of the perception of mild degrees of Threat on performance. *Journal of Abnormal and Social Psychology,* 1959, 47.
15. Cunningham, M.D., The effects of bilateral EEG biofeedback on verbal, visual-spatial and creative skills in learning disabled male adolescents. Dissertation, Oklahoma State University, 1977.
16. Diamond, S., J. Diamond-Falk, & T. DeVeno, Biofeedback in the treatment of vascular headache. *Biofeedback and Self-Regulation,* 1978, 3: 385-408.
17. Fahrion, S.L., Autogenic biofeedback for treatment of migraine. *Mayo Clinic proceedings,* 1977, 52: 776-784
18. Frostig, M. & D. Horne, *The Frostig program for development of visual perception, teachers guide.* Chicago: Follett, 1964.
19. Hammer, S.L. School underachievement in the adolescent: a review of 73 cases. *Pediatrics,* 1967, 40:373-81.
20. Harris, A.J., *Effective teaching of reading.* New York: David McKay Co., 1962.
21. Harrower, M., Reading Failure: A warning signal. Cited by Kaliger and Kolson, *Reading and learning disabilities,* Columbus: Charles E. Merrill, 1969, p. 44.
22. Jacobson, E., Teaching and learning: new methods for old arts. National Foundation for Progressive Relaxation, 1973.
23. Kephart, N.C., *The slow learner in the classroom.* Columbus: Merrill, 1960.
24. Koppitz, E.M., *The Bender gestalt test for young children.* New York: Grune and Stratton, 1963.
25. McMillan, D.L., The problem of motivation in the education of the mentally retarded. *Exceptional Children,* 1969, 37.
26. National Advisory Committee on Dyslexia and related Reading Disorders, Reading Disorders in the United States. Washington, D.C. HEW, 1969.
27. Russell, H.L. & J.L. Carter, Biofeedback training with children: consultation, questions, applications and alternatives. *Journal of Clinical Child Psychology,* 1978, 7: 23-25.
28. Sheer, D.E., Classification and training of learning disability children on the basis of specific EEG activity. National Institute of Education, HEW, Grant No. NEG0030012, 1977.
29. Silvaroli, N.J., *Classroom reading inventory,* 3rd ed., Dubuque: William C. Brown Co., 1976.

CHAPTER 14

CREATIVE RELAXATION: A STRESS REDUCTION TECHNIQUE FOR CHILDREN

Joy N. Humphrey, M.S.

In this chapter the author explains the use of creative movement as a means of reducing stress in children. She takes into account the methods involved in this technique as well as the presentation of a number of specific examples.

Children as well as adults need some type of relaxation in order to relieve the tension encountered in their daily lives. It is the purpose here to explore various facets of relaxation along with those kinds of conditions which tend to produce a relaxed state. Special emphasis will be placed on *creative relaxation* and how teacher and parents can use this technique to reduce stress in children.

THE MEANING OF RELAXATION AND RELATED TERMS

A relatively new term, *relaxation response,* has been coined by Herbert Benson.[3] This involves a number of bodily changes that occur in the organism when one experiences deep muscle relaxation. There is a response against "overstress" which brings on these bodily changes and brings the body back into what is a healthier balance. Thus, the purpose of any kind of relaxation technique should be to induce a relaxation response.

From the point of view of the physiologist, relaxation is sometimes considered as "zero activity," or as nearly zero as one can manage in the neuromuscular system. That is, it is a neuromuscular accomplishment that results in a reduction, or possible complete absence of muscle tone in a part of the body or in the entire body. It has been suggested that a primary value of relaxation lies in the lowering of brain and spinal cord activity, resulting from a reduction of nerve impulses arising in muscle spindles and other sense endings in muscles, tendons, and joint structures.

The meaning of the terms *relaxation, refreshment,* and *recreation* are often confused. While all of these factors are important to the well-being of the human organism, they should not be used interchangeably to mean the same thing. *Refreshment* is the result of an improved blood supply to the brain for "refreshment" from central fatigue and to the muscles for the disposition of their waste products. This explains in part why mild muscular activity is good for overcoming the fatigue of sitting during a baseball game and arising for the "seventh inning stretch," and for hastening recovery after strenuous exercise as in the case of an athlete continuing to run a short distance slowly after a race.

Recreation may be described as the experience from which a person emerges with the feeling of being "re-created." No single activity is sure to bring this experience to all members of a group nor is there assurance that an activity will provide recreation again for a given person because it did so the last time. These are more the marks of a psychological experience. An important essential requirement for a recreational activity is that it completely engross the individual; that is, it must engage his or her entire undivided attention. It is really escape from the disintegrating effects of distraction to the healing effect of totally integrated activity. Experiences that produce this effect may range from a hard game of tennis to the reading of a comic strip.

Some individuals consider recreation and relaxation to be one and the same thing, which is *not* the case. Recreation can be considered a type of mental diversion that can be helpful in relieving tension. While mental and muscular tension are interrelated, it is in the muscles that the tension state is manifested.

For many years recommendations have been made with regard to procedures individuals might apply in an effort to relax. In consideration of any technique that is designed to accomplish relaxation, one very important factor that needs to be taken into account is that learning to relax is a skill. That is, it is a skill based on the kinesthetic awareness of feelings of *tonus* (the normal degree of contraction present in most muscles that keeps them always ready to function when needed). Unfortunately, it is a skill that very few of us use and practice—probably because we have little awareness of how to go about it.

One of the first steps in learning to relax is to experience tension. That is, one should be sensitive to tensions that exist in his or her body. This can be accomplished by voluntarily contracting a given muscle group, first very strongly and then, less and less. Emphasis should be placed on detecting the signal of tension as the first step in "letting go" (relaxing).

USING RELAXATION WITH CHILDREN

Until relatively recent years, the use of relaxation as a means of stress reduction appeared to be used primarily with adults; however, in more modern times relaxation procedures have been found to be very useful with children. Moreover, there is some objective evidence to support the idea that the practice of relaxation with children can be beneficial for them in various ways. For example, one study found that there could be significant changes in attentiveness of school children when relaxation training was used.[2] Other studies have shown that various measures of anxiety can be lowered as a result of the use of relaxation procedures.[6,8] It has also been found that there is improvement of self-help skills of retarded children after using relaxation exercises accompanied by music.[5]

Mental Practice and Imagery in Relaxation

Mental practice has been described as the symbolic rehearsal of a physical activity in the absence of any gross muscular movement.[12] This means that a person imagines in his own mind the way he will perform a given activity. Imagery is concerned with the development of a mental image that may aid one in the performance of an activity. In mental practice the person is likely to think through on his own what he is going to do. With imagery another person (teacher) may suggest a condition, and the performer then tries to effect a mental image of the condition. (As will be seen later, a form of imagery and mental practice plays an important part in *creative relaxation*.)

The use of mental practice in performing motor skills is not new. Research in this general area has been going on for more than half a century. This research has revealed that imagining a movement will likely produce recordable electric action potentials emanating from the muscle groups that would be called up if the movement were to be actually carried out. In addition, most mental activity is accompanied by general rises in muscular tension.[5]

One procedure in the use of mental practice for relaxation is that of making suggestions to one's self. For the most part, as children, we first learn to act on the basis of verbal instructions from others. Later, we learn to guide and direct our own behavior on the basis of our own language activities—we literally talk to ourselves, giving ourselves instructions. This point of view has long been supported by research[9] and postulates that speech as a form of communication between children and adults later becomes a means of organizing the child's own behavior. That is, the function that was previously divided between two people—child and adult—becomes an internal function of human behavior.

A number of researchers report success in using imagery as an aspect of relaxation with children. Kanfer and Goldstein used imagery to advantage in their work on self-instructional training with hyperactive and impulsive children.[7] Schneider and Robin had success with imagery in the development of a self-control program.[11] They developed the technique of training disruptive children to have impulse control by pairing imagery and relaxation.

In what he terms the "release only" phase of relaxation training, McBrien[10] used instructions involving imagery as follows:

> Just imagine you are lying on your back on soft green grass . . . you are so comfortable as you look up through the branches and leaves of a shade tree at the deep blue sky . . . you can see soft, white, puffy clouds floating by. (Further instructions to focus on the pleasant feeling of relaxation would then follow.)

Another way imagery can be used to promote a relaxed state is by making short *comparative* statements to children such as "float like a feather" or "melt like ice." The creative adult and child will be able to think up many such comparative statements to assist in producing a relaxed state. Incidentally, such statements are an integral aspect of the technique of creative relaxation.

CREATIVE MOVEMENT

In order to provide the reader with an understanding of its meaning, it is perhaps appropriate to provide a literal description of *creative movement*. The English word *creative* derives from the Middle English word *createn* and the Latin word *creatus,* both of which imply a bringing into existence. The term *movement,* when applied to the human organism, simply means a "change in body position." Therefore, when we put the two words *creative* and *movement* together, the interpretation is bringing something into existence or being creative by expressing one's self by means of body movement. This creative action can pertain to the whole body or various body parts, and this procedure is basic to creative relaxation as a means of stress reduction in children.

One of the utmost concerns to educators in our modern democratic society is the problem of how to provide for creative expression so that a child may develop to the fullest extent of his potentialities. Democracy is only beginning to understand the power of the individual as perhaps the most dynamic force in the world today. It is in this frame of reference that creativity should come clearly into focus, because many of the problems in our complex society can be solved mainly through creative thinking.

Creative experience involves *self*-expression. It is concerned with the need to experiment, to express original ideas, and to think. Creativity and childhood enjoy a congruous relationship because children are naturally creative. They imagine. They pretend. They are uninhibited. They are not only original, but actually ingenious in their thoughts and actions. Indeed, creativity is a characteristic inherent in the lives of practically all children. It may range from some children who create as a natural form of expression without adult stimulation to others who may need varying degress of adult guidance and encouragement.

There are a variety of media for creative expression (art, music, and writing) that are considered the traditional approaches to creative expression; however, the very essence of creative expression is movement. Movement as a form of creativity uses the body as the instrument of expression. For the young child, the most natural form of creative expression is movement. Because of their very nature, children have a natural inclination for movement, and they use this medium as the basic form of creative expression. Movement is the child's universal language, a most important form of communication and a most meaningful way of learning.

Some Principles of Learning Applied to Creative Movement

There are various basic facts about the nature of human beings of which we are now more cognizant than we were in the past. Essentially, these facts involve some of the fundamental aspects of the learning process which all good teaching should take into account. Older concepts of teaching methods were based largely upon the idea that the teacher was the sole authority in terms of what was best for children, and that children were expected to learn regardless of the conditions surrounding the learning situation. For the most part, modern teaching replaces the older concepts with methods that are based on certain accepted beliefs of educational psychology. The following principles provide important guidelines for arranging learning experiences for children, and they suggest how desirable learning can take place when the principles are satisfactorily applied to the use of creative movement.

1. *The child's own purposeful goals should guide his learning activi-*

ties. For a desirable learning situation to prevail, one should consider certain features about purposeful goals that guide learning activities. Of utmost importance is that the goal must seem worthwhile to the child. This will involve factors such as interest, attention, and motivation. Fortunately, in creative movement activities these factors are "built-in" qualities. Thus, the child does not necessarily need to be "aroused" with various kinds of motivating devices.

2. *The child should be given freedom to create his own responses in the situation he faces.* This principle indicates that problem solving is a very important way of human learning and that the child will learn mainly only through experience, either direct or indirect. This implies that the child should be provided with every opportunity to use his own judgment in the various situations that arise in the creative movement experience.

3. *The child agrees to and acts upon the learning that he considers of most value to him.* Children accept as most valuable those things which are of greatest interest to them. This principle implies in part, then, that there should be a satisfactory balance between *needs* and *interests* of children in their creative movement experiences. Although it is of extreme importance to consider the needs of children in developing experiences it should be kept in mind that their interest is needed if the most desirable learning is to take place.

4. *The child should be given the opportunity to share cooperatively in learning experiences with others under the guidance, but not the control, of the teacher.* The point that should be emphasized here is that, although learning may be an individual matter, it can well take place in a group. This is to say that children learn individually, but that socialization can be retained. This can be achieved even if there are only two members participating, such as the teacher or parent, and the child.

5. *One should act as a guide who understands the child as a growing organism.* This principle indicates that one should consider learning as an evolving process and not just as instant behavior. If a teacher or parent is to regard his or her efforts in terms of guidance and direction of behavior that results in learning, wisdom must be displayed as to when to "step in and teach" and when to step aside and watch for further opportunities to guide and direct behavior. The application of this principle precludes an approach that is adult-dominated. In this regard, an adult could be guided by the old saying that "children should learn by monkeying and not by aping."

It is quite likely that one will have good success in using creative movement to reduce stress through creative relaxation if attempts are made to apply these principles. The main reason for this is that effort in helping children learn through creative movement will be in line with those conditions under which learning takes place most effectively.

CREATIVE RELAXATION

There are at least two different versions of what can be termed *creative relaxation*. In his interesting book, *High Level Wellness*, Donald B. Ardell considers it to be an awakening of different parts of the breathing body, a gentle way of reaching the flow of vital energy deep within where experience and creativity penetrate each other.[1] He further considers it as a movement meditation of the innate relationship between the breathing body and gravity; one means of harmonizing thought, feeling, and movement.

The approach to creative movement presented in this paper was developed by the present author and an associate (the editor of this volume) for the purpose of reducing stress in young children. It combines a form of imagery and tensing and releasing. A child or a group of children with various degrees of adult guidance creates a movement(s) designed to tense and relax individual muscles, muscle groups, or the entire body. The procedure is applicable in the home to be used by the parent as well as applicable in the school setting to be used by the teacher.

Creative relaxation simply means that there are contrasting creative movements that give the effect of tensing and letting go. An illustration is provided here for a better understanding of the concept.

This example shows the contrast (tensing and letting go) of the muscles in an upper extremity (arm). The leader could start by raising a question such as the following: "What would you say is the main difference between a ball bat and a jump rope?" This question is then discussed and will no doubt lead to the major difference being that a ball bat is hard and stiff and that a jump rope is soft and limp. The leader might then proceed as follows: "Let's see if we can all make one of our arms be like a ball bat." (This movement is created.) "Now, quickly, can you make your arm be like a jump rope?" (The movement is created by releasing the tensed arm.) The experience can then be evaluated by using such questions as: "How did your arm feel when you made it like a bat?" "How did your arm feel when you made it like a jump rope?"

The creative person can produce a discussion that will increase an understanding of the relaxation phenomenon. This is but one example and others will be presented in the following discussion.

CREATIVE MOVEMENTS FOR GENERAL AND SPECIFIC RELAXATION

For purposes of discussion here *general* relaxation involves the entire body, and *specific* relaxation is concerned with an individual muscle or a group of muscles. Specific relaxation as used here should not be confused with what some persons call *differential* relaxation. Those who use this term generally consider it to be concerned with relaxing all muscles except those that are actually needed for the particular occupation at hand. Perhaps it should be mentioned that the terms *general* and *specific* are used arbitrarily in this discussion. This is to say that others may prefer to use different terms for this same purpose, and in the absence of standardized terminology, it is certainly their prerogative to do so.

In considering the examples of creative movement experiences that are recommended here, it appears important to make some general suggestions for their use. The following descriptive list is submitted for this purpose.

1. Because of their very nature, most creative movement experiences tend to be relaxing. The reason for this is that they are conducted in an informal atmosphere with a minimum amount of formal structuring.
2. Although most children are naturally creative, some will manifest more creativity than others. This means that, depending upon the nature of a particular creative experience, along with the creative level of a child, there is a need to determine the extent of adult guidance needed in each situation. With practice, most adult leaders will be able to make a judgment that is in the best interest of the children. (The term *leader* is used as a general term for an adult and could be a parent, teacher, or other adult).
3. A very important aspect in conducting creative movements with children is the leader's voice. The manner in which a leader speaks, along with the intonation of certain words, can have a profound influence on children's creative responses. For example, a soft tone of voice tends to make children respond with a slower movement. A sharp or loud tone tends to cause

children to respond more vigorously. Even the words can have an influence on children's responses. For instance, words like *hard* and *soft* and *heavy* and *light* are likely to inspire feelings and emotions that will result in varying responses. The important thing to keep uppermost in mind is that there should be contrasting experience—tensing and letting go. The voice can have a pronounced influence on this experience.

4. The format for conducting the various activities is intended only as a general way of organizing the experiences. For this reason, the suggested procedures should be considered as a guide and not necessarily as a prescription to be followed. In other words, individuals should inject their own creative ideas into the procedures for conducting the experiences. The suggested format consists of (a) the name of the activity, (b) suggested leader input, (c) some possible children's responses, and (d) suggested evaluation procedures.

5. The question of *where* to conduct the activities is important. Some can be conducted while sitting in a chair or on the surface area. Others may require more space. The nature of the activity itself will ordinarily indicate where the activity might best take place. One very important consideration in this regard is that, for those activities that suggest that the child might respond by falling to the surface area, a soft landing surface should be provided for this purpose. This could be a rug or other suitable soft landing surface.

(NOTE: Creative movement responses of children are pretty much an individual matter; that is, each child is likely to respond in the way that the experience means to him personally. Therefore, a creative movement experience can be conducted with a group of children with each child creating his own more or less unique response. At the same time, any of the suggested activities can be presented to a single child. Although the activities can be used with individual children or with groups of children, the indication in the descriptions of the activities is that they are for a group of children).

Examples of Creative Movements for General Relaxation

Activity:

HARD AND SOFT. A major purpose of this activity is to help the children distinguish between the terms *hard* and *soft*. The opening discussion can be oriented in this direction.

Introduction:

The leader can ask the children if they know the difference between hard and soft.

Responses:

Children might respond by naming some things that are hard and soft. (If this does not happen, the leader can guide the discussion with certain questions.)

Leader:

Is a rock hard?
Is the pavement hard?
Can it be made soft?
(The purpose here is to help those children who do not know the difference, or how to explain the difference, to be able to distinguish between hard and soft. All such questions will be governed by the original responses of the children.)

Leader:

We have talked about some of the things that are hard and some that are soft. I wonder if you could do something to make yourself hard?

Responses:

Children respond by creating shapes and positions that depict their bodies as being hard.

Leader:

Now, can you do something that will make your body feel soft?

Responses:

Children do several things that give them the feeling of a soft body.

Leader:

All right. Very good. I am going to say the word *hard,* and when you hear it, I want you to make yourself feel hard. After that, I will say the word *soft,* and then you make yourself feel soft. (The leader calls out the word *hard* and has the children hold their position for three or four seconds before calling out the word *soft.* The leader should take advantage of appropriate intonation of the words *hard* and *soft.*)

Evaluation:
> A discussion can be developed with questions such as the following:
> How did you feel when you were hard?
> How did you feel when you were soft?
> Did you feel better when you pretended you were hard or when you were soft?
> Could you feel the difference?

Activity:
> COLD AND HOT. In working with children in creative movement, it has been found that there are certain conditions that cause children to react more or less "naturally" to specific situations. The activity COLD AND HOT is a case in point. When children are asked to respond to *cold* they tend to react with a "tensed up" body condition. When responding to *hot* they tend to react with a more relaxed state. This is probably because children have had the actual experience of being cold and hot.

Introduction:
> The leader can introduce the discussion by referring to certain climatic or seasonal conditions that will depict cold and hot. Some introductory questions could include the following:
> Is a piece of ice hot or cold?
> Is the sun hot or cold?
> If you have been out on a cold winter day, how did it make you feel?
> How does it feel to be out on a hot summer day?
> Can you think of some things that are cold or hot?
> (The leader attempts to guide the discussion in the direction of a person's feelings when the body is cold and/or hot.)

Responses:
> Some children are likely to suggest that they shiver when cold and sweat when hot. Others will tell about their experiences with things that are hot and cold.

Leader:
> You have told a lot of things about cold and hot. Now, how would you like to show us how it feels to be cold and how it feels to be hot? When I say the word *cold*, please show us what you would do

with your body. When I say the word *hot,* show us what your body would do. (The leader continues with this procedure as the children create body movements that express hot and cold.)

Evaluation:

Did you feel "looser" when you were cold or when you were hot? George, you made your body into a ball when I said "Cold," and when I said "Hot," you flopped over and spread out your arms. Why did you do that? Could you tell us if you had any different feeling when you were pretending to be hot and pretending to be cold?

Activity:

RAIN AND SNOW. Although this activity is somewhat like the previous ones, it differs because it is likely to be an experience in which most children have participated on their own. Experience has shown that when children are asked to imitate rain, they tend to make their bodies tense. When imitating snow, they appear to relax the body. It could be speculated that the reason for this is that they generally associate rain as *heavy* and snow as *light.* The discussion could be guided in this particular direction.

Introduction:

One good way to introduce this activity is to ask the difference between rain and snow.

Responses:

Some typical responses are the following:
Rain is wetter than snow.
Rain comes down harder than snow.
Snow is white; rain does not have a color.
It is more fun playing in the snow than it is in the rain.
My mother doesn't care if I play in the snow, but she does not like to have me play in the rain.

Leader:

You have suggested some very interesting ways in which snow and rain are different. Now, how do you think it would make you feel to pretend you are rain—and then snow?

Responses:

Children express different feelings.

Leader:
> You have told many different ways it could feel to be like rain and snow. Now, let's pretend we are one and then the other. I will say "Rain," and then I will say "Snow." (The leader alternates calling out "Rain" and "Snow" as the children try to create movements in the form of these elements.)

Evaluation:
> Which did you like best—pretending you were rain or pretending you were snow?
> How did it feel to be like rain?
> How did it feel to be like snow?
> When did it feel more restful—when you were rain or when you were snow?
> Did you feel heavier when you were rain?
> Did you feel lighter when you were snow?
> Which one gave you the better feeling?

Activity:
> PEANUT BUTTER AND MILK. This activity is similar to the preceding one because the substances (peanut butter and milk) are concerned with contrasting consistency. Peanut butter is thought of as a thick substance, while milk is thought of a thin substance.

Introduction:
> The discussion can be introduced by raising questions about the two foods as follows:
> How many of you drink milk every day?
> How many of you have eaten peanut butter?
> What is the difference between the two?
> What do you think would happen if we tried to pour peanut butter like we pour milk?

Responses:
> Children generally respond in terms of the thickness of peanut butter and the thinness of milk. Typical responses are the following:
> You don't spread milk like you spread peanut butter.
> You can't make a sandwich out of milk.
> You eat peanut butter, but you drink milk.
> You can eat a peanut butter sandwich, and then drink milk.

Leader:
> Those are all good ideas. Now, how do you think it would feel to make your body like peanut butter and then like milk? Let's try it. I will say "Peanut butter," and then I will say "Milk," and you try to change from one to the other.

Evaluation:
> How did you feel when you made yourself like peanut butter?
> How did you feel when you made yourself like milk?
> Was it easier to make yourself like peanut butter or like milk?
> Which was more fun?

Activity:
> THE KITE. This activity is concerned with a kite in flight being kept up by the wind. This is compared to when the wind ceases and the kite begins to descend.

Introduction:
> In the introductory discussion the leader poses questions such as the following:
> What is a kite?
> How many of you have ever had a kite?
> Did you ever try to make a kite?
> How can you make a kite fly?
> What makes a kite stay in the air?
> What happens when a kite begins to fall?

Responses:
> There will be many various responses, with the leader attempting to guide the discussion in the direction of the purpose of the activity.

Leader:
> How do you think it would feel to be like a kite up in the air?

Responses:
> Children express their feelings, and the leader encourages them to demonstrate. (Children will perform in many different ways with the most prevalent way being to take a forward-leaning stance with arms outspread to the sides. This tends to cause the muscles of the body to become tense.)

Leader:
> You are all very good at being a kite. Now, let's try being a kite in the air, kept up by the wind, and a kite after the wind stops blowing. When I say "Up," it will mean that you are a kite in the air, and when I say "Down," it will mean that the wind has stopped and the kite comes down.

Evaluation:
> How did you feel when you were a kite in the air?
> How did you feel when the wind stopped?
> What was the difference in your body when you were a kite in the air and when you were a kite when the wind stopped?

Activity:
> THE BALLOON. This activity involves a balloon being blown up to capacity and then the air suddenly being released. A very important feature of this activity is that it helps a child learn about controlled breathing, which is so important to muscular relaxation. This activity provides for rhythm in breathing as the child inhales deeply, then exhales, and becomes relaxed when the air is released from the balloon.

Introduction:
> To begin the discussion the leader can use questions such as the following:
> Did you ever blow up a balloon and then let it go?
> What happens if you blow it up too hard?
> What happens when you let it go?
> (It might be a good idea for the leader to start the discussion with a real balloon. It can be blown up and then let go with the questions and discussion from this point.)

Responses:
> Children will provide many responses verbally, but many times they will immediately try to show what a balloon does when it is let go with air in it.

Leader:
> Good! You are acting like you are a balloon. Now, let's blow up like a balloon, and when I say "let go," everyone do what a balloon would do when the air comes out.

Evaluation:
>Did you feel tight when you took the air in like a balloon?
>How did it make you feel when you were holding the air?
>How did it make you feel when you let go?
>Was it a better feeling to hold the air in or to let it go?

Examples of Creative Movement for Specific Relaxation

The reader should notice that some of the activities for specific relaxation involved a certain degree of structuring. This means that children should still be free to explore various ways of performing an activity. At the same time, the leader should provide enough guidance in the creative response to direct the performance of an activity in a manner in which the objective of the activity will be reached.

Muscles of the Head, Face, Tongue, and Neck

Children particularly enjoy activities in this muscle group because it gives them an opportunity to make "funny faces" legitimately.

Activity:
>BIG EYES. In this activity the eyes are opened as wide as possible for a period of about four to six seconds. Also, the person can look to the right, left, above, and below.

Introduction:
>The leader can name the activity and ask the children what they think it means.

Responses:
>Some children will immediately respond by opening their eyes very wide.

Leader:
>When I say "Big Eye," try to open your eyes wide and hold it until I say "Little Eye."

Evaluation:
>How did it feel to have a big eye?
>Did it feel different to have a little eye?

Activity:
> THE SNEEZE. The muscles are contracted on either side of the nose as in sneezing. The skin should be wrinkled upward over the nose as hard as possible.

Introduction:
> The activity can be introduced by discussing how one looks when sneezing. There can also be a discussion of what causes one to sneeze.

Responses:
> The children consider this to be a very funny activity, and they will respond in a variety of ways. Some will immediately try to do a forced sneeze.

Leader:
> I want you to show how you would look when you are getting ready to sneeze. When I say "Ready," everyone pretend to get ready to sneeze. When I say "Sneeze," everyone pretend to sneeze.

Evaluation:
> Did your face feel tight when you were getting ready to sneeze? How did your face feel after you pretended to sneeze?

Activity:
> THE FROWN. There are many ways to perform this activity which include (1) stretching the left corner of the mouth up and out, (2) stretching the right corner of the mouth down and out, (3) stretching the left corner of the mouth down and out, and (4) stretching the lower lip down hard while trying to keep the lip flat.

Introduction:
> A discussion can begin about smiling and frowning, with consideration of how they are alike and different, why people smile and frown, and what it means to keep a "straight" face. Also the leader can mention the different kinds of frowns suggested above.

Responses:
> While children will respond verbally, more often than not, they will immediately respond by frowning and smiling.

Leader:
> Let's play a game in which we will use different kinds of frowns. Remember the different kinds of frowns we talked about. When I say "Frown," make any kind of frown you please, and hold it until I say "Straight." This means that you should quickly change from the frown to a straight face.

Evaluation:
> Was your face stiff when you frowned?
> Did your face feel loose when you changed from a frown to a straight face?
> What do you think happened?

Activity:
> THE HARD WHISTLE. The movement in this activity is with the lips, as in whistling, but it is done by tensing the lips vigorously.

Introduction:
> The discussion can begin by asking how many can whistle. This can be followed by a consideration of what causes the whistling sound.

Responses:
> The responses can be noisy because those children who can do so are likely to begin immediately to whistle.

Leader:
> Did you notice the shape of your mouth and lips? They formed a circle. Now, let's try what we will call the hard whistle. What does that suggest to you?

Responses:
> Children give various comments on the position of the lips in the hard whistle.

Leader:
> Let's try the hard whistle when I say "Whistle." When I say "Stop," let your lips go back to the regular position.

Evaluation:
> What kind of feeling did you have on your mouth and lips when you did the hard whistle?

Did your lips feel tight?
How did they feel when you stopped?

Muscles of the Upper Extremities

Activity:

THE SQUEEZER. This activity involves squeezing an imaginary object. It is simply concerned with making a tightly clenched fist and then releasing to an open hand.

Introduction

The discussion can start with the leader asking what is meant by the word squeeze, how the squeeze is accomplished, and under what conditions it is done.

Responses:

Children will give all sorts of responses, some of which include the following:
You squeeze lemons.
You squeeze tight on a bat when hitting a ball.
I like to squeeze a toothpaste tube.
I once squeezed a cherry and the seed popped out.

Leader:

There are certainly many things to squeeze and ways to squeeze them. The kind of squeeze I am thinking about is one in which you would use your whole hand to squeeze something, let's say like a small rubber ball. Let's try it. When I say "Squeeze," everyone pretend to squeeze something in your hand. You can use both hands to pretend you have something in each hand. Then I will say "Open," and you can stop squeezing and let your hand come open.

Evaluation:

Did your hands get tired when you squeezed hard? How did it feel when I said "Open?"

Activity:

THE RUBBER BAND. One way to be like a rubber band is to clasp the hands tightly in front of the chest with the elbows pointing out to the sides. The idea of the rubber band is shown when the performer tries as hard as possible to pull the hands apart.

Introduction:
    A discussion can focus on rubber bands and their uses. Different sized rubber bands can be presented and stretched to various lengths. (This is exciting for the children because they wonder if the rubber band is going to break.)

Responses:
    Children will enter eagerly into a discussion about rubber bands because practically all of them will have had some sort of experience with them.

Leader:
    I wonder how it would feel to be a rubber band and stretch like one? Let's try some movements that would make us be like a rubber band.

Responses:
    Children do a large variety of movements depicting a rubber band.

Leader:
    I noticed that some of you held your hands together like your arms were a rubber band. (If this does not happen, it could possibly be suggested by the leader.) Let's try to stretch the rubber band until it breaks. When I say "Start," try to stretch very hard like a rubber band. When I say "Snap," pretend that the rubber band breaks.

Evaluation:
    Did your arms get tired quickly when you were stretching them like a rubber band? Did your hands and arms feel tight? How did it feel when I said "Snap?"

Activity:
    THE WEIGHT LIFTER. This activity is concerned with lifting an imaginary weight, while at the same time straining, as if actually lifting a heavy weight. The kind of lift thought of here is known as the "curl." The lifter stands upright. The weight is on the floor in front. The performer bends at the knees, stoops, and picks up the weight with both hands, "curling" it to the chest.

Introduction:
> The discussion can be introduced by asking what is meant by the term *weight lifter*.

Responses:
> Since weight lifting has become a popular event, many children will have seen the activity on television. They are very interested in the strength it takes to lift the heavy weights.

Leader:
> (The discussion is focused on various ways to lift weights with emphasis on the curl.) What do you think we mean when we say that one way of lifting a weight is the curl?

Responses:
> Some children will know immediately, and the discussion can be directed to why it is called the curl. (Weight is curled by the arms up to the chest.)

Leader:
> Let's see if we can be weight lifters and try to curl. When I say "Curl," pretend you are lifting a heavy weight. When I say "Stop," pretend to drop the weight.

Evaluation:
> Did your arms feel tight when you were lifting the weight? Did your arms get a tired feeling? How did it feel when the weight was dropped?

Muscles of the Lower Extremities

Activity:
> ANKLE SNAP. In this activity the ankle is flexed (bent) very hard toward the body in order to stretch the muscles at the back of the legs from the knee down. This position is held for a short period, and then the foot is extended outward for a short period. Finally, the position is released, relaxing the muscles. Each ankle can be flexed and extended separately.

Introduction:
> The discussion can center around the various extremities of the body with reference to how the different kinds of joints can bend

(be flexed). The activity can be named, and the leader can ask what they think is meant by it.

Responses:
The kind of introduction mentioned above will likely result in many kinds of responses indicating experiences children have had with various body joints.

Leader:
(The leader takes into account the different responses and then attempts to direct these to the activity.) You have suggested many things that can be done with the ankles. Could you show us some of these things?

Responses:
Children react with different ankle movements. If the leader notices a movement similar to the ankle snap, this is pointed out.

Leader:
Let's play the ankle snap game. When I say "Stretch in," try to do this, and when I say "Stretch out," try to do that. When I say "Snap," quickly stop stretching the ankle.

Evaluation:
Did you stretch as hard as you could? How did it feel? Did you feel a change when I said "Snap?" How did that feel?

Activity:
KICK UP. This activity is best accomplished from a sitting position in a chair or the edge of a desk or table. The sitting position should be such that the edge is under the knee. One leg is extended and held for a short period. The extended leg should be very stiff. After the short period, the leg is allowed to bend back to the original position. Each leg can be extended separately.

Introduction:
The discussion can begin by asking about kicking as a movement. Particular reference can be made to its use as a skill in certain kinds of activities.

Responses:
> Children are likely to mention games in which the skill of kicking is used, such as football, soccer, and the popular game of kickball played in many schools.

Leader:
> (After the discussion about kicking in general, the question is raised about kicking from a sitting position.)

Responses:
> This will, of course, evoke many different reactions because children will not be likely to think of kicking being used in this manner.

Leader:
> There is an activity called the kick up. What does this mean to you? Let's try it. When I say "Kick up," will you please do so, and hold it until I say "Down."

Evaluation:
> How did it feel to kick up? Did your leg feel stiff? Did your leg get tired when you held it up? How did it feel when I said "Down?"

In summary, it should be mentioned that all of the activities presented here have been field-tested with many children. They have met with a great deal of success as a means of relieving tension and, thus, of helping to reduce stress.

The activities for creative relaxation that have been suggested should be considered as representative examples of an almost unlimited number of possibilities. These activities have numerous possible variations that will be immediately noticed by the discerning reader. Therefore, it is recommended that these activities be used as a point of departure for the development of other movements for creative relaxation. (NOTE: For complete and extensive details on this subject the reader is referred to: Humphrey, James H., and Joy N. Humphrey, *Reducing Stress in Children Through Creative Relaxation*, Charles C Thomas Publisher, Springfield, Illinois, 1981.)

REFERENCES

1. Ardell, D. B., *High level wellness*, New York: Bantam Books, Inc., 1979, p. 44.

2. Bednarova, N., An investigation concerning the influence of psychotonic exercises upon the indices of concentration of attentiveness, *Teor. Prax. Vychov.*, 1968, 16 437–442.
3. Benson, H. *The relaxation response.* New York: William Morrow and Company, Inc., 1975, p. 18.
4. Brown, B. B., *Stress and the art of biofeedback.* New York: Bantam Books, Inc., 1978, p. 31.
5. Cratty, B. J., *Physical expressions of intelligence.* Englewood Cliffs: Prentice-Hall, Inc., 1972, 144–145.
6. Johnson, D. I., C. D. Spielberger, "The effects of relaxation training and the passage of time on measures of static and trait anxiety. *Journal of Clinical Psychology,* 1968, 222–239.
7. Kanfer, F., A. P. Goldstein, *Helping people change: a textbook of methods.* New York: The Pergamon Press, 1975.
8. Keat, D. B., Broad spectrum behavior therapy with children: a case presentation, *Behavior Therapy,* 1972, 3.
9. Luria, A. R., Development of the directive function of speech in early childhood. *Word,* 1959.
10. McBrien, R. J., Using relaxation methods with first grade boys. *Elementary School Guidance and Counseling,* 1978, February, 27–32.
11. Schneider, M., A. Robin, *Turtle Manual,* Stony Brook: State University of New York, 1974.
12. Whiting, H. T. A., *Acquiring Ball Skills.* Philadelphia: Lea & Febiger, 1969, p. 82.

SUBJECT INDEX

Adolescence, 32
Adaptive homeostasis, 258–259
Adualism, 22–23
Anger, 200
Animism, 23

Basal metabolic rate, 15–16
Biofeedback, 278–299
    electroencephalographic, 293–297
    rationale, 278–279
    research, 279–281
    use with learning disabled children, 283–299
Body arousal, 261–263
Brain function and stress, 140–144

Child's perceptions of change, 86–87
Competition, 10
Conditions of learning, 40–41
Coping road map, 190–193
Creative movement, 304–307
    for general and specific relaxation, 308–323
    some principles of learning applied to, 305–307

Defense against stressful events, 121–123
Dependent child, 52–53
Developing autonomy, 26–27
Development of the LES-A, 98–121
Divorce, 79–93
    and environmental factors, 81–82
    assessment of related to environmental change, 82–85
    cumulative effects of environmental change in, 87–88
    effects of on children, 80–81
    problems in assessing related to environmental changes, 85–86

Egocentrism, 24–25
Elective mutism, 235–237
Emotional arousals and reactions, 199–203
Emotional behavior, 208–211
Emotional development, 197–203
    evaluating influences of the environment on, 210–211
    guidelines for, 205–206
    opportunities for in the home and school environment, 206–208
Emotional immaturity, 191–197
Emotional needs of children, 203–205
Emotionality, 197–199
    characteristics of childhood, 197–198
    factors that influence, 201–203

Family functioning, 144–145
    and IQ, 144
Family stressors, 65–66
Fatigue, 201–202
Faulty bracing, 269–271
Fear, 199; 213–245
    adult attitudes towards children's, 216
    and learning principles, 214–215
    of heights, 243–244
    of loud noises, 243–244
    of snakes, 242–243
    of the dark and nightmares, 237–240
    use of systematic desensitization in treatment of, 213–240
Float ride, 287–289
Freedom to learn, 25–26

Genetic plan, 29–32
Growth and development, 19–43
    theories of, 20–42
        behavioral, 35–42
        classical and operant, 35–36

    implications of, 39–40
  cognitive, 20–27
    implications of, 25–27
  psychoanalytic, 27–33
    implications of, 33–35

Home conditions that can cause stress, 5–8
Humiliation, 12
Hyperactivity, 16

Impulsive child, 53
Individual differences, 88–90
Individuality, 167–172
  accepting, 167–168
  comparisons of, 185–190
  profile, 172–193
  interpretation, 173–179
  why some adults do not accept, 168–172

Jealousy, 200–201
Joy, 201

Learning styles, 180–185
Life events, 105

Math anxiety, 11–12
Maternal mental health, 68–72
  as a meditator for life stressors, 68–70
Measuring stressfulness of child's environment, 97–124
Measuring stressors, 64–66
Measuring well-being, 66–68
Mental practice and imagery, 303–304
Mind/body integration, 259–261
Modality preference, 179–180
Muscle tension reduction research, 281–283
Multiple phobias, 244–245

Nature of growth, 28–29
Natures vs. nurture, 165–167

Passive-aggressive child, 53–54
Phobic disorders, 216
Predictors of children's happiness, 70–72

Predictors of children's problems, 70–71
Principles to help children learn about stress, 161–163

Quieting Reflex, 252, 276
  meaning of, 253–258

Reading and muscle tension, 292
Readiness, 196
Recreation, 302
Relaxation, 302–324
  creative, 307–308
  meaning of, 302
  using with children, 303–304
Repressed child, 54

School learning environment, 14–18
  that can induce stress in boys, 14–15
School phobia, 227–230
Self-concerns of children, 4–5
Signaling systems, 267–269
Stranger anxiety, 23
Stress
  a response model, 49–54
  and brain function, 140–144
  and competence, 127–147
  and coping, 135–138
  and divorce, 79–83
  and growth and development, 19–43
  and income, 71–73
  and implications for competence, 140
  and mathematics, 11–12
  and reading, 11
  and task performance, 132–135
  and the child in the educative process, 8–9
  behavior responses of children to, 48–59
  caused by parents, 6–8
  causes of in children, 3–18
  dealing with emotional in childhood, 195–211
  factors that mediate it, 138–140
  home conditions that can cause, 5–8
  impact of on children, 129–132

plan for the development of concepts, 160–161
principles to apply to help children to learn about, 161–163
regulation of, 145–147
response scale, 54–59
self-concerns of children that can cause, 4–5
stages of development as sources of, 22–25
school anxieties that can cause, 8–18
teacher behaviors that induce in children, 9–10
teaching children about, 157–163
Stress response model, 49–54
Stress response scale, 54–59
    clinical use of, 57–59
    reliability of, 57
    validity of, 55–56

Stressful environments, 64–76
    impact of on children, 64–72
Subject anxiety as a stress inducing factor, 10–13
Systematic desensitization, 216–245
    adaptations of for use with children, 219–222
    in medical settings, 230–234
    in the classroom, 222–230

Teacher behaviors that induce stress in children, 9–10
Teaching children about stress, 157–163
Test anxiety, 13–14; 222–227
Time pressure, 12
Type A Behavior, 263–267

Understanding thinking, 26

Worry, 199–200